CHANGE AND THE MOI⎯⎯⎯ ⎯⎯⎯⎯⎯BUSINESS

CW01572469

To Diava

thanks for all your support.

13/6/12

Also by Neil Harris

EUROPEAN BUSINESS

CHANGE AND THE MODERN BUSINESS

Edited by

Neil Harris

MACMILLAN
Business

First published 1997 by
MACMILLAN PRESS LTD
Houndmills, Basingstoke, Hampshire RG21 2XS
and London
Companies and representatives
throughout the world

ISBN 0–333–68091–X hardcover
ISBN 0–333–68092–8 paperback

A catalogue record for this book is available
from the British Library.

10   9   8   7   6   5   4   3   2   1
06   05   04   03   02   01   00   99   98   97

Copy-edited and typeset by Povey–Edmondson
Tavistock and Rochdale, England

Printed and bound in Great Britain by
Antony Rowe Ltd
Chippenham, Wiltshire

Contents

List of figures

List of tables

Preface

'One thing is clear: we don't have the option of turning away from the future. No one gets to vote on whether technology is going to change our lives. No one can stop productive change in the long run because the marketplace inexorably embraces it. Governments can try to slow the rate of change within their own borders by restricting the use of certain technologies, but these policies risk leaving a country isolated from the world economy, preventing its companies from being competitive and its consumers from getting the latest products and the best prices.

I believe that progress will come no matter what, we need to make the best of it – not try to forestall it.'

(Bill Gates (Chairman and Chief Executive Officer, Microsoft Corporation), *The Road Ahead*, 2nd edn, Penguin Books, 1996)

■ Change as a central characteristic of modern business

The common theme of this book is change and its impact on the business organisation. This involves exploring a number of issues such as:

- what causes change?
- how does change impact on a business and why?
- how might a business respond to existing change and anticipate potential change?
- what implications do the actions of one firm have for others in the same market, and for its consumers?
- what likely changes might be anticipated in the medium-term future?

This is not, therefore, a specialist book aimed just at the economist, business strategist or marketer. Rather its philosophy is to provide a broad-based examination of areas particularly relevant to modern business operations. It draws on a number of different specialisms and uses these to explore the issues identified above. Each chapter of this book is written by an expert in his or her field who takes theories of business behaviour to provide frameworks or models to apply to contemporary case studies. The reader may therefore use these models to evaluate business change, both in particular circumstances and generally.

■ **Intended readership**

The inevitability of change and its accelerating pace makes this book essential reading for anyone interested in business theory and practice. It is aimed particularly at years two and three of undergraduate business courses and for students on MBA (Master of Business Administration) programmes. It is also very suitable for providing underpinning knowledge at NVQ (National Vocational Qualification) Levels 3 to 5, and for students at year two of HND (Higher National Diploma) courses. However, the book also offers valuable insights for the business practitioner and for the general reader who is interested in taking his or her knowledge of business behaviour further than just the financial pages of a newspaper.

■ **The structure of the book**

The market drivers of change are various and particularly include information technology. Its impact is explored in the context of the services sector of economies, particularly financial services, and in marketing. Chapters 2 and 4 examine the financial services industry while Chapter 3 explores the impact of change on the services sector of developed economies and, especially, the definition and qualities of services management. Chapter 5 discusses the influence of information technology on the promotion, distribution and sale of products.

Additionally, changes in more broad-based technology have impacted significantly on production and transport processes with the development of lean production, explored in Chapter 7, and the replacement of traditional shipping by new cargo carriers, which Chapter 10 examines. This, in turn, has considerable implications for the labour force and has contributed to the development of human resources management as an important facet of managing a business, as discussed in Chapter 6.

Another major market driver of change is competition. Certainly competition in the EU has become very much more significant with the near completion of the Single European Market. However, it is the global nature of competition which will be most important in the next twenty years, with its impact already to be seen in car and white-goods production and shipping. With EU economies increasingly providing services not producing goods, the impact of new technology, the global capital market and cheap labour will enable Pacific Rim competitors to compete even more in domestic markets. The nature of competition and its internationalisation and globalisation, and its impact in causing structural change in an industrial sector , is explored in a number of chapters in this book, particularly 1, 2, 4, 5, 7 and 10.

Other change drivers, which are analysed in this text, are grounded in national and EU legislation. One area is the growth of intellectual property and the need for businesses to know their legal rights and how to defend these. This is discussed in Chapter 9. Another area is the environmental effects of business activities and the need for businesses to meet new legislative challenges. Chapter 8 examines this. In both cases these need to be addressed in businesses' strategies.

The other major characteristic of global competition is the impact of cultural differences. At the macro level, in spite of the moves to a global culture as characterised by mobile phones, McDonalds, speaking American English and watching Hollywood films on satellite tv, cultural diversity is significant both at UK and global levels. Most importantly for business, the influx of Japanese and South Korean direct investment into the UK and the remainder of the EU has introduced cultural differences 'at the back door' where industrial relations based on the single union plant, and other issues such as quality circles, have been absorbed into mainstream industrial life. Chapter 7 particularly explores these issues at the micro level. Chapter 1 looks at organisational culture and the use of Johnson's Cultural Web to analyse it, while Chapter 4 examines information systems and the organisational culture.

Just as a number of key themes exist in this book so a number of common analytical tools are employed by its authors. PEST/PESTLE analysis is used in Chapters 1, 2 and 6 to explore the environment within which businesses operate, albeit in different contexts. In Chapter 1 it is applied to the French water company GDE, in Chapter 2 to the UK building societies sector of financial services and in Chapter 6 to human resources management.

The influence of American academic Michael Porter is strong in analysing the impact of change in two main areas. In Chapters 1, 4 and 10 it is important in terms of his Five Forces Model. In Chapter 4 this is used in the context of the Royal Bank of Scotland, while in Chapter 10 it is used to analyse the UK shipping industry. Porter's value chain analysis is used in Chapters 1 and 4 as a means of exploring how business activities add value to operations of a business and hence enable it to gain competitive advantage.

In the same way product/service differentiation strategies are used to analyse the operations of GDE in Chapter 1 and services management in Chapter 3.

The reader should bear in mind that theoretical developments seek to provide a better understanding of business behaviour. However, theory does not fit neatly into compartments which, when bolted together, give total understanding of how all businesses behave. Moreover, theories have weaknesses and are, at times, criticised for their lack of realism – a consequence of making necessary but limiting assumptions. Empirical testing of theory against reality is the accepted way of determining its relevance and validity, but this poses pitfalls in a number of areas. Data may not be available or may not be in the form required – hence proxy data must be used which may not map exactly against the theoretical requirements. Again, findings may be inconclusive leaving doubt as to the validity of the testing of the theory.

In practice, therefore, theories compete with each other, and while some may explain certain aspects of business behaviour better than others, in different areas they may be less effective. Consequently the reader must exercise critical judgement and awareness and actively pursue other theories for himself or herself to test the validity of these against those advanced in this book.

■ Conclusions

The warning of Bill Gates, that change is inevitable and unstoppable – and that we must live with it and make the best of it that we can – began this introduction. That may sound reactive and, in part, it is because change is most commonly imposed externally. However, one of the themes of this book considers the ability to adapt to such change, to take it forward and to utilise it for one's own benefit as a proactive response to such externally generated change.

It has often been said that we are now living through a second industrial revolution. The first, dating from the late eighteenth century, was based on capital instead of labour, fuelled by fossil fuels, and mass-produced goods to achieve economies of scale. The current revolution is information technology based with individualised production to achieve economies of scope. As important an output as physical goods is information. Ed Bales, Co-founder, Motorola University, USA, recently argued that 'technology (hardware and software) is now available to all corporations equally on a global basis. The competitive edge will go to the corporations that have the best people (mindware) managing the technology' (Keynote speech, 3rd 'Educational Innovation in Economics and Business' conference, Florida, December 1996). In other words, within their business environment, organisations can initiate change and gain competitive advantage.

However the ability to maintain it requires constant adaptability and, most importantly, investment in people.

So, if we do not change we stagnate – and others will overtake us, whether businesses or countries. This is the theme of this book, and the theoretical tools this book provides seek to help the exploration of this concept of change.

■ Acknowledgements

As editor, my thanks go to my co-authors for their involvement in this book when higher education is having to adapt to rapid change and resource constraints, particularly time. Their enthusiasm, support and prompt response to my editorial requests has been much appreciated. Particular thanks go to Adrian Webb for stepping in to fill the gap so competently when one author withdrew at short notice. Ian Taylor of the Education Development Service, Southampton Institute provided considerable help with the graphics, while Stephen Rutt, Publishing Director of Macmillan Business, was, as usual, helpful and supportive but not intrusive.

Last, but not least, on behalf of the authors who wrote this book, a sincere thanks is offered to all families who had to endure spouse, partner or parent hunched over a keyboard for long hours producing his or her chapter. This book is dedicated to them.

NEIL HARRIS

Notes on the contributors

Gary Akehurst is Professor of Marketing at the University of Portsmouth Business School, Department of Business and Management. He is a Fellow of the Tourism Society, a Member of the Institute of Management and Member of the Chartered Institute of Marketing. He is also editor of the *Service Industries Journal*. He has published extensively in journals and as co-author of books. He has also undertaken consultancy work nationally and internationally.

John Cross is Senior Lecturer in Strategic Management, Southampton Business School. He has recently undertaken substantial work producing a range of case studies one of which is incorporated into the chapter he has produced for this text. He was recently awarded the title of most inspirational teacher at Southampton Institute. Currently he is developing a sports management programme in conjunction with sporting professional bodies to meet industry needs.

Neil Harris is Head of Economics and Business Modelling, Southampton Business School. His research interests are European business, European economics, and business education. He has had articles published in refereed journals and has given papers at international conferences in the UK and overseas. His book *European Business* was published by Macmillan Business in 1996.

Ashok Ranchhod is Head of Marketing, Southampton Business School and has led the programme to develop its MBA. He has published widely in refereed journals and lectured extensively and given papers in Europe, the US and India. He was previously the managing director of a biotechnology company. His research interests centre around marketing and biotechnology.

Mervyn Rowlinson is Senior Lecturer in Transport Economics in the Maritime Faculty, Southampton Institute. He has delivered papers at international conferences, his work has been published in refereed journals and he has written discussion papers for the Labour Party. He is an active researcher, particularly in the fields of marine transport and small and medium sized enterprises.

Heather Stewart is Senior Lecturer in Accounting, Southampton Business School, and a management accountant. In 1994 she completed her MBA at

Henley Management College. Her masters' dissertation was on lean production and her research forms the basis for her contribution to this volume.

Richard Thomas is Head of Academic Operations, Southampton Business School. He has published extensively, acting as series editor and writing several books in the 'Step by Step Guides' series published by Stanley Thornes. He has recently co-authored a book *Business Information – Technologies and Strategies* while his book *Quantitative Methods for Business* was published in 1997.

Brian Thornton is Senior Lecturer in Human Resource Management, Southampton Business School. A former senior local government officer, he has substantial and recent industrial experience in the field of HRM and has written a number of internal and position papers for employers.

Adrian Webb is a Consultant, part-time lecturer in Southampton Business School, and writer on European environmental, regional and transport issues. He has been widely published and contributes regularly to *European Policy Analyst* (formerly *European Trends*) published by the Economist Intelligence Unit Ltd. He has wide experience as a researcher, and as an administrator in local government and the water industry. He also speaks five languages.

Mark Wing is a lecturer in the Law Faculty, Southampton Institute. He is responsible for teaching intellectual property law and European Community law, especially on the LLM course in intellectual property, of which he is the course leader.

Glossary of abbreviations

ABP	Associated British Ports
ACE	Alliance for Beverage Cartons and the Environment
AMA	American Marketing Association
APEAL	Association Professionelle des Producteurs Européens d'Aciers pour Emballages
ARPA	Advanced Research Project Agency
ATM	Automated Telling Machine
BCME	Beverage Can Makers Europe
BPR	Business Process Re-engineering
CAD	Computer Aided Design
CAM	Computer Aided Manufacture
CASE	Computer Aided Software Engineering
CCT	Compulsory Competitive Tendering
CDPA	Copyright, Designs and Patents Act (1988)
CIM	Chartered Institute of Marketing
CLES	Centre for Local Economic Strategies
CME	Computer Mediated Environment
CPC	Community Patent Convention
CSO	Central Statistical Office
CTM	Community Trade Mark
EAA	European Aluminium Association
EC	European Community
EIS	European Information Service
EMAS	Environmental Management and Audit Scheme
ENDS	Environmental Data Services
EPC	European Patent Convention
EPOS	also EFTPOS: Electronic Funds Transmission at Point of Sale
EU	European Union
FOC	Flag of Convenience
FTP	File Transfer Protocol
GATT	General Agreement on Tariffs and Trade
GDE	Générale des Eaux
GDP	Gross Domestic Product
GRT	Gross Registered Tonnes
HRM	Human Resource Management
ILO	International Labour Office
IMVP	International Motor Vehicle Program
ISL	Institute of Shipping Logistics

ISO	International Standards Organisation
IT	Information Technology
JIT	Just in Time
LIFO	Last in First out
NDLS	National Dock Labour Scheme
NGO	Non Governmental Organisation
NIC	Newly Industrialised Country
OECD	Organisation for Economic Cooperation and Development
PCT	Patent Cooperation Treaty (1970)
PEST	Political, Economic, Social, Technological
PESTLE	Political, Economic, Social, Technological, Legal, Environmental/ Ethical
RBS	Royal Bank of Scotland
ROCE	Rate on Capital Employed
SMEs	Small and Medium-sized Enterprises
SPC	Supplementary Protection Certificate
SWOT	Strengths, Weaknesses, Opportunities, Threats
TQM	Total Quality Management
TRIPS	Trade Related Aspects of Intellectual Property
TSB	Trustee Savings Bank
UNCTAD	United Nations Committee on Trade and Development
UNICE	Union of Industrial and Employers' Confederations of Europe
WTO	World Trade Organisation

CHAPTER 1

Modern developments in business strategy

John Cross

■ 1.1 Introduction

All organisations, large or small, public or private sector, manufacturing or services industries, today operate in a constantly changing environment. It is difficult to think of an organisation that is not subject to change, although some are obviously affected more than others. In his publication *The Origin of Species*, Charles Darwin suggested that those adapting best to change will be the ones to survive; this applies as equally to organisations as it did, in Darwin's case, to organisms in the biological world. Companies which are proactive rather than reactive to change have more chance of survival, due to being able to predict perhaps imminent environmental changes and be ready for them, whether this is taking advantage of possible opportunities or guarding against potential threats that might arise. Strategic Analysis, as a part of business strategy, is an iterative process and it is this constant appraisal not only of the external environment but also of internal capabilities and resources, that may ultimately lead to some sort of competitive advantage in the market place. Effective companies constantly monitor the environment to understand better the industry in which they operate. No organisation can predict future changes with any degree of certainty but environmental scanning can help reduce uncertainty to a limited extent.

Business strategy concerns the whole organisation rather than individual functions or sections (see also Chapter 4.3 for a discussion of strategy in relation to Information Technology). As with effective decision-making, strategy requires collecting current and relevant information. There are those who consider this a waste of time and strategic planning a pointless exercise since the environment in certain industries often changes on a daily basis. Other successful entrepreneurs, certainly in the early stages of their organisational life-cycles, opt for a more intuitive approach to strategy. While there are numerous examples of failure associated with lack of market research in favour of gut feeling, there are also examples of enthusiasm leading to success. Richard Branson and Alan Sugar bear witness to this, although they now probably use more formalised planning processes. Luck, either in timing or a certain situation leading to an unexpected but welcome outcome, can also contribute greatly to success and leave observers with the impression that strategy has been masterminded to perfection. An example to illustrate this is Anita Roddick and Body Shop. In the early days of Body Shop, competitive advantage was unwittingly built around the fact that there were no throw-away containers for their cosmetics since customers supplied their own.

At a time when social responsibility had just become fashionable, this might have been considered strategic genius but in fact was due to Anita and husband Gordon Roddick being short of funds to provide packaging. Their strategy was to re-invest early profits into packaging at a later date; in practice they never had to implement this. Partly as a result of their success significant change has taken place not only in the cosmetic industry but also in other related ones where environmentally friendly products and biodegradable or recyclable packaging are largely now the norm through customer demand. Could effective strategic analysis rather than luck or gut feeling have provided the same success?

Clearly the answer is somewhat dependent upon a firm's ability to predict trends and customer needs and wants. An alternative view on strategy is that put forward more recently by Stacey (1993). He argues that conventional strategic analysis may have worked in static environments but in the modern business arena the environment is often uncertain and chaotic and that it takes extraordinary management to succeed. Stacey suggests that successful companies have adapted to large-scale change often by discovering innovative strategies which have emerged without directed intention and planning.

Current thinking on Business Strategy has never been more active and, apart from many journals such as the *Harvard Business Review* and *Strategic Long-Range Planning*, literally hundreds of strategy texts can be found on the shelves of high street bookshops. Business Strategy is very subjective and perhaps best explained as an iterative process. Several factors impinge on future strategy not least current strategy, but more significantly culture and structure which largely determine an organisation's ability to adapt to change.

This chapter will consider the process of effective business strategy for the organisation through the use of well tried and tested analysis frameworks. Used in isolation they offer only a snapshot of the situation but used in a complementary manner they build and provide a more extensive picture of organisational capability to adapt to an ever changing environment. (The reader is also referred to Chapter 4 where strategy is explored in relation to Information Technology.)

■ 1.2 Strategy and change in practice

It is currently difficult to read business journals without being made aware of certain management 'buzz words'. Whereas the 1980s were times of corporate takeovers, the introduction of new technology, Just-In-Time production (JIT) (see Chapters 5.3 and 7.1 for a more detailed discussion of this) and 'sticking to the knitting' for Tom Peters' disciples, then the 1990s have seen startling changes. Corporate collapse and de-layering or downsizing are terms to suggest that only very effective organisations are likely to survive into the twenty-first century. Even the successful diversified Hanson corporation of the 1980s, which seemed to have the Midas touch, has been forced to break up its vast business empire by divesting certain divisions. Big is no longer beautiful and there are those who believe that Small and Medium Enterprises (SMEs) are best placed to take advantage of the changes of the 1990s and the next decade. The adoption of Total Quality Management (TQM) over the last decade has paved the way for greater effectiveness in certain industries (see Chapter 7 for a detailed discussion with reference to the car and orthopaedics industries). TQM is an organisational approach to improve quality through implementing certain necessary changes in practices, systems, structure and particularly culture. However, the end result in many situations has been disappointing considering the investment. In more recent times Business Process Re-engineering (BPR) has been hailed as another revolutionary approach to aiding organisational effectiveness.

The idea of BPR is that operations should be organised around the processes, which add value for the organisation, rather than on a functional basis. This reduces problems associated with purely concentrating on efficiency of individual organisation functions rather than the overall effectiveness of the organisation. BPR has resulted in changes from plant layout to job design, but again, similarly to TQM, BPR has failed to live up to expectation after much early promise. Used initially as a comparative benchmarking process with other organisations, much of its potential may have waned due to bad publicity where in some quarters it was perceived to be an excuse to de-layer an organisation. BPR is essentially the re-alignment of structures to fit the work that they do. The main reason, however, for the relative failure of many BPR attempts is that organisations are extremely complex which often results in many unforeseen and detrimental side effects. There are those who suggest that BPR is simply change management re-packaged and re-named for the 90s. Champy himself suggests that 'Reduced to its bare bones, re-engineering is about the radical reinvention of a company's processes. It's about starting over, starting from scratch' (Merriden 1996).

He also suggests that some companies have used his theories as an excuse for substantial cuts in manpower without undertaking the rigorous review of processes that re-engineering demands. Champy's perception is that European managers find tough re-engineering decisions harder to make than their US counterparts, and have a certain inability to get to grips with necessary redundancies. Much of success might well hinge on changing culture, and according to Champy (Merriden 1996), 'unless you can work out how to get managerial behaviour to change, re-engineering gets stuck at the top of the organisation'. He suggests that the main problem with this is that 'typically, real culture change is more like a five-year cycle'. BPR also falls down where many managers play safe with change instead of starting with a new sheet of paper. Champy concludes 'Managers come back to me and argue for incremental change. To me, incrementality is the high risk proposition.'

Another major business change in the 1990s concerns the Single European Market (see also Chapter 8.2). This has seen radical change since the trade barriers were substantially dismantled at the end of 1992. There are now more opportunities for European firms to compete both inside and outside of the European Union (EU). Employees have freedom to work more easily within the union and mobility of labour has meant that organisations can be more selective when recruiting specialist skills. UK firms must now think European because along with potential opportunities come threats of competition from areas previously never considered. When Compulsory Competitive Tendering (CCT) was revolutionising public sector organisations in the early 1990s, extremely competitive bids were placed from across the channel. For example, when tenders were invited from Hampshire County Council to cut and maintain school playing fields it was a bid from Holland which proved most competitive. More recently the Rennes-based French water organisation, Générale des Eaux (GDE), bid for one of the Railtrack franchises in the UK. The GDE organisation is a case-study at the end of this chapter. Any current UK book of change should have at least a European focus in part and the GDE case will provide this focus. It illustrates how the most successful companies have to plan strategically both carefully and wisely and perhaps diversify as never before to maintain growth when existing markets become more limited. GDE is a good example of this.

One question often asked is how have UK organisations adapted to changes within Europe? While the real answer may be difficult to ascertain there is nevertheless a reluctance by some UK firms to become seriously involved, whether just through apathy or pure ignorance to grasp the fact that the game is played in a different arena with a different set of rules. There is now a real need for British management, aside from usual expertise requirements, to be competent in language skills and knowledge of European business culture. For those brave enough to take on the European challenge effectively there is both opportunity and competition. However, some EU member states perceive the UK to be not always thinking European and this is reflected in how some British companies pursue business in the EU. Whatever the truth the EU has certainly changed the prospects for UK firms since 1992.

For those organisations not averse to expanding into mainland Europe, the European challenge will involve having to find out much more with respect to markets, competition and regulations rather than assuming that European business will merely be the expanding of existing company practices across the Channel. It is much more than that and for those prepared to make the research effort it can be lucrative in terms of new markets. Some UK firms may decline the European challenge and may prefer instead to re-focus strategy within the home market rather than venturing into the unknown. Others may take it up to reciprocate where continental firms have taken some of their business in the UK.

Doing business effectively in mainland Europe necessitates the need for a solid understanding of European employment law, sourcing new suppliers and distribution channels and possibly having to tailor UK products to different types of customer demands. It may also be necessary to be familiar with import and export administration practices, different terms of payment and almost certainly alien ways of marketing the product to a different culture audience. For small firms, where profit margins may be lean these complications, together with fluctuating European exchange rates, may be too much of a risk. Some of the better known larger companies have only experienced limited success with such ventures, and Laura Ashley are such an example. Their underlying theme which has brought success in the UK, does not necessarily suit the needs and wants of different types of European cultures which might have different attitudes and values with respect to overseas consumer products. Currently more successful are Marks & Spencer, in Europe and globally, and the motor exhaust and tyre chain, Kwik-Fit. Similarly European mainland firms have not found success that easy in the UK. The French chain of hypermarkets, Carrefour, did initially find some success and in more recent times the names of Aldi and Ikea have become more familiar to British shoppers. Pre-EU quotas, tariffs and nationalistic prejudices may have accounted for many of the failures. The time lag associated with dismantling of barriers to trade is now complete and it may only be cultural ones that need to be scaled before a wider range of organisations are successfully competing across the geographical frontiers of Europe.

Strategy in the real world rarely runs like clockwork. A planned strategy may be put into practice with the expectation that it will run its expected course. However, within the timescale of the plan, the organisation may need to make slight changes which move it away from the original strategy. This may lead to the business becoming successful at managing this deviation and perhaps result in a lucrative new situation. It has thus moved towards an emergent strategy which could not have been predicted when planning initially took place. Imposed strategies might also rise, again difficult to predict, through changes within the industry such as market or product maturity, or even a hostile takeover. It may be that an opportunity occurs which is too good to miss. Thus an organisation may follow in part or in whole an opportunistic strategy. Overall then, in only a small number of cases does strategy, through the strategic planning process, follow a straight line. In practice the realised strategy will probably comprise a mix of the above and some, if not all of the intended strategy, may be unrealised for whatever reasons.

Since effective strategy seeks to ensure that an organisation stays in tune with its changing environment, then understanding that environment is of paramount importance. This will be considered in more detail in the next section but, if a firm allows itself to become too far out of step with its environment, then there is the risk of strategic drift occurring. When this happens often a large or revolutionary change will be required to bring the firm back into line. This can be problematic as most strategic managers prefer small scale or evolutionary step changes because there is significantly less risk of failure involved and career prospects may be at stake. This can lead to a state of flux with company prospects deteriorating even further unless revolutionary change, which might include pursuing more than one strategy, is enforced.

Strategic planning then is not about following only one single strategy although in some situations this has its merits. Several strategies might be pursued simultaneously. There can be situations where organisations are blinded by earlier success or complacency; IBM prior to its crisis in 1992 can be included here. This is outlined in the Icarus Paradox whose author (Miller 1995), draws a parallel between Icarus, the mythical figure who persisted in flying towards the sun with disastrous consequences as it melted his wax wings, and well known successful companies which persist in pursuing previously successful strategies until they too become unstuck. Miller quotes Digital, ITT, Rolls-Royce and Chrysler in his paradox, but there are many others.

There is a case for arguing that business success is a cyclical feature and that successful strategies, as Miller highlighted above, only last for so long before tinkering or replacement is needed. Certainly organisations not prepared to undertake radical change when necessary in the short term are unlikely to survive. In the long term not all current successful organisations will continue to be in business in twenty or thirty years time as others are likely to emerge to take their place. This poses a number of questions. Can business success or failure ever be predicted? Are certain industries more secure than others? At the present rate of extinction, hundreds of businesses die every week in the UK alone and it is a fine line which distinguishes between the success or survival of one organisation and the failure of another. The use of theory and analysis alone can never provide survival, and should never be promoted as such. However they can bring a certain amount of order and precipitate original and critical thinking skills which might provide the innovation necessary for survival. Any organisation with an inability to produce acceptable profit is going to fail in the long term. It is reasonable to expect that sufficient warning of such a situation would arise but all too often the tell-tale signs are misinterpreted or not acted upon quickly enough to allow turnaround, and corporate collapse ensues. The fact still remains that businesses have to cater for and satisfy customer requirements in an effective manner. The customer is king is a cliché but organisations which keep a focus on this tend to be the successful ones. Good market research data, including customer perception of the organisation and its products and services, is often the starting point in enabling a company to provide the products and services which the customer wants, at the right price and in the right places.

The successful companies are customer-led, constantly trying to innovate at every opportunity to gain a lead over competitors, maintain customer loyalty and extend customer base at the expense of competitors. Nowhere is this more evident than in the supermarket sector. In January 1997 both Tesco and Sainsbury's were considering adding free life insurance cover for customers of their Clubcard and Reward Card respectively. Hence the breadwinner's surviving family would be provided with free weekly groceries for life under these schemes. In fiercely competitive markets it is innovations such as these which may just edge toward market leadership. The customer is very much part of the success equation. Sainsbury's suggest that it is five times more time-consuming to win back a customer than to gain them in the first place. Many organisations now operate customer care training programmes.

Successful organisations over a consistent period are likely to have top quality staff behind them. With the revolutionary change within many industries nobody can command a job for life anymore. Staff now may well be paid on performance, and mobility of labour together with head hunting has seen some rapid staff turnover in a range of industries. Those organisations less risk aversive might well buy in the personal expertise needed for success with diversification ventures. Richard Branson at Virgin is never afraid to move into new markets where Virgin has little or no expertise. However, rather than slowly develop internally, the company prefers to search out the top quality staff required for the task and secure their services from other organisations. Clearly continual retention and recruitment of top quality staff can only aid the success and long-term future of any company and those which recognise the need for its incorporation as part of the strategic planning process will be most successful.

Whether Strategic Planning can ever be the answer to effective organisations remaining effective or poor performers improving is open to debate. The strategic plan can be compared to an individual's Curriculum Vitae (CV). It only ever highlights what has been achieved in the present and past with no guarantees relating to future achievements and performance. From the origins of strategic planning, around 1965, there have been those who have considered that it is never a guarantee for business success and hence survival. Mintzberg (1994) outlines many pitfalls of the planning process. The author argues that the process can destroy commitment, narrow a company's vision and in some cases discourage change which might be essential for future survival. Earlier work by Mintzberg and Quinn (1991) emphasised the need for appropriate organisational structures for firms to become effective and hence successful. Mintzberg also suggests that an appropriate climate or culture is necessary for success and that an inappropriate one is often the reason why strategy can fail.

In his video *Crazy Ways for Crazy Days*, Peters (1995) suggested that the only certainty concerning the future for organisations was one of great uncertainty. The environment has seen many largely unpredicted changes in recent times and many of these would have been unheard of a decade or two ago. These changes are obviously part of, and can affect, business strategy; they form the basis of the next section.

■ 1.3 The Changing Environment

Effective organisations tend to have an understanding of the environment in which they have to operate. However, it is not enough to get it right once as the environment is constantly changing almost daily in some industries. What proved an effective strategy last year, or even last month, or week in some situations, may be inappropriate for the future due to change. Even the very successful companies cannot rest on their laurels as IBM discovered in 1992. Organisations previously in sheltered environments within the public sector have, through privatisation, been thrown into new and highly competitive environments and have had to cope quickly and effectively with a steep learning curve. They have had to change from operating in simple, static type environments to one that is more complex in competitor make-up and dynamic with associated product, price and technology changes.

In August 1996, although it occurred once before briefly in 1971, the British government intervened in the Post Office dispute to suspend for one month their monopoly on letter delivery. Although such a brief suspension is unlikely to change the industry environment radically it has nevertheless alerted competitors such as TNT to the possibility of planning for a potential opportunity to enter this industry.

British Rail was also subject to radical change in 1994 when the whole structure was dismembered as part of privatisation. Railtrack retained ownership of the infrastructure and any organisation could bid for various area franchises. In 1996 the largest French water organisation Générale des Eaux bid, albeit unsuccessfully, for one of these UK Railway franchises. Although not easy for industry competitors to predict, this illustrates how the business environment is now subject to quite radical changes. In this case a predatory organisation seeking growth is prepared and confident enough to venture overseas in a non-related diversification capacity. As well as its core business of water services, GDE is now involved in water related construction and engineering (mainly in France but also abroad), energy management, electrical contracting and power generation (France and USA), waste management, urban maintenance (France and Spain), construction (UK, Germany and France), real estate management (France), communications (France), media and entertainment, leisure, healthcare and other community services. GDE has been actively diversifying its business portfolio as opportunities have availed themselves through environmental change.

Once the nature of the environment has been identified the organisation is better prepared for some of the challenges of a general nature. However, further appraisal of the environment is necessary to be better positioned in terms of business strategy.

Figure 1.1 illustrates an organisation's environment that needs to be considered and breaks it down to the macro-environment and the micro-

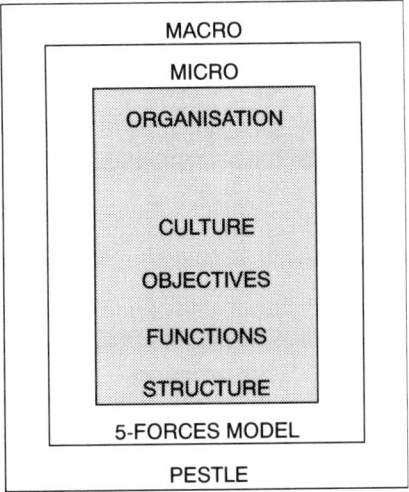

Figure 1.1   An organisation's environment

environment. The macro or wider environment can affect all organisations, not only those in a specific industry, whereas the micro environment is concerned principally with a specific industry.

PESTLE analysis is useful in establishing whether any of these six areas has affected or is likely to affect the organisation either presently, or in the future, and the implications of this. The areas, with general examples, are:

POLITICAL	(e.g. Act of Parliament or change of government)
ECONOMIC	(e.g. inflation rate change)
SOCIAL	(e.g. more women now working)
TECHNOLOGICAL	(e.g. use of new technology)
LEGAL	(e.g. EU legislation introduced)
ECOLOGICAL	(e.g. use of environmentally safer raw materials)

These areas are applied in more detail at the end of the chapter with the GDE case-study. They are also employed in Chapter 2.2 (as PEST) in relation to the financial services industry and in Chapter 6.4 regarding human resources.

The micro or industry environment is more specific to an industry and was developed by Porter (1980). He suggests that for a company to be successful it first needs to 'get a handle' on its industry through the Five-forces model (Figure 1.2) and then decide on what basis it is going to do business through the generic strategies model which will be reviewed later (this model is also employed in Chapter 4.4 concerning the use of technology to secure competitive advantage and in Chapter 10.4 to explore changes in the UK's maritime industry).

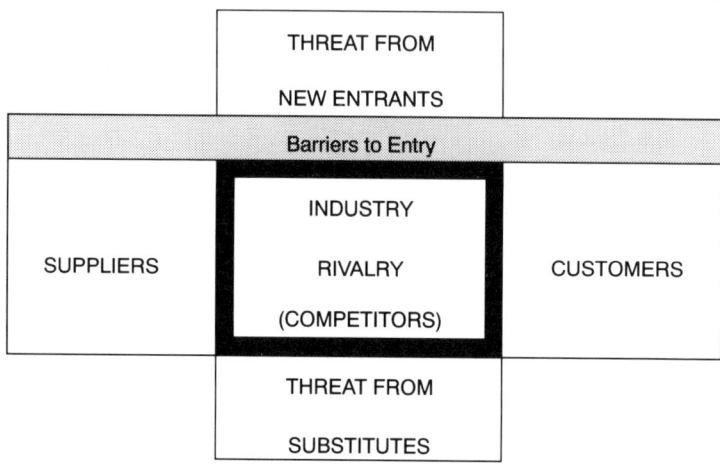

Figure 1.2   The five-forces model
Source: M. E. Porter, *Competitive Strategy*, Free Press, 1980.

A good place to start with this model is with the Industry Rivalry segment and it is useful to list the present competitors. Consideration should now be given to the threat from new entrants area and this will be dependent upon the barriers to entry that the industry has erected. High entry barriers, which might include capital costs, or new technology, or a high use of patents within the industry or a host of other aspects, tend to restrict the number of new players. Obviously low barriers could allow a whole range of would-be competitors to enter the industry.

It is also important to understand whether the relationship between the industry and *suppliers* favours one or the other. Where there are many suppliers and the cost of switching is insignificant, then the power lies with certain firms within the industry. A low number of suppliers can alter the equation. Equally important is whether the customers (buyers) have power over the sellers. Many sellers offering similar products or services means that the customers may be spoilt for choice. However, when there are few producers or sellers it means that the customer is limited in terms of shopping around. Hence in a monopolistic setting there are very few alternatives. Finally, the threat from substitutes should never be ignored. A substitute may be chosen by customers when it is perceived as offering similar benefits. It is not the same but similar. Hence back in the 1970s when a bad coffee harvest meant that coffee prices in the UK were very high, some consumers switched to tea or soft drinks as an alternative.

The Five-forces model facilitates a better understanding of the industry in which an organisation competes. It is then necessary to build on how competitive advantage has been obtained and maintained. This may be achieved by a range of factors that are better explained using Porter's 'Value Chain Analysis' to be found in the next section and in Chapter 4.3 (Porter 1985). All effective organisations seek some sort of advantage over competitors. This can be achieved, according to Porter (1985), either through cost leadership or by differentiation. If large purchasing power leads to cheaper raw materials, i.e. economies of bulk purchase for example, this often results in slightly lower than average industry prices that perhaps smaller competitors cannot match. That is, competitive advantage has been achieved. Differentiation occurs when a firm produces a good or service which is perceived by the customer as different and hence worth purchasing. This might involve quality, styling, design or image. Porter's 'Generic Strategies' highlights the fact that a company can also focus in a niche market by only providing a single or narrow range of products or services. Whether a narrow or wide range is decided upon the company must determine what business philosophy to follow. The customer will become confused if the firm is not convinced itself whether to do business on a cost leadership (lower prices) or a differentiation (perhaps a quality image) basis. The worst possible thing to do according to Michael Porter is to be stuck in the middle of the matrix.

Business strategy, as mentioned earlier, is involved with monitoring the environment so that the organisation can stay in tune with it. However, this means that there are implications for resources and the capabilities of the organisation and these are discussed in the next section.

■ 1.4 Frameworks for analysing internal capability

Although there is sometimes an element of doubt surrounding the validity of using certain frameworks to aid strategic analysis, it may also be said that these provide useful insights to a particular organisation's current position, if used in an unambitious manner. They provide a skeleton to which to add the flesh. Used singularly they exhibit limitations but, if used collectively, they can be complementary in building an overall picture. However, care should be taken to avoid using frameworks in an inflexible manner when more relevant information might be available. A balance between theory and practice should ensure no analysis paralysis occurs in relation to a particular organisation.

■ Organisational culture

Culture within organisations is very much based upon history, the environment that the company has been operating in, the way that operations are carried out and the type of organisation that it is. Culture is an intangible which permeates an organisation and extends much further than attitudes, beliefs, behaviour and values. Even by labelling a type of organisational classification in terms of

Handy (1976), or Miles and Snow (1978), there will be occasions when change will not be predicted or well received by certain organisational cultures. An organisation structure can be changed overnight as it can be re-drawn and issued the next day or at almost any time. Changing a business's culture is not so straightforward. It can take many months, or even years to change within an organisation, since culture is perceived as 'that's the way we do things round here'. Culture change will only take place when the critical mass of employees has changed. In some situations, if strategy is dependent upon culture change, it can be forced through at a cost as in the case of Halfords in the mid-1980s. Most original Halford employees were dismissed overnight at considerable financial cost to the company. The next day saw a new era with new personnel who would welcome new strategies and who were part of the critical mass of the new culture. Often culture can be the stumbling block to success with growth. In January 1997 Ford decided to downsize production at the Halewood plant in favour of their existing plants in Genk and Valencia. True, the cost of labour might well have been cheaper but in an era when effective organisations are badly affected by labour strikes, Ford UK manufacturing plants have a history and culture of industrial relations problems which are not about to disappear overnight. Ford were not prepared to take unnecessary risks when there were alternatives.

The 'Cultural Web' (Johnson 1988) (Figure 1.3) allows all organisational aspects which comprise culture to be considered under one framework. It suggests that all aspects impinge on each other and contribute towards the recipe for success for the enterprise. History and the learning experiences of managers involved with business strategy influence, and have a bearing on, future decision making so this framework can be beneficial in highlighting areas that are resistant to change. In particular rituals and routines should identify aspects that are highly valued and almost taken for granted that would be difficult to change. Stories as well as power structures involving key personalities also tend to add weight to a valued culture. Symbols including company logos and a distinct

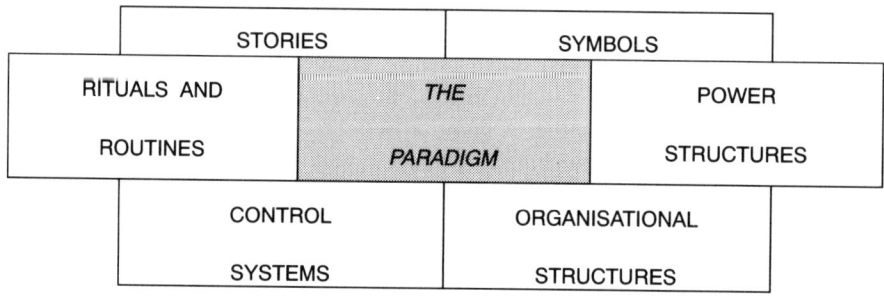

Figure 1.3   The cultural web
Source: G. Johnson, 'Rethinking Incrementalism', *Strategic Management Journal*, 1988.

company jargon all add to the desirability of the culture for many personnel. The paradigm within which the organisation operates outlines what it does well as part of its recipe for success and suggests that any change to the recipe would result in a downturn in success at the present time.

The reader is also referred to Chapter 4.2 and 4.7 where organisational culture is explored in the context of the use of information systems.

■ Rich picture

Once a certain amount of knowledge regarding a particular organisation has been obtained it is worthwhile representing the situation as a cartoon-style diagram, often referred to as a Rich Picture. This allows the complete scenario to be outlined on one sheet of paper and forces the creator to apply lateral thinking which may be beneficial in problem solving. This idea is based on soft system thinking (SSM) suggested by Hicks (1991). Earlier researchers included Checkland and Scholes (1990) who contributed much to the process of Soft Systems Methodology.

A pictorial representation or Rich Picture (see Figure 1.4) is better than a written description, according to Hicks because:

- A picture can show more information in the same space.
- It shows patterns, arrangements, connections and relationships far better.
- It permits the whole of the problem situation to be seen in all its complexity, and gives a feel of its overall shape.
- It provides a representation of the problem situation that can be readily shared with others.

A Rich Picture does not have to be a work of art as long as it makes sense to the creator and often vivid symbols may be used to emphasise certain situations.

■ The McKinsey Seven-S framework

Another framework useful in aiding understanding of many key organisational aspects is McKinsey's Seven-S framework (Waterman, Peters and Phillips 1980) (see Figure 1.5). It provides an initial checklist for analysis, although it should be remembered that the seven areas are all inter-related and a significant change in one area will probably affect the others. It allows the user to see how existing strategy utilises the other six areas effectively or ineffectively and how the success of future strategy change will almost certainly require changes to be made in other key areas such as structure.

■ Value chain analysis

As mentioned previously all successful organisations seek some sort of competitive advantage within their industry. There are several ways of achieving this but in more recent times there has been much discussion relating

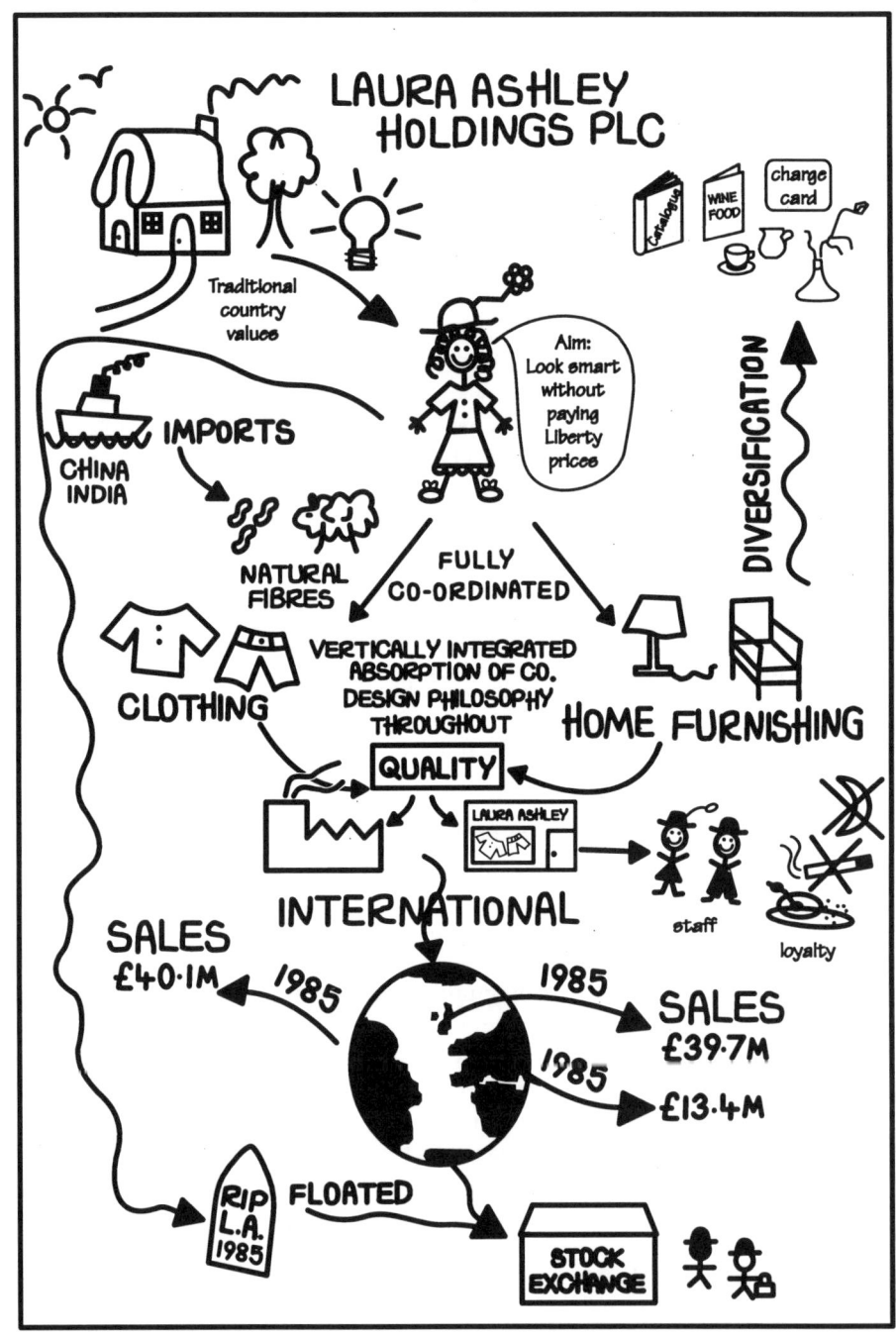

Figure 1.4   A rich picture for Laura Ashley Plc in 1990

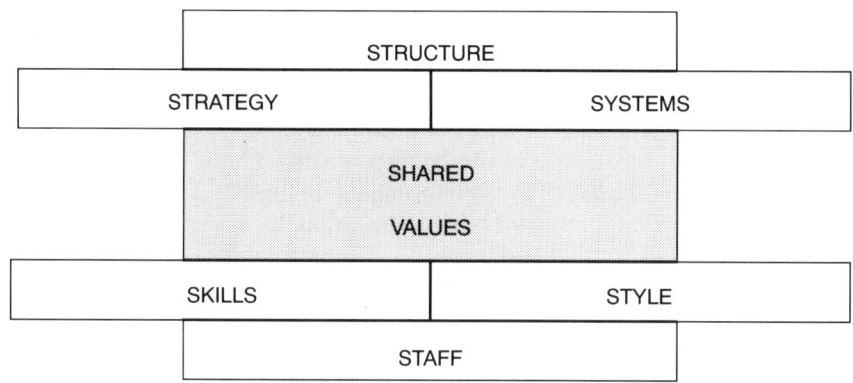

Figure 1.5   The McKinsey Seven-S framework
Source: Waterman, Peters and Phillips, 'Structure is not organisation', *Business Horizons*, 1980.

to Porter's Value Chain (Porter 1985). Whatever the arguments, for and against this, it does allow a systematic approach to organisational activities which, if handled effectively, can provide a source of competitive advantage for the enterprise. In short the primary activities, whether they include the manufacture of motor vehicles or consultancy services, are initially separated from the support activities commonly found in most types of firms, such as IT and Personnel services (see also Chapter 4.3).

The value chain looks at all the operations on a step by step basis and identifies and answers two key considerations. Firstly, is value added at various sequential stages and, if not, then is there at least no erosion of value at each stage on which to build? Secondly is it straightforward to identify weaknesses or inefficiencies in the chain of operations which ought to be improved to create or aid competitive advantage? Used on this basis the value chain can be a powerful analytical tool. It should also identify where effectiveness in one area can aid significant improvements in others which can lead to synergy and again help towards competitive advantage. Overall it can ensure a consistency of value and quality at all stages of operations.

■ Financial appraisal

Organisations need to compare their current performance with both the previous year's performance and also with competitors in their industry. Financial analysis will provide certain performance indicators of interest to external and internal stakeholders. This section seeks to provide awareness of the importance of financial appraisal within the area of business strategy. Figures alone often bypass the fact that return on capital employed (ROCE), for example, overlooks other key areas such as risk and business ethics when following a specific strategy. Financial appraisal does, however, provide an indication of the present state or health of the firm and therefore whether financial resources are available for a strategy of growth, for example. Generally the most appropriate sources of information are to be found within the profit and loss accounts and the balance sheets. These two often provide most of the data required for performance analysis. The balance sheet illustrates the economic state of an organisation in a standard form, at a moment in time, and highlights the sources of finance utilised by a firm as well as any assets which have been acquired. However, it is really only a window of the situation at a particular time. The profit and loss (P&L) account outlines the size of any profit or earnings for a particular trading period and also indicates those factors which have caused profits to rise or fall.

Although there is currently much debate as to how much weighting should be applied to financial information as an input to business strategy, it is nevertheless an important source. According to Luffman, Lea, Sanderson and Kenny (1996) five major areas are of particular importance to strategic appraisal and these form the basis for Ratio Analysis.

- Is the business profitable?   (Profitability ratios)
- Is the trading position satisfactory?   (Trading ratios)
- Is the business solvent?   (Liquidity ratios)
- Is business properly funded with effective use of funds?   (Gearing ratios)
- Are shareholders earning satisfactory returns?   (Shareholder ratios)

Whenever these ratios are used for various time periods, to ensure consistency the same ones should be used each time rather than choosing an alternative ratio. The ratios themselves just paint a picture for an organisation; the interpretation of that picture is the role of the business strategist who will have to weigh up many variables before future strategy is formulated. Not least of these variables is the expectations of the many stakeholders, internal and external, concerned with the enterprise. Will the shareholders prefer higher profits at the expense of any business ethics and to what extent is it advisable to take into account the stance of the local community against the need for quick company profit? These and other stakeholder issues are addressed in the next section.

■ 1.5 Stakeholder Mapping

If a stakeholder is considered as any individual or organisation which can affect or be affected by a particular organisation then it is clear that the influence of stakeholders on business strategy can be enormous. As Stacey (1993) points out, the main strategies put forward 'will turn out to be successful only if their consequences are acceptable to the organisation's most powerful stakeholders.

These consequences must be acceptable not only in the obvious terms of financial performance but also in terms of meeting other stakeholder expectations, including the impact on their power positions and their cultural beliefs. If a pattern of actions is not acceptable to powerful groups from any of the stakeholder categories then the strategy may well fail.'

This adequately summarises the strategic importance of the stakeholder when formulating strategy and reminds us that strategy is a political act, as well as an analytical process. The starting point focuses on mapping out the organisation's stakeholders, in other words those with some sort of stake or interest in the fortunes of that enterprise. Obviously certain stakeholders will be more important in terms of power and influence and these often stand out as the key stakeholders. However, having suggested that change is now very much part of all organisations then certainly the amount of influence that key stakeholders can impose may radically change, perhaps overnight in some cases as, for example, in the print industry. Equally other stakeholders, at some stage perhaps considered insignificant, can become very much influential where strategy is concerned. Hence, as Mintzberg (1994) indicates, it becomes necessary not only to identify the stakeholders but also their stake in the organisation, their criteria for judging organisational performance, how well the organisation performs against those criteria, how these stakeholders influence the organisation, and how important these various stakeholders are.

The implications of not being able to predict the various stakeholder reactions to strategy formulation are enormous. When appraising various options for the future it not only becomes necessary to consider what the organisation could do but also what the organisation should do given the various involvements and expectations of the key stakeholders. A potential strategy which is likely to be controversial to the main stakeholders may well be doomed to failure from the outset. Two useful frameworks for mapping stakeholders are those suggested by Mendelow (1991) and adapted by Johnson and Scholes (1997). These are the power/dynamism matrix and the power/interest matrix.

■ The stakeholder power/dynamism matrix

This aids assessment as to how political effort might be channelled when strategy formulation takes place. There is obvious danger and risk associated with strategies which might prompt an unpredictable response from stakeholders with high power, as in quadrant 'D' of Figure 1.6. Obviously stakeholders placed in the other quadrants are likely to be easier to negotiate with.

Although quadrant 'D' stakeholders might provide problems in certain situations they are powerful allies whenever their support is gained concerning other strategies. It might well prove beneficial to sound out any awkward stakeholders with potential new strategies whenever the occasion arises.

■ The stakeholder power/interest matrix

The power/interest matrix, shown in Figure 1.7, considers stakeholders in terms of power level and level of likely interest to the strategies which an organisation formulates. It provides an indication of required organisation posture to these various stakeholders to help ensure success. The strategy makers should be aware, and this is where problems might arise, that stakeholder positions are not fixed and repositioning can occur at any time. Hence, quadrant 'C' stakeholders need to be kept satisfied because if lobbying of any sort takes place the raising of their level of interest, coupled with their existing high level of power, means that they have now become key players in the game. It is the ability of the strategist to successfully predict both the potential repositioning of stakeholders and their likely response to proposed new strategies or change which singles them out as being visionary and often determines the success or failure of their organisation.

Again the likelihood of new strategies being rubber-stamped by the key players in the stakeholder game is dependent on how well those strategies tie in with the expectations. If those expectations are not met then the key stakeholders in this particular scenario may well become strategy blockers.

■ 1.6 Strategic options and choice

Since business strategy is mainly concerned with building an organisation's competitive position within the various industries in which it competes, it follows that the organisation should continually look for a criterion of adding value whenever there are options and choice to consider. All successful firms, by virtue of an ever changing environment, need almost constantly to change in some shape or form. Those who constantly resist are unlikely to remain competitive in the long term. Thus, after an analysis of the current situation has taken place, the decisions which often need to be made are not only 'what could we change' but very much 'what should we change'.

Considering the discussion of organisational stakeholders in the previous section it becomes very apparent that, although a wide range of options may be available which the firm could pursue, there is likely to be a much more limited range of options which the firm should pursue in order to appease key stakeholders. Much will depend on where or in which direction the organisation wishes to venture. During the last two decades, in some quarters, it has been considered to be macho for a company to pursue growth by means of acquisition or merger. There have also been debates as to the various merits of external versus internal growth and whether UK companies should become more European if not global. The international versus multinational aspects have also been argued. Is there merit in an organisation doing business abroad but being based in the UK or is there benefit in having a multinational set-up

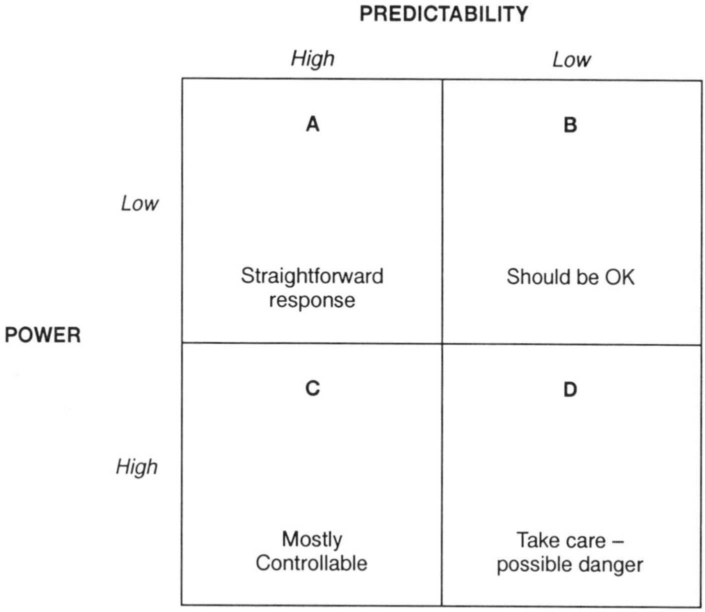

PREDICTABILITY

	High	Low
Low	**A** Straightforward response	**B** Should be OK
High	**C** Mostly Controllable	**D** Take care – possible danger

POWER (row label, left side)

Figure 1.6   Stakeholder power/dynamism matrix
Source: G. Johnson and K. Scholes, *Exploring Corporate Strategy*, Prentice-Hall 1997.

INTEREST

	Low	High
Low	**A** Harmless at present	**B** Do not alienate
High	**C** Consult with	**D** Sound out

POWER (row label, left side)

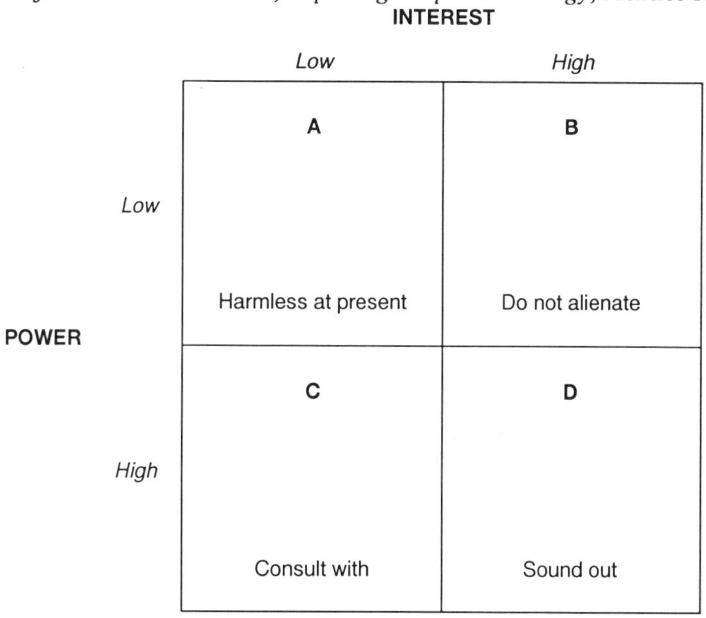

Figure 1.7   Stakeholder power/interest matrix
Source: G. Johnson and K. Scholes, *Exploring Corporate Strategy*, Prentice-Hall, 1997.

which has bases in the various foreign countries. There is just not one best answer, as the optimum solution will be based on a whole range of situation factors. What is in fact perhaps the best option for one company may be suicidal for another.

In order for profits of an enterprise to improve there are three ways to achieve this.

(a) sell more products or services (if possible)
(b) increase the price (but this might reduce sales!)
(c) reduce the cost of inputs and production

There may be little opportunity to increase price as in (b) above unless the product or service in question is perceived by customers to have a unique selling proposition (USP) or is at least differentiated enough from competitor products that customers would not switch with a price increase. Effective companies should always be looking to improve supply costs and production costs ((c) above) as a standard course of action and as an aid to achieving competitive advantage. It is therefore worth exploring (a) in more detail, and the use of Ansoff's (1968) product/market matrix (Figure 1.8) allows this to be done.

A firm can attempt to penetrate the existing market place more either by discounting or by greater promotion. This, however, is limited to the short term regarding possible success. The firm can decide to continue serving its current customers by offering new products or services, as the existing ones mature or become obsolete, but this can become very costly and with no guarantee that new products will successfully emerge. A cheaper alternative is to continue producing existing products and find new markets in which they are still valued. Hence a company manufacturing recently obsolete technology, with no

		PRODUCT	
		Existing	New
MARKET	*Existing*	LOW RISK MARKET PENETRATION	HIGHER RISK PRODUCT DEVELOPMENT
	New	LIMITED RISK MARKET DEVELOPMENT	HIGHEST RISK DIVERSIFICATION

Figure 1.8   Product/market development matrix
Source: H. Igor Ansoff, *Corporate Strategy*, Penguin, 1968.

trading prospects in the Western world, might find viable markets in the developing nations. Similarly the decline in the tobacco markets of the West has been offset by increasing sales in Africa and Asia. Alternatively diversification, consisting of new markets for new products or services, can be sought. Diversification can be related or non-related where risk is increased the further the enterprise moves away from the comfortable and known.

As well as seeking growth organisations can also attempt to consolidate or even withdraw from existing markets. In fact none of the discussed options are mutually exclusive and it is often the case that effective, and hence successful, companies tend to mix and match a range of options rather than placing all their eggs in one basket. The chosen options should not be competitive but indeed complementary to each other. As Sudarsanam points out: 'the particular choice that a firm makes depends on its evaluation of the attractiveness of the market that it wishes to enter or deepen its commitment to, its own competitive strengths, and the potential for value creation when these strengths are matched to the demands of the market. The core competencies or distinctive capabilities of the firm have a decisive influence on its strategic choice' (Sudarsanam 1995).

In terms of strategic choice organisations must be realistic in following only viable options wherever possible. There might be a tendency to want to get into sexy high-profile industries when there is very little logic behind it. Normally if there would appear at first glance to be a dozen or so options then a process of sensible elimination should reduce this to five or six sound possibilities. These then need more serious appraisal before a final choice is made. Where quantitative information or comparison is available then this can help but in many cases only subjective or qualitative information is available. There are a number of evaluation criteria which can be utilised and those outlined by Johnson and Scholes (1997) are as good as any and include suitability, feasibility and acceptability.

Suitability can be used to assess whether the proposed strategy will solve the current problems and add value or generally improve competitive standing of the enterprise. Feasibility should indicate whether the resources are either in place or the finance available to buy them in and whether there is confidence in the capability of the organisation to successfully implement the proposed strategy. The third criterion, acceptability, is related to expectations of the key stakeholders. Is it likely to be acceptable to them without a fair amount of compromise? It is unlikely that a new strategy will be acceptable to all stakeholders and a quick glance at the matrices discussed in the previous section should indicate who the real power brokers are.

It should be remembered that wherever possible stakeholders should not be alienated as any repositioning could make them powerful enemies or strategy blockers in the future. All new strategies as part of any planning process require control to monitor whether they are on target and schedule. Effective business strategy requires regular monitoring. Since it is largely an iterative process all organisations should constantly review the situation to keep the enterprise in tune with the changing environment which can render a strategy which is effective one day obsolete and ineffective the next. The French water company, GDE, have done this effectively and are a good example to use as a strategic case-study.

■ 1.7 Case study: Générale des Eaux (GDE)

■ History and background

In France the production and distribution of drinking water, as well as the collection and purification of waste water, are communal public services which local authorities can either undertake themselves or delegate to a specialised private water company, such as Générale des Eaux (GDE). Whether it is a question of meeting a seasonal demand, such as the arrival of the summer holiday makers at seaside resorts, or avoiding water shortages in drought stricken areas, Générale des Eaux's forty years of experience in the industry makes the company the first choice for local authorities throughout France. The main players in the industry are currently GDE, followed by Lyonnaise (with half GDE's turnover) and SAUR, the smallest of the trio.

Générale des Eaux was founded in 1853 by Napoleon III (the nephew of Napoleon Bonaparte) with the specific intention of improving the irrigation of the French agricultural system and of distributing water to the towns. Today GDE is a world leader in water technology, be it the supply of water to heavy industry such as steel and electricity production, the purification and supply of drinking water or the treatment of waste water products. Based in Rennes, GDE still fulfils its original role in the supplying of 5 billion cubic metres of water each year to French farmers for the irrigation of their crops.

Water contracts are a relatively recent phenomena in France. In the period 1983–93, Générale des Eaux increased its investment by 900 per cent, and over this time the operating profit before depreciation increased by 330 per cent. This rapid growth was funded by the decentralisation policy of the Mitterand government which came to power in 1981. The changes in law introduced by the socialist government enhanced the powers of the local authorities allowing communities to privatise their water distribution networks. This has allowed the private sector's market share to increase to nearly 85 per cent. The heavy investment costs, which depreciate over 20–30 years, have been offset by transferring the usual five-year contracts into concession agreements.

Générale des Eaux is expanding its water services outside France and has subsidiaries in Spain, the United States and Great Britain. In the latter it owns the Three Valleys, North Surrey and Tendring Hundred water companies and has major interests in the Folkestone and District, South Staffordshire and Mid Kent water companies and the Bristol waterworks. It is also expanding into other services and has interests in construction, energy, property management, refuse collection and street cleaning, and transport and parking industries as well as health and audio-visual communications.

Today, Générale des Eaux employs some 200,000 people worldwide (a five-fold increase on the 1980 figure) and has an annual turnover of FF135 billion compared with approximately FF26 billion in 1981. In the water industry alone Générale des Eaux employs 22,000 people, and manages 1,600 purification plants for the treatment of waste products.

■ Water services in France

Générale des Eaux is the main water company in France and is used by 35 per cent of French people. Rennes, the Headquarters of GDE, has no underground water supplies and has to rely on dams, rivers and reservoirs for its sources. GDE supplies 27 million cubic metres of water per year; average consumption per head is 55 cubic metres per year supplied by 2,500 kilometres of distribution network.

The end of the First World War spurred high demand, and in the 1920s water meters were introduced. In the 1990s all households in Rennes now have them. The quality of water is affected by agriculture through the use of too much pesticides, nitrates and slurry. The EU has introduced certain regulations governing the treatment of these chemicals which has led to increased investment in areas such as activated carbon, hydrogen peroxide and ozone. Such investments may warrant an increase in meter charges, but the end result is an improved service to the consumer.

■ The water industry in Europe

GDE is the world's largest supplier of water. Water activities are expanding in France and abroad due to environmental concerns in the industrialised nations. Many recent contracts which have been taken out in France are long-term, and competition from outside would find it difficult to penetrate the water market as French companies are already well entrenched. However, the French private sector is now providing municipal services through expansion outside France. A brief overview of the existing situation and potential opportunities for foreign investment within the water services industry in Europe is as follows.

□ 1 France

Private companies act as concessionaires by designing projects and specifications, raising capital, building infrastructure, managing assets, bearing risks and subsequently pocketing profits. The municipalities (local authorities) delegate virtually all their public service duties to a private company. GDE has been granted the concessionaire for the running of the water supply plant in Rennes. The plants are owned by the local authorities and management contracts usually run for 10–15 years. This can be longer or shorter and is decided by the local authorities whether a concessionaire is granted. Renewal of equipment in plants is the responsibility of the private company, and until now a high standard of water has been achieved to meet EU regulation under the GDE umbrella.

Recent increases in water prices have been due to:

- expensive methods for the collection of water
- charges based on actual volumes consumed
- the powers of regional water authorities having increased in defining and promoting water policy
- reduced contractual flexibility of French local authorities and companies such as GDE in preparation for the opening up of the industry in Europe to increased competition in the European water industry.

GDE is the top company in water supply in France but, due to the static nature of the industry, they have also looked beyond France, as city services around the world become privatised.

□ 2 United Kingdom

Opportunities for foreign investment in the UK are greater with the privatisation of water companies; this has enabled GDE to invest here. They own three water companies, employing some 1,500 people, and supply 900 million litres of drinking water each day. Rather than delegated management, as in France, management by private companies which own the infrastructure is the current practice in England and Wales. There is much hostility directed towards the private companies at the present time, due to water shortages coupled to increased profits.

□ 3 Germany

No prospects of rapid change are likely in the near future as operating services are currently under local government control or through private companies supervised by local authorities. However, opportunities for foreign investment may well arise in the future.

□ 4 Spain

An increasing number of local authorities are considering delegating management of services to the private sector. However, there is currently fierce competition in this area, and several contracts are already run by GDE.

□ 5 Italy

Little profit potential is foreseen in this area, as the existing water services are not anywhere near as effective as some European counterparts at present and so potential foreign investors may well be cautious.

□ 6 Eastern Europe

Management contracts in Eastern Europe are currently blocked by difficulties in identifying the licensing power, decision makers and general key stakeholders necessary for joint ventures from abroad. Also there is not enough international financing to take into account the bad state of installations. To bring the services up to date would required a drastic increase in water prices which would not be tolerated. However, GDE is presently providing some service, the level of which will depend on whether payment for services is forthcoming and how feasible the renovation of certain installations is likely to be.

■ General operations presently within France

Générale des Eaux primarily provides the service of water supply and waste water treatment for millions of consumers, both residential and industrial. The plants and equipment which they use to provide this service are operated and maintained on behalf of local authorities.

□ 1 Water supply

Water is collected behind dams and piped to local treatment works. Operations then occur to clean the water and bring it up to a safe standard for the use of consumers. There are various specialist processes employed to ensure that the required standard is met. Water is then piped to meters in consumers' homes.

□ 2 Waste water disposal

Waste water is piped from consumers to local treatment works where it is cleaned. This operation involves various processes, at the end of which the clean water is returned to natural water supplies whilst the solid element is taken away by road for disposal.

□ 3 Support services

In addition to the product there are a range of associated services that the company also have to provide. For example, they are responsible for maintenance and repair of plant and pipeworks up to and including the consumers' meter, meter reading, invoicing consumers for the use of product and services, and monitoring water quality in rivers.

The quality initiative is not limited to products. It is also aimed at the overall service provided to the consumer. Areas already highlighted for improvement are the simplification of procedures, i.e. drawing up subscription contracts, improved communication by phone and mail, more flexible appointment times and improvements to response times.

■ Marketing GDE

Marketing continues to play an important role, even in companies such as GDE where choice of service is somewhat limited. It is important that marketing techniques are used effectively to ensure customer satisfaction whenever possible (see also Chapter 5.1 regarding the four 'Ps').

☐ 1 Price

Prices are closely monitored by the watchdogs throughout Europe. In France the price is set at the start of the contract and only allowed to change if investment is required or inflation occurs. In the UK, prices are set by individual authorities monitored by OFWAT. Even if two authorities offered distinctly different prices it would be impossible for the water consumer to use a different company's water.

☐ 2 Promotion

Water and sewerage services are a necessity to the water consumer. As already stated consumers cannot easily change suppliers. Therefore, promotion is only required to gain or retain contracts. There is effort being made to market Compagnie Générale des Eaux outside France to increase their foreign investments which already stand at 25 per cent.

There is little scope for competition within France as margins are lower than the rest of Europe. In an effort to gain foreign markets, the division has adapted the very successful way in which it operates in France to fit better the methods used in Europe. This appears to be successful in many countries within the EU, e.g. Spain and the UK, although Germany still limits its public utilities to German companies.

☐ 3 Product development

The spate of legislation and guidelines from the EU on water quality has meant heavy investment by all water authorities. Générale des Eaux has developed advanced treatment techniques based on ozone, activated carbon and membranes, all of which have been tested. Quality assurance procedures and automatic control systems have contributed to the progress made in water quality. The company is also heading a European project, TEDS, aimed at standardising the exchange of analysis results between data banks by direct computer links.

In waste water treatment research into improving techniques in recycling sludge into fertiliser, new detection and automated systems, and treatment of waste by ultra violet rays is currently on-going.

☐ 4 Distribution

There is scope both in Continental Europe and the UK for better distribution of water. In the UK it has been common for consumers not to be able to obtain the water which they require due to drought. In France this problem has not arisen due to high rainfall over the last two years causing flooding. In France, the two major water companies have been experimenting with linking water networks better to meet demand. This also creates even higher barriers to entry into the French market.

In France, due to stories of corruption, doubts have arisen about having the private sector provide municipal services. However some countries are still enthusiastic about French investment and foreign markets now account for 25 per cent of investments in the division.

■ Personnel and HRM issues

Générale des Eaux regard their employees as a highly professional group of people who are keen to provide excellent levels of service and quality. Whether in France or abroad, retaining a highly decentralised policy is at the heart of the group. This structure is designed to make sure responsibilities are shared out and to build cohesion so that each employee has a sense of participating in shared goals. Further efforts were made in 1993 to strengthen this feeling, as the difficult economic situation made it more necessary than ever to encourage cooperation in initiatives and reinforce solidarity between activities and workforces.

The group as a whole employed a workforce of 204,307 in 1993 compared with 201,497 in 1992, an increase of 1.4 per cent. The percentage increase for the group's personnel outside France was higher – 66,157 people were employed in 1993, an increase of 2.7 per cent on the previous year. Employees abroad represented 32.4 per cent of the total personnel employed in 1993, compared to 31.9 per cent in 1992. In France, the group employed 138,150 people in 1993, compared to the 1992 figure of 137,103.

The reader is also referred to Chapter 6, where human resource management issues are discussed in depth.

■ Financial aspects

☐ 1 Water supply contracts

As previously mentioned, These are negotiated with various municipal authorities and normally last 10–15 years, unless company investment is involved, in which case contract lengths may extend to 20–30 years. The normal arrangement is for the municipal authority to make the initial capital investment in plant, which GDE then maintains and operates on its behalf. Both domestic and industrial water supplies are metered by GDE and the ensuing charges cover the supply and treatment of water, together with an allowance for dealing with leakages and other problems. Industrial organisations are able to obtain discounts as volume users. Three per cent to 4 per cent is GDE's normal profit margin for this type of activity, but this figure is higher in other areas of the group's operations.

According to information obtained from a company research report by the French organisation ODDO, made in January 1995, French margins are among the lowest in the world and the report argues that there is little fear of them being reduced much further when contracts are negotiated. It describes water company margins as being 'comfortable without being abusive' and reports that GDE's 'technical know-how and geographic presence assure it a virtually impregnable position'. Because of these factors, ODDO has concluded that the profitability of the water division is not under threat.

☐ 2 Costs to the customers

In 1996, the yearly water bill for an average family was about £200, and although there was a modest increase in net sales, the average volume of water per consumer fell slightly in comparison with the previous year. Although the weather had some influence on this result, consumers were also affected by sharp increases in water invoices.

☐ 3 GDE sales

Excluding fees paid to local authorities, GDE's water distribution sales figures increased two and a half times during the ten-year period from 1983 to 1993, mainly due to an increase in business volume. In 1993 it was reported that GDE had increased its subscribers in France by 2.7 per cent over the previous year and now supplies about 30 million people with water and 19 million with waste water services. In addition, sales in the rest of Europe have continued to rise, particularly in the UK (FF1.3 billion in 1993) where government policy is more in favour of having private companies involved in providing municipal services.

In terms of GDE's water related sales figures, France accounts for 72 per cent and the rest of Europe for 22 per cent of the total. The UK and Germany between them make up two-thirds of the foreign European total and GDE also has concessions in Spain, Italy, the Benelux countries and in a number of Central and Eastern European countries, including Russia.

■ The future for GDE

Since even the most industrially developed countries continue to use their rivers and oceans as a sink for toxic waste and chemicals, the issues surrounding the quality of drinking water will continue to be debated in Europe and, more importantly, worldwide. The ultimate goal is one towards total quality water and so it is likely that the major players, such as GDE, will need to play key roles. Indeed it is difficult to imagine that any future major decisions for the industry will not involve Générale des Eaux. It will also be interesting to see whether GDE decides to diversify into new predatory ventures outside the water industry as it continues to pursue a strategy of growth, initiated by previous Chairman Guy Dejouany. According to Dejouany (1994), 'Since the beginning of the year, GDE shareholding in Cofira, UGC, Electrafina, and British cable networks have increased. The Group has also taken shareholdings in UAP and in Havas, and has subscribed to the Saint-Gobain capital increase and an issue of Alcatel Alsthom convertible bonds.'

'The French water industry model is applicable on a far broader scale – and the Group has in fact made use of similar approaches in other activities. There is still enormous scope for further application, even in France.' Dejouany continues, 'The investment policy which GDE has followed over the past few years has changed the Group considerably, opening it up to new areas, and giving it a truly international base. The group is now among the market leaders in sectors linked to the concerns of today: the environment, urban life, and communications. We will therefore remain faithful to our vocation, and open to the promising prospects which are appearing throughout the world.'

■ 1.8 Using frameworks on the GDE case study

This case study needs to be investigated in more detail and the frameworks outlined in sections 1.3 to 1.5 are very suitable for this purpose, as indeed they are for many other cases. However, due to chapter limitations only a selection of some of these frameworks are applied to the Générale des Eaux case study and these will consider both internal and external aspects. The set questions at the end of the chapter will continue the investigation and analysis and highlight the relevance of analytical techniques applied to organisations.

■ External: the macro-environment

The PESTLE analysis, in section 1.3 (also employed in Chapters 2.2 and 6.4), considers those aspects that have been important in the past and the changes that may be significant in the future. Although the company group operate worldwide the analysis here has been mainly concerned with the French environment due to chapter length constraints.

☐ 1 Political

The Ministry of Environment is responsible for co-ordinating, planning and developing the French water industry and it is subject to public opinion with respect to environmental issues. A long tradition of state ownership and intervention is gradually giving way to privatisation and increased liberalisation. However, if change is forced through too quickly then pressure groups might lobby influential stakeholders to slow the pace of change. Corporate tax has fallen from 50 per cent in 1986 to 33.33 per cent in 1993 though reductions have been balanced by cuts of 10 per cent in aid to industry. High taxation has pushed France into high automation, which fits well with the water industry. Standard VAT (TVA) is currently 20.6 per cent. Changes in political power are not likely to alter dramatically views on services provision or the business environment.

☐ 2 Economic

France is the fourth largest economic power after the USA, Japan and Germany with the lowest inflation rate (1.7 per cent) in the EU. The high value of the Franc has created high labour costs which affects the ability to compete internationally. A high unemployment rate (12.4 per cent in 1995) especially with the young is not beneficial and may mean that some of GDE's customers have problems in paying bills which might affect company strategy in a small way.

☐ 3 Social

The Paris conurbation accounts for one-fifth of the population which is otherwise widely dispersed with the country having a significant agricultural base. Basic conditions of employment are not vastly different to the UK but there is a fixed minimum wage. Although only 20 per cent of the French workforce are registered members of the trades union movement, it is particularly active and regarded as influential. There is scope for companies to show willing to resolve current social problems such as high unemployment and GDE have set up locally based employment initiatives.

☐ 4 Technological

France has adopted a long-term view and is investing heavily in education, infrastructure and technology. As far as the latter is concerned, corporations undertaking research receive encouragement in the form of tax concessions. This support is engrained in French tradition and is only likely to be abandoned if economic circumstances dictate severe cutbacks. Hence, technological advances and change are likely to be associated with GDE on a continuing basis.

☐ 5 Legal

Recent legal issues concerning GDE include:

• Greater transparency and more business information to be made available to local authorities issuing delegated management contracts and to consumers.

- Guarantees that all management companies' contractual expenditure will be dedicated to improving water services.
- EU requirement to allow foreign competition in the award of contracts.
- New European and national standards for waste water treatment.
- A Bribery scandal concerning GDE chairman. Clearly in an industry where business is awarded by contract then competitors such as GDE need to have a positive corporate image ethically and an ability to demonstrate high managerial standards.

☐ 6 Ecological

Across most of the EU there are public concerns about water pollution from fertilisers and pesticide and about conservation of water resources. These problems are being addressed through the European Eureka programme and environmentally friendly technology is positively encouraged. In 1992 the French government announced an ambitious ten-year waste management programme again reflecting considerable concern for environmental issues. It has a special emphasis on recycling and energy recovery with FF15 billion to be spent on waste management systems. Environmental issues are likely to continue to be of paramount importance to most of the EU general public.

■ The micro or industry environment

The micro or industry environment is best analysed using Porter's Five-Forces Model (also employed in Chapters 4.4 and 10.4). In section 1.3, Figure 1.2 illustrates this with consideration given to the competitive environment in relation to Générale des Eaux's core business of water.

☐ 1 Threats of entry

The threat of entry into a market or market segment depends to some extent on the barriers to entry and also exit. If the venture fails and it is not fairly straightforward to exit without a high cost of bad press as well as finance, then this in itself may prove to be a barrier to entry. Within the European water industry there are strong EU demands for open competition between EU members. Additionally numerous existing water supply contracts are soon to expire, bringing with them the considerable threat of competition from non-French companies. Nonetheless there are still significant barriers to entry in place.

Being a large and resourceful company in France, GDE represents a considerable intangible asset and barrier to others. Entrant companies will still need to register in Paris and thus be subject to French control. There is also the considerable accumulated expertise GDE has gained from working with the French system and building up contacts. It has also built up quality to better meet French customers' perceived needs.

☐ 2 Power of suppliers and buyers

The Five-Forces diagram shows a stable suppliers' power position with the key activity related to abstraction consents. Buyers' power is more variable with the municipalities having particularly high influence on the award of contracts and consumers having low power but with the potential of increased influence through trends in the introduction of customer charters.

☐ 3 Competitive rivalry

Competition is likely to increase with the threat of new entries. It is also likely to increase from GDE's main rival, Société Lyonnaise des Eaux, as it will be under similar pressure to retain market share. Increased rivalry might be expected in a mature market. Both companies have strong core traditions in the industry and have not yet built up sufficient alternative markets to dispense with the core business. There could be pressure to reduce prices which could have consequences for profit margins already low despite efficient and effective operations. Acquisition of smaller companies might start to occur (e.g. Saint Gobain and Bouygues/SAUR). Differentiation of services/products could become even more important and GDE have concentrated on quality backed up by strong innovative R&D which has given them a considerable head start and competitive advantage. Lyonnaise, like GDE, has been expanding into world markets such as entry into the lucrative UK market. In the home market Lyonnaise has a similar standing to GDE relying on a substantial reputation but also suffering scandal stories.

☐ 4 Threat of substitutes

Since all customers need water there are no real alternatives. Even if one considered increasing sales of bottled water as an alternative this would only have a bearing in metered areas within the EU. However, many major water companies either own or have substantial shares in the bottling companies.

Already it is possible to envisage an overall picture of the environment in which GDE currently competes. To summarise the situation further the *external* key aspects of a SWOT analysis are presented:

■ Key issues of GDE – opportunities and threats

☐ 1 Opportunities

- Acquisition of small, weaker French companies
- Worldwide markets including lucrative UK and untapped Third World areas
- Government encouragement for R&D and environmental improvement schemes
- Increased privatisation coupled to slight recovery of French economy.

□ 2 Threats

- High wage levels affecting competition abroad
- Worldwide recession in construction industry affecting water related construction
- Legal obligations for greater accountability and transparency
- Expiry of contracts and prospect of foreign entrants and greater Lyonnaise rivalry
- Problems of pollution of water supply and reduced water resources
- Increasing customer knowledge and bargaining power
- Increased priority for lower prices as opposed to high technological standards.

■ Internal aspects

In order to understand best an organisation's current situation a whole range of frameworks may be considered for use. A Temporal Analysis is as good as any to start with. By outlining events in a chronological order it becomes more straightforward to understand the events and aspects which have had a bearing on the organisation to date.

A brief Temporal Analysis is as follows:

- GDE was established in 1853 to help French municipalities organise water supplies.
- In late 1970s GDE began acquiring interests in the engineering and construction fields.
- In 1995 Guy Dejouany, Chairman since 1976, was at the centre of bribe allegations which concerned the award of water supply contracts in Saint Denis, Reunion's capital. This scandal prompted a change of chairman. The succeeding chairman was Chief Executive Officer/Managing Director, Jean-Marie Messier, who had joined the Group shortly before the end of 1994 from Lazard Freres, the Paris-based investment bank.
- GDE is now the leading water distributor in France and provides a complete range of municipal and industrial water management and other public services.
- The Group now operates 2,250 subsidiaries including 600 outside France.
- In 1997 GDE ranks first in the world in distribution of drinking water and first in Europe in thermal power.

■ Seven S's analysis

McKinsey's framework (Figure 1.9) is valuable in enabling a broad insight to be gained of the key elements that make the company what it is. These elements are all linked so that a change in one is likely to have an effect on the others. French shared values of pride and achievement are obtained, for example, by the utilisation and effectiveness of the other Ss.

■ The cultural web

The Cultural Web can be a useful analytical framework for understanding the way in which beliefs and assumptions can guide and sometimes constrain the development of a particular strategy within an organisation such as GDE (see

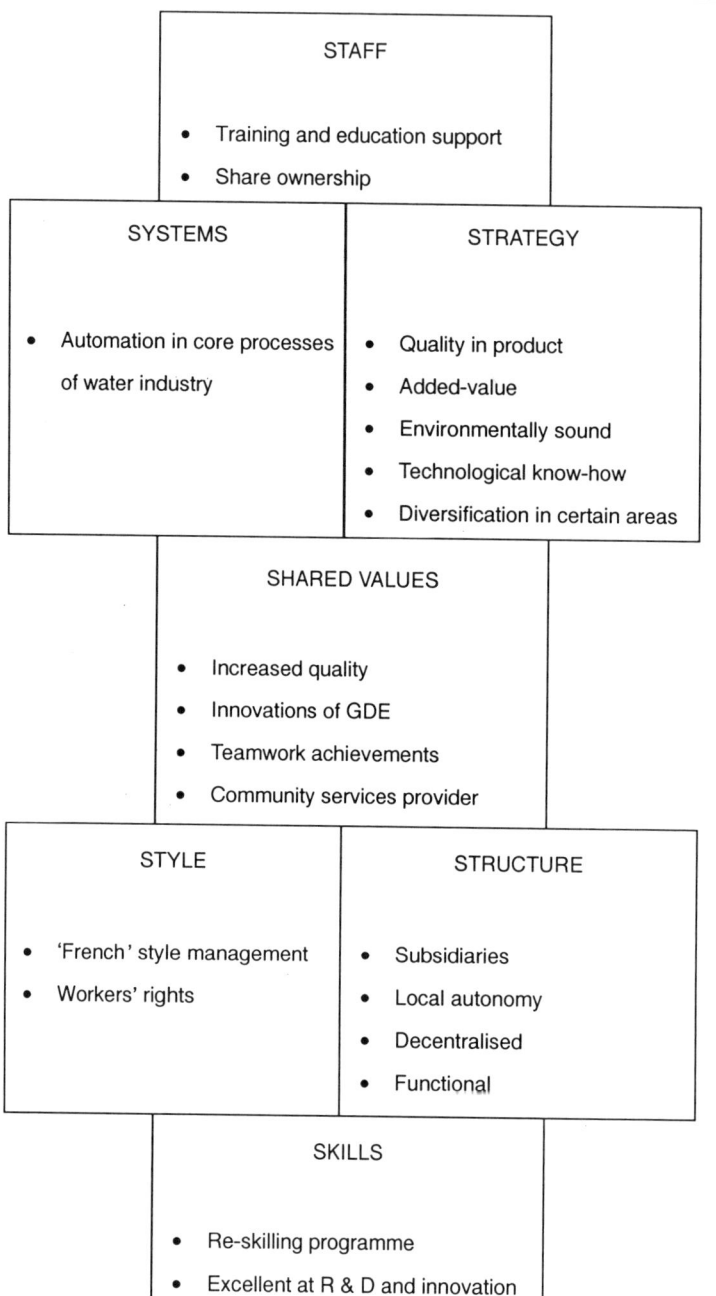

STAFF

- Training and education support
- Share ownership

SYSTEMS

- Automation in core processes of water industry

STRATEGY

- Quality in product
- Added-value
- Environmentally sound
- Technological know-how
- Diversification in certain areas

SHARED VALUES

- Increased quality
- Innovations of GDE
- Teamwork achievements
- Community services provider

STYLE

- 'French' style management
- Workers' rights

STRUCTURE

- Subsidiaries
- Local autonomy
- Decentralised
- Functional

SKILLS

- Re-skilling programme
- Excellent at R & D and innovation

Figure 1.9   McKinsey's 7s framework for GDE
Source: Based on the model in: Waterman, Peters and Philips, 'Structure is not Organisation.'

Figure 1.10). Company culture is encapsulated in the paradigm of the organisation (see also Chapter 4.2 and 4.7). In the case of GDE decentralisation and initiative are a key part of corporate culture. A diversity of activities is seen as necessary to obtain competitive advantage internationally. This raises the question of whether there is any difference in the culture of the core section of GDE and the rest of the Group.

The bribery scandal made the company very anxious about the way in which it was perceived both by the business world and its staff. Consequently the environmental innovations achieved by GDE under Dejouany were replaced by

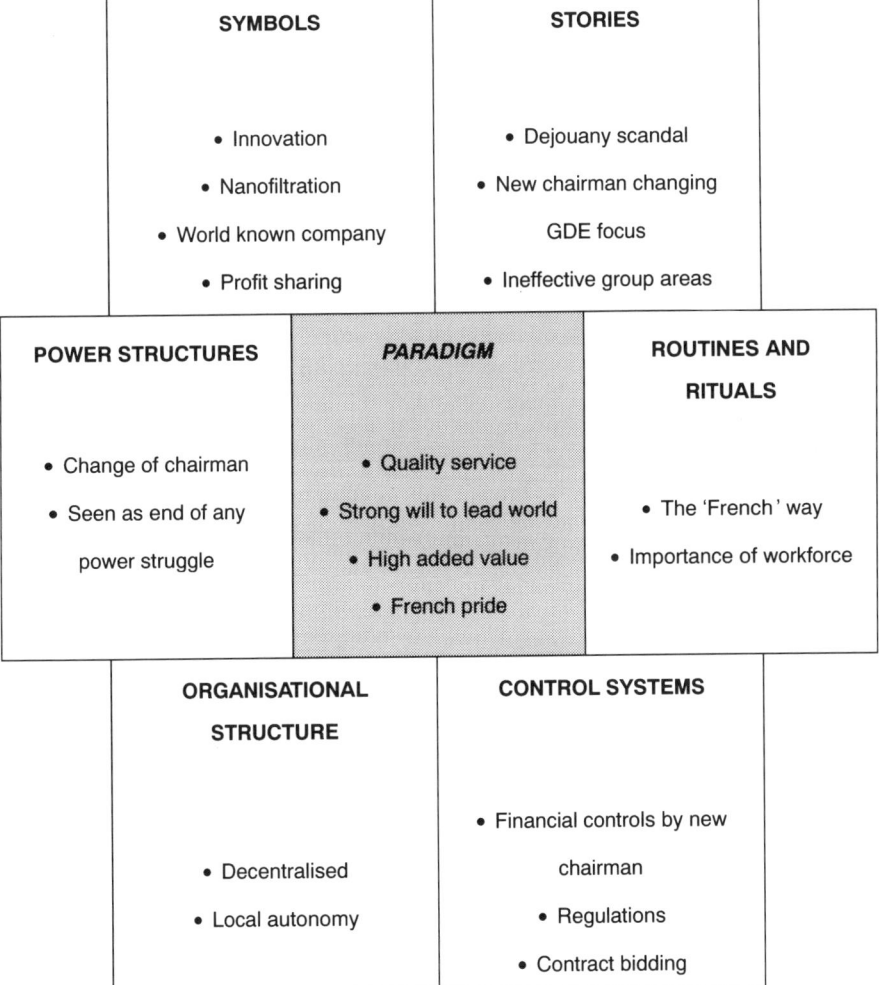

Figure 1.10   The cultural web applied to GDE

more risk-aversive strategies, perhaps to be expected of a new chairman with a financial banking background. Conscious effort has also been made to engender pride in the workforce and demonstrate complete propriety in GDE's activities to the outside world. Control systems of the organisation reflect this emphasis with regulated processes and central financial controls. In return for compliance with this regulated framework there are employee rewards of company ownership through profit sharing schemes and other benefits. The paradigm of the cultural web is the recipe for success and in the case of GDE is built around French pride and quality of service in its quest as a world leader in its industry.

■ Product analysis

GDE's core business of water services comprises the treatment, purifying and distribution of drinking water and wastewater treatment. Primarily this was provided only in France but it is now also being rapidly expanded internationally through the Group's subsidiary companies with a strong presence in the UK and USA.

The Group has overall diversifications in energy management, electrical contracting and power generation (France and USA), waste management, urban maintenance (France and Spain), construction (UK, Germany and France), and media and entertainment, leisure, healthcare and other community services. Thus, while the product range stays relatively static in the water sector, GDE's Group product range is undergoing rapid expansion in the 1990s.

■ Life cycle analysis

The water service industry in France has reached a state of maturity. GDE largely shares the market with its main competitor Lyonnaise des Eaux.

■ Stakeholder mapping

This analysis of GDE stakeholders will focus on the power/interest matrix and a snapshot at the present time looks something like Figure 1.11, although as indicated earlier the position of some stakeholders will vary over time. Municipalities, for example, have high power when contracts are being awarded but this is reduced at other times although their power is still relatively high.

An analysis of the power/dynamism matrix (see Figure 1.6) looking at the predictability of the GDE stakeholders would be beneficial in providing more information on the situation.

■ Summary of GDE case study

Using some of the frameworks applied to Générale des Eaux has started to indicate the present position that the organisation finds itself in with respect to competitors and markets. It is recommended that all of the frameworks

LEVEL OF INTEREST IN STRATEGY

	Low	High
Low	Minimal Effort • Customers • Community • Small shareholders	Keep Informed • Local management • Employees • Trades unions • Group subsidiaries • Suppliers
High	Keep Satisfied • Large shareholders • Banks • Government • Key departments	Key Players • Chairman & Board • Group management • Municipalities

POWER (row label on left)

Figure 1.11   Stakeholder power/interest map of GDE

discussed in this chapter are applied to the GDE case study and indeed to any other strategic case study which requires analysis for that matter. Comprehensive analysis of GDE should highlight the following aspects in relation to the company.

- GDE is in a strong position in the French water market holding high market share. However, this might be threatened by expiry of contracts with municipalities and new foreign entrants bidding for new contracts. Its knowledge of the French systems gives it a strong competitive position though with respect to foreign companies.
- Finding competitive advantage and core competencies to distinguish itself from Lyonnaise is less easy as the two companies have developed side by side. It intends to create differentiation in product and service by concentration on improved quality, through product development and quality customer service, and added value. This is also supported by developing a quality culture.
- In addition to market development abroad the company has increased its product/service range by acquisitions in France and other countries. This offers the possibility of benefit from the transfer of skills and technology.
- In general the organisation seems highly capable of taking advantage as a predatory company, of the main opportunities of profitable international markets.

- The most powerful stakeholders are the Group Board and Chairman who presently through display of strong and assertive leadership assume almost total control over strategy formulation. However, although they explain decentralisation as providing the means to be responsive to municipalities and customers, there needs to be appreciation in the overall strategy of the influence these stakeholders can impart. For example the municipalities become particularly powerful at the time of award of contracts.
- The company's weaknesses seem to leave it vulnerable to the identified threats of greater competition, sluggish demand and tighter standards.

■ 1.9 Conclusions

In a rapidly changing environment organisations need to adapt to these changes to survive. However, short-term survival is no guarantee for life, and constantly staying in harmony with the business environment may provide the opportunity not only for survival but also growth. Reactive leadership is really only short-termism and the successful and effective companies which pursue growth take a far more proactive stance. Entrepreneurial skills and innovation can provide the initiative for such success but in some industries may be considered to be too risk seeking. There is no real recipe for success in business today and a successful formula for one company may be poison to another. Also an opportunity to one organisation may not be so to another which is short of the necessary resources needed to make it a success. Hence, there are no definite rules to follow other than the obvious need for survival or it is the end of the game.

Whether Small and Medium Enterprises (SMEs) are better placed, in the 1990s, to take advantage of the turbulent environment is open to debate. Certainly they are likely to be more flexible to change than the larger corporations but they may have insufficient financial clout for significant growth. However, big is no longer considered beautiful in some current quarters of business. The focus is very much on effective organisations, where Just-In-Time (JIT) delivery is now very much seen as standard practice.

In the constant search for everlasting success, organisations seek innovation not only in their offerings of products and services to the customer but also in the processes which provide these organisational outputs. Business Process Re-engineering (BPR) has had some success in aiding effectiveness but plenty of criticism as well. It has allowed firms to appraise and compare their systems and processes but has not necessarily provided the answers to the many uncertainties. This is because total success with BPR revolves around organisational ability to change culture and that can take more time than some firms are prepared to accept. Gut reaction may have been just as effective in the short term. What is certain is that in the UK alone hundreds of organisations are extinguished every week and just as many others seek the solution for long-term survival. Whether formalised strategic planning, with all of its analytical frameworks, is the answer to many firms is very much open to debate. There might be the danger that, taken to extremes, analysis paralysis occurs, but on the other hand it does allow for the whole picture to be made available to the strategic decision makers. Whether a sensible decision is then made is a different matter. Business Strategy which encompasses these strategic decisions, amongst other things, concerns the whole organisation in trying to ensure that the firm's competences and capabilities are made effective use of given the current business environment. The chapter explores a whole range of strategic frameworks from the value chain, which highlights value adding operations and linkages, to the cultural web which investigates the activities that have led to the recipe of success for the company. Some of these operations and activities might need to be tinkered with in line with proposed strategic change necessary for survival.

Strategy rarely runs like clockwork. Even the best-thought-out plans may need to be amended in light of even further environmental changes. One major recent change has been the formation of the single European market and dismantling of some of the barriers to trade associated with it. This has meant a European challenge for firms prepared to do their homework on market research to enable them to compete effectively in a new market place. Although this has undoubtedly led to greater opportunities to UK-based organisations it has also led to threats to the UK markets from would-be overseas competitors as well. One such organisation, Générale des Eaux (GDE), the French water company, is now very much perceived as a predatory company currently looking to grow with non-related diversification as well as related growth through penetration in the water industry throughout Europe. It recently felt confident enough to bid for one of the UK Railtrack franchises, and even though, on this occasion, it was unsuccessful, GDE is still seeking further growth through non-related areas. The chapter highlights GDE as a case-study and uses various frameworks to analyse and better understand the type of firm it is and the current external environment in which it operates.

Finally the role of stakeholders within Business Strategy is outlined and the importance of understanding how they can block as well as rubber-stamp any potential strategies put forward for implementation.

The chapter is not designed to train the reader as an expert strategist but to provide an understanding and awareness of Business Strategy in general. The examples reinforce some of the key aspects of the chapter and illustrate that often a blend of theory and practical experience can prove invaluable when seeking success in business. Getting the balance right is all important and some organisations consistently do it better than others.

■ Questions for discussion

1.   Complete the SW-OT analysis of GDE by outlining the key *internal* strengths and weaknesses of the organisation.

2. Draw a rich picture of the current situation of GDE.
3. Building on the information provided for the Five-Forces model, discuss where GDE's services would fit Porter's Generic Strategies matrix.
4. Combining all of the available analysis of GDE, use the Ansoff grid to consider future business options which the organisation might realistically pursue.
5. Discuss whether the existing cultural web of GDE might need to be adapted assuming the company pursues a strategy of growth.

■ Bibliography

Ansoff, H., *Corporate Strategy*, (Harmondsworth: Penguin, 1968).

Checkland, P. and Scholes, J., *Soft Systems Methodology in Action* (Chichester: John Wiley, 1990).

Dejouany, G., 'Compagnie Générale des Eaux, Chairman's Review of Operations', June 1994.

Hammer, M. and Champy, J., *Reengineering The Corporation* (London: Nicholas Brealey Publishing, 1995).

Handy, C., *Understanding Organisations* (Harmondsworth: Penguin, 1976).

Henderson, B., 'Strategy and the Business Portfolio', *Long Range Planning*, February 1977.

Hicks, J., *Problem Solving in Business and Management* (London: Chapman & Hall, 1991).

Johnson, G., 'Rethinking Incrementalism', *Strategic Management Journal*, January–February 1988.

Johnson, G. and Scholes, K., *Exploring Corporate Strategy*, 4th edn, (Hemel Hempstead: Prentice-Hall, 1997).

Luffman, G., Lea, E., Sanderson, S. and Kenny, B., *Strategic Management*, 3rd edn, (Oxford: Blackwell Business, 1996).

Mendelow, A., Proceedings of 2nd International Conference on Information Systems, Cambridge, MA, 1991.

Merriden, T., 'The Gurus – James Champy', *Management Today*, October 1996.

Miles, R. and Snow, C., *Organisation Strategy, Structure and Process* (Maidenhead: McGraw-Hill, 1978).

Miller, D., *The Icarus Paradox* (New York: Harper Business, 1995).

Mintzberg, H., *The Rise and Fall of Strategic Planning* (Hemel Hempstead: Prentice-Hall, 1994).

Mintzberg, H. and Quinn, J., *The Strategy Process* (Hemel Hempstead: Prentice-Hall, 1991)

Peters, T. *Crazy Ways for Crazy Days*, video and BBC TV presentation (London: BBC, 1995).

Porter, M., *Competitive Strategy* (New York: Free Press, 1980)

Porter, M., *Competitive Advantage* (New York: Free Press, 1985)

Stacey, R., *Strategic Management and Organisational Systems* (London: Pitman Publishing, 1993).

Sudarsanam, P., *The Essence of Mergers and Acquisitions* (Hemel Hempstead: Prentice-Hall, 1995).

Waterman, R., Peters, T. and Phillips, J., 'Structure is not Organisation', *Business Horizons*, June 1980.

CHAPTER 2

The economics of organisational change

Neil Harris

■ 2.1 Introduction

In recent years the UK financial services industry has undergone rapid changes due to the impact of information technology and resultant concerted efforts to control costs by reducing labour. The blurring of traditional boundaries between banking, insurance and building societies has intensified competition and, in the case of the building societies sector, led to a spate of horizontal mergers and acquisitions. Additionally, some societies have sought to abandon their mutual status and become public limited companies (Plcs) and banks. The move to increased concentration of financial service providers is likely to continue and also apply to insurance companies and possibly banks.

The purpose of this chapter is to use economic theory to explain this behaviour, employing a structure–conduct–performance methodology. This focuses on the theory of oligopolistic markets and, in particular, the tendency of businesses in such markets to merge and undertake acquisitions. The neoclassical model of profit maximising business behaviour is assumed as the underlying rationale. Arguments advanced by building societies for these mergers and acquisitions are tested against the theory and empirical evidence. The limitations of the methodologies and models employed are also discussed.

The chapter concludes by seeking to identify change agents in the medium term in the financial services sector and how the main players might respond to these.

■ 2.2 Why organisations change – rationale and implications

It is a cliche but none the less true that, in modern business, the one constant is change. The variables or market drivers generating change may be external (or exogenous) to the business or they may be internal (or endogenous).

■ External factors

If the former they are likely to include:

- **Political factors** – such as a change of government with the consequent adoption of new policies – as with the switch of emphasis from direct to indirect taxation under UK governments since 1979; an increasing emphasis on the regions within the European Union (EU); deregulation of financial services in the 1980s; and the waves of privatisation across Europe since the mid-1980s.
- **Economic factors** – for example, since the 1970s, the economies of the EU, and especially the UK, have experienced deindustrialisation in their heavy industries due to competition from lower cost newly industrialised countries. To some extent this decline has been offset by the growth of the service sector, such as the financial services industry, which is typical of mature economies.
- **Social factors** – as businesses adjust to ageing UK and EU populations; the growth of the dual income family with no children or the birth of the first child delayed to later in life; the decline of marriage and the increasing divorce rate with its implications for the housing market. All of these impact on businesses' product mix, marketing, and strategic direction generating potential economic costs and benefits.
- **Technological factors** – particularly through the use of Computer Aided Design (CAD) and Computer Aided Manufacture (CAM); improved global communications; the replacement of labour by new technology at both workforce and managerial levels promoting the waves of downsizing or delayering of the 1980s and 1990s; the attendant feature of contracting out as specialist firms supply services previously undertaken in-house, e.g. accounting; information technology; human resources. Additionally new ways have been developed of bringing products to consumers such as cable or satellite shopping channels or the use of the Internet; and new payments mechanisms such as smart cards (e.g. the Mondex electronic purse currently being developed and tested by Midland and NatWest banks).

These forces are also analysed in Chapter 1.3, 1.8 and Chapter 6.4. They and other external factors create enormous pressures on businesses requiring them to respond as quickly as possible or, more importantly, to anticipate change and hence adopt appropriate strategies in anticipation of these changes. They also have substantial economic implications.

■ Internal factors

Internal factors may also be the cause of change although, in many cases, these are likely to be responses to prior external factors. In turn, costs and revenues may be generated. The decision of a firm to go public may be to raise funds for expansion but is likely to be motivated by its competitors' behaviour and hence the market in which it operates. The decision to merge with a rival to achieve scale economies or to integrate vertically backwards with a components supplier may be driven by the desire for more secure supplies or to provide a better base for expansion into foreign markets, but is likely to be motivated, in part, by the potential actions of competitors.

Nonetheless, internal factors do play an important part in their own right. For example many threats to UK banking are perceived to come from internally driven factors and are the consequence of poor management and weak risk control rather than external factors as discussed above (CSFI 1996). This covers such issues as bad lending, slack internal controls, concern with size rather than profitability and unwise mergers and diversification. The factor perceived by bankers as the greatest cause for concern was over-capacity.

One way by which a firm may grow in size is internally, i.e. by making profits and ploughing them back into the business. However in the last twenty years most growth has not been internal so this is not discussed in the context of this chapter.

■ 2.3 The financial services sector of the UK economy

Before considering the theory to analyse the behaviour of building societies it is useful to provide some background detail of the financial services industry and of the building societies sector.

■ Financial services

Financial services may be viewed as a number of overlapping sub-sectors, of which building societies are one; the other two are banking and insurance (Figure 2.1, p. 51). Until the mid-1970s these tended to be relatively discrete; since then they have increasingly competed in each other's markets to the extent that their product/service bases and potential customers overlap considerably. Banks have competed directly with building societies in offering mortgages and with insurance companies in offering life and other insurance products (the so-called bancassurers). In contrast, direct providers such as Direct Line (part of the Royal Bank of Scotland group), which established itself by the provision of telephone-based insurance services, are now offering telephone banking and mortgage services. Pearl Insurance offers a deposit account operated by Midland Bank, Scottish Widows set up its own bank in 1995 and in October 1996 Prudential Banking was launched.

Additionally a number of building societies have entered the traditional markets of insurance companies while some are currently seeking to become banks. For building societies the advantages of insurance diversification are perceived to be the use of their own well-known names, their large customer bases and their branch networks. These enable them to sell their own label products and services rather than being tied to those of insurance companies. Indeed, Abbey National, the former building society, which became a bank in 1989, now obtains 42.5 per cent of its profits from non-traditional activities (*The Times*, 8 August 1996).

In broad terms the financial services sector of the UK economy has therefore undergone fundamental changes in recent years, changes which will continue into the next century. These include:

(i) the increasing concentration of financial services providers through a series of takeovers and mergers, particularly in the building society and insurance sectors. These have included, in banking, Lloyds Bank and the TSB Group's £13 billion merger and, in insurance, the acquisition of Provident Mutual by General Accident in 1995, Clerical Medical by the Halifax Building Society, and the merger between Royal Insurance and Sun Alliance, completed in 1996. Additionally, at the time of writing, there is a proposed merger between Refuge Assurance and United Friendly. Building society mergers are discussed below in section 2.7.

These mergers and acquisitions are essentially horizontal in nature. The best, and yet a disastrous, example of vertical integration in financial services was the building societies' high cost acquisition of estate agency chains just before the late 1980s collapse of the UK property market. In a number of cases high operating losses caused their resale within five years, at times back to their original owners, and often at large losses in terms of sale price.

(ii) a change in the nature of financial services provision as centralised 24-hour telephone and computer based services grow at the expense of high cost branch networks.

(iii) a consequent reduction in the number of retail branches and of employees in financial services.

In banking the number of staff employed was 460,000 in 1989; by 1996 it had contracted to 370,000. Estimates of numbers employed by the start of the new decade are as low as 295,000 (*Sunday Times*, 2 April 1995).

For the insurance sector estimates suggest 100,000 jobs will be lost during the next decade, while estimates of job losses in the building societies sector are 10,000, which realistically look to be very conservative (BBC 2; *The Money Programme*, 3 March 1996).

In some cases staff are retrained or redeployed within the same organisation although in many cases they are not. Most importantly it is the nature of jobs available which is changing within financial services. Many routine clerical jobs are disappearing and more emphasis is placed on the provision of financial advice and the marketing of products and services such as pensions (due to SERPS and government incentives as well as an ageing UK population); plastic cards; mortgages (as the housing market recovers); and shopping via the Internet, once secure payments methods have been developed.

(iv) the previously noted increasing overlap of product and service provision by different sectors of the market.

These changes are due to a number of reasons:

- deregulation of UK financial markets since the 1980s. The Building Societies Act 1986, which widened the range of building society activities, and the Financial Services Act 1986, which led to the Big Bang in the investment industry, have

created a 'level playing field' (Davis 1995) enabling banks, building societies and insurance companies to compete in each other's previously separate areas.
- the increased application of information technology to financial services. This has manifested itself in such ways as the widespread use of automatic teller machines (ATMs), 24-hour telephone banking, the growth of debit cards replacing cheques and cash, and the development of smart cards. (Chapter 4 discusses the Information Technology strategy adopted by the Royal Bank of Scotland.)
- an increasingly competitive environment and culture in financial services, and also in the UK economy as a whole, dictating the need to cut costs as the most effective way to improve profit margins.

Moreover these developments are not peculiar to the UK alone. Globally retail banking has been very inefficient in the past (as measured by a number of variables including the cost to income ratio) due to a consequence of decades of protective regulatory frameworks (*Evening Standard*, 8 June 1995). This has resulted in overbanking in many countries, measured by the number of the population per bank branch. Within the EU in Belgium, for example, the market is concentrated and overbanked (one branch per thousand of the population), although the most internationalised market in Europe; France is overbanked with 26,000 branches, one of the highest number in relation to population size in Europe; Greece is over-concentrated, very regulated, underdeveloped and uncompetitive; while Spain is overbanked (one branch per 2,300 people), very regulated and inefficient (Dixon, 1991). Indeed it was this which, in 1994, prompted Bill Gates, the co-founder of Microsoft, to liken the banking industry to the dinosaurs, while Martin Taylor, the chief executive of Barclays has argued that 'the European Union must have the thick end (*sic*) of 100 major retail banking institutions. There probably needs to be only twenty' (*Sunday Times*, 2 April 1995).

What has not yet demonstrated itself is significantly increased EU competition within the UK financial services industry in anticipation of the completion of the single market in financial services. However, with the proposed introduction of the single currency and the freedom from dependence on establishing costly retail branch networks, which lowers entry barriers, this is likely to develop significantly in the early part of the next decade.

■ The building societies

Building societies have a long tradition dating back to the end of the eighteenth century. They were established as associations of more prosperous craftsmen to enable the latter to buy their own homes in the newly industrialised towns and cities. Some of these associations subsequently terminated themselves when they had achieved their objectives. From 1845, however, permanent societies were formed. Their mutual status derives from these origins since its savers, or borrowers, or both, effectively own a building society, rather than shareholders, as with a company.

During the twentieth century, and especially the last 25 years, the number of building societies in existence has progressively contracted (see Table 2.1). This has coincided with a movement away from regionally based building societies. The contraction, and hence increased concentration, parallels a similar contraction in other UK industries such as brewing, the utilities and retailing. The reasons for this are discussed in section 2.7 below.

It has been suggested that the number of building societies could be as low as two dozen by the end of the decade (*The Banker*, vol. 1, no. 1, September 1995). In the 1990s two distinctive developments have occurred which are likely to change the essential nature of the building societies sector. These are the growth of mergers leading to greater concentration and the movement of a number of societies from mutual status to plc and bank status.

□ 1 Abandonment of mutual status

The abandonment of mutual status, initially by the Abbey National and subsequently by the Halifax Building Society and others, changes the fundamental characteristic of building societies. With plc status the society's first responsibility is not to its savers and borrowers but rather to its shareholders. While initially these are likely to be substantially the same, due to the issue of free shares as an incentive to savers and borrowers to support the abandonment of mutual status, in practice many private shareholders are likely soon to sell and institutional investors will become more and more influential. This links well with the neoclassical model of business behaviour discussed below.

The 1986 Building Societies Act deregulated building societies enabling them to provide all types of financial services which previously they had not been empowered to do: e.g. unsecured loans; unit trust management; insurance services, as broker or agent; land services, e.g. estate agents (Deakins and MacKay 1995). It also empowered them to raise 40 per cent of their lending from wholesale funds, in contrast to earlier when lending was essentially funded

Table 2.1   Decline in number of building societies in last twenty-five years

YEAR	NO. OF SOCIETIES
1900	2 286
1970	471
1972	456
1982	227
1989	126
1992	95
1994	84
1995	81

Source: *The Banker*; Henderson (1993); Deakins and MacKay (1995); *The Economist*.

from deposits. The question to be asked then is why, if building societies are more empowered to compete head on with banks by diversifying into other businesses, do they need to abandon mutual status?

The response to this by societies converting to plc status is that if they were to try and diversify further as mutuals they would be using their reserves as risk capital. Those converting or contemplating conversion see their future as one stop shops or financial supermarkets, where, for consumers, all financial products and services may be obtained in one location. By becoming a plc and bank a building society secures status in the City, can more effectively raise external funds, offer more competitive products, and in the words of Jon Foulds, Chairman of what was then the Halifax Building Society, is enabled to be an innovator not a follower of personal financial services, e.g. pension selling and financial advice regarding tied products. However unlike retail banks it will not have corporate customers (BBC Television, Panorama, 29 April 1996). In other words the argument is that mutual status is not compatible with aspirations to be a financial services 'one stop shop'.

Critics of this policy, such as the Consumers' Association, argue that in practice customers lose when a building society converts to a bank. Returns to savers are less while rates paid by borrowers are higher for a bank compared with a building society, resulting in less competitive products. The other real criticism of moves to plc status is that the major beneficiaries are senior management and directors who receive substantial salary increases and attractive share options once mutual status has been given up. Managerial theories of organisational behaviour such as Williamson's managerial utility theory have long argued that managers seek to maximise their utility – such as salary, job security, status and prestige – rather than owners' profits. So long as a satisfactory level of profits is achieved they have the discretion to pursue their own goals and shareholders will accept this (Williamson 1964).

It is interesting to note that a number of insurance companies are now considering abandoning mutual status, the Halifax Building Society takeover of Clerical Medical leading the way. This has given the Halifax a presence in the IFA (Independent Financial Advisers) part of the insurance market to complement its presence in the tied sector through Halifax Life. Scottish Equitable demutualised in 1994 and Norwich Union has signalled its intention to demutualise and undertake a £5 billion float on the stock exchange in 1997 (*The Banker*, April 1996). Other insurers have always been proprietaries so the two forms of privately owned and publicly quoted businesses have coexisted in the insurance market for years.

□ 2 Greater concentration

Table 2.2 presents the twenty leading building societies in the UK in 1995.

Compared with the previous year there have been a number of significant changes. The Halifax (number 1 in 1994) and the Leeds Permanent (number 5 in 1994) building societies have merged under the name of the Halifax. In 1994 the

Table 2.2   Top 20 UK building societies 1995

SOCIETY	ASSETS (£000)	PRE-TAX* PROFITS (£000)	MORTGAGES** (£000)	CAPITAL*** PERCENTAGES %	COST TO INCOME RATIO %
1. Halifax	98,387	933,200	75,558	7.99	38.40
2. Nationwide	35,700	287,500	27,693	8.00	47.60
3. Woolwich	27,317	279,100	21,512	8.00	42.61
4. Alliance & Leicester	21,032	245,000	16,359	8.95	60.86
5. Bradford & Bingley	15,597	141,500	12,140	7.50	49.50
6. National & Provincial	13,885	151,500	10,663	7.70	51.49
7. Northern Rock	11,541	144,500	9,407	6.47	33.33
8. Britannia	10,927	97,400	8,224	7.70	46.30
9. Bristol & West	8,536	58,200	6,985	7.40	45.57
10. Yorkshire	6,367	76,517	5,149	8.10	40.52
11. Birmingham Midshires	6,273	45,000	3,537	8.10	59.55
12. Portman	3,514	35,500	2,574	7.75	45.72
13. Coventry	3,379	40,706	2,718	7.71	40.52
14. Skipton	3,030	26,044	2,152	7.01	37.90
15. Leeds & Holbeck	2,609	14,512	1,853	6.86	39.23
16. Chelsea	2,596	27,300	1,835	7.60	46.15
17. Derbyshire	1,843	21,031	1,486	7.91	51.75
18. Norwich & Peterborough	1,557	13,877	1,161	7.00	52.38
19. Cheshire	1,510	19,085	1,221	8.36	37.03
20. West Bromwich	1,508	9,074	1,199	7.89	53.02

Key: *   Profit on ordinary activities before tax.
       **   Class 1 (advances secured on residential property) and Class 2 (other advances secured on land).
      ***   Gross capital as a percentage of shares, deposits and loans.
Source·   The Building Societies Association.

(unmerged) Halifax had assets of £72,151,000, pre-tax profits of £975,000 and mortgages totalling £58.5 million. In comparison, in its last year of independent existence, the Leeds Permanent had assets of £20,620,000, pre-tax profits of £245,000 and mortgages of £16.24 million.

The Cheltenham & Gloucester Building Society has merged with Lloyds bank although it continues to trade under its old name. In its last year as an independent organisation its assets totalled £19.4 million, its pre-tax profits £219,000 and its mortgages £15.9 million. Interestingly its cost/income ratio, at

31.8 per cent, was significantly the lowest of the top 30 building societies (the next nearest was Northern Rock with 34.3 per cent).

Additionally the Abbey National has acquired the National & Provincial Building Society (number 9). There were also exploratory talks between the National & Provincial and Leeds Permanent Building Society concerning a merger but these foundered due to differences in management philosophies. The Bank of Ireland also indicated its intention, in April 1996, of acquiring the Bristol and West Building Society. Additionally, in September 1996, the Prudential Corporation, the largest life insurer in the UK, restated its interest in acquiring a building society.

Further, at the time of writing, the Woolwich Building Society intends to become a Plc in mid 1997, while the Northern Rock intends to float in October 1997. Additionally the newly acquired Bristol & West is becoming a public limited company as is the Alliance & Leicester Building Society, the latter also being rumoured to be interested in acquiring the Bradford & Bingley Building Society.

The above poses the questions of why this spate of mergers and acquisitions has taken place and how effectively does economic theory explain this? If the economic model examined in the next sections of this chapter is to be useful it must also permit an explanation of the why building societies behave as they do and enable predictions to be made about future performance.

■ 2.4 The structure–conduct–performance (SCP) methodology

This analysis examines the characteristics of an industry to determine the structure of the market in which its goods and services are sold. From this it is possible to determine how it, and the buyers and sellers which comprise it, are likely to behave – in other words its conduct. As a consequence predictions may then be made about the probable performance of the market.

Economic theory seeks to explain business behaviour either from a static viewpoint, i.e. at a moment in time, or from a dynamic viewpoint, i.e. over time. Although this analysis explores business behaviour and equilibrium from a static viewpoint it does seek to address some of the important dynamic implications relating to mergers and acquisitions.

■ 2.5 Structure

The structure of a market refers to how it is organised. To determine its competitive structure a number of variables must be considered. These include how many businesses supply the product onto the market; their relative size; the nature of production costs; how far they have diversified into other markets, enabling cross-subsidisation of loss making ones; the extent to which entry and exit barriers exist and their height; and the elasticity of demand for the goods/ services produced.

This is a simplification, of course, and as Gowland and Paterson (1991) argue, there are other structural variables to be considered including the role of imports (i.e. alternative suppliers) and the structure of foreign markets (with opportunities for increased production to supply to them), the speed of technological change, the structure of buyers of the industry's products (and whether they have market power), the structure of suppliers of the inputs (and whether they have market power), the turnover of customers (measuring the effectiveness of advertising among other things), and the capital/output ratio and nature of the production function (with implications, among other things, for entry barriers). Nonetheless, for the purposes of this chapter, only the first group will be examined partly through limited space but also since these are the most significant in this particular case.

■ The number of suppliers and relative size

The importance of examining market structure is to determine to what extent competition exists and hence how prices and levels of outputs are determined, the extent to which non-price competition is employed, such as product differentiation through advertising and branding, etc. Traditional economic theory provides a range of market structures determined by the number and size of suppliers operating in each market and their degree of market power, from monopoly with a sole seller or with a group of firms acting as sole seller on the one hand, to a very large number of firms selling homogeneous products at the other extreme (perfect competition). Perfect competition, which is also characterised by its large number of economically small buyers (who with sellers are therefore price takers), no entry and exit barriers and perfect knowledge typifies competition in its 'purest' sense without restrictions where all can compete on equal terms. In practice it exists only rarely and so theories of imperfect competition are used to explain the real world – these do not meet all the criteria required for a market structure to be perfectly competitive.

Between monopoly and perfect competition lie the two market structures of monopolistic competition and oligopoly. In practice many industries may be described as oligopolistic in nature; they are dominated by a few large firms which may or may not collude to fix prices, output etc. This does not preclude the existence of other smaller firms in the industry whose behaviour is likely to be influenced, at least in part, by the dominant firms – as in the building society sector. Indeed one key characteristic of oligopolistic industries is the mutual interdependence of businesses ie what one does will impact on others in the industry and in turn their response will feed back to the first organisation.

Certainly the large businesses in an oligopolistic industry are likely to exercise some influence over market price. Smaller businesses are likely to be price takers in that they have to accept the prices set by the large ones. Nonetheless they are likely to pose a challenge collectively to the large suppliers even if individually one firm is likely not to have much of an impact. This is because, through their advertising and/or focusing on a market segment, either geographically or in terms of products or services, they may be able to compete effectively and profitably at the margin of the large businesses' activities, even though the benefits of economies of scale are beyond them.

In this sense then the real nature of competition is better explained by the theoretical models of oligopoly (although there is not one coherent and integrated theory) than by perfect competition.

The building society sector of the financial services industry consists of suppliers of which some are national organisations with substantial economic muscle, as shown in Table 2.2. At the other extreme are small regionally based mutual societies, such as the Marsden Building Society, in Nelson, Lancashire, or the 26-branch Dunfermline Building Society in Scotland. With only limited branch networks offering a much narrower range of services, they focus on core building society activities of deposit taking and mortgage provision. As such they may be viewed as more typical of the earlier regionally based building society sector.

Overlapping with the building society sector are retail banking and insurance which provide similar services, as shown in Figure 2.1. The deregulatory impact of the 1986 Financial Services Act, and the fact that many banks and insurance companies are long-established organisations with large financial resources, make the building society sector a very competitive oligopolistic market. This

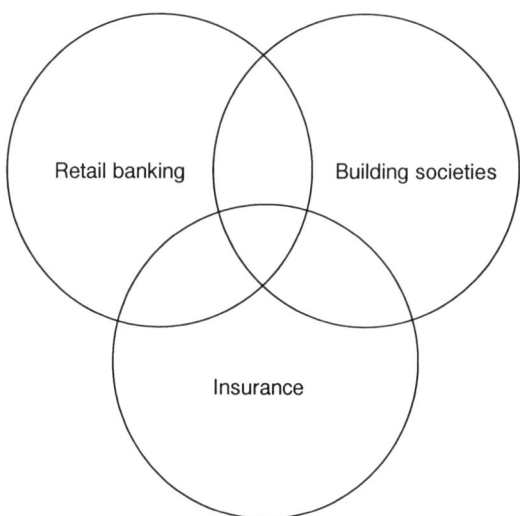

Figure 2.1   The financial services industry

can be seen in terms of the reduced price fixing capabilities of the building societies in the 1990s compared with the 1970s.

Twenty years ago building societies operated a cartel for fixing interest rates; by 1983 this had broken up (Deakins and MacKay 1995; Coles 1996). Nonetheless until very recently societies still tended to keep their rates close to each other and to compete more on non-price grounds through competitive marketing strategies to achieve market segmentation. However, the recent action by a number of mutual building societies, such as the Newcastle Building Society and the Yorkshire Building Society, to lower their interest rates to borrowers but not to depositors, and to finance this from their reserves, has given them a competitive price advantage over the large societies which are seeking to secure plc and bank status, and which will, therefore, distribute part of their reserves to members as a sweetener to accept these proposed changes when they become public limited companies.

This is further reinforced by the provisions of the 1997 Building Societies Act which removed the five-year takeover protection period for any building society which converts to a bank and then seeks to take over another financial services provider. Additionally under the terms of this legislation, societies retaining their mutual status will be able to compete more effectively with banks and diversify into new activities such as operating a rural post office, whereas previously they could only have an agency in one (*The Times*, 19 March 1997).

□ 1 Theories of oligopolistic markets

The theory of oligopolistic markets lacks the concision of other market theories. This is because of a variety of different market structures which exist under the generic heading of oligopoly. For example a particular market may have a cartel operating to fix its members' prices or output quotas (known as collusive oligopoly because the firms collude with each other). Conversely another market may find firms competing with each other on price or non-price (eg advertising) grounds without any attempt at cooperation between them (known as non-collusive oligopoly).

Because of these differing conditions a number of different theoretical models have been developed over time to try and explain how oligopolistic firms behave. For non-collusive oligopoly, which is relevant to the financial services industry and building societies, these have included Cournot's duopoly model (1838), Bertrand's duopoly model (1883), Chamberlain's 1930s oligopoly or small group model and Sweezy's kinked demand curve model (1939).This last theory was subsequently employed by Hall & Hitch to explain stickiness within a certain range of prices.

It is the latter theory which is still widely used in introductory economics textbooks today although it has theoretical deficiencies. For example it seeks to explain why firms are reluctant to move from a stable market price but it fails to explain how that price was determined initially. It also fails to acknowledge that price stability may be due to other factors than those defined in the model.

In the 1950s Stackelberg's duopoly model was published as a development of the Cournot model. More recently the Cournot model has come back into favour and is, for example, used by Deakins & MacKay (1995) to determine the quantity of services provided by banks and building societies. As they note its value lies in its ability to predict the behaviour of firms and its determination of a stable market equilibrium (ie the amount of services each firm supplies onto the market and from which position there is no tendency to move).

More recently game theory has been developed to explain how businesses which do not collude behave in oligopolistic markets.

- Within this theory a business makes assumptions as to how other businesses in its market will behave in response to what it does; on the basis of these assumptions it will choose a best strategy.
- It doesn't need to know what the other businesses will do but it does need to be able to measure the effects of what they do to determine the expected value of the payoff (or returns) from each alternative policy it adopts.
- Of course it cannot be an exact value of payoff since no business has perfect knowledge of what will come about.
- Depending on its assumptions a business may adopt one of a number of different strategies.

The author is mindful of the fact that the above section is rather theoretical for a non economist. He therefore suggests that any reader who wishes to pursue further the theories identified above refer to any of the excellent books mentioned in the bibliography and particularly Koutsoyiannis (1987). The reader is also referred to Chapter 10.3 where increased concentration is explored in the context of the UK shipping industry. Porter's Five Forces model used there to analyse industrial structure may be compared with the Structure–Conduct–Performance methodology employed in this chapter.

☐ 2 Mergers

Although the building society sector has been likened above to non collusive oligopoly, when mergers and takeovers are examined, the most appropriate model is that of collusive oligopoly and particularly the joint profit maximising cartel (Koutsoyiannis 1987). Indeed the difference between a cartel and a merger has been described as only one of degree (Stigler 1970). As Koutsoyiannis notes, a merger involves creating a new business from a number of existing independent ones. The new business may or may not decide to change the output of each of the constituent elements. For example, following the Halifax–Leeds Permanent building societies merger nearly all the branches initially closed through rationalisation came from the old Leeds Permanent, reflecting the weaker partner in the relationship. Each business will be allocated output levels where its marginal cost is equal to the common marginal revenue of the newly merged business. In that sense, Koutsoyiannis argues, the only real difference between a cartel and a merger is that the former is illegal in the UK and US whereas a merger normally is not. However, mergers are usually justified on the grounds of using resources more effectively and achieving economies of scale. Also the ability of a merger to exploit its increased market power to seek monopoly profits will be constrained by potential entrants to the market, i.e. Baumol's contestable markets theory which is discussed below. However, she adds a rider that the implied reallocation of resources and output may not actually take place, although in practice it normally has in financial services.

The motives for mergers are discussed in section 2.7 below.

The effects of a merger can be examined by the diagrams in Figure 2.2 which draw on the model used by Koutsoyiannis.

As an illustration, two building societies located in Southern England, the Sarisbury Building Society and the Titchfield Building Society, have merged creating a new public limited company which has also just secured bank status. Imaginatively named Titchfield & Sarisbury Bank Plc its objective is to maximise profits. Although each former society spent money on marketing to create a distinctive image for its financial products and services, for the purposes of this analysis they may be assumed to be homogeneous and aggregated as one commodity.

All decisions regarding the quantity of financial goods and services provided are of course made by the new bank including the amount supplied by each of the former building societies. The bank's economics department will estimate the demand (denoted D/AR standing for Demand/Average Revenue) and marginal revenue (MR) curves as shown in figure 2.2 (c). The bank's supply curve (denoted ΣMC) is obtained by aggregating each former building society's marginal cost (MC) curve. Where $\Sigma MC = MR$ determines the level of goods and services provided by the bank.

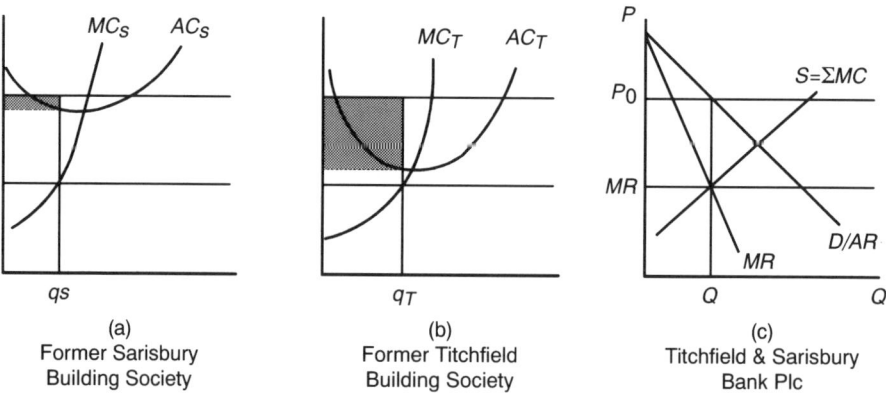

Figure 2.2 **Output allocation model for post-merger sections of a new organisation**

For each former building society (shown in Figure 2.2 (a) and (b)) its share of output will be determined by where its *MC* curve equals the bank's *MR*. For the former Titchfield Building Society this is at *qt*; for the former Sarisbury it is at *qs*. Together $qs + qt = Q$, which is sold at price *P* (where the bank's Demand and Supply curves intersect). The former Titchfield Building Society has lower costs and hence produces more that the former Sarisbury. The shaded area in 2.2 (a) and (b) above the Average Cost (*AC*) curve show the profits each part of the new bank contributes to the total.

There are a number of difficulties associated with this model. In practice, calculating the demand curve of the new bank for a range of different products and services (instead of merely one as assumed here) may pose difficulties, certainly in the short run. Secondly strategic considerations may, in practice, override economic ones. In our example, if the branch network of the two former building societies overlaps, it may be that the majority of the closures affect only one of them – say the Sarisbury. As Koutsoyiannis noted, rationalisation may not occur, so the new bank may experience scale diseconomies; this will cause $S = \Sigma MC$ to shift upwards and to the left, reducing *Q* and raising the price(s)/charges levied. In turn the bank will then lose market share to other financial services providers. In practice, because the financial services market is increasingly competitive, the ability of the new bank to raise its prices/charges will be relatively limited – so it may just have to accept lower profit margins, at least in the short term.

■ The nature of production costs

The most important aspect of cost conditions is whether economies of scale exist in an industry. These are illustrated by a declining long-run average cost curve, i.e. lower costs per unit of output. Introductory textbooks discuss economies of scale in the context of plant economies, e.g. relating to labour specialisation and the division of labour within the productive process, or to where inputs of other factors may be reduced per unit of output, or to the existence of plant indivisibilities where machinery can only be used economically at high levels of production. Indivisibilities can also relate to management and administration however. Economies of scale can only apply to monopolistic and oligopolistic markets because of the minimum size needed to achieve them.

Other causes of economies of scale relate to the organisational structure of a business where, subsequent to a merger or takeover, the two head offices are combined, including corporate functions such marketing, information technology and human resources. The absence of a large overlap, inhibiting the merger of computer systems for example, may prevent such scale economies being achieved (causing x-inefficiencies, which are discussed in section 2.8).

In financial services, reductions in the number of retail outlets, where these overlap geographically, is a different example of cost reductions. Rationalisation on this scale can effect significant economies and may remove potential diseconomies of scale.

Financial economies are another example of scale economies. A large organisation finds it easier to raise external funds than a smaller one, and at more favourable rates. This argument has been used by building societies both to support mergers and also to justify moves from mutual to plc status as a precursor to subsequent anticipated growth. In the same way pecuniary economies may arise from a reduced price per unit of input as a result of large-scale purchase of consumables such as stationery.

Scale economies also relate to output distribution as well as production. Hence the impact of the information technology revolution on financial services. Although the number of current accounts is nearing saturation level other areas of financial services continue to offer growth potential. To the extent that these can be promoted through telephone banking, output growth is feasible at lower costs, both through new technology and through further downsizing of staff.

The difficulty of arguing the importance of economies of scale as a key cost condition determining the structure of a market is actually measuring whether they occur. As Davies (1991) argues, one problem is data suitability – that which is available measures costs in accounting terms rather than in terms of the economic concept of opportunity cost. Again firms' costs are largely historical whereas what is needed for an individual firm is costs at alternative levels of output currently and with the same fixed factors. Davies also makes the point that cost differences between firms may reflect different levels of capacity utilisation rather than differences in scale economies.

George, Joll and Lynk (1992) stress that the statistical approach to estimating scale economies measures average production costs of different sized firms or plants. This requires a large number of observations to make the results significant yet will bias results towards relatively small optimum size of plant to achieve scale economies – which is supported by findings. Other problems relate to the different mix of products/services firms supply, different input prices paid and different accounting procedures used by different firms to value fixed capital. As a result statistical estimates (as these are known) do not compare like with like and hence doubt is cast upon their validity.

Other ways of analysing scale economies are the survivor approach and the engineering approach. The interested reader is referred to George, Joll and Lynk (ibid).

The achievement of scale economies has been used consistently as a rationale for building society mergers. 'An Alliance & Leicester spokesman said "everyone is talking to everyone, because the building society industry is looking for economies of scale."' (*The Guardian*, 5 April 1995). The main logic of this is the existence of excess capacity within the financial services sector. With mergers reducing the number of outlets and hence creating larger leaner organisations growth potential develops and hence the opportunity for scale economies.

In reality there are also risks of diseconomies of scale especially if organisations are created which are too large. In 1995 talk centred on mergers of three or even four building societies at a time to provide scale economies. If the point of minimum efficient scale is passed then extra provision of financial services and products will create unit costs which grow faster than any increase in output of goods or services. This is particularly relevant to information technology with the acquisition of new all compatible computer systems which often fail to achieve their performance goals or are abandoned (*The Times*, 24 July 1996, Interface p. 2). The other major risk, a direct consequence of mergers, is the proliferation of a bureaucracy generating costs but not output.

■ Diversification into other markets

As Pass and Lowes (1994) argue, where businesses have diversified into other markets they secure a competitive advantage over those which have not. They are able to use the profits from established markets where their products sell well to cross-subsidise goods or services in these new markets where they are less successful. This will strengthen their position in the latter in relation to that of existing and new competitors. (The reader is also referred to Chapter 10.7 where diversification is discussed in relation to UK shipping.)

Although cross-subsidisation may not make economic sense in the medium to long term, because resources are not being used with maximum efficiency, in the short term the business may well perceive that the tactical advantages of cross-subsidisation outweigh this. Certainly diversification is a key feature of financial services markets. Although providers do not make available confidential information about the profitability of individual products it is safe to assert that there are examples where financial services providers have moved into new markets and been forced to subsidise these heavily. The early provision of credit cards by the clearing banks in the 1970s was one example while building society forward vertical integration into the estate agency market in the 1980s was another. In each case profitable core activities subsidised these new ventures, a parallel with the economic argument for subsidising new or infant industries. Of course, as businesses move towards devolved profit centres the scope for cross subsidisation reduces.

■ Entry and exit barriers

Entry barriers are restrictions limiting the entry of new firms to an industry. As such they are most commonly associated with monopolistic and oligopolistic market structures. The higher these entry barriers are the more difficult entry becomes until, in extremis, when a barrier is infinitely high all entry is excluded. Entry barriers act as a tax, in effect raising the capital and/or operating costs of a new firm, reducing its competitiveness and profitability and hence discouraging entry into the new market.

Existing firms in an industry with entry barriers are therefore able to secure long-run excess or monopoly profits. If free access to new entrants exists, as in perfect competition, then these firms will enter and compete away the excess profits, enabling all firms only to make normal profits. A number of different types of entry barrier exist including legislation; product differentiation through advertising, free offers etc. which creates brand loyalty; and economies of scale where the production costs of existing suppliers and hence the prices they charge are so low that new entrants cannot match them. In the past the acquisition of high street premises was a significant entry barrier to new financial services providers. However, as noted elsewhere, with the advent of telephone banking and other financial services provision, the height of this barrier has declined very substantially.

When exit barriers exist there are costs incurred in leaving that market. Depending on the nature of the activity and the speed with which a business wishes to withdraw these costs can be substantial. They may include sale of premises, specialised plant and other equipment which has limited alternative use, unsold stocks and works in progress which have to be written off, redundancy payments for staff, etc. Retail banks have experienced these costs significantly in recent years as branch networks have been reduced. If exit barriers are estimated to be high then a firm may be discouraged from entering that market in the first place.

The theory of contestable markets was developed by Baumol in the early 1980s and has direct relevance to the above. He argued that the number of firms in an industry is not what is crucial. Any market structure can approximate perfect competition provided that a firm can enter and leave the industry at zero cost without restriction, i.e. no entry or exit barriers exist. In that case, if monopoly profits exist, a firm can enter, compete them away and leave the market. The very threat of potential entry to firms already in the market will therefore prevent them from exploiting their established position to secure excess profits.

In financial services the need for banks to secure authority from the Bank of England before they may accept deposits is a clear example of a legislative entry barrier (building societies are excluded from this while insurers are authorised by the Department of Trade and Industry (DTI)). This requires them to convince the Bank as to their solvency, probity and the competence of their management. The 1986 Banking Act also required any institution using the name bank to have paid up capital of at least £5 million.

Similarly entry barriers exist in the form of brand loyalty by consumers to particular financial services providers. Indeed the majority of customers have, in the past, stayed loyal to the bank with which they have a current account for all their lives – although this is probably as much due to inertia through customer perception of limited choice through an homogenous product, as to customer satisfaction, since recent surveys have indicated significant levels of customer dissatisfaction with some clearing banks' services.

Since there is now considerable overlap between banking, insurance and the building societies, entry barriers are lower for existing financial services providers than they would be for a new entrant. Even a business such as BAT (British American Tobacco), which in the 1980s sought to diversify from the declining cigarette market by the acquisition of Eagle Star Insurance, had to incur large costs from the initial purchase. However, the impact of information technology has lowered entry barriers substantially as with the development of telephone banking. This has also facilitated the entry of new players such as Virgin with its personal equity plans, Marks and Spencer Financial Services with its credit card, insurance, personal loans, etc., and, in October 1996, the proposal by the supermarket chain Sainsbury's to provide full telephone banking services in conjunction with the Royal Bank of Scotland. Potential competition from other EU countries, although not yet significant, is likely to increase in importance as the EU's financial single market comes fully into effect, and with continuing developments in information technology. This supports the relevance of Baumol's model of contestable markets to this case.

■ Elasticity of demand

In an oligopolistic industry firms face a downward sloping market demand curve and also downward sloping individual demand curves. Products or services supplied by each firm may be intrinsically similar but nonetheless are perceived by consumers as inherently different due to advertising and branding. The effectiveness of advertising will in turn determine the elasticity of the demand curve of each firm and the amount of each product demanded at each alternate price.

Elasticity of demand may be defined as the responsiveness of demand to a change in the price of the good or service (price elasticity of demand), or to some other variable such as income or the price of other goods or services. If price elasticity of demand is considered it is influenced by factors including the number and closeness of substitutes, the proportion of income spent on the good or service, and the time people take to respond to any price change.

The oligopolistic nature of the building societies sector and financial services in general, and the wide range of competing services, could suggest that market demand is likely to be elastic. However, with financial services such as current accounts, mortgages, credit cards and personal equity plans (peps), market demand does not vary significantly as prices change. Partly this is through inertia and partly because financial service providers tend to keep their prices fairly close to each other. Heavy advertising, branding and sponsorship by major providers does create significant customer loyalty. Also mortgages, endowments, etc. are longer term and so customers are locked into them. Hence both the firm's demand curve and the market demand curve are likely to be relatively inelastic. In other areas, such as car insurance, where people are more likely to switch from provider to provider in spite of heavy advertising, the firm's demand curve is likely to be elastic although market demand is likely to be inelastic.

The time period people need to adjust to price changes is also significant in that the longer the period the more price inelastic demand is likely to be. This can be seen with mortgages. In the short run as rates increase people will reduce expenditure on other consumer items to compensate. In the long run, however, as price (interest rate) increases are maintained demand for house purchase, and hence new mortgages, may fall. Also, in time, as people are unable to maintain existing mortgage payments, they are forced to switch to rented accommodation.

■ 2.6 Conduct

If the structure of a market refers to how it is organised then its conduct relates to the behaviour of businesses and consumers as they interact in that market. For example if analysis of a market determines that its structure is oligopolistic then it is possible to predict the behaviour of businesses within that market. This would include that the large businesses will be price makers since their output is a significant part of the total and, with static analysis, the level of output of each business will not be determined by the point of least cost (minimum cost) production on its long-run average cost curve. Also advertising will occur since this creates in consumers' minds the perception that the product is heterogeneous. This characterises the building society sector.

As previously noted, there are a number of different types of oligopolistic model. Depending on whether businesses collude or not will determine the conduct in a market. Non-collusive oligopoly may lead to price warfare, for example, while collusive oligopoly may lead to such conduct as tacit or formal collusion, through price leadership in the former case and cartels in the latter, and limit pricing as an entry barrier. In both types of oligopoly non-price competition plays an important role as a means of achieving market segmentation. There may also be a tendency to mergers and takeovers with collusive oligopoly. Nonetheless this is still consistent with the structure–conduct–performance methodology.

Among the key variables to be considered in examining the conduct of businesses are their objectives. For example are they seeking to maximise profit, sales revenue or asset growth; the extent to which businesses collude or operate cartels; linked to this is the pricing policy adopted; the levels of output produced; the extent and type of marketing employed, including advertising and branding; the role of research and development programmes in creating competitive advantage; and opportunities for scale economies which will offer cost advantages.

Most of these have already been discussed in section 2.5 as consequences of market structure, which is how conduct is viewed in the structure–conduct–performance paradigm.

■ The neoclassical model of the firm

One factor determining business conduct is its objectives, such as profit maximisation. Neoclassical theory assumes that the business seeks to maximise profits which are the rewards or income of its owners. Implicit in this is that the owners both own and manage the business and so interests coincide. This has been the assumption made in this chapter so far.

In reality the coinciding of ownership and management/control functions has become directly relevant in recent years both in privatised companies and, more recently, in some financial services organisations, particularly those moving from mutual to plc status. This is because senior executives are becoming part-owners through the opportunity to exercise share options.

The simplest neoclassical model of profit maximisation assumes that a business seeks to maximise short-run profits, i.e. relating to the period when fixed inputs such as computer hardware or the number of retail outlets cannot be changed. However it is more realistic to consider the maximisation of profits in the long run or, more accurately, the discounted flow of anticipated future earnings accruing to shareholders. In practice, decisions regarding the profits of one period are likely to impact upon future periods and so on the whole stream of future profits. This will be clearly seen in the analysis of building society mergers below.

There has been much criticism of neoclassical theory in the past on a number of grounds. For example do firms in practice seek just to maximise current profits or are there other issues that must be taken into account? As can be seen from above, this has been addressed by considering the discounted flow of anticipated future earnings accruing to shareholders, which can be modified to include also increases in share valuation. Nonetheless, as Gowland and Paterson (1991) note, this is not appropriate for such organisations as co-operatives, public sector bodies or, in this chapter, mutual building societies. Another criticism is whether the behaviour of directors varies if they are, or are not, shareholders. Increasingly directors are shareholders through incentive option schemes or as a result of mergers, and this brings together the assumed division between shareholders (owners) and managers which managerial and behavioural theories raise. Further, there is evidence that shareholders' interests must be considered by businesses since by the short-term horizon of the Anglo-Saxon model of the firm (discussed elsewhere in this chapter) there is considerable stock market pressure to deliver short-term profits (including rising share prices) to keep shareholders content (ibid). For these reasons the neoclassical model is the one most widely accepted and used.

Nonetheless other theories have been developed to explain business behaviour. Broadly these may be divided into two main schools namely managerial models and behavioural models. It is not the intention of the author to analyse these here. The interested reader is therefore referred to the bibliography at the end of this chapter for more in-depth analysis.

■ The modified neoclassical model to explain building society behaviour

Mutual building societies do not have shareholders and hence do not have to maximise profits for these. Their owners are the depositors who have voting rights at the annual general meeting (AGM) and, as such, tend to be private individuals rather than institutional investors as with a plc. Their return is twofold: firstly the financial one of the interest earned on their deposits, and secondly the non-financial one of security compared, for example, with possibly higher but also riskier returns from the stock market. The interest earned will vary with movements in market interest rates but will not reflect more business transacted by the society or reduced costs. When the property market is booming and societies make higher profits these have normally been added to reserves or loaned, not distributed to the depositors directly. However, indirectly the depositor has secured higher non-financial returns through the security of the knowledge that his/her society now holds these higher reserves.

Nor do these reserves accrue to directors as higher financial or non-financial returns. Indeed, when comparing the earnings of directors of the Abbey National and the Halifax Building Society since the former became a bank, the remunerations of its directors have risen much faster and to a much higher level than those of the Halifax's directors (BBC, *Panorama*, Battle of the Bonuses, 29 April 1996). This has been a major focus of criticism by the depositors with mutuals which seek to convert to plc status.

Increasingly, as mutual status has come under pressure from converting societies, building societies have sought ways to return some profits to their owners. Coles (1996) argues that two main models exist to achieve this. In one the standard mortgage rate is reduced to a level below that of competitors – as the Nationwide Building Society has done. The second model is to give loyalty discounts on mortgages which have been held with the society for a number of years. This has been employed by such societies as the Britannia, Northern Rock and the Cumberland.

Coles (1996) also argues that mutual societies are extremely accountable to their members (although not seeking to maximise shareholders' returns in the long run), and that comparisons with the accountability of Plcs are invalid for a number of reasons. Especially Plcs are, in practice, not as accountable as they are in theory. This is further reinforced by the 1995 Treasury Review of the 1986 Building Societies Act with its emphasis on increased building society accountability.

What implications do these arguments have for the neoclassical theory of the firm? This author argues that the theory is still appropriate to mutual building societies even though their reserves have not until recently been directly distributed to the depositor owners. Their return is significantly in the form of security, a main reason for depositors placing their funds with a society, and interest payments are accepted as determined by the market and hence largely beyond an individual society's control. Moreover, since the society's reserves form the basis for the bulk of its lending, depositors have not until recently expected these to be distributed to them as higher returns. For the building society its rationale is to maximise non-financial returns to the depositors in the form of security, and also reserves (through the delegated authority of its depositors) which are a proxy for profit but, in practice, are largely loaned to mortgage holders. More recently attempts by mutuals to return some funds to owners have pushed them further into a more similar operating philosophy to that of Plcs. In this sense the neoclassical theory of the profit maximising firm can still be applied to building societies.

■ 2.7 Acquisitions, mergers and diversification – market-driven change

■ Defining aquisitions, mergers and diversification

Mergers and acquisitions are a form of business or market conduct and so it is appropriate to examine them at this stage of the structure–conduct–performance methodology. The underlying motives of acquisitions and mergers may differ but, in practice, the results are relatively similar. An acquisition or takeover involves one firm (the predator) seeking to gain control of another (the victim) through the acquisition of a majority of the victim's shares. Unless the victim is rescued by the intervention of a third party (known as a white knight), either through an invited and competing takeover or through a merger (which by definition is mutually acceptable to both), an acquisition is hostile. This will involve the board of the victim company appealing to its shareholders to resist any offers which the predator makes – usually these will involve a rise in the price of the victim's shares increasing pressure on the victim's shareholders to accept the takeover bid. Halifax Building Society's securing Clerical Medical is a clear example of an acquisition. In the case of acquisition of a building society or insurance company with mutual status all the owners have to be consulted, usually depositors and policy or mortgage holders.

In contrast, a (horizontal) merger occurs when two or more businesses which supply the same goods or services agree to merge their activities and create a new organisation. At times this may seem little different in its effect to that of a takeover. Although the Halifax and Leeds Permanent Building Societies merged the *Financial Times* commented that 'it looks as though the Leeds will not so much merge as be submerged' (*Financial Times*, 31 July 1995). Since horizontal mergers are most directly relevant to financial services and building societies it is these which will be examined in this section.

Diversification may be effected either through acquisition or through merger. Its essential and distinctive characteristic is that the acquiring business diversifies into business areas unrelated to its current activities. This will not be examined in any depth in this chapter.

■ The theory underpinning mergers and acquisitions

A number of arguments have been proposed as rationales for mergers and takeovers. Underpinning many of these is the neoclassical theory of the firm which has been advanced through this chapter as the most effective explanation of business behaviour or conduct. To remind the reader, this argument is that a merger or acquisition will occur if it maximises profits for the newly formed business in the long run or, more accurately, the discounted flow of anticipated future earnings accruing to shareholders. This will reflect both distributed profits (to shareholders) and the share price, particularly relevant to newly converting building societies.

Due to uncertainty and imperfect knowledge in the market, risk exists. Hence managers, especially in financial services which is traditionally a conservative industry, will pursue the above objective subject to the constraint of avoiding excessive risk. The joint profit maximising model of collusive oligopoly is, as noted previously, the most effective model to explain this since mergers reduce competition.

Managerial theories, which suggest that senior managers act to their own agenda, have been advanced recently as a rationale for building societies converting to banks. However, due to share options, such managers become part-owners of the newly capitalised organisation, and so their behaviour is consistent with the neoclassical model. Further, as discussed previously, the Anglo-Saxon model of the business, as embodied in UK and US organisations, has frequently been accused of short-termism, rather than taking the longer-term perspective of continental European (especially German) and Japanese businesses (Handy 1994). This is consistent with profit and share price maximisation.

An examination of the theoretical motives for mergers will now be undertaken and related to the building society sector to explain the recent increase of these and takeovers. In many cases these can be linked to the neoclassical model. This analysis can then be used to predict the sector's performance as the final part of the structure–conduct–performance methodology.

■ Motives for mergers

Although a number of discrete motives are advanced here to explain merger or acquisition activity in reality these are not likely to be mutually exclusive. When two organisations merge, or when one acquires the other, a number of coinciding and overlapping motives is much more likely to be the case.

Koutsoyiannis has advanced two main reasons for the occurrence of mergers and takeovers, namely:

□ 1 To achieve economies of scale

Section 2.7 discussed how economies of scale has frequently been advanced as a rationale for building society mergers. By reducing unit costs, profits will be increased, other things remaining equal, and so will returns to shareholders as dividends or increased share prices. As Peter Robinson of the Woolwich

Building Society argued 'there is a virtuous circle in economies of scale and within the same geographical spread' (*The Guardian*, 5 April 1995). Linked to this are the gains arising from synergies in sales and distribution, investment and management as a consequence of a merger, i.e. the benefits arising when it is more advantageous to combine activities than to undertake them separately. Ansoff (1979) notes, however, that synergic gains need to be estimated rigorously, calculating the benefits in additional revenue, or savings in costs or investment, wherever possible. This is easier said than done and often claimed gains are left unquantified as in the Halifax–Leeds merger where 'they (i.e. spokesmen of the two societies) say that the benefits will outweigh the extra short run costs which the merger will involve' (*Financial Times*, 7 April 1995).

☐ 2 Rationalisation

This means using existing resources more efficiently. As well as reducing unit costs through the increased scale of operation, post-merger rationalisation and hence cost reduction opportunities are also afforded. For building societies these economies of scale include reduction of branch networks where there is geographical overlap, rationalisation of administrative and computer systems (although system incompatibility of the latter may initially generate extra costs), the closure of one head office, pooling of marketing costs, etc. Most significant is the opportunity to reduce staffing levels through a programme of early retirement, voluntary redundancies, redeployment, etc. even though, when the merger is announced, senior managers normally promise that there will be no labour reductions.

Sloman (1994) notes that in practice empirical evidence suggests most mergers achieve little if any cost reductions. This is due to a failure by the merged organisation to exploit potential economies of scale due to a lack of rationalisation or due to diseconomies of scale arising from lack of control by managers, often as a result of lack of sufficient knowledge of the new business. In the case of building society and other financial services mergers this latter seems improbable. Nonetheless, with the Halifax and Leeds Permanent merger, John Miller, Executive Director of the Leeds Permanent Building Society, argued 'there will be no huge rationalisation in terms of the branch presence'. In practice 42 branches were closed before the merger, 39 of which came from the Leeds Permanent (*Financial Times*, 1 March 1995). The Abbey National's acquisition of National & Provincial Building Society saw the closure of 120 of National & Provincial's 324 branches with, again, a pledge of no job losses.

☐ 3 Other motives

Many other theories have been advanced as reasons for mergers and takeovers. They have included the desire to increase market power, to increase the geographical coverage of market for the new organisation, to reduce the chance of being the victim in a takeover by another organisation, to grow in size for its own sake (empire building) and, at times, happenstance – i.e. quite simply taking advantage of an opportunity which presents itself.

Quite often a number of these are put forward simultaneously by the merging parties. If the Halifax–Leeds Permanent merger is again taken as an example it is possible to see such motives as:

- increased market power: 'getting our retaliation in first' – concerning protecting its lead in the mortgage market and expanding its presence in the retail market: Mike Blackburn, Halifax Chief Executive (*The Economist*, 3 December 1994). 'We want a bigger share of the personal customer wallet' (ibid) (*Financial Times*, 4 February 1995).
- increased geographical coverage: 'he said that a merged society . . . would have more branches than any rival': Malcolm Blair, Leeds Permanent Building Society chairman (*The Guardian*, 24 January 1995).
- to reduce the chance of being taken over by another organisation: 'the bigger and stronger you are the more difficult it is for someone to take you over, and the more likely it is that your continuing independence is assured': Mike Blackburn (*Financial Times*, 4 February 1995).
- to be price maker: when the Abbey National acquired the National & Provincial Building Society Peter Birch, Abbey National's chief executive, argued that the increase in market share would enable it to continue to take a leading role in 'price setting rather than price taking' (*Financial Times*, 11 July 1995). The Abbey has a 13 per cent market share against the newly merged Halifax's 20 per cent, making these the two most influential societies in setting prices.
- happenstance: 'the Leeds, the UK's fifth largest society, was left looking slightly foolish, somewhat adrift and without a chief executive after its 1993 plans to merge with National & Provincial Building Society were cancelled because of a clash of management cultures' (*Financial Times*, 4 February 1995). This provided an excellent opportunity for the Halifax to move in, helped by the fact that its chief executive, Mike Blackburn, was formerly chief executive of the Leeds Permanent.

Re-examining the goals of the business in the neoclassical model the main constraint was 'subject to the need by managers to minimise risk'. This can be achieved, in part, by reducing uncertainty. The underlying feature of many of the above motives is that they use merger and acquisition strategies to minimise uncertainty as generated by political, economic, social and technological factors discussed at the beginning of this chapter.

For example, to increase market power and secure their customer base, two businesses may decide to merge, reducing competition and hence securing larger market share and the ability to charge higher prices, i.e. further above the business's marginal cost curve. This is a direct consequence of the business's demand curve becoming more inelastic and is likely to be reinforced by non-price-competitive strategies.

Although particular examples are not usually to be taken as evidence of the general, nonetheless it is useful to examine the motives of contemporary building society mergers. Following the announcement of the merger of Lloyds Bank with the Cheltenham & Gloucester Building Society, Brian Pitman of Lloyds argued 'we believe the deal will upset the competitive equilibrium in our favour'. In other words, by increasing their size and market power relative to that of their competitors, risk in the market would be reduced.

Figure 2.2, which was examined earlier in this chapter, demonstrated how output will be allocated among merging building societies in the same way as among members of a cartel, so as to maximise profits. Reviewing the motives above, the desire to achieve economies of scale, and the desire to undertake rationalisation (even if it is not actually achieved) are both consistent with profit maximisation. In the same way, other motives for mergers or acquisitions, with their emphasis on reducing uncertainty, are linked indirectly at least with profit maximisation. This is not to deny that other motives exist but, certainly in many cases, the motives are consistent with the rationale of the business in the neoclassical model.

Gowland and Paterson (1991) review the literature which analyses why mergers and takeovers occur. One theory argues that mergers reduce information and transaction costs compared with if the new business had continued to operate as two separate entities. A competing theory suggests that mergers are essentially about corporate control, i.e. which managers are going to run a business. The less efficient managers are, the lower the profits they make, the more their business's share price falls relative to other more efficient firms, and the more vulnerable they are to takeover.

The logical consequence of many merger theories, argue Gowland and Paterson, is that they should lead to an increase in profits. Yet evidence from the UK suggests that in many cases this does not happen; in the US, analysis of over 6,000 mergers suggests that they result in 'a small but significant decline in post-merger profitability'. Nonetheless this does not deny, they argue, the hope of increased profit before the merger takes place. What does occur however is an increase in the stock exchange value of the merged company compared with that of its constituent elements pre-merger; certainly shareholders of the acquired company benefit and probably those of the acquiring business.

The conclusion of this, Gowland and Patterson summarise, is that most mergers are financial in nature. They benefit shareholders in that they raise the stock market value of the new company compared with its pre-merger constituent elements, but they do not raise profits. This certainly appears consistent with the motives of the owners of mutual building societies when they vote in favour of mergers and conversion to plc status. The reason for the financial nature of mergers is a consequence of uncertainty or is dependent on some characteristic of the tax system. Tax, stock exchange anomalies and sub-optimal debt ratios are probably the most important reasons they suggest.

The reader should also examine Chapter 10, especially section 10.7 regarding mergers in the UK shipping industry.

■ 2.8 Performance

On the basis of determining the structure and conduct of a market then types of market and business performance may be predicted. As Pass and Lowes (1994) argue, this involves such variables as production costs, marketing (advertising and promotion) costs, prices, profit levels, product performance and technological innovation.

Using this structure–conduct–performance methodology it can therefore be predicted that if a market structure is a non-collusive oligopoly, as is the building society sector, with entry barriers becoming lower for businesses in allied sectors, then its conduct may well tend towards mergers and acquisitions as new firms seek access and the acquisition of existing expertise and customers. Further, existing societies may also resort to mergers and acquisitions as means of fighting off competition and making themselves less vulnerable to predatory attacks. In this case the theoretical model of collusive oligopoly is the most appropriate. As a defence they may also seek to diversify into other financial services sectors.

With the increased concentration arising from such conduct predictions can then be made as to the performance of businesses in this market. The remainder of this section will explore this in the context of the building societies sector of the financial services industry.

The issue of mergers and acquisitions has already been discussed and a model presented to explain the behaviour of a newly merged business. Where problems arise in examining building society performance is in terms of the availability of data much of which is commercially confidential. Additionally there is the problem of definitions – as Pass and Lowes (1994) argue, what is a fair price or normal profit as a rate of return?

Taking the variables discussed by Pass and Lowes (ibid) we may apply these to the building societies sector of the financial services industry.

■ Production costs

The issue of economies of scale has already been discussed in this chapter as one reason advanced by the building societies for the spate of merger activity. Linked to this is the perceived need to rationalise to achieve optimum size of business to realise these economies due to overcapacity in this sector. This is being aggravated by entrants from the overlapping sectors of banking and insurance, and from new players, as entry barriers reduce in height partly due to new information technology. Additionally, the 1997 Building Societies Act which removes the five-year protective shield for building societies who bid for another financial services business, is likely to contribute still further to increased concentration.

Attempts to achieve scale economies may be offset by the existence of x-inefficiencies which exist when actual production costs exceed potential costs.

Certainly in the building society sector and the financial services industry, however, generally increased competition is likely to keep x-inefficiencies low in the long run. In the short run, however, increased concentration may see x-inefficiencies as newly merged organisations struggle to rationalise their operations.

As Pass and Lowes note, size is not all. In all industries small businesses can also survive, at times with lower unit costs, due to exploitation of market niches for example – something that was discussed previously in this chapter with the Dunfermline Building Society. Indeed with the intention of some societies to become one stop financial service shops it is probably more appropriate to talk of economies of scope rather than economies of scale, i.e. reduced total average costs due to producing more and different products (Harris 1996) (see also Chapter 6.9). Moreover in so far as unit costs may be reduced by progression along the learning curve as new technology is introduced for example, subject to management's ability to learn effectively from experience, this will apply equally to large and small firms – one of the dynamic aspects of assessing market performance.

For building societies, cost/income ratios are one important measure of their financial success – see Table 2.2. In discussing the acquisition of the Cheltenham & Gloucester Building Society by Lloyds Bank in 1995 one argument was that it had the lowest cost/income ratio at 31.8 per cent compared with a building society average of 48 per cent and a ratio of over 60 per cent for Lloyds Bank (and most other banks) – one reason why banks are shedding labour is to bring their ratios down (*The Banker*, May 1994).

The conclusion of this is that competition and IT will drive down production costs as businesses shed labour and seek other ways to increase profits.

■ Marketing costs

Marketing has traditionally been a main way in which building societies have competed against each other in the past at least to maintain and preferably to expand their market share. This is particularly important in the light of the above discussion of scale economies since marketing reinforces the demand against which unit cost reducing production takes place. As Pass and Lowes argue, in traditional static analysis, these expenditures are perceived as generating extra costs which are passed on to consumers as higher prices. However, if a dynamic perspective is taken then it can be argued that the extra or marginal costs of marketing are more than offset by extra or marginal revenue created by the extra demand.

For new entrants to financial services, such as Marks & Spencer and Virgin, although marketing undertaken by existing suppliers might be perceived as a barrier to entry, their financial muscle and their reputation for quality and their popularity with consumers have given them a head start over some less well known suppliers already well established in this industry. As competition intensifies and barriers between different financial services providers reduce, the marketing of their services, and of their identities, is likely to become more important. (See also Chapter 5.)

■ Prices and profits

Pass and Lowes argue that it is difficult to apply realistically the concept of normal profit to a range of industries which have quite different expectations of what constitutes normal – hence each needs to be looked at individually and over time to reduce the impact of business cycle fluctuations. In particular, pricing policies and profitability need to be considered in the context of the extent of risk in the market, efficiency gains, expenditure on research and development, improvements in quality and range of products, etc.

In the past, competition has been mainly on non-price grounds. However this is changing to some extent as the market becomes more competitive and so, inevitably, drives prices down. To cite the example of the Halifax it has 'used its muscle to compete in the mortgage market far more aggressively on price, hurting both banks and smaller societies' (*The Economist*, 3 Dec. 1994, p. 87). Societies now normally offer tiered rates of interest to encourage larger deposits.

In terms of profit levels, the tendency in the building society sector to increasing concentration might initially look as if societies were using this to increase profits. In practice the lowering of entry barriers and increased competition from other financial services providers, creating a market more contestable in nature, and the persistent downturn in the housing market have prevented this from happening. For the early 1990s a series of years of declining profits were experienced. This has recently remedied itself to some extent – both the Halifax and the Leeds Permanent making record profits in 1994 for example, the last full year before merger plans were announced. Indeed more recently the growth in building society profits generally has outpaced asset growth. This means that there has been a significant increase in capital ratios (Lister 1995). For building societies who have become banks, the need to satisfy new shareholders will create extra pressures to increase profitability.

■ Product performance

One interesting aspect of building societies' performance in the 1990s is the attempt of many to widen the range of financial products and services provision, undoubtedly driven by increased market competitiveness due to deregulation. Conventional economic analysis can fail to address the issue of improved quality but increased depth of provision (quality) is at least as important as wider provision (more goods and services). As was noted previously, the ability to measure quality improvements effectively is problematic. More recently remortgages and cheaper loans to larger borrowers were used in the mid-1990s to offset some of the effects of the recessed housing market; other products have included more societies offering unit trusts to offset low interest rates. Widening of the provision of financial services and products, partly through further mergers and acquisitions, is likely to continue.

■ Technological innovation

As has been discussed in this chapter, certainly building societies and financial services providers generally have been proactive in adopting new technology but still have a long way to travel; 24-hour telephone based financial services offer considerable scope for future growth while attempts at home based interactive services have not proved too successful so far. Stan Dolberg, Forrester Research, argues that 'the value of trading via the Internet will increase from \$10 billion in 1996 to \$196 billion by 2000. By 1998, most organisations will be doing commerce on line.' ('Doing Financial Business on-line', *Financial Times*, June 1997). As such traditional retail building societies, insurance companies and banks will face an even more competitive environment from businesses familiar with the Internet, they will need to match these new financial services providers, such as software companies, and develop innovative new products and services. At the same time they will still need to provide tradtitional financial services from real rather than virtual premises, although these will continue to contract in the near future.

The dynamic importance of technological innovation is fundamental both to suppliers and consumers. For the former it is a means to generating new demands for new goods and services (i.e. widening the market) while also anticipating potential future competition from other EU financial services providers. For consumers it offers greater choice, more flexibility of provision and, through economies of scope, lower prices.

As Pass and Lowes argue, what this does is to create extra pressure on these businesses to undertake large programmes of research and development to try and secure competitive advantage. (See also Chapter 4.)

■ 2.9 Criticisms of the structure–conduct–performance methodology

The major criticism of the above model, argue Gowland and Paterson (1991), is that one cannot assume a direct and linear causality from structure to conduct to performance as the methodology suggests. The direction could be the reverse of what has been indicated. For example the technologically innovative firm Microsoft is currently undertaking a very extensive R&D programme to develop world wide web browsers and other software, having realised that a strategic error had been made by overlooking the Internet as the growth area of the 1990s (conduct). If they are as successful here, as they have been with mainframe and PC software, they may end up as an effective monopoly, in which case performance determines conduct.

These criticisms have been taken much further with the development in recent years of what is termed New Industrial Economics (Begg, Fischer and Dornbusch 1994). Game theory, which is discussed elsewhere in this chapter, is part of this. Other concepts include pre-commitment (a voluntary arrangement entered into by firms joining a cartel to discourage cheating, for example by agreeing to limit output), credibility (where a firm is punished for cheating on a cartel of which it is a member) and strategic entry deterrence (where a business in a market discourages others from entering by influencing their expectations of how it will behave). These have emphasised the point made in the previous paragraph that one cannot always assume a linear causal relationship from structure through conduct to performance. Rather, structure and conduct are frequently determined at the same time. Secondly, potential entry (contestable markets) which includes imports, will affect the competitive nature of a market. Hence an oligopolistic market which can be easily entered, such as the building society sector, may behave much more like a perfectly competitive market than a traditional oligopolistic one.

In spite of this, the structure–conduct–performance model does offer useful insights into market and business behaviour and so is still widely accepted in managerial economics. It is perceived as a rigorous and effective methodology for analysing market behaviour, which is why it is employed here.

■ 2.10 Conclusions: the financial services sector – which way forward?

Various models might have been used in this chapter to analyse the building society sector. In practice a structure–conduct–performance methodology has been employed and the neoclassical profit maximising model of the firm adapted to reflect the distinctive nature of building societies. The benefits of using economic theory are that it is rigorous and effective in explaining the structure of the building society sector, how building societies behave and their performance over time. However, as discussed above, there are criticisms of the methodology.

A number of conclusions may be drawn from the above analysis:

- Due to falling entry barriers, facilitated in part by information technology, there has been an increasing overlap between the three main sectors of financial services, banks, building societies and insurance companies.
- Mergers and acquisitions have caused a major contraction in the number of building societies as rationalisation has been seen as a competitive strategy to

remove surplus capacity, maintain market share and secure customer bases; yet through lower entry barriers the building society sector has become more competitive.

- Building societies have advanced economies of scale as the main rationale of mergers and acquisitions. However, as neoclassical theory explains, given the structure of the building societies' market, the desire to reduce uncertainty is also a major contributory factor.
- Empirical evidence suggests, however, that most mergers do not achieve significant cost reductions, either through a failure to rationalise or through experiencing diseconomies of scale.
- Most mergers, research suggests, are financial in nature for the benefit of shareholders (including newly created shareholders in our model of building societies), through increased share value in anticipation of increased profits. In reality, however, mergers do not normally raise profits.
- Competitive forces are likely to intensify in the foreseeable future, creating still further pressures for financial service providers. Indeed it is likely that in ten years' time one will see a much smaller number of societies in existence.
- The labour force in financial services is likely to continue declining substantially as it is replaced by information technology.
- Traditional branch networks will contract significantly (a number of those remaining becoming automated), and the provision of telephone and other new banking services, including from new suppliers such as retail chains, software and cable companies and other EU banks, will intensify (Chetham, 1995; *Financial Times*, 21 January 1996). These new players will more than offset any tendencies to increased concentration as a consequence of mergers and acquisitions. Indeed it has been argued that 'within ten years banks may be "virtual" existing only within a computer' (*Daily Mail*, 3 February 1996).

(My sincere thanks are due to my colleagues Chris Downs, Mervyn Rowlinson and Harjinder Virdee for their helpful comments on earlier drafts of this chapter.)

■ Questions for discussion

1. Why has the financial services sector of the UK economy undergone such significant change in the last ten years?
2. Discuss critically the advantages and disadvantages offered by the use of neoclassical theory to explain the economics of organisational change in the building societies sector.
3. What economic costs and benefits does horizontal integration offer firms in the financial services sector?
4. Analyse the response of the Halifax Building Society to the competitive pressures it has faced in recent years.
5. Is further change likely in the financial services sector? Explain your answer.

■ Bibliography

Anderton, Brian, *Current Issues in Financial Services* (Basingstoke: Macmillan Business, 1995).

Anon, 'Lloyds Mortgage Challenge', *The Banker*, May 1994.

Ansoff, H. Igor, *Strategic Management* (New York: Macmillan, 1979).

Baumol, W. J., *Business Behaviour, Value and Growth* (New York: Macmillan, 1959).

Baumol W. J., Panzar, John C. and Willig, Robert D., *Contestable Markets and the Theory of Industry Structure* (New York/London: Harcourt Brace Jovanovich, 1982).

Begg, David, Fischer, Stanley & Dornbusch, Rudiger, *Economics. 4th edn* (Maidenhead, Berks: McGraw-Hill, 1994).

Bird, Graham and Bird, Heather, *Contemporary Issues in Applied Economics*, (Aldershot: Edward Elgar, 1991).

Bishop, Matthew and Kay, John, *European Mergers and Merger Policy*, (Oxford: OUP, 1993).

Centre for the Study of Financial Innovation (CSFI), *The Building Societies: Do They Have a Future?* (London: CSFI, 1995).

Centre for the Study of Financial Innovation (CSFI), *Banking Banana Skins III* (London: CSFI, 1996).

Chetham, Jacqui, *The Future of the UK Financial Services Industry* (London: FT Financial Reports, 1995).

Coles, Adrian, 'Mutual Meltdown?', Text of a speech by the Director-General of the Building Societies Association to the Prebon Yamane Housing Finance Seminar, London, 19 October 1995.

Coles, Adrian, 'Building Societies: Assessing the Changes, Looking to the Future', Text of a speech by the Director-General of the Building Societies Association to the 11th IBC Annual Building Societies Conference, London, 18 March 1996.

Davies, Howard., *Managerial Economics*, (2nd edn). (London: Pitman, 1991).

Davis, John, 'The Problem of Costs and Cost Identification', in Anderton, Brian (ed.), *Current Issues in Financial Services* (Basingstoke: Macmillan Business, 1995).

Deakins, David and MacKay, Stephen, 'Marketing and Corporate Strategies for Financial Institutions', in Anderton, Brian (ed.), *Current Issues in Financial Services* (Basingstoke: Macmillan Business, 1995).

Dixon, Rob, *Banking in Europe: The Single Market* (London: Routledge, 1991).

Dunkley, Peter and Gutman, Peter, *The Monetary and Financial System* (Worcester: Osborne Books Ltd, 1990).

Earl, Peter E., *Microeconomics for Business and Marketing* (Aldershot: Edward Elgar, 1995).

Easton, Geoff, *Learning from Case Studies*, 2nd edn (Hemel Hempstead: Prentice-Hall, 1992).

The Economist, 3 Dec. 1994, p. 87, 'It's high noon on Britain's high street: the struggle for control of Britain's retail financial-services industry has entered a new stage'.

Financial Times, 'Doing Financial Business on-line', June 1997.

George, Kenneth D., Joll, Caroline and Lynk, E. E., *Industrial Organisation: Competition, Growth and Structural Change*, (4th edn) (London: Routledge, 1992).

Gowland, David and Paterson, Anne, *Microeconomic Analysis* (Hemel Hempstead: Harvester Wheatsheaf, 1991).

Griffiths, Alan and Wall, Stuart (eds), *Applied Economics – An Introductory Course*, 6th edn (Harlow, Essex: Longman Group Ltd, 1995).

Handy, Charles, *The Empty Raincoat: Making Sense of Modern Business* (London: Arrow Books, 1994).

Harris, Neil, *European Business* (Basingstoke: Macmillan Business, 1996).

Henderson, Roger, *European Finance* (Maidenhead, Berks: McGraw-Hill Book Company, 1993).

Hertje, Arnold (ed.) *Innovation, Technology and Finance* (Oxford: Basil Blackwell for the European Investment Bank, 1988).

Jacquemin, Alexis *et al.*, *Merger and Competition Policy in the European Community* (Oxford: Basil Blackwell, 1990).

Koutsoyiannis, A., *Modern Microeconomics*, 2nd edn (Basingstoke: Macmillan, 1987).

Lister, Geoffrey, 'Here to Stay', *The Chartered Banker*, September 1995.

Marris, R., 'A Model of the Managerial Enterprise', *Quarterly Journal of Economics*, 1963.

Marris, R., *Theory of Managerial Capitalism* (London: Macmillan, 1964).

Moschandreas, Maria, *Business Economics* (London: Routledge, 1994).

Pass, Christopher and Lowes, Bryan, *Business and Microeconomics* (London: Routledge, 1994).

Ryan, Bob, Scapens, Robert W. and Theobold, Michael, *Research Method and Methodology in Finance and Accounting* (London: Academic Press (Harcourt Brace Jovanovich Publishers), 1992).

Sachwald, Frederique (ed.), *European Integration and Competitiveness* (Aldershot: Edward Elgar, 1994).

Sloman, John, *Economics*, (2nd edn) (Hemel Hempstead: Harvester Wheatsheaf, 1994).

Stigler, George, *The Theory of Price*, 3rd edn (London: Macmillan, 1970).

Valdez, Steven, *An Introduction to Western Financial Markets* (Basingstoke: Macmillan, 1993).

White, David, 'Building Societies: The Future', *Chartered Banker*, vol. 1, no. 1, pp. 9–14.

Williamson, O. E., *The Economics of Discretionary Behaviour* (Englewood Cliffs, New Jersey: Prentice-Hall, 1964).

Also:

The Chartered Banker
The Economist
Financial Times
Daily Mail
The Guardian
The Observer
The Times

and:

BBC, *Panorama*, 'Battle of the Bonuses', 29 April 1996.

CHAPTER 3

Services management

Gary Akehurst

■ 3.1 Introduction: the growth of the service economy

'No matter what industry they're in, the customers they serve, or the countries they operate in, all firms are – to a greater or lesser extent – in services. They can't afford not to be: profound changes in the competitive environment and in customer values have put services squarely at the centre of today's corporate strategies and operational agendas. The stakes are obvious: attracting customers, retaining them, and keeping a unique competitive edge. The challenge? Implementing strategies for these services in an efficient, yet cost-effective way.'

(Vandermerwe and Lovelock 1994, p. xxxiii)

While there is no generally accepted definition of 'services', for the purposes of this chapter services are defined as business transactions which have intangible as well as possibly tangible elements. This definition includes both business services and consumer services, that is, services provided by one business to another (for example, an advertising agency) and services provided for consumers (for example, hotels, banks and shops). It would be a mistake however, to believe that all services are consumer services, and indeed, the fastest growing part of the service sector is business services. (The reader should also see Chapters 2 and 4 where financial services are examined, Chapter 5 where marketing is discussed and Chapter 10 where UK maritime industries are analysed.)

Shostack (1977) reminds us that there are very few 'pure' goods or services and she introduces the concept of a continuum running from tangible dominant products to intangible dominant products. This focuses on what is the essential core of the product being sold, whether a physical, tangible product which has been augmented or enhanced by a service (for example, a video machine purchased in a shop with after sales warranties) or a more intangible product such as an insurance policy (although even here there is a tangible hard copy policy document backing up a core service). Berry (1980) further reminds us that while the performance of many services is reinforced or supported by tangibles, nevertheless, what is being purchased is a performance.

Gummesson (1987, p. 22) suggests, perhaps tongue in cheek, that 'services are something which can be bought and sold but which you can not drop on your foot'. Amusingly, Gummesson is reminding us of those attributes or characteristics of services which define the offering, which are part performance – intangibility, inseparability (real time performance), perishability (real time nature which cannot be stored), heterogeneity (often dependent on human involvement in the delivery and consumption process, with a service which may be customised or non-standardised) and transfer of ownership (temporary use of the service or access to it, with what is 'owned' being the benefit derived from consuming the service but this benefit may or may not be enduring) (Gabbott and Hogg 1997, p. xi).

Services lie at the heart of one of the most fundamental changes in the structure of economies this century. Three out of every four jobs in the US in 1985 were in service industries (Daniels 1991, p. 1), and Tom Elfring (1988, p. 27) has shown that the percentage of total UK employment generated by the service sector has risen from 35 per cent in 1870, to 44 per cent in 1960 and 65 per cent in 1984, with comparable figures for the US being 26 per cent, 61 per cent and 72 per cent respectively. At the current time around 70 per cent of UK employment and 75 per cent of US employment is in the service sector. It is a similar picture with the service sector contribution to national incomes. Even back in 1861, the UK service sector's share of national income was already 46.7 per cent (while its share of total employment was 31.3 per cent) with South East England having some 44.4 per cent of its employment in services (Lee 1984). Business services alone account for around 6 per cent of European Union GNP and 14 per cent of the value added for all market sectors (Commission of the European Communities 1990). Some 20 per cent of the UK's GDP is generated by City of London financial and related services.

Efforts have been made to build an 'all-encompassing theory of the service sector' but are the service industries too diverse? Following the work of Daniels and Thrift (1987) three broad sets of service sector theories can be detected:

(i) **the 'post-industrial' or 'service economy', stages of economic growth thesis.** The demand for goods tends to rise less rapidly than the demand for services as income rises. Over time a majority of the labour force is engaged in service activities with an inexorable shift towards service industries and service occupations (Fisher 1935; Clark 1940; Bell 1974).

(ii) **the theory of the 'self-service economy'.** The growth of a service consuming society will continue but based upon a fundamental trend towards 'self-service' via the substitution of goods for services, fuelled by a continuing rise in productivity (Gershuny and Miles 1983). This suggests that the continuing rise in services employment should not be taken for granted.

(iii) **the Marxist theory of the service sector.** Here the service economy is nothing more than an outgrowth of the basic capitalist industrial system. Changes in production methods and the labour process gives rise to a growth of services, which in turn change the process of circulation. As enterprises grow larger and production methods and labour have become more efficient, so a whole raft of services have sprung up which accelerate the circulation of goods (retailing, banking and finance, transport, information, management consultants). Also as the state has grown so have services arising out of the state (education, health and government administration).

Unfortunately no one has yet devised an all-embracing and rigorous theory of service sector development and possibly never will, but this should not stop attempts to explain and describe these profound societal changes.

'The service sector, also known as the "tertiary" or "residual" sector, has long been the stepchild of economic research. This was unfortunate but tolerable during the 19th and early 20th centuries when the shift from agriculture to industry was in full swing and services were of lesser importance. Since the end of World War II, however, the service sector has become the largest, and, in many respects, the most dynamic element in the U.S. economy. Furthermore, most of the industrialised nations of the world appear to be following, with some lag, the pattern set by the United States. Thus, the emergence of this country as the first "service economy" has created a new set of priorities for economic research.' (Fuchs 1968, p. xxiii)

Fuchs was not, of course, the first writer to issue a call to arms as far as services research is concerned. Colin Clark for instance, issued a challenge in 1940 that 'the economics of tertiary industry remains to be written' but Fuchs' book on the service economy, published in 1968, was influential in drawing attention to this most glaring and potentially worrying gap in our knowledge of developed and developing economies. The service sector has, however, been studied from time to time (Stigler 1956; Browning and Singelmann 1975; Gershuny 1979; Gershuny and Miles 1983, to name but a few), and various service industries have been quite extensively researched, notably retailing, transport and tourism (see, for instance, Channon 1978; Senior and Akehurst 1988; Akehurst and Alexander 1995; 1996a; 1996b; 1996c; Akehurst and Gadrey 1987 and Gadrey, Gallouj and Weinstein 1995).

Even as late as 1987 in the geography discipline, a discipline recognised by many as having made useful contributions to service sector research, two authors wrote:

'It has become something of a rictual to begin a paper on the geography of the service sector by posing a question – why has so little work been carried out on the geography of the service sector relative to its importance in the economies of so many localities? Just because the question has been asked so many times does not make it any the less pertinent, however. Indeed the question becomes even more puzzling when it is remembered that services have been a prominent sector of the British economy since at least the mid-nineteenth century.' (Daniels and Thrift 1987, p. 1)

So while services may not be new, or of recent origin, their contribution to economic life has been consistently underestimated. When services were belatedly included in the 1986 Uruguay Round of the General Agreement on Tariffs and Trade (GATT) (see also Chapters 6.4 and 9.3), the Organisation for Economic Co-operation and Development (OECD), the United Nations Committee on Trade and Development (UNCTAD) and the International Labour Office (ILO) suddenly realised that they had very little hard evidence on the contribution to economic and business life of services. The absence of detailed and disaggregated statistical series and other substantive information proved to be a considerable drag on the GATT negotiations, even more so when it was realised that without detailed knowledge of the major portion of their economies, GATT countries were finding it peculiarly difficult to know how to build up their competitive trading strengths (Daniels 1991, p. 9). Furthermore, it was not until 1990 that there was a comprehensive directory of the world's largest service corporations (UN Centre on Transnational Corporations 1990); and yet Fuchs, back in 1968, had said 'perhaps the most urgent need of all is for more and better-quality data concerning the service industries' (Fuchs 1968, p. 13).

This chronic understatement of services within economic development can be attributed in part to three factors. First, classifications of economic activity in national statistics have not kept pace with the fundamental restructuring of production which has taken place since the nineteenth century (indeed, the author was a member of a small team brought together in 1989–90 by Eurostat, the statistical division of the European Commission of the European Union, to collect tourism statistics in preparation for the designated 'European Year of Tourism 1990' because it had been found that very little was known about the dimensions of tourism, an activity which accounts for around one in ten jobs within the European Union [Eurostat 1990]). Second, it is often difficult to trace service transactions either because telecommunications have been used or the transaction may have taken place within large, very complex and often transnational corporations engaged in a globally wide range of economic activities; and third, there is a belief, articulated by Adam Smith among others, that services are in some way parasitic or have at best a supporting role in economic development (Daniels 1991).

Services, both consumer and business, are essential and intrinsic to the working of modern economies, and as can be shown, are in many respects the major activity in these economies. These activities are changing fast and need sensitive and creative management. Consider just a few examples:

- education, health, leisure and recreation facilities help sustain and enhance the quality of the labour force
- transport infrastructure enables the efficient distribution of goods within localities, regions and countries, and between countries
- the capital markets provide the finance for enterprises of varying sizes and complexity

- accommodation facilities provider shelter and sustenance to those people on the move
- the banking system provides the essential lubricant to keep economies functioning by facilitating exchange.

Economies have changed fundamentally both in terms of what is being produced and how it is being produced. There have been changes in both demand and supply caused in part by changing real incomes, the rate of technical progress, the rate of investment, internationalisation and specialisation to name but some factors. An important intermediary role has been played by technology (including information, telecommunications, transport and electronics). Technology has enabled service providers to deliver their products more quickly, more reliably over far greater distances and at lower cost (Daniels 1989, p. 3). Technology has improved accessibility to services and other products and enhanced customer awareness of alternative sources of services. For a stimulating discussion of these fundamental issues see Vandermerwe (1993).

Various labels have been given to this apparently rapid transformation of economies into primarily service-based economies, such as 'deindustrialisation' (see also Chapter 10.7), 'the service economy', and 'post-industrial society'. The label 'deindustrialisation' is particularly inappropriate in that one debate has focused on the apparent decline in manufacturing activity as somehow symptomatic of an undesirable development, that services are an evil drag on real economic activity. In truth, the development of services is inter-twined with manufacturing such that it is wrong to consider one sector (manufacturing) as somehow 'good' and services as somehow 'bad'. Both sectors (and in many ways we cannot neatly divide the economy into apparently two opposing forces) feed off, support and reinforce the other. Services are used to augment and enhance manufactured products, to improve their usage among consumers and to facilitate exchange – the example of after sales service comes to mind. To an increasing extent consumers are purchasing a 'product package' – a package of both tangible (physical) and intangible (service) benefits. Sometimes a physical entity is not exchanged at all, merely an entitlement or ownership of a financial instrument.

The process of economic transformation has however, been long-term; after all, many service activities and trades have existed since time began. The importance of the current transformation is, however, founded in the huge global economic and social implications of these changes focused particularly on information technologies, changing production inputs, operating flexibilities, and employment divisions. Services are the very engine of change, affecting all manner of processes, markets, products, jobs and activities. Researchers are attempting to make sense of these profound changes, because in truth we do not know enough about them, and yet we have the belief that service industries will create more jobs and reduce unemployment. We need to understand the macro issues of economic growth, service output, service productivity, and the diffusion of information technologies, and the micro issues of the management of service businesses, quality of services, training of service personnel, and so on.

The old economic order, or certainly that existing from the late nineteenth century to the 1970s, was founded essentially on a number of basic features (Akehurst 1989):

- standardised output often with factory assembly lines
- in-house or in-company services with very little outsourcing
- markets very localised or at most at national level
- large corporations with vertical integration of production
- technical progress moving relatively steadily with occasional 'quantum leaps' when a new invention occurred
- production fundamentally based on physical (tangible) inputs and outputs
- primarily blue-collar factory employment
- regulated service functions.

It is not surprising therefore that, until comparatively recently, researchers were primarily concerned with manufacturing industry and businesses within it; but the world was changing. The old and lingering distinctions between the usefulness or not of services versus goods really owes more to belief than to fact, and is indebted more to the arbitrary, and frankly, inappropriate national standard industrial classifications which have failed to capture the way the economy has changed and, in particular, how production has changed. The old view was of a primary sector (agriculture and mining), a secondary sector (manufacturing) and, the residual, a tertiary sector (Fisher 1935; Clark 1940).

The new view is one of complementarity, with services being complementary not ancillary or an adjunct to manufactured products (Daniels 1991). The days of 'a spurious analytical dichotomy' (Foxall 1984) are gone, but it leaves the analysis of services management in need of theoretical reassessment and empirical verification. McKenzie (1987) is surely wrong in saying that 'the emergence of the service economy may be as much an artefact of the classification system as it is a real phenomenon'. Researchers, in part, desire to redress the overwhelming bias in favour of manufacturing which still pervades most thinking on business performance, and which provides many of the examples and case studies most used in empirical testing. They have therefore attempted to list comprehensively the characteristics of services such as intangibility, simultaneous and inseparable production and consumption. For quite a time, such a classification list was brought out as some kind of self-evident truth which needed no further explanation; what it did was provide a starting point for empirical work. It is not the purpose of this chapter, however, to overwhelm the reader with lists of definitions and classifications so beloved of academics but more to set the scene in terms of the nature of services and how businesses are changing.

What this new emerging global industrial order comprises are:

- customised goods and services, bundled in increasingly different ways (as opposed to standardised goods and services)
- a strong customer focus and development of long-term relationships between businesses and their customers
- increased externalisation of services, as in-house services are out-sourced (giving rise to a new generation of producer services firms)
- increased networking and linkages between organisations and individuals across continents
- growing internationalisation and competition, growing interdependence of national economies, with the emergence of transnational corporations (especially in banking, finance, insurance and telecommunications) and often with no need to be located in the same geographic areas as consumers
- vertical disintegration with a growth of small and medium-sized enterprises
- flexible production methods, with the nature of production changing from 'materialisation' (or dominant physical inputs and product characteristics) to know-how/information-based inputs
- predominantly white-collar employment with increasing home-based working
- deregulation and liberalisation with new forms of regulation where market imperfections are present
- smaller government sectors with more private services previously provided by the state.

At the very heart of these profound and often disturbing changes is 'know-how'. To survive, businesses require timely knowledge or 'know-how', i.e. timely and pertinent information delivered to the right user, which has been processed in a way immediately useful to that end-user in their decision making (Sveiby and Lloyd 1987). Know-how is capital and helps ensure survival in the contemporary business environment, which is rapidly changing – the size distribution of firms, mergers and take-overs creating multi-functional, multi-product service organisations which trade globally, such as securities trading. At the very heart of these changes is competition not on just a local or regional level but across continents. Competition has intensified the pressure to innovate, to lower costs to remain competitive, to enhance and modify existing products, and to add new products to a constantly changing product line. These changes have promoted diversification and specialisation with extensive promotion of the diversity, quality and complementarity of the services offered. Increased specialisation and internationalisation of these know-how inputs often require an organisation to look outside its own resources to business services firms, to utilise the services of designers, consulting engineers and logistics specialists, to name but a few.

As products become more differentiated in order to appeal to very specific market niches, so product lives are shortening as product lines are broadening. This places increased emphasis on timely product development, strategic planning, marketing, production flexibility and more efficient management practices. We are witnessing a 'dematerialisation of production', that is, an increase in knowledge within products rather than physical inputs (Daniels

1991, p. 6) and within deregulated markets where services such as finance and telecommunications are traded internationally. Researchers are showing empirical evidence that the 'economic vitality' (i.e. the ability to change, adapt and grow to promote competitive advantage) of towns, cities, regions and countries, is 'built upon a close relationship between goods production and services as well as upon exports of service industry output' (Daniels 1991, p. 7; Beyers 1989; Daniels 1986; Illeris 1989; Ochel and Wegner 1987).

All these societal and economic changes raise profound questions as to how organisations in the future will be managed. While we cannot crystal-ball-gaze into that future, we can at least consider some of the ways that services can be managed as efficiently as possible for the greater good of all. Whether the wealth created by the change to a predominantly service economy will be shared by all or just a fortunate few is not something that can be answered here but there seems little doubt that politicians in many countries across the world will be challenged to provide mechanisms for a more equitable distribution of societal and economic gains generated by the gathering 'services revolution'.

■ 3.2 What is services management?

At first glance, the modern economy is extremely diversified. All products however, have to lesser or greater extent core tangible and intangible elements, and deliver to customers a bundle of benefits. The more tangible the product, the greater is the permanent ownership of the product (Lovelock 1996, p. 4). Many products are complex in both design and usage but one thing is clear – very few manufactured products do not have a service (intangible) element, and very few services do not have a tangible element. Shostack (1977) as mentioned earlier, proposed a continuum, from tangible dominant (for example, a car) to intangible dominant (for example, an insurance policy), while Sasser, Olsen and Wyckoff (1978) proposed a continuum based on the proportion of selling price attributable to service elements (as a reflection of the value added by these service components).

Whatever the classification system used, it is coming to be recognised that adding services to products and managing these services, creates a competitive advantage while helping to resolve customer needs.

According to Lovelock (1994, p. 11) and other writers, there are four broad categories of services based on whether people or objects are being processed, each of which requires subtly different management:

1. direct physical contact with customers (for example, health care and restaurants)
2. contact with people's minds (for example, education and broadcasting)
3. processing of physical objects (for example, repairs, retailing and transportation)
4. processing of information (for example, banking, insurance and accounting).

Such distinctions between services make us think long and hard about the service process and the ultimate service output in terms of what happens to the customer or other object being processed. It makes us think about the benefits being delivered to the customer.

In earlier years there had been an over-emphasis on the differences between services and goods focusing on output perishability (for example, a hotel bedroom not sold by the end of the day is revenue lost for eternity), intangibility, heterogeneity and simultaneity of production and consumption. Lovelock (1996) again has recently led the way by providing a better and more practical insight into services management by highlighting eight generic differences inherent in services:

(i) **Nature of the product.** This emphasises that a service, while being focused and rooted in time, is not necessarily ephemeral. The nature of a service is summed up by Berry (1980) as 'a deed, a performance, an effort' compared with a good as 'an object, a device, a thing'. The use of the word 'performance' gives us clues as to how a service may need to be managed in order to secure customer satisfaction. A performance, however, can be variable and is ephemeral.

(ii) **Greater involvement of customers in the production process.** The process of bringing together, assembling and delivering a service often actively involves the customer as an intrinsic and fundamental part – for example, self-service in superstores, co-operating with service personnel and the resulting variability of physical contact with an organisation's personnel.

(iii) **People as part of the product.** Where there are high contact services, customers interact with service personnel and other customers in all kinds of ways. The quality of contact personnel is critical in these encounters with the customer (for example, their training, management and empathy with customers). Managing the service encounter between contact personnel and customers, labelled the 'moment of truth' by Normann (1991) and Carlzon (1987), is fundamental to securing customer satisfaction, personnel motivation and commitment, financial success for the service organisation and securing its competitive advantage over other organisations.

(iv) **Greater difficulties in maintaining quality control standards.** Where services are consumed simultaneously with production, it can be difficult to ensure high quality is being consistently maintained, unlike manufactured goods on an assembly line.

(v) **Difficult for customers to evaluate a service.** Physical goods exhibit characteristics of shape, feel and smell which can usually be experienced or examined prior to purchase. Certain services can only exhibit their true worth and quality after purchase or during consumption. Even then, some service characteristics and benefits may be difficult to evaluate; for example, while many people who have purchased a house may well have a strong view about the worth of estate agents, it can be more difficult to evaluate the worth of legal advice given by a lawyer. Difficulties in customer evaluation mean greater risk for the customer. Service managers need to strive hard to reduce this risk by giving clear information which helps customers evaluate alternatives prior to purchase, encourages first time buyers and demonstrates a service provider's sincerity, reliability, competencies and trustworthiness. They also need to offer unconditional service guarantees where customers have been dissatisfied.

(vi) **Absence of inventories for services.** A 'performance' cannot be stored. A manager must however, have the capacity, such as facilities, personnel and equipment, ready to create and deliver a service when it is required. Matching service capacity with demand levels is a difficult but important managerial task – too little capacity and disappointed customers could be turned away, probably never to return; too much capacity and the costs to the business could be crippling.

(vii) **Relative importance of the time factor.** Customers in restaurants, hospitals and banks are experiencing service delivery in real time. These customers have reasonable expectations of the service being delivered in reasonable time with waiting times minimised where possible.

(viii) **Structure and nature of distribution channels.** Often service businesses are managing customer contact personnel, with all the attendant behavioural problems, rather than contracting out the 'retailing task' to intermediaries.

■ 3.3 Designing service products and their management

In the past the design and managing of a service delivery system was often undertaken by skilled operations managers. We now recognise that while there may well be a service delivery system comprising of a front of house and back of house (or backstage and front stage) complete with technical resources such as facilities, equipment and contact personnel; nevertheless, we must add to these essential elements other points of contact. These include the organisation's marketing communications as well as random exposure to contact personnel, word-of-mouth recommendations and media stories. By adding these communication elements to the service operations system we have in effect a fully functioning service marketing system. Figure 3.1 shows a service marketing system for a high contact consumer service.

Flowcharting is a very useful way of understanding how a service is designed, created and delivered. All the principal functions to create and distribute a service are identified together with the responsible organisational unit and personnel, and depicted in a graphical form. It enables managers to gain a thorough understanding of all underlying service processes both visible and invisible to the customer, and in so doing, managers come to understand more thoroughly the customer's experiences within the service process being created, sustained and controlled. Exposure to service flowcharting often comes as quite a shock to even very experienced service managers and, as empirical research

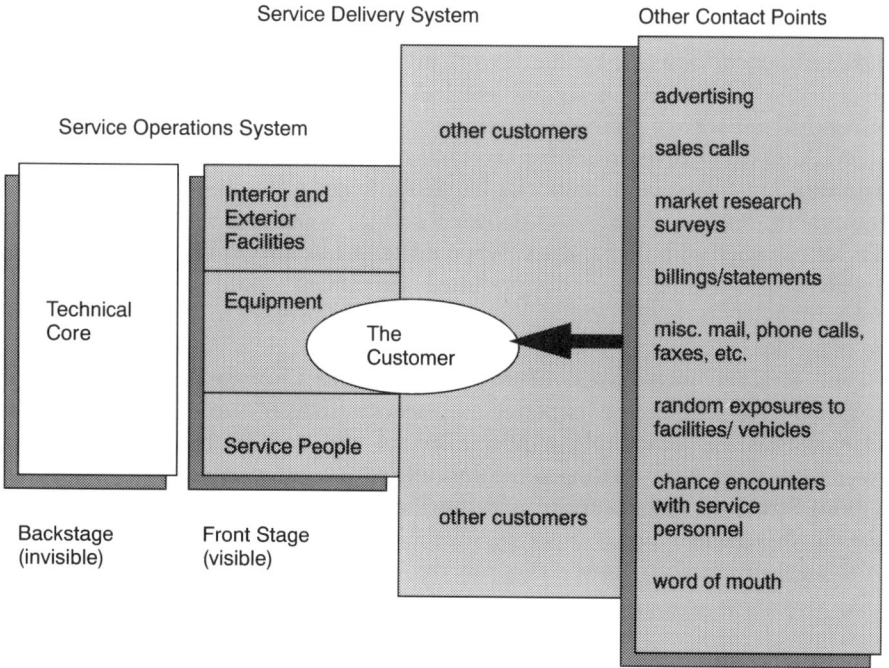

Figure 3.1   Service marketing system for a high contact consumer service
Source: Lovelock, *Services Marketing*, Prentice-Hall International, 1996, p. 55.

shows time and again, managers may often fail to perceive the provided service in a way that the customer does. It does no harm for managers to see the service through the steps taken by a customer and, in so doing, improve on processes, speed them up if necessary and eliminate unnecessary steps so saving the customer time and needless frustrations. One clear advantage derived from service flowcharting is that managers come to see how often their service offering is highly compartmentalised, being composed of a series of discrete activities often undertaken by many different personnel rather than a whole experience or performance as hoped for by the customer.

One variation of flowcharting is a mapping technique called 'blueprinting' developed by Lynn Shostack in the United States (Shostack 1984a; 1984b; 1985; 1987). Basically by preparing a blueprint or flowchart we can see the whole dynamic and developing service process as experienced by the customer. Blueprinting refers to any product delivery process actually experienced by a customer but Shostack has developed this blueprinting technique further within the context of service products. In this context we should strictly talk of service blueprinting rather than blueprinting *per se*, in order to distinguish what concerns services managers (and their customers) and what is of interest to managers (and their customers) of possibly more tangible products.

Lovelock (1996, p. 61) makes a distinction between service mapping where an existing service process is shown and service blueprinting where planning a new or revised service process is undertaken and there is a need to depict how it should ideally function. We will use the term 'service flowcharting' as a generic term for a range of very useful graphical and managerial techniques.

Figure 3.2 illustrates a small service flowchart which illustrates customers coming to a budget or economy hotel.

The following features are often developed (although Figure 3.2 is relatively simple and does not show all such features):

- The timing and linear sequencing of relationships between functions and customer activities are depicted; each interaction with the customer is depicted.
- Managers need to ask what the customer really wants at each stage in the process, eliminating those activities which are not required.
- Two zones are often depicted – a zone of visibility (visible to the customer and where they are most likely to be active participants) and a zone of invisibility (processes and activities which may be hidden from the view of customers).
- Points of critical importance or potential failure are identified, often called 'failpoints' or 'critical incidence points'. These points must be carefully managed if the customer is to be satisfied with the service delivery (that is, critical to customer perceptions of service quality).
- Acceptable levels of tolerance for each event and action are often shown with steps to be taken in the event of failure, although this last area can tend to clutter up the flowchart and obscure the essential points of managerial concern.

Christopher Lovelock (1996, p. 64, originally presented in Lovelock 1994, p. 155) provides a basic checklist for flowcharting the customer experience which is adapted and summarised below:

1. Define the purpose of the flowchart, focusing on what managers wish to learn and why, thinking clearly about what sorts of customers and under what usage conditions.
2. Compile a list of the activities which comprise the experience of customers, keeping it broad rather than too detailed in steps or activities; recognise that different flowcharts may be necessary for alternative customer service experiences – a segmentation of flowcharts in effect.
3. Chart each step in the customer's experience in the sequence in which it is normally encountered, noting carefully customer and contact personnel complaints which may well provide important clues or evidence of critical points or failpoints.
4. It is often helpful to show a parallel flow indicating points in the service process where information is collected and records created, accessed and updated.
5. For every front-stage activity, chart backstage supporting activities, essential in examining service quality problems and in developing internal marketing programmes.
6. Validate descriptions by soliciting inputs from customers and contact personnel – at this stage, mismatches between different perceptions of the service experience may well emerge
7. Supplement the flowchart with a brief narrative describing the activities and their interrelationships.

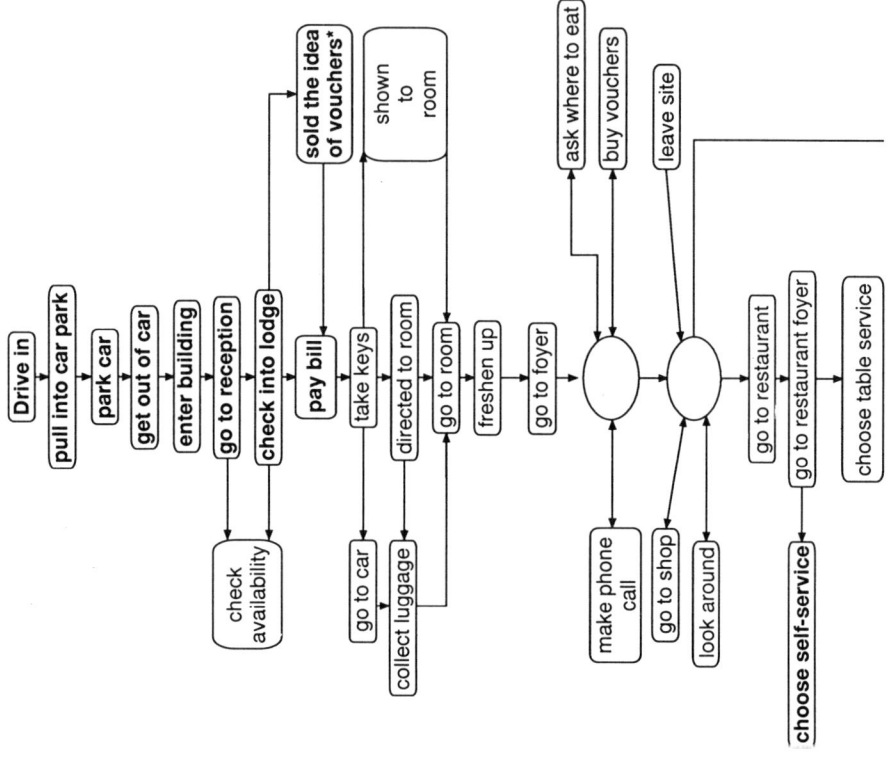

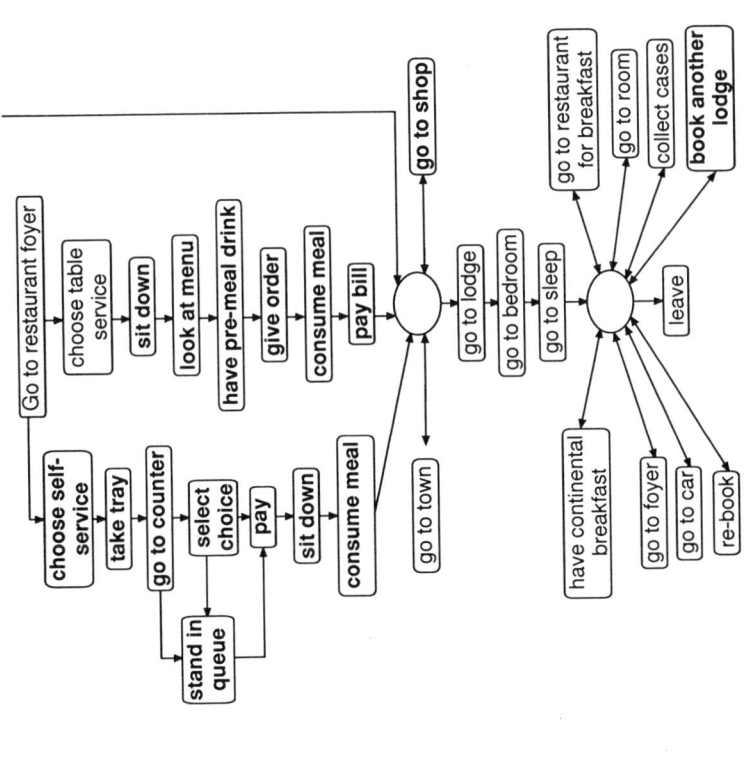

Figure 3.2 Service flowchart
Source: Senior and Akehurst (1992)

■ 3.4 Defining service quality and how it can be promoted

One of the most productive areas of services management since 1985 has been in the definition, measurement, enhancement and promotion of the quality of services. One model in particular, SERVQUAL, introduced by 'Paru' Parasuraman, Len Berry and Valerie Zeithaml in the United States in 1985, has generated an explosion of empirical research in search of this 'Holy Grail' of sustained competitive advantage. This model is briefly examined below, where its principal features and possible limitations are explored.

Service quality has a particular importance to consumers and service organisations which is very clear, perhaps summed up as 'fitness for the purpose', although the concept itself is not easy to define. In service organisations attention given to quality can possibly contribute to market share, lower costs and improve productivity (Garvin 1983). For consumers, service quality can possibly help differentiate one competing service from another.

The word 'quality' has different meanings for different people in different circumstances, such that there is no single definition; indeed, searching for such a single all-embracing definition is doomed to failure from the start. Lovelock (1996) proposes five different approaches to service quality:

- transcendent view – quality is equated with excellence and superb achievement or delivery
- product-based approach – quality is some kind of precise and measurable variable where differences in quality reflect differences in some element or attribute within the service and 'conformance to requirements' (Crosby 1979)
- user-based definition – quality lies in the eyes of the beholder and equals maximum satisfaction for the consumer
- manufacturing-based approach – quality is conformance to internally developed specifications within the organisation
- value-based definition – quality is a relative value-based 'affordable excellence' (Lovelock 1996, p. 99), recognising a trade-off between performance and price.

Gronroos (1982) helpfully outlined two fundamental types of service quality; first, technical quality or what the customer actually receives from the service and second; functional quality or the way the service is delivered.

All these definitions are helpful but are not the only definitions which can be found in the management literature. However they show the many-faceted nature of service quality and, given these different views of quality, it is even more important that managers are clear in their own mind what is being promoted.

Parasuraman, Zeithaml and Berry (1985) move us on from trying to define the elusive concept of quality and focus on those characteristics of services that customers use to evaluate service quality. This has proved to be a more fruitful and rewarding approach to take because it places the customer at the heart of managerial deliberations and acts as a reminder that, ultimately, it is the customer who generates revenues and promotes business changes. Five groups are identified:

1. tangibles – clues given by the appearance of physical facilities, equipment, personnel and marketing communications
2. reliability – ability to perform a promised service with dependability and accuracy
3. responsiveness – willingness of staff to give good, prompt service and ensure customers are helped to satisfy their needs
4. assurance – courtesy, competence and trustworthiness of staff with freedom from risk and doubt
5. empathy – good communications and understanding of customer needs.

Reliability in service delivery and usage consistently appears to be the most important characteristic as far as consumers are concerned and should be also for managers. In short, a service must never promise more than can be delivered. Although this simple business reality appears to be common sense, it is often overlooked by managers keen to secure a customer's business. In manufacturing, formal inspection of products is relatively easy and, consequently, quality control can measure actual performance of the product against specifications. But uniformity can be difficult in services delivery, and indeed, some services are completely customised to a customer's exact requirements (Lewis and Booms 1983).

There are other distinguishing features of service quality, each of which needs managing. First, most services cannot be inspected or verified in advance of a sale in order to ensure quality or fitness for the purpose intended. Second, performance of a service may vary from delivery to delivery while consistency of service personnel behaviour may be difficult to ensure over a given time period. Third, there may be less managerial control over service quality where there is an active participation of the customer.

Much research then has been undertaken in order to understand how a service will be evaluated by the customer. Once we understand how these service quality perceptions are formed and compared with customer experiences of service performance, that is, comparing expectations with evaluations of the service delivery process, then managers have more solid evidence to work on. The equation to remember is:

$$\text{Customer satisfaction} \ = \ \frac{\text{Perceived service}}{\text{Expected service}}$$

If perceptions, or actual experience, of the service are greater than expectations before the service is experienced then a customer will be happy and may well purchase the service again. If perceptions are less than expectations, however, a customer may well be disgruntled or miserable and may well never return to purchase the service again from the providing organisation (Lovelock 1994, p. 111). The problem is how to measure expectations and perceptions of disparate groups of consumers and managers in a rigorous and standardised way. The SERVQUAL instrument offers the promise of such an approach.

From relatively tentative research beginnings, researchers set out in the latter 1980s and into the 1990s to gain insights into:

1. what consumers perceive to be the key attributes of service quality (although recognising the problem that two consumers may perceive a service differently and expectations can be unreasonable)
2. what managers perceive to be the key attributes of service quality
3. possible mismatches between the perceptions of consumers and service managers.

The SERVQUAL model tries to identify the gaps between what customers expect of a service in terms of quality and their perceptions of what they actually experience. With reference to Figure 3.3, five gaps are identified:

- **Gap 1: consumer expectation – management perception gap.** Often there are differences between what managers perceive customers are expecting in a quality service and what customers are actually expecting such as the right to privacy or confidentiality and security in financial transactions. There is no excuse for managers who do not know what their customers need and expect.
- **Gap 2: management perception – service quality expectation gap.** Differences exist between management perceptions of customer expectations and service quality specifications, that is, managers may set service quality specifications based on what they believe a customer is requiring. These discrepancies may be the result of market conditions, resource constraints or sheer management indifference (Parasuraman, Zeithaml and Berry 1985, p. 44).
- **Gap 3: service quality specifications – service delivery gap.** Execution fails to match predefined standards; the pivotal role of contact personnel is of great importance where service delivery is heavily dependant on people, and where service delivery and performance is immediate and directly involves the customer as a willing party in the transaction.
- **Gap 4: service delivery – external communications to consumers.** Media advertising, public relations and other communications may affect customer expectations of a service; over-promising can lead to real problems because customer expectations are raised to levels which cannot possibly be met, and therefore a gap may exist between service delivery intention and what is communicated about that service to customers.
- **Gap 5: expected service – perceived service gap.** The difference between actual performance and customers' perception of that performance; good quality can often be unobtrusive resulting in the customer not realising what good service they have received.

The SERVQUAL model has been further refined, extended and empirically tested (Zeithaml, Berry and Parasuraman 1988; Parasuraman, Zeithaml and Berry 1988; Carman 1990; Parasuraman, Berry and Zeithaml 1991; Babakus and

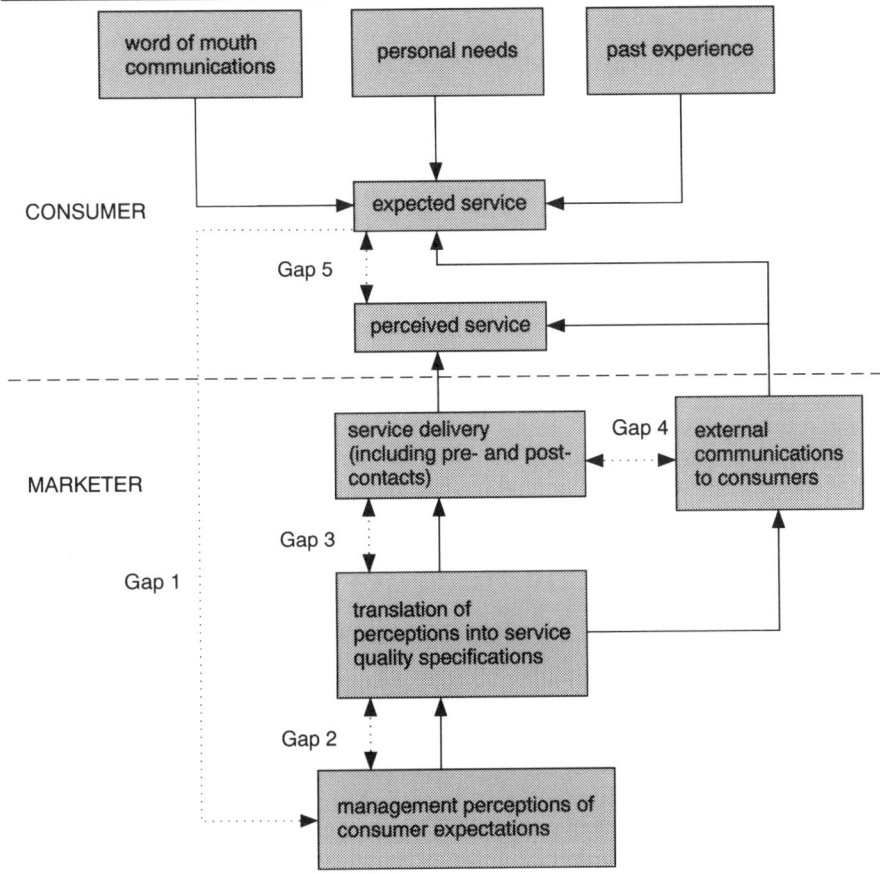

Figure 3.3 SERVQUAL model
Source: Parasuraman, Zeithaml and Berry, 'A Conceptual Model of Service Quality and its Implications for Future Research, *Journal of Marketing*, 49, 1985.

Boller 1992; Zeithaml, Berry and Parasuraman 1993) but has recently come under increasing criticism, notably by Brown, Churchill and Peter (1993) and Cronin and Taylor (1992). The Cronin and Taylor criticism is potentially the most damaging by focusing on a performance-based measure of service quality, with service quality being an antecedent of customer satisfaction, while customer satisfaction has a significant effect on purchase intentions. It is this important relationship between service quality, customer satisfaction and purchasing behaviour, and the causal order of the relationship, which remains to be thoroughly empirically tested. Whether SERVQUAL in its current formulation is up to the task is, at the time of writing, open to question, but for the moment, SERVQUAL remains a useful instrument for exploring these important operational and strategic issues.

While this consideration of service quality may appear at first sight to be unnecessarily complex, nevertheless, what lessons are there here for managers? To summarise, Lovelock (1994, pp. 113–14), as always, neatly highlights the essentials:

- ask your customers what they need, that is, carry out market research and ensure you have a fully functioning marketing information system in place
- translate these customer needs into clear service specifications
- use training and quality control procedures to make sure that delivery conforms to service specifications
- brief the marketing communications personnel very carefully in order to avoid over-promising
- manage customer expectations so they do not have hugely unrealistic expectations about the service being delivered, and especially the benefits accruing (a difficult task this)
- ensure that customers recognise what service they are receiving, drawing attention, if necessary, to the quality of service performed for them.

■ 3.5 Service encounters, service personnel and recovery from service failures

Many but not all services require the physical presence of the customer. Unfortunately, much of the service management literature uses consumer service examples in the retail, banking and hospitality sectors while tending to neglect the substantially larger business services sectors where actual customer presence is not necessarily required for service delivery to take place. In high contact services the encounter becomes the only means by which customers can assess service quality, while in low contact services the encounter is just one element in the total production and consumption process.

Shostack (1985) defines a service encounter as 'a period of time during which a consumer directly interacts with a service'. This Shostack definition includes all aspects of the service organisation with which the customer may interact, including personnel, the physical assets and other tangible evidence of the service and service organisation. This definition can be expanded somewhat to delineate the period of time during which an organisation's human and physical resources interact with the customer in order to create service benefits for the satisfaction of that customer's needs. We recall from earlier discussion that the service offered is a complex mix of tangible and intangible elements that make up the total functional, psychological and social benefits of the service delivered. How this service encounter is managed is critically important.

Often service production cannot be separated from its consumption so this producer–consumer interaction assumes great importance. The service process itself helps to shape and define the benefits received by the customer; for example, how customers are checked-in at an airport prior to flying is clearly part of the benefit paid for and received. In direct contrast, a manufacturer may only come into contact with customers very briefly at the point where goods are exchanged for payment. Generally, manufacturers act through intermediaries without having direct contact with customers, while stocks are normally held to meet fluctuating customer demand (unfortunately, many service organisations cannot store their services). This customer-service organisation interaction can either be a series of discrete transactions over time or an on-going relationship. Generally, service organisations strive to develop an on-going relationship; for example, retailer customer loyalty cards may nurture such a relationship while yielding useful marketing information about customer spending habits.

Developing long-term relationships with customers in a mutually beneficial partnership, generally called relationship marketing is, therefore, especially important. Dwyer, Schurr and Oh (1987) identify five stages in a business relationship:

- awareness
- exploration
- expansion
- commitment
- dissolution.

Knowing that there are distinct stages in customer-organisation relationships, managers can devise appropriate strategies which move customers through to the committed or loyal phase:

- show reasons for choosing your organisation
- on entering the relationship, a series of promises are made to each other
- first encounter with the customer triggers recording of information about the customer which is useful for assessing future needs and building up a database of customer profiles
- frequent users should receive graded incentives: that is, the more frequent the usage, the better the incentive)
- look for ways to turn discrete service delivery into continuous service delivery; for example, moving a daily rail ticket purchaser to a monthly or yearly season ticket
- use financial incentives as a reward for maintaining the relationship; for example, graduated discounts and privileged membership schemes
- do not neglect the attraction of non-financial incentives; for example, special preview events
- look for ways to develop trust and lessen perceived risks.

Facilitating customer loyalty is important particularly where there are complex services. Complex services are inherently risky so anything a service organisation can do to reduce perceived risk is to be welcomed by customers. Customers may well be reassured by preferential treatment, for example, frequent hotel guest or flyer programmes, or semi-automatic responses to requests for service such as maintenance contracts provided the service organisation monitors results during and after service delivery.

High contact encounters are particularly demanding for both contact personnel and management. Customers are on site and quality control is critical because the customer is concerned as much with the process of service delivery as with the end-result. During the encounter the management of customer demand is critical because delays and frustrating waiting in queues, for instance, can have adverse consequences for developing perceptions of good service quality and harmonious on-going customer-organisation relationships. On the other hand services performed on physical objects, such as car servicing, is a large part of the production process which is completely unseen by the customer. In such circumstances the customer may be reduced to initiating the service process and retrieving the results. Here the process may be of very little concern but the end-result is. So handling of pre and after-sales is of special importance.

Earlier we examined briefly how services can be designed and how failpoints or critical incidents assume a particular importance which cannot be underestimated. We can describe critical incidents as specific interactions between service organisation contact personnel and customers that are especially satisfying or dissatisfying (Bitner, Booms and Tetreault 1990). Incidents are not confined, however, to the contact personnel–customer interface but also other resources of the service organisation. At each critical point in the service process customers are evaluating the service provider and forming an opinion of service quality. Each encounter may involve a large number of critical incidents, each of which must be managed with care. Consider the following simplified example of customer interaction with an airline, on a flight from London Heathrow to Miami, Florida:

pre-ticket sales
decision to make journey
select travel agency or airline
initial telephone enquiry
making reservation
issue of ticket
payment
post-ticket sales, pre-service consumption
travel to airport
check-in of person and baggage
ticket inspection
issue of boarding pass
passport control
departure gate advice
quality of airport announcements, signage and other information
quality of waiting conditions
consumption of flight service
welcome on boarding aircraft
assistance in finding seat
assistance with stowing hand baggage
safety information and demonstration

reliability of departure time
attention to security and reassurance
attentiveness of in-flight service
quality of food and drink
quality of in-flight entertainment
quality of announcements
safe and comfortable aircraft operation
fast transfer from aircraft to terminal building
post-consumption of flight service
arrival at destination
baggage reclaim and handling of lost baggage
information and signage at arrival airport
customs control
leave airport

This example is based on Palmer (1994, pp. 152–3) and Lovelock (1996, pp. 158–62).

Our simplified example above shows all kinds of failpoints or critical incidents (and no doubt the reader can think of many more from their own experiences of the joys of flying). Where critical failures occur, for whatever reason, strategies are needed to effect rapid service recovery. In such instances contact personnel need to find out quickly what went wrong; contact personnel must have the ability (reinforced regularly by training) to genuinely empathise with customers and be empowered to act. This last point is vital and yet it is often the one thing that managers are reluctant to ensure happens. Some service managers see empowerment of contact personnel as some kind of diminution or restriction of their 'right to manage' or a curtailment of their managerial control. An intelligent manager will think otherwise and so turn a failed critical incident into a positive advantage. Usually this is by ensuring quick action, where necessary, speedy and fair compensation, followed by the opportunity for the customer to provide valuable feedback. Such feedback does need, however, to be acted on and used to good effect the next time the critical incident is performed or encountered.

A service has been likened, as we saw earlier, to a performance. Some writers talk of the 'service drama' and each service encounter as a theatrical drama. The theatre analogy is a useful one because it reminds us that each of the 'actors' in the performance has a role to play. Roles are assumed as a result of learning from past experiences and conditioning by society and culture. We each have multiple roles to play (parent, employee, customer, etc.) and each role has a set of expectations. These expectations are brought to the service encounter. Customers have role expectations of contact personnel while personnel have expectations of customers. Over time these role expectations may change but the quality of the service encounter reflects the extent to which each party's role expectations have been met. Earlier we saw that the quality of a service is seen as the difference between service expectations and perceived delivery.

Other customers in the service process also assume an importance. Often services are consumed in public and individual customer behaviour can affect other customers. Such customer–customer interaction can be successfully managed in order to enhance the perceived quality of the service being provided. For example, holiday companies may wish to specialise in 18-to-30 holidays and may actively select customers on the basis of their ability and willingness to interact positively with other customers and may actively facilitate positive customer–customer interaction, for example, between conference delegates. Certainly a service organisation can determine, overtly or covertly, rules of behaviour expected from customers.

Some services lend themselves to a certain industrialising of the service encounter and so enhance productivity but keep labour costs down. There is a trade-off with this approach, however, where maximisation of customer choice and flexibility of available services is traded for a comparatively limited range of services with tightly specified operating procedures, less human contact and where machines or technology are used where possible – for example, hole-in-the-wall cash machines. For the service organisation, an additional benefit is a reduction in the variability of service outcomes and consistent brand values.

Finally, we must remember that the service encounter in all its various forms is about successfully managing customer demand and organisational capacity. It means giving careful attention to managing peaks and troughs in demand and matching supply to it. Peaks and troughs need evening-out, equipment and personnel need scheduling to maintain maximum flexibility and the capability to switch these resources between alternative uses. Pricing may need to be varied between peak and off-peak periods, and queuing and reservation systems need good and sensitive management, good communications, with both customers and contact personnel, and an acute awareness of cross-selling opportunities. For a good relatively recent study of critical service encounters, see Bitner, Booms and Mohr (1994).

■ 3.6 Strategic services management – the strategy of the augmented service

This final section briefly introduces one aspect of strategic services management – adding value to core products with supplementary services to enhance customer value added and significantly improve the service organisation's competitive advantage. In the words of Christopher Lovelock (1994) it means becoming 'a product plus company'. It is often performance delivered on the supplementary services which differentiates a service organisation from its competitors. But sustaining competitive advantage cannot be attained solely through tactical manoeuvres; there must be a well-thought-out strategy. This requires the service organisation to think holistically by looking carefully at the totality of their customer's experiences, the service processes and how technology is used to enhance the service provision. It also means thinking in terms of customer, distributor and investor relationships rather than just a series of discrete transactions.

Core products will vary from organisation to organisation but supplementary services are often common across different industries. These supplementary services help define competitive performance which ultimately feeds through to better business performance. Lovelock (1994) likens these supplementary services to the petals on a flower – they attract attention, and even if the core is fine, wilted petals create a poor impression for customers.

Lovelock (1994, p. 269) outlines eight supplementary services or 'petals':

- **information** – to obtain full value from a service, customers, especially first-time users, need relevant and timely information about it – directions, instructions, reminders, schedules, prices, conditions of sale, warnings, reservation confirmations, summaries of account activity, and so on
- **consultation** – dialogue to probe true customer requirements, developing customised solutions to customer needs
- **order taking** – accepting applications, orders and reservations, requiring politeness, speed and accuracy
- **hospitality** – purchasing people-processing services involves entering the 'service factory' and staying until service delivery is completed; this means taking care of the customers, greeting them, providing waiting and washroom facilities, security and possibly entertainment (according to service delivered)
- **caretaking** – looking after customer possessions, cloakrooms, baggage handling, valuables safekeeping, child care, caring for purchases (packaging, delivery, installation and repairs)
- **exceptions** – services falling outside the routine service delivery, special requests (customised treatment), problem-solving, complaints handling and restitution for performance failures; intelligent managers capitalise on exceptions by planning in advance for these highly profitable activities
- **billing** – incomplete, inaccurate or illegible bills will annoy or disappoint, with such failures adding insult to injury if the customer is already dissatisfied
- **payment** – self-service by the customer (cash machines, prepaid cards and tokens), customer interaction with contact personnel (cash, credit and cheque handling).

These 'petals' are vital add-ons that can improve profitability or other performance indicators:

- the 'petals' are augmentations of the core product that enhance the core; customers may well pay handsomely for such enhancements
- they are responses to customer needs;
- they are facilitating services that enable customers to use the core product more effectively.

Finally, some managerial implications of augmented services are listed below which the reader may wish to ponder:

- As a manager, what 'flower' do you offer your customers?
- Should supplementary services be optional extras with additional charges?
- Should customers be offered a menu featuring a la carte items and different price combinations (a pick and mix)?
- Most 'petals' are data or information-based which has enormous implications for both service innovation and competitive advantage, giving opportunities to enhance service and productivity through the intelligent application of information technology.
- How do we introduce innovative extras designed not merely to satisfy customers but also to delight them as well?
- How can we cope with supplementary services which can be readily copied by competitors and over time become absorbed into standard customer requirements?
- How can we plan capacity to ensure we match resources to fluctuating demand which may be inherent in our markets but which can be exaggerated by supplementary services?

Close attention to excellent quality of core and augmented services together with effective marketing communications and a well-thought-out human resources strategy will ultimately ensure not just organisational survival but excellent performance. This is a happy result worth striving hard for, both for the organisation and its customers.

■ 3.7 Case study: Brownloaf MacTaggart – the next chapter in a sorry saga

This case study has been adapted from that published in Akehurst (1994, pp. 187–94) 'Brownloaf MacTaggart – Control and Power in a Management Consultancy'. The original case study had been written to explore issues of managerial control and power. The simplified case below raises questions of service quality within a management consultancy. The name of the consultancy is not the true name for legal reasons but all events and problems are real.

Watkins International is a long established firm of chartered accountants and management consultants, with international interests in accountancy and audit services, corporate finance, insolvency services, taxation and management consultancy. This case is concerned with one division of Watkins International, the Brownloaf MacTaggart Management Consultancy Division (BM), which, until merger with Watkins in 1988, had been a successful small engineering consultancy practice.

Moving from being a small, closely knit company to a small insignificant division in an international corporate empire has created considerable tensions. Managerial control has changed rapidly from one of benevolent dictatorship to one of corporate uniformity.

This case is concerned with issues of service quality among a group of highly qualified and highly energetic and enthusiastic professional consultants. Personnel are highly motivated towards meeting client expectations and needs but an over-elaborate quality management system and highly constrained budgets make for less than consistent service quality. The partners, however, appear to be more concerned with increasing turnover than with delivering good service. In management consultancy this is unusual. The question is whether this business can survive in its present form.

Watkins was established as a chartered accountancy practice in 1893. Following decades of moderate growth it entered the management consultancy market in 1955 primarily as a 'spin-off' from audit and taxation work. In the following years this diversification proved to be profitable. What had started as a very small side-line activity has developed into a multi- divisional management consultancy business employing in the UK alone some 700 people. World-wide Watkins employs around 70,000 people through a network of firms and associate firms. The international firm has at least one office in most countries, and in the early 1990s had established new offices, particularly in Eastern Europe.

Watkins has endeavoured to grow primarily by acquisition and internal growth, but acquisition has been by far the most successful strategy, particularly in the 1980s when a software development company and BM were acquired. The firm now has five consultancy divisions in the UK covering information technology and software engineering, public sector management, financial services and treasury, leisure and retailing, and general engineering.

Brownloaf MacTaggart & Co had started business in 1962 as a two-person partnership. Alex MacTaggart had been a successful production engineer, who had assiduously built up a long list of good contacts while working for blue-chip engineering companies. Duncan Brownloaf had been a successful engineering company salesman selling diverse products such as hydraulic pit props and mining pump equipment. The two men combined their strengths by taking small premises in Walsall, in the West Midlands. The business flourished, and in 1977, now employing 20 people, two additional employees were admitted into partnership – Heinrich Grubber and William Smallpiece.

The BM business flourished, establishing a good reputation for creative and practical solutions for engineering businesses across the world. Projects tended to be fairly small in value, averaging £10,000 to £15,000 (at current prices), with occasionally larger assignments, but clients were prestigious and BM gained a reputation as one of the top three in its specialised field.

Having admitted the two new partners both founder partners began to think of retirement. In 1980 the company moved into bigger offices in the heart of Birmingham. One month after the move both Alex MacTaggart and Duncan Brownloaf were effectively retired.

The BM name was continued for goodwill reasons, and the new partners set about planning for the future but both were worried about future strategy.

Should they stay as a small stand-alone company or actively seek merger or acquisition? In 1988 the future direction was settled. Watkins International had been looking to acquire an existing engineering consulting company. Merger negotiations were started with BM. These negotiations proved to be unusually protracted. Besides issues of partner capital, there were a number of issues surrounding managerial autonomy. Surprisingly, merger was nearly aborted by the insistence of the BM partners that young Eric Reliant be admitted into partnership. The partnership qualities of Eric were not, however, immediately obvious to the senior partners of Watkins. He tended to be a disorganised blue-sky thinker, or 'head in the clouds' visionary. What he lacked in technical engineering skills he more than made up for in low-life cunning.

With agreement reached on the admission to partnership of Eric Reliant, the way to merger was clear. Following merger life appeared to continue much as before. BM occupied the same premises and, to all intents and purposes, operated as the same company. The BM name was retained but they now operated as the Brownloaf MacTaggart Division of Watkins International.

For eighteen months it was business as usual. The head office of Watkins was two miles away – in many respects out of sight and out of mind. Surprisingly Watkins did not rein in its new division. Procedures stayed more or less the same although the house style of reports to clients now had to conform to strict and elaborate Watkins' requirements. The name of the overall firm had changed but the three partners continued to behave as if BM was an independent company.

Watkins International began to introduce firm-wide standardised practices early in 1990. First the time-sheet recording system linked to client billing was changed from a manual system to a computerised system; later, standardised routines and forms were introduced for a number of administrative procedures, including holiday requests, staff appraisal, expenses and assignment control. All curricula vitae were placed into a computerised database linked to a proposal (or bidding for work) administration system. Surprisingly, despite the relative sophistication of this system, matching the personnel with the requisite experience to project requirements is rather hit and miss, and depends more on an informal reward and punishment system.

In May 1991 Watkins secured three floors of a prestigious ten-floor office block located adjacent to their head office in Birmingham. In August and September 1991 all Watkins' management consultancy divisions were located on one floor of the new office. Some 700 people, including all management consultancy support staff such as accounts, personnel and office management, are housed in a huge open-plan office, although partners have individual, if small, offices. Individual consultants are assigned to a desk, each desk accommodating at least two consultants. If both consultants are in the office, working space becomes a simple matter of early desk possession. All consultants are required to log on to a computerised staff locations system, which records contact telephone numbers and physical location for every hour of the working day. The same system acts as a message recording point when consultants are working outside the office.

The change from a relatively small office away from the main management consultancy to the big company environment came as quite a shock to several BM staff. There was a realisation, perhaps for the first time, that they were working in a large, rather impersonal, increasingly automated and tightly regulated environment. Above all they were expected to sink or swim in a fiercely competitive environment. There was also a realisation that although they might be well-known in the engineering industry, within the Watkins' empire they were minute in terms of size of turnover, number of projects, number of employees and profitability.

The length and severity of recession, not just in the UK but also in other developed countries, was beginning to cause difficulties in the BM division and also in the information technology and software engineering division. Many engineering businesses were being taken into receivership, and while managing businesses under receivership became for a time highly profitable for BM, other more profitable work needed to be generated. The traditional feasibility study and other development type work had steadily become less easy to obtain and, in the early part of 1995, there was virtually no on-going development work. While international work had provided a cushion during the depths of the recession, UK-based work had seriously declined since the beginning of 1993. The BM divisional plan for the five years to 1997 had envisaged a doubling of turnover from £3.5 million to over £7 million; the number of BM consultancy staff staying the same at 30 (including 3 partners) and 4 support staff, and the average consultant utilisation rate, or percentage of employable time charged to a client, increasing from just under 60 per cent to 65 per cent. At a divisional meeting early in 1993 BM staff were warned that, although staff numbers were forecast to remain the same, new staff were to be recruited.

To improve its competitive advantage in a stagnant management consultancy market, by being seen to conform to the highest service quality delivery standards, in 1992 Watkins introduced a new quality management system. This was an effort to secure BS 5750 Part 1 certification (the British Standards quality award). This new system required a complete rethink of the way consultancy assignments are managed, and introduced an essentially mechanistic approach to quality management based on an accountant's view of correct filing, record keeping and random assignment audits. Elaborate quality procedures became progressively refined during 1992 and encapsulated in a beautifully printed Watkins Quality Manual. This manual was revised five times in as many months and, not surprisingly, many consultants became confused as the quality system appeared to be used by partners as part of a reward and punishment system. It was all too easy to miss completion of a form, or completion of a section of a form, or to neglect to obtain a partner's signature on a form or miss a quality plan review. The threat of periodic quality audits now hangs over every consultant and, instead of using the quality management system as a means of improving services to clients, many consultants have become increasingly antagonistic towards it. The whole quality management system has become a bureaucratic nightmare instead of the aide to successful service quality and client satisfaction that it should be.

The allocation of consultancy assignments within the BM Division is either on 'the warm body' principle, i.e. who is available, or is part of a none too subtle punishment and reward system. Generally there is a perceived hierarchy of jobs. A succession of either top-rated jobs for prestigious clients or small insignificant jobs managed by poor job managers, can make or break a Watkins career in around four months.

It is against this background of difficult trading conditions in an uncertain environment, together with the absorption of a relatively small firm into an international management company with all its standardised procedures, and where mistrust, intimidation and fear are common emotions, that BM appears to be trying to boost its number of clients. Recognising that something needs to be done, the firm has ordered an extensive review of its quality management system with a particular emphasis upon identification and management of service failpoints, and service recovery (perhaps linked to service guarantees). The senior partner at the firm's recent technical conference heralded the new age of 'relationship marketing' and asked Divisional partners to go away and develop appropriate plans and mechanisms in order to deliver this.

Postscript   The situation in Watkins and the Brownloaf MacTaggart division continues much as described in the case, although in 1995 the Division was moved out of Birmingham and relocated in small premises in Shrewsbury. This clear marginalisation of the Division has not gone unnoticed. Business continues to be relatively slow and further cost-cutting exercises have taken place principally by reducing the number of employees. Identification of service failpoints has been erratic with an imprecise grasp of what service quality management is all about.

There is now the very real possibility of a management buy-out in the BM division led by Heinrich Grubber. Currently the BM division is awash with buy-out rumours and one of the partners, Eric Reliant, has decided to leave. In all probability, over the next two years, staff turnover, whether voluntary or involuntary, will reach 30 per cent per year, as the economy picks up. The BM partners are unlikely to seriously analyse and resolve their management problems but this will not stop them offering advice and solutions to the management problems of clients. This is a classic case of 'physician heal thyself'.

■ 3.8 Conclusions

To understand the growing and important area of services management requires an understanding of many disciplines – of marketing, operations management, human resources management and organisational behaviour to name but a few. This chapter has outlined some of the special and enduring characteristics of services, recognising that all business transactions have a service element within them but some business transactions have a greater tangible or intangible core than others. How service quality is perceived by customers, how we as managers can assess, promote and measure service quality is crucial to the success of modern business whatever the nature of their business transactions. Satisfying needs of particular market segments is the name of the game.

Customer care, customer satisfaction, meeting customer needs, developing long-term relationships and customising products are all vital elements and foci in contemporary businesses: they are also the key to enhanced productivity and profitability. How elements are changed over time has important consequences for customer perceptions of service quality, but we must not ignore differences within the service sector and similarities across the goods and services sectors (Wright, 1996, p. 35). Clearly services are not homogeneous. Within the broad group of intangible dominant products there is plenty of heterogeneity in terms of the extent of direct contact with the customer, the nature and level of the intangible elements, and the use of information technology and other equipment in delivering the product. Many writers (for example, Wright 1996) suggest strongly that managers should emphasise the total market offering, that is, the aggregation of all benefits received by the customer, which results from the core product and augmentations (whether tangible or intangible). Customers seek utility or satisfaction from products and it is these benefits they seek – they do not necessarily care whether the core product is tangible or intangible – and nor are all businesses seeking to increase face-to-face contact with customers (take, for example, the introduction of bank cash machines or automatic teller machines to reduce personnel–customer contact).

Lewis (1996, pp. 59–60) helpfully outlines the stages involved in customer care programmes. In reading through these steps, much of this chapter is 'operationalised' and brought to life:

1. Identify the service and customer care dimensions which are important from customer research and ways that customer perceived risk in purchasing your product can be reduced.
2. Measure the importance of these dimensions.
3. Translate customer needs and expectations into products, service specifications and standards.
4. Set standards which are measurable and service delivery systems prepared where potential fail points are clearly identified and sensitively managed.
5. Manage employees, especially front line staff with care.
6. Manage the service delivery process paying particular attention to handling complaints with sensitivity and promptness, using service recovery techniques to good effect and using information technology to enhance accuracy, speed, efficiency and credibility.

7. Monitor the care programme to include systems to research and evaluate customer satisfactions and dissatisfactions, and employee performance.
8. Review customer care objectives and organisational structures in the light of operational experiences.

When set out in list form, these features of good service delivery appear to be common sense (and in many ways they are) but it is surprising just how many businesses neglect these steps – to institute them, improve on them, and constantly strive to improve service delivery. Services management brings its own rewards to the modern business in terms of customer loyalty, improved new sales and repeat business generated through improved customer satisfaction. It also reduces costs and improves profitability (for those organisations where profit is a driving objective). It brings increased job satisfaction for employees and knowledge of a job well done.

The case study illustrates in vivid terms where customer and employee satisfaction are ill-served by a management ill-equipped to manage its operations in a services dominated world, where services are one of the keys to enhanced and sustainable competitive advantage. By working through the case study and attempting the questions at the end, the reader will be understanding and seeing in a small way the application of these fundamental principles.

■ Questions for discussion

1. Advise the partners of Brownloaf MacTaggart as to how they could improve their service delivery system in order to consistently deliver high quality and reliable services. Could you sell such improvements to the career grade management consultants?
2. What critical incidents points or failpoints can you identify in a management consultancy service?
3. Are service guarantees, where customers are guaranteed compensation or other restitution in the event of service failure, feasible in management consultancy services?
4. The senior partner of Watkins International asks you to address his firm's next technical conference on what are the essential features of a service marketing system as opposed to a service operations system. Pinpoint the differences and say why moving to a service marketing system is fundamental to delivering a quality service.
5. Outline the 'petals on the flower' augmented services that you would recommend be developed to supplement core products in the Brownloaf MacTaggart Division, explaining how these, together with effective marketing communications, may secure the firm competitive advantage and a secure market position.

■ Bibliography

Akehurst, G., 'Service Industries', in Jones, P., (ed.), *Management in Service Industries* (London: Pitman, 1989) pp. 3–35.

Akehurst, G., 'Brownloaf MacTaggart – Control and Power in a Management Consultancy', in Adam-Smith, D., and Peacock, A. (eds), *Cases in Organisational Behaviour* (London: Pitman Publishing, 1994).

Akehurst, G., and Alexander, N., (eds), *The Internationalisation of Retailing* (London: Frank Cass, 1995).

Akehurst, G., and Alexander, N., (eds), *Retail Marketing* (London: Frank Cass, 1996a).

Akehurst, G., and Alexander, N., (eds), *Retail Structure* (London: Frank Cass, 1996b).

Akehurst, G., and Alexander, N., (eds), *Retail Employment* (London: Frank Cass, 1996c).

Akehurst, G. P., and Gadrey, J., (eds), *The Economics of Services* (London: Frank Cass, 1987).

Akehurst G., and Senior M., 'Perceptual Blueprinting in the United Kingdom', in Scheuing, E. E., Gummesson, E. and Little, C. H., (eds), *Proceedings of the Quality in Services Conference* (St. John's University, New York and Service Research Centre, University of Karlstad, Sweden, 1992) pp. 177–92.

Babakus, E. and Boller, G. W. 'An Empirical Assessment of the SERVQUAL Scale', *Journal of Business Research*, 24 (1992) 253–68.

Bell, D., *The Coming of Post-Industrial Society* (London: Heinemann, 1974).

Berry, L.L., 'Service Marketing Is Different', *Business*, 30, May-June (1980) 24–9.

Beyers, W. B., *The Producer Services and Economic Development in the United States: The Last Decade* (Seattle: US Department of Commerce, 1989).

Bitner, M. J., Booms B. H., and Mohr, L. A., 'Critical Service Encounters: The Employee's Viewpoint', *Journal of Marketing*, 58 (1994) 95–106.

Bitner, M. J., Booms, B. H. and Tetreault, M. S., 'The Service Encounter: Diagnosing Favorable and Unfavorable Incidents', *Journal of Marketing*, 54 (1990), 71–84.

Brown, T. J., Churchill, G. A. and Peter, J. P., 'Improving the Measurement of Service Quality', *Journal of Retailing*, 69 (1993), 127–39.

Browning, H. C. and Singelmann, J., *The Emergence of a Service Society* (Springfield: National Technical Information Service, 1975).

Carlzon, J., *Moments of Truth* (Cambridge, MA: Ballinger Publishing, 1987).

Carman, J. J., 'Consumer Perceptions of Service Quality: An Assessment of the SERVQUAL Dimensions', *Journal of Retailing*, 66 (1990), 33–5.

Channon, D. F., *The Service Industries* (London: Macmillan, 1978).

Clark, C. A., *The Conditions of Economic Progress* (London: Macmillan, 1940).

Commission of the European Communities, *European Tourism Year* (Brussels: CEC, 1990).

Cronin, J. J. and Taylor, S. A., 'Measuring Service Quality: A Reexamination and Extension', *Journal of Marketing*, 56 (1992), 55–68.

Crosby, P. B., *Quality is Free: The Art of Making Quality Certain* (New York: New American Library, 1979).

Daniels, P. W., *The Supply and Demand for Intermediate Services by Merseyside Firms: A Preliminary Study*, (Liverpool: Department of Geography, University of Liverpool, 1986).

Daniels, P. W., 'Spatial Patterns of Producer Services: Recent Research and New Directions', *Working Papers on Producer Services No. 14* (Portsmouth: Portsmouth Polytechnic, 1989).

Daniels, P. W., *A World of Services, an inaugural lecture*, (Portsmouth: Portsmouth Polytechnic, 1991).

Daniels, P. and Thrift, N., 'The Geographies of the UK Service Sector: A Survey', *Working Paper Series on Producer Services* No. 6 (Liverpool and Bristol Universities, 1987).

Dwyer, F. R., Schurr, P. H. and Oh, S., 'Developing Buyer and Seller Relationships', *Journal of Marketing*, 5, April (1987).

Elfring, T., *Service Sector Employment in Advanced Economies* (Aldershot: Gower, 1988).

Eurostat, *Tourism in Europe. Trends 1989* (Luxembourg: Office for Official Publications of the European Communities, 1990).

Fisher, A. G. B., *The Clash of Progress and Society* (London: Macmillan, 1935).

Foxall, G., *Marketing in the Service Industries* (London: Frank Cass, 1984).

Fuchs, V. R., *The Service Economy* (New York: National Bureau of Economic Research, 1968).

Gabbott, M. and Hogg, G., *Contemporary Services Marketing Management. A Reader* (London: Dryden Press, 1987).

Gadrey, J., Gallouj, F. and Weinstein, O., 'New Modes of Innovation. How Services Benefit Industry', *International Journal of Service Industry Management*, vol. 6, no. 3 (1995) 4–16.

Garvin, D. A., 'Quality on the Line', *Harvard Business Review*, 61, September–October (1983) 65–73.

Gershuny, J., *After Industrial Society: The Emerging Self Service Economy* (London: Macmillan, 1979).

Gershuny, J. I. and Miles, I. D., *The New Service Economy: The Transformation of Employment in Industrial Societies* (London: Frances Pinter, 1983).

Gronroos, C., 'A Service-Oriented Approach to Marketing of Services', *European Journal of Marketing*, 12 (8), (1978) 560–88.

Gronroos, C., *Strategic Management and Marketing in the Service Sector* (Helsingfors: Swedish School of Economics and Business Administration, 1982).

Gummesson, E., 'Lip Services – A Neglected Area in Services Marketing', *Journal of Services Marketing*, 1 (1987), 22.

Illeris, S., *Services and Regions in Europe* (Aldershot: Avebury, 1989).

Lee, C. H., 'The Service Sector, Regional Specialisation and Economic Growth in the Victorian Economy', *Journal of Historical Geography*, 10 (1984), 139–56.

Lewis, B. R., 'Customer Care in Services', in Glynn, W. G. and Barnes, J. G., *Understanding Services Management* (Chichester: John Wiley, 1996) 57–88.

Lewis, R. C. and Booms, B. H., 'The Marketing Aspects of Service Quality', in Berry, L., Shostack, G. and Upah, G., (eds), *Emerging Perspectives on Services Marketing* (Chicago: American Marketing , 1983) 99–107.

Lovelock, C., *Product Plus* (New York: McGraw-Hill, 1994).

Lovelock, C., *Services Marketing* 3rd edn (London: Prentice-Hall International, 1996).

McKenzie, R. B., 'The Emergence of the "Service Economy": Fact or Artifact?', in Grubel, H. G., *Conceptual Issues in Service Sector Research: A Symposium* (Vancouver: The Fraser Institute, 1987).

Normann, R., 'Service Management: Strategy and Leadership', in *Service Businesses*, 2nd edn, (Chichester: John Wiley, 1991).

Ochel, W. and Wegner, M., *Service Economies in Europe: Opportunities for Growth* (London: Pinter, 1987).

Palmer, A., *Principles of Services Marketing* (London: McGraw-Hill, 1994).

Parasuraman, A., Zeithaml, V. A. and Berry, L. L., 'A Conceptual Model of Service Quality and its Implications for Future Research', *Journal of Marketing*, 49 (1985), 41–50.

Parasuraman, A., Zeithaml, V. A. and Berry, L. L., 'SERVQUAL: A Multiple-Item Scale for Measuring Consumer Perceptions of Service Quality', *Journal of Retailing*, 64 (1), (1988) 12–40.

Parasuraman, A., Berry, L. L. and Zeithaml, V. A., 'Refinement and Reassessment of the SERVQUAL Scale', *Journal of Retailing*, 67 (1991), 420–50.

Sasser, W. E., Olsen, R. P. and Wyckoff, D. D., 'Understanding Service Operations', in *Management of Service Operations* (Boston: Allyn & Bacon, 1978).

Senior, M. and Akehurst, G., 'The Development of Budget/Economy Hotels in the UK: The Consumer's Perception of Quality', *Quality in Services Conference* (QUIS 1) (University of Karlstad, Sweden, 1988).

Shostack, G. L., 'Breaking Free From Product Marketing', *Journal of Marketing*, 41, April (1977), 73–80.

Shostack, G. L., 'A Framework for Service Marketing', in Brown, S. W. and Fisk, R. P., (eds), *Marketing Theory, Distinguished Contributions* (New York: John Wiley, 1984a).

Shostack, G. L., 'Designing Services that Deliver,' *Harvard Business Review*, 62, January/February (1984b), 133–9.

Shostack, G. L., 'Planning the Service Encounter', in Czepiel, J. A., Solomon M. R. and Surprenant, C. F., (eds), *The Service Encounter* (Lexington, MA: D.C. Heath/Lexington Books, 1985), pp. 243–53.

Shostack, G. L., 'Service Positioning Through Structural Change', *Journal of Marketing*, 51, January (1987), 34–43.

Stigler, G. J., *Trends in Employment in the Service Industries* (Baltimore: Johns Hopkins University Press, 1956).

Sveiby, K. E. and Lloyd, T., *Managing Know-how: Add Value by Adding Creativity* (London: Bloomsbury Press, 1987).

United Nations Centre on Transnational Corporations (UNCTC), *Directory of the World's Largest Service Companies* (New York: Moody's Investors Service and UNCTC, 1990).

Vandermerwe, S., *From Tin Soldiers to Russian Dolls* (Oxford: Butterworth-Heinemann, 1993).

Vandermerwe, S. and Lovelock, C., *Competing Through Services* (New York: Prentice-Hall, 1994).

Wright, L. K., 'Avoiding Services Marketing Myopia', in Glynn, W. J. and Barnes, J. G. (eds), *Understanding Services Management* (Chichester: John Wiley, 1996).

Zeithaml, V. A., Berry L. L. and Parasuraman, A., 'Communication and Control Processes in the Delivery of Service Quality', *Journal of Marketing*, 52 (1988), 35–48.

Zeithaml, V. A., Berry, L. L. and Parasuraman, A., 'The Nature and Determinants of Customer Expectations of Service', *Journal of the Academy of Marketing Science*, 21 (1993), 1–12.

CHAPTER 4

Information systems and business change

Richard Thomas

■ 4.1 Introduction

This chapter will explore how the use of technology can place excessive demands on any business in addition to being a tremendous benefit. In particular, the way a company is organised can affect its competence in adapting to new circumstances. The ability to evolve in the light of the changing conditions created by technology is vital for today's organisations. The application of technology based systems offers an organisation the capability to redefine the characteristics of markets, enhance the scope of the business, and provide significant competitive advantage. The use of technology has a synergous effect on the business structure and the organisation's strategic goals, being both affected by, and affecting these elements.

The systems design methodology adopted is an important factor in the resulting effectivenness of information systems. In addition to budgetary and resource issues, the problems encountered with information systems are often caused by a combination of factors such as a lack of strategic overview, management and organisational issues. The incorporation of strategic planning is a vital element in the development phase for new information systems.

This chapter will analyse these issues and consider how the use of technology can transform a business examining both the positive and negative aspects of such a reorganisation.

■ 4.2 The organisation and appropriate information systems

■ Organisation structures

An organisation can be defined simply as a group of people combined together to achieve a set of common goals. Descriptions of organisations tend to concentrate on the relationship between their three primary elements: structure, people, and objectives. The structure of an organisation develops and adapts subject to a range of factors including maturity, culture, size, complexity, and objectives. Organisations can be structured in a multitude of configurations. One obvious organisational structure incorporates the ideas of functional specialisation. For instance, the main business functions such as Marketing, Finance, Human Resources, and Production would be the responsibility of one or more individuals. Separating these functional areas has the advantage of being able to concentrate skills and expertise in a confined area which may make management of them easier. However, a disadvantage of this type of structure is that it encourages an insular approach to any given specialism and makes communication and collaboration between functions much more problematic.

Conventional organisation structures include the hierarchical and matrix approaches (Thomas and Ballard 1995). An hierarchical organisation would incorporate a number of levels of decision-making involving strategic, tactical and operational managers. For instance, the organisation could consist of a director, functional managers, department heads, first-line managers, and staff. Communication in such an organisation is generally only up to a specific line manager, down to subordinates, or within a given team. Taller or flatter structures can be obtained using this approach by either adding or removing levels. Hierarchical structures tend to be less adaptive and may be difficult to change. Alternatively, the matrix structure approach enables individuals or teams to be answerable to a number of managers in varying functional areas allowing greater flexibility and enhanced communication.

■ Relationship between organisations and information systems

There is a strong relationship between the organisational structure of a company and the information systems adopted, which is complex and may not be easily defined. However, a number of basic factors are clear. Firstly, the type and scope of an organisation dictates the range of information requirements for specific stakeholders and thus the organisation affects the design of any information system developed. Secondly, it must necessarily be influenced by developing new technologies and may need to adjust in order to take advantage of the potential information systems available.

Clearly, there is a two-way relationship between organisations and information systems. The organisation has a direct impact on the information system since all decisions involving the system's design and development are made or approved by those within. Managers in the organisation decide on the type of systems required and on the range of tasks to be performed. These managers are, of course, part of the organisation and are directly influenced by it. The type of organisation will therefore affect these decisions. For example, an innovative organisation is likely to introduce a range of new computer systems whereas a more traditional type may be slower to realise the benefits and more reluctant to undertake the necessary changes in procedures. More specifically, the information system is designed to satisfy the organisation's requirements. Thus, a small company specialising in a specific product or service, and employing twenty staff, will have far different information needs than a multi national company involved in a range of diverse products and a global customer base. The organisation's structure will also affect its information requirements; taller hierarchical structures will require more rigid, defined information flows, whereas flatter, more fluid structures will require greater flexibility in requirements.

Conversely, the information system is almost certain to modify the organisation in a number of ways. For example, a new system can drastically change the specific skills required by existing staff in a range of posts. Furthermore, the information system is likely to change the work-force profile of the organisation; new staff with appropriate knowledge and skills will be employed, and some existing staff may be made redundant as a result of the information system implementation. Information systems can often lead to greater autonomy for staff in making decisions on their own work patterns and result in a more flexible, self-initiated working environment. Those staff who have a high level of competence in the use of information systems are often able to extend their influence in the organisation. The information system will also produce other changes in the behaviour of employees, such as increasing competition between certain groups of stakeholders and a change in the goals and working practices of selected staff. The improved flow of information in all sectors of the organisation may lead to a flattening of the hierarchical structures and greater flexibility of the work-force to move within and between functional areas. The introduction of an information system may change the actual organisational structure in other ways (Drucker 1988). For example, the system may necessitate an increase in the number and range of skills of middle managers with a corresponding decline in the number of semi-skilled and unskilled posts available. Alternatively, the number of middle managers could decline with an increase in the number of semi-skilled jobs required (O'Brien 1993).

There is often an apparent resistance to change in an organisation and the introduction of a new information system is often seen as the catalyst for change. Consequently, there can often be resistance to the introduction of such systems. Resistance can be embedded in the organisation's structures and can lead to the failure of systems when not properly introduced. It is clearly not sufficient to buy in new hardware and software without the appropriate management of the required changes. Early research in implementing change considered the relationship between components in an organisation. For example, Leavitt (1965) added technology to the organisational components people, objectives, and structure, described earlier in this chapter. The interrelationship of these four elements is vital and it is often proposed that the only path to the implementation of new technology is to change all four elements simultaneously. It is generally not possible to initiate significant changes in technology without radical changes in some or all of the other components (Laudon and Marr 1995). Furthermore, what is required is a strong commitment from senior management in the organisation to provide support and encouragement at each phase of the development (Adams and Thomas 1996).

In general, this section has provided an overview of some of the aspects of information systems and their significance in organisations. In terms of the development of new systems this area should not be under-emphasised. In order to implement a successful system it is important to consider a range of factors including the structure and type of organisation, the environment and external influences, and the goals and working methods of any interested groups.

■ Information systems and the organisational culture

The previous sections have introduced the effects of information systems on people and business structures. Possibly a more fundamental effect involves the potential changes in organisational culture that can be instigated by implementation of new information systems. To understand these potential changes it is important to define the term 'culture'. For the purposes of this chapter use will be made of a commonly employed definition as described by Sathe (1985) and many other commentators. This is 'the set of important assumptions (often unstated) that members of a community share in common'. Such assumptions include the beliefs and values of its members. These assumptions then interrelate to form the culture of an organisation. Such assumptions can act as a filter through which the members in an organisation view the realities facing the company. Such a definition of culture does not allow us to analyse the effect of information systems in any objective detail. It is necessary to consider some of the important dimensions of culture as outlined below (Weber 1988) and how these may apply to the implementation of information systems. The following elements relate to the beliefs and values of individuals in the organisation:

(i) **Innovation and action orientation:** The urgency to take actions and the importance of encouraging innovation. Information systems are likely to improve the speed of response for particular tasks (e.g. customer handling) though they may be a deterrent to innovative thinking. Speedy action such as that requiring a change in business processes or systems may be hindered and delayed by the complexity of the required information systems changes.

(ii) **Risk taking:** The importance of making risky decisions and embarking on high-risk ventures. The information system may be a deterrent to risk-taking and could be more suitable for a stable, 'safe' business environment. The use of information systems (e.g. in the form of decision support systems) can involve the balancing of risk against outcomes often erring on the side of caution. For instance, expert systems may produce an output of potential decisions listed in ascending order of risk with a tacit aversion to risk taking.

(iii) **Integration and lateral interdependence:** The importance of co-operation and communication between elements, e.g. Departments, in the company to achieve organisational targets. Information systems may encourage closer liaison between individuals and business units within a company. The common use of company-wide databases and the networking of information sources will tend to enhance the integration of the organisation and foster a closer working relationship between diverse elements.

(iv) **Top management contact:** The significance of the relationship between managers and subordinates. This relates to the level of openness enjoyed by subordinates and the candid nature of communication between all levels in the management hierarchy. A desire for open communication is vital for many information systems to flourish. At the development stages managers at all levels must be candid about their requirements and concerns. Fear of reprisals due to disagreement with senior managers at any stage may be a barrier to effective system implementation.

(v) **Autonomy in decision making:** The importance of delegating responsibility for decisions. Employees at all levels may have a degree of freedom in the decisions they make without constant reference to their line managers. Information systems may not facilitate an individual's belief in his/her autonomy since improved information will allow senior managers direct access to current decisions and their effects.

(vi) **Performance orientation:** The importance of targets set for individuals and their accountability for achievement. This is related to whether individual targets are clearly defined and whether objectives are measured through formal procedures such as appraisals. The application of information systems can be viewed as a means of measuring performance against set objectives and as such this may be a barrier to successful development. The 'Big Brother' approach to the use of systems in monitoring performance can be an obstacle and deter effective use, fostering user resentment against the systems.

(vii) **Reward orientation:** The view of reward compared with performance. How are individuals paid and how does this compare with other organisations? Is there an element of performance related pay, and does this produce an equitable system of reward? Information systems can be used as the primary tool in the development and application of objective performance related pay systems and the management culture of many of today's organisations reinforces the importance of such systems. However, the bulk of the workforce may not be as keen to co-operate with the measurement of performance, in particular when linked directly to reward, and again this can be a deterrent to successful implementation.

An attempt has been made in this section to introduce the relationship between a number of elements in the organisational culture and the use of information systems. Whilst it is useful to consider these aspects in relation to change in the organisation it should be stressed that culture is not an easy concept to measure and its effects on an information system are unclear. There may be a perceived culture which differs from the actual culture in a company. For example, consider one of the dimensions – Top management contact – described above. It may be that individuals in the organisation perceive that there is openness in their contact with managers and that they are encouraged to air their views honestly. In practice, the senior managers may be negative towards criticism and in general will not tolerate it. Also, in order to be effective, an information system should be designed with the organisational culture in mind. It is not advisable to attempt to manipulate the culture to fit the information system; rather the information system must be adjusted to be acceptable to the culture. However, as previously suggested, in the long term the information system may be a vehicle for change in the cultural fabric of the organisation. (The reader is also referred to Chapter 1.4 and 1.8.)

■ 4.3 Strategy and the value chain

The design of appropriate information systems should evolve from an organisation's business strategy. Consequently it is useful to consider briefly the way in which a business strategy is developed. Developing a strategy involves consideration of the attributes and direction of the whole business (Thomas and Ballard 1995). Strategic decisions will consider questions such as: What will be our main markets in the future; what will our customers want? Who will be our competitors; what resources will we require? To answer such questions the senior managers in an organisation need to obtain information from a range of sources. A model of strategic management described by Johnson and Scholes (1989) incorporates the three interrelated elements of strategic analysis, strategic choice, and strategic implementation. Strategic analysis involves factors such as the environment, the organisation's resources and culture. Strategic choice involves the generation and evaluation of options, and the selection of a strategy. Strategic implementation involves the acquisition and use of resources, analysis of the required organisational structure changes, and the management of people and systems.

Every organisation has its own set of unique activities designed to provide goods and services required by customers. The value of any organisation can be measured in terms of its success in generating business. Its activities are linked together in a chain and should add value to operations. This 'Value Chain', described by Porter (1985), should enable an organisation to obtain competitive advantage. Activities in the value chain are separated into primary and secondary groups. Primary activities are those that add directly to the value of the product or service to the customer, such as the purchase of raw materials, production methods, marketing, sales and the distribution of goods. Secondary activities can also play a vital role in the value chain, such as acquisition of appropriate resources, recruitment of staff, and the monitoring and controlling of all activities. The combination of primary and secondary activities is a critical factor in the success of an organisation. For example, it is not sufficient to have an excellent product if the pricing is excessive or sales staffing is insufficient.

Porter identified a number of ways in which a business could manipulate its Value Chain in order to gain competitive advantage. Such methods include:

- **Cost leadership** Ensuring the appropriate pricing for a given quality for products and services.
- **Differentiation** Highlighting the uniqueness of the product or service compared to the competitor's provision.
- **Focus strategy** Concentrating on a specific customer base and targeting the necessary resources.

An analysis of the Value Chain is an important element in developing and implementing the organisation's business strategy (see also Chapter 1.3 and 1.4).

■ 4.4 Using technology for competitive advantage

An organisation can gain competitive advantage by enhancing any of the activities in the value chain. Competitive advantage involves the dominance of one competitor over other participants in the same market. Porter (1985) describes competitive advantage as offering a product of superior value to customers. In an earlier publication, Porter (1980) suggested that competition depends on five basic forces:

(i) **Threat of new entrants:** Consideration of the ease of entry into a given market. If a market is easy to enter then existing competitors do not have competitive advantage. For instance, markets which require significant initial investment have a substantial barrier to new entrants. The computer industry is a good example of a market requiring high start-up costs with a high risk (see also Chapter 3's discussion of contestable markets).

(ii) **Intensity of rivalry among direct competitors:** The effect of the concentration of competitors in a market. For instance, fewer competitors can mean less competition. An extreme case of this would be a monopoly in which the organisation can dictate price and quality of product.

(iii) **Pressure of substitute products:** The range of substitute products will affect a company's profitability. For example, the banking industry has substitute products such as a range of credit cards and debit cards, and in the insurance area substitute services such as direct telephone sales have made significant inroads on traditional sales methods.

(iv) **Bargaining power of buyers:** The buyers (or customers) may have sufficient power to bring down prices, improve the quality of the product and insist on enhanced services. This would clearly affect the profitability of a company.

(v) **Bargaining power of suppliers:** Suppliers of companies compete in terms of price, quality, and service offered. This in turn affects the competitive advantage of any organisation. Greater competition between suppliers will benefit the organisation in terms of the improved quality of goods and services for customers (see also Chapters 1.3, 1.8 and 10.4).

Primarily an organisation can gain competitive advantage by pricing and product differentiation. The same product produced more cheaply, or a unique product at a reasonable price, will enable a company to gain competitive advantage. The use of new technology and sophisticated information systems can assist in this process (Tom 1991). For example, to be able to offer a product at a low price the organisation must employ tight financial controls, stringent monitoring procedures and large-scale manufacturing processes. Alternatively, differentiation of a product may involve enhanced service to the customer including improved response rates, faster production and delivery techniques. These elements can be implemented with the aid of appropriate information systems and technology-based approaches.

■ 4.5 Technology and strategic alignment

Companies develop business strategies to address the competitive forces outlined in the previous section. By a strategic planning process a corporate strategy is evolved which in turn leads to an appropriate information strategy. To achieve the optimum from new technology there should be a clearly defined set of strategic goals defining the areas in which competitive advantage can be gained. Following the specification of clear goals, appropriate technology-based options can be considered. This does not mean that information technology should simply be added to existing systems. In fact, this approach generally leads to significant problems and ultimate failure. What is needed is a flexible approach, often requiring a fundamental change in the working processes and organisational culture within the company. The primary element in such a change are the individuals (stakeholders) involved. It is necessary to consider changes in the behaviour of those involved in installing, maintaining and using the systems. A change in the processes and behaviour of the stakeholders for any given system will necessarily have an impact on the organisational culture. There have been many high-profile failures of systems because of the lack of organisational flexibility (Thomas and Ballard 1995).

There is often a false assumption that an increase in the application of IT will automatically lead to improvements in productivity and quality. Indeed many studies have concluded that the reverse is often the case and that an introduction of technology has coincided with a reduction in productivity and a slowing down in growth. Those companies who also attempt a degree of organisational and structural change to coincide with an introduction in technology tend to perform much better.

A study undertaken at the Massachusetts Institute of Technology during the 1980s on the relationship between organisational change and technology produced some interesting results (Scott-Morton 1991). Figure 4.1 illustrates the productivity achieved by a number of car manufacturers compared with the degree of organisational change and level of technology used. The technology systems in this example involved the automation of the production and related processes.

As expected, the company with a low level of automation had the poorest productivity. However, the difference in the two General Motors production sites was very marginal despite the massive automation adopted at Michigan. Furthermore, other companies who had lower levels of automation achieved significantly higher productivity by concentrating on organisational change with limited expenditure on automation. The Nissan plant achieved superior productivity with a similar level of automation to Michigan by combining organisational changes with the introduction of new systems. The highest productivity was achieved by Toyota who concentrated on organisational and cultural changes with minimum expenditure on automation.

Such studies indicate the need for careful consideration of organisational and cultural issues rather than an unplanned rush into technological innovation. The following section considers the development of information systems and the associated changes that have been necessary for successful implementation.

■ 4.6 System development and business change

As previously discussed, the way in which a business is organised can have a profound influence on the effectiveness of new technology. In particular the

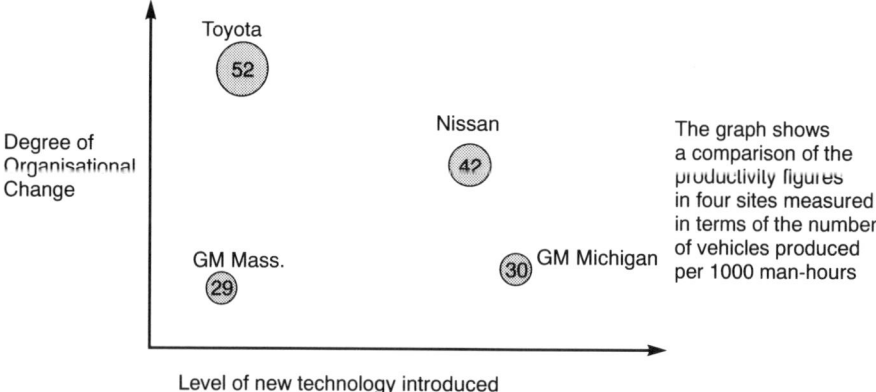

Figure 4.1   Relationship between organisation and technology
Source: Scott-Morton, *The Corporation of the 1990's: Information Technology and Organisational Transformation*, Oxford University Press, 1991.

organisation must learn to adapt to meet changing requirements in order to remain competitive. Failure to adapt may result in business decline. Information technology can be both the catalyst for, and the result of, change. The impact of IT is an element in a three-way process involving changes in the strategic goals and business structure of an organisation. The organisation with an existing structure may begin by developing strategic goals which will define essential information technology requirements. The resulting use of IT may generate new market opportunities and lead to a restructuring of the organisation which may then lead on to a redefinition of the business goals resulting in new IT requirements, and so the evolution continues.

■ Levels of IT application and organisational change

The application of new technology can be a powerful medium in affecting change in an organisation. However not all IT applications lead to major structural or cultural shifts. Scott-Morton (1991) discussed the relationship between IT, business strategy and the organisation incorporating the following stages undertaken by a business in utilising technology for competitive advantage. The stages described, from localised exploitation to business scope redefinition, indicate, in order of increasing significance, the effect of technology on the overall business.

☐ 1 Localised exploitation

This is the use of a specific IT application in one or more isolated areas within the business. For example, the finance department may introduce a new accounting system, or the sales department develop a customer database. Development of such systems could be performed by one or more individuals within a business area, and it is often the case that systems across the company will be incompatible. Such IT development can be *ad hoc* and is unlikely to have a profound impact on the business as a whole although it may lead to improvements, such as savings in time and reductions in costs, in specific functional areas at the operational level.

☐ 2 Internal integration

During this phase a number of processes in the business may be integrated by a systematic application of IT. The separate elements computerised in the first stage may be linked together providing more efficient use of information resources. For example, a customer database could be linked to stock files, order files, invoicing data, and financial reporting. One major advantage at this level is that the company has systems across the functional areas which are now compatible allowing further development of systems to assist in other functions.

At this stage the company may have an embryonic information plan to support its strategic goals. The result of such internal integration is usually an improvement in the overall business process without necessitating any major change in the way the business operates or is structured.

☐ 3 Business process redesign

The use of IT during this stage becomes increasingly significant resulting in changes in the way the business operates. Processes within the organisation need to be rethought in order to make the most efficient use of the technology available. The technology is not simply an add-on to the current business practices but actually provokes a review of the overall business systems. Strategic plans will need to be reviewed in the light of a changing emphasis though no significant changes in the target market or business opportunities should be apparent. The organisational structure may need to be modified due to a change in the business operations. This may directly affect staff, some of whom will no longer be required, whilst others will be expected to acquire new skills. New technology can be introduced to reduce the level of organisational complexity (Keen 1991). For instance, problems such as too many managerial levels, complex working methods, and an over-reliance on paper-based communications can be addressed.

☐ 4 Business network redesign

At this penultimate stage the boundaries of the whole business are blurred by the use of technology. The information systems not only affect the internal operations and processes of the business but cloud the traditional boundaries. Stronger links are established with external organisations to an extent where the organisations' information systems are meshed together. For example, a company may link the stock control system directly to external suppliers for automatic ordering and additional financial systems may be integrated for automating invoicing and payments. Such radical changes will produce a widening of organisational boundaries and a change in the traditional business structures within the company. An example of this type of radical change is illustrated in the case of the Baxter International organisation described by Laudon and Laudon (1996). Baxter International is a major supplier of hospitals in the USA providing all required items of stock. Baxter installed terminals in participating hospitals enabling its customers to order directly from the on-line catalogue. The system generates delivery, costing, invoicing and stock information and provides estimated delivery times for each order. The participating hospitals were reluctant to use alternative suppliers once linked to the system due to its ease of ordering, and speed of delivery. The system transformed Baxter International enabling them to become a close working partner with the hospitals. There was a blurring of the organisations since a development of the system enabled Baxter to take over and manage its customers' supplies and warehousing functions.

☐ 5 Business scope redefinition

In addition to the changes in internal structures and processes this stage signals a major transformation in the way the company operates and the scope of its markets. This period may involve a significant shift in the primary business objectives of the company. A traditional example of this phase in the evolution of an information system is the American Airlines SABRE project (Thomas and Ballard 1995). American Airlines developed an information system which was installed at many travel agents nationwide providing information on airline routes and availability. The system known as SABRE eventually provided a significant competitive advantage for the American Airlines company. Furthermore, the SABRE information system was so successful that it was valued higher than the aircraft part of the business. Consequently the use of information technology in this case generated a completely new market for the organisation. Such a radical shift in business objectives will result in a significant reorganisation of the company. Areas which were considered core to the business may now become secondary, whereas totally new areas may be incorporated. This will have a considerable effect on the required management structures and channels of communication within the organisation.

■ Problems with information systems

It is well known that the majority of information systems do not fully meet expectations. Failure can involve a range of elements in a spectrum from cancellation of a systems project at the early stage to full implementation followed by complaints from dissatisfied customers and a lack of the expected benefits. Major problems with development projects also include overspend on the initial budget, and overruns on the expected time-scales. These problems are caused by a range of elements including those described by Dhammi (1994):

- **Strategic problems:** A lack of a strategic overview or disagreement between a number of stakeholders, e.g. Departments concerning strategic objectives.
- **Organisational change:** Failure of the organisation to adapt to the changing environment caused by the introduction of new technology.
- **Supplier problems:** Difficulty in obtaining the required systems from suppliers at the appropriate time and agreed cost, and the general unsuitability of suppliers selected.
- **Poor management:** Ineffective management of change particularly when integrating the new systems with existing organisational structures and cultures.
- **Technophiles:** Too much faith and emphasis on the ability of technology to solve problems without careful consideration of more appropriate options involving changes in the procedures or low level technological solutions.
- **User skills:** A lack of support from end-users and insufficient skills to ensure the effective operation of systems.

This list can be augmented with other related factors such as:

- **Technophobia**: Apprehension by potential users of the technology and fear of the effect on their role and job security.
- **Lack of participation**: Little involvement from users in the early stages of system design and development resulting in poor specifications being produced and general user resistance.
- **Poor control systems**: Ineffective control mechanisms and insufficient monitoring procedures in place resulting in lack of information on the progress of the system development.

These areas indicate a wide range of factors that individually or collectively may affect the viability of information systems produced. However, it is clear that the majority of these factors relate to people issues. This fact has been discussed earlier, but it is worth emphasising that technical aspects (such as software and hardware considerations) are in a sense less important than the aspects of user participation, involvement, and ownership of the systems. With a positive attitude from all the stakeholders the technical problems can be rectified. However, conversely, if negative attitudes are prevalent then it is almost immaterial whether or not there is a 'good', robust system in operation. The system can be technically superior, and the development methodology theoretically sound, but without user support and commitment it is destined to fail.

■ Overview of systems development

To alleviate many of the problems outlined in the previous section it is vital to adopt stringent measures in the design and development of information systems. In general, as described by Tom (1991), a successful project will require a number of elements including:

- A project team possessing the required skills to develop the system.
- A management team able to integrate the necessary skills.
- An appropriate development methodology for implementing the total project.

The methodology adopted for the system development is highly significant. Tom (1991) has argued that a typical development life cycle would incorporate the following elements: strategic planning, information planning, system design, system development and installation, and systems support and maintenance. These elements are described briefly below:

(i) **Strategic planning**: This area considers the long-term aims of the company and culminates in the development of business objectives and the setting of corresponding strategies. Following the specification of an organisation's strategic direction the information requirements can be identified (see also Chapter 1).

(ii) **Information planning**: This stage should ensure that the organisation's long term information requirements will be satisfied. Current and future requirements are identified and appropriate information systems strategies are developed. Each project can be defined in terms of scope, required data models, work plans, costs and benefits.

(iii) **System design:** The work undertaken during this phase is the basis for future development and installation tasks. A variety of solutions to problems can be considered and compared. Functional specifications are prepared including details on input and output requirements, file organisation, security needs, and performance criteria. Technical specifications are produced defining the hardware requirements, program modules, and database design.

(iv) **System development and installation:** This involves the production of systems designed previously. New software is developed, systems installed and tested, documentation produced and staff trained.

(v) **System support and maintenance:** Following acceptance of the system by users this phase involves monitoring of all elements. Modifications and additions to the system are made when required. Performance of the system is closely monitored and evaluated and periodic status reports are produced.

This traditional approach to development has a number of drawbacks. Clearly, the procedures adopted do not ensure that time-scales are adhered to, or projects completed within budget. Also it has been recognised that strict adherence to a structured approach may lead to a distortion of the real project objectives. For example, the production of precise, standardised documentation is the backbone of many traditional approaches. While this is an advantage a number of organisations have experienced a situation in which the documentation becomes more important than the user's requirements and management needs. Monitoring of the development process can also be difficult by those not in the Systems area. It is essential to build in review points, not only to monitor whether the project is proceeding as planned, but also to evaluate the system requirements and ensure that they still meet the ever-changing needs of the organisation.

Additional development techniques, such as prototyping and CASE, have evolved in order to solve some of the problems of the traditional approach. The use of CASE (Computer Aided Software Engineering) tools can automate a number of steps described in the development life-cycle. In particular, using these tools results in a change to the time spent on different elements in the process. For example, it has been found that additional time is spent on the planning and design processes whereas less time is dedicated to the development and maintenance of software. The introduction of prototyping methods has speeded up the development process. Prototyping involves the creation of 'mini-systems' that may incorporate a few of the required functions. The aim is to allow the user to have a working system very quickly and additions and modifications to the prototype can be implemented in collaboration with the user. This has a number of benefits: the user is much more closely involved with the design and development stages, time-scales and corresponding costs tend to be reduced drastically, and there is a enhanced user acceptance of the final systems. Furthermore there is a significantly improved sensitivity to changes in the business requirements due to managers and users at all levels being actively involved in the prototype development. Of course, the development of prototypes may involve the use of CASE tools and other fourth generation software techniques.

The choice of a specific methodology adopted for the development of new systems depends on a number of factors including the size and structure of the organisation, the level of IT application in the company, and the importance of the proposed system to the business's strategic goals. For example, a single user system is likely to be developed employing a prototyping approach which involves the individual affected. Additional support from the in-house systems experts may be available for training and advice though it is unlikely that any significant effort will be expended other than by the individual concerned. Alternatively, a company-wide integrated system will require a more formalised approach possibly using CASE tools. Stand-alone systems to be used on a company-wide basis may be available off the shelf and require little development resources. For example, application packages such as spread-sheets, word-processing, and graphics software may be available for individual use. A standardisation of the packages used will at least ensure compatibility across the organisation.

■ 4.7 Case study: The Royal Bank of Scotland

■ Introduction

The Royal Bank of Scotland (RBS) is one of the top five banks in the UK competing with the NatWest, Barclays, Lloyds-TSB and Midland banking organisations (see also Chapter 2). Employing over 21,000 staff, the core market for this group is in the UK, with interests also in Europe and the USA. The RBS has achieved tremendous growth in recent years and has a vision of becoming the 'best performing financial services group in the United Kingdom' (Corporate statement, RBS Group Progress Report 1995). Few would argue that the group are not able to achieve such a goal, as the management, products and services offered are of the highest quality. Founded in 1727, with headquarters in Edinburgh, the RBS has a reputation for high standards, stability and dependability which provides an excellent cornerstone for future growth. However, the group has not rested on its laurels and has continually expanded its range of products and services to remain competitive in this difficult market. The group has achieved significant growth by reorganising management structures and processes, the appropriate application of technology based systems, careful management of change and innovative developments in products and services. During the five-year period 1991–5 the group benefited from a seven-fold increase in its operating profit, achieving over £600 million during 1995.

The RBS Group consists of UK Banking, Direct Line Insurance and Citizens Financial Group. Direct Line Insurance has been trading since the early 1980s and has been a major success for the company. It has provided an innovative approach to selling insurance and is currently the largest insurer of private motor vehicles in the UK. Citizens Financial Group, the RBS's subsidiary in the United States, is a leading provider of personal and corporate banking services in the North-East of the US, and incorporates a mortgage banking company based in Atlanta. The UK Banking arm is split into three divisions: Branch Banking, Corporate and Institutional Banking, and Operations. The Branch Banking Division (BBD) offers a range of banking and financial services to private and commercial customers. The Corporate and Institutional Banking Division (CIBD) manages the corporate customers offering a range of products such as corporate banking, securities services, and development capital. The Operations Division provides a range of services to the UK banking businesses and offers a number of products to external clients.

The RBS provides an interesting case study for the application and implementation of information systems. While mistakes have been made in the past, the group has endeavoured to create integrated systems with close attention being given to the needs of customers and staff. Whilst many development projects can fail because of the over-emphasis on technical issues at the expense of the human factor, the RBS has not fallen into this trap and has successfully re-engineered its processes including the use of new technology and changes in the organisational culture. This case study will consider a number of aspects of the development and implementation of systems in the RBS and concentrate on activities within the Operations Division as described below.

■ The Operations Division

The Operations Division in the RBS, headed by Norman McLuskie, provides a range of services including supporting the technology requirements of the RBS group. Figure 4.2 shows the structure of the RBS group and illustrates how the Operations Division fits into this structure.

In relation to the use and development of information systems it is interesting to note two departments within the Operations Division: Technology and Operations Support. These two departments are involved in the majority of systems development projects for the group and will be considered in more detail subsequently.

■ Operations Support

The Operations Support Department, founded in 1991 and managed by Alan Duff, incorporates areas such as cost management, business management, productivity and project management. Essentially, this department supports the operations of other sections in the RBS group and has expanded into external consultancy in a number of areas. Business consultancy in the department

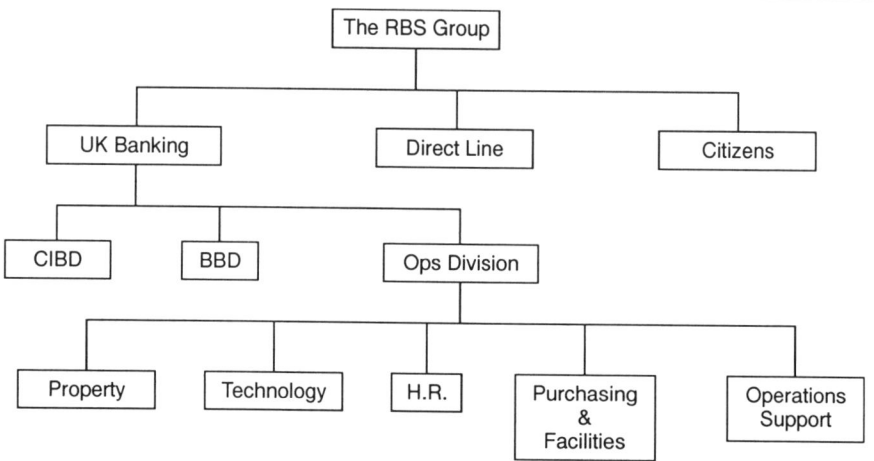

Figure 4.2   Organisation chart: Royal Bank of Scotland Group

underwent a restructuring during 1994 and, using the expertise gained in supporting the Divisions, it started offering a range of consultancy services to external organisations. Such services include advice on business process re-design, management information systems, business solutions, organisational design and project management. Figure 4.3 shows some of the services offered by Operations Support and illustrates the central theme of 'Issues and Solutions' emphasised by the consultancy staff.

The Operations Support team now exceeds 85 who, in addition to detailed financial services knowledge, have experience in local government, manufacturing, public utility and service industries. The team includes specialist programmers, analysts, technical writers, consultants and project managers.

Operations Support has been involved in a range of systems design and developments for a variety of departments and divisions within the RBS group. Essentially the department is involved in the development and support of small systems utilising stand-alone and networked micro-computers. Support for the larger systems within RBS is the responsibility of the Technology department described later. Operations Support is both pro-active and reactive to the needs of its customers who may be internal or external to the RBS group. Business strategies developed by the senior management team at RBS are translated into plans and objectives which can be supported by the Operations Support team. This may involve Operations Support consulting with staff in other departments to develop solutions. Alternatively, the impetus for a new project often comes from the departments themselves when Operations Support are contacted and asked to assist in the design and development of a new system to

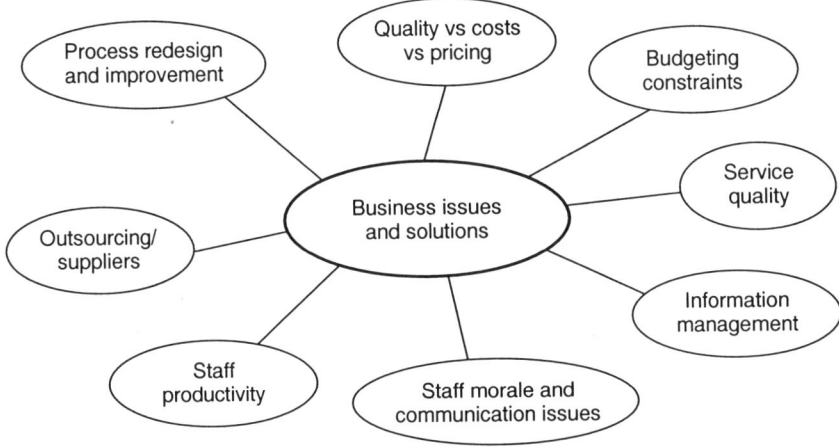

Figure 4.3   Operations support consultancy

satisfy given requirements. A sample of the projects in which Operations Support have been involved at RBS are given below:

- **Profitability project:** The 'Vostro' profitability project involves the development of a profitability system providing automatic quarterly profit and billing statements for approximately 650 banking connections. The system utilises data obtained from mainframe, micro and manual inputs. The data is accessed using a SQL database by a 'smart' software program and presented in spreadsheet format.
- **Payment services:** Development and maintenance of a new tender system model for use in the tendering process to give a closer fit in terms of inputs, outputs, hardware platform and control methods. The new system developed uses Excel and will provide greater flexibility and improved capability linking to local area networks.
- **IT security:** providing support and assistance in the implementation of the Security Policy throughout the RBS group. This project involved the collection of information and the production of policy documentation, and the dissemination of information to relevant staff including the presentation of training programmes.
- **Documentation:** Project Alpine involves ensuring that the documentation of the software and systems to be installed in the RBS Zurich office conforms to agreed quality standards. In addition to the support of systems documentation, Quality Assurance documentation will be provided for subsidiary suppliers and training sessions will be organised for RBS staff.

This sample of work undertaken by Operations Support indicates the breadth of skills available in this area. A range of external information system projects have also been completed including systems analysis and design, software development, implementation and support. A range of services and products are available, including:

- **Data collection:** from computerised and manual sources
- **Data formatting and reporting:** involving the presentation of electronic data in order to provide meaningful management information
- **End-user systems:** providing advice on a range of IT projects
- **Cost estimation:** reviewing potential work and providing price and time-scale estimates for the completion of work
- **Interactive end-user systems:** designing and building PC models enabling users to extract, examine and report customised data
- **Technical specifications:** providing detailed specifications for systems projects
- **Training:** on PCs for a range of software packages
- **After sales support:** giving support and after sales service for any of the products and services listed

It can be seen that Operations Support provides key support to assist in the systems development process. A variety of software packages and development tools are used including Microsoft Office, Visual Basic, Access, and SQL Windows.

The RBS has an important resource in this department. Staff within the department are committed and quality is assured through the consultancy approach to their work. No guarantees are given in terms of work being available to Operations Support from internal RBS departments or divisions. Individual business managers can opt to look elsewhere and employ external consultants on particular tasks. Consequently, in some cases Operations Support compete directly with external consultancy groups and may be required to tender for specific projects within the company. This has ensured that the department has not stagnated and the skills available and processes adopted are continually being reviewed and updated in the light of the latest developments. This has facilitated and promoted a continuation of the change process in other parts of the RBS organisation.

■ Systems development

It is interesting to note the way in which staff in Operations Support help clients in the development of new systems. For example, John Kerr, a Client Manager in Operations Support, describes how a typical project begins: 'A business comes to us and asks us to undertake a development project. The business has a lot of information but is unable to make the best use of it because the information systems may have been inherited or simply evolved over many years.' This typical situation describes an information gap in the organisation. In some cases it may mean that, although the information is available, it is in an unsuitable format to assist in operational areas, management decision making or developing policy. For instance, in the RBS it is vital to have appropriate financial information for clients such as credit balances, overdraft details, loans, and other ancillary services. Such information, collected together in a cohesive manner and readily available, will greatly assist a manager visiting a client and enhance the professionalism and credibility of the complete service.

Operations Support have gained ISO 9001 registration with the British Standards Institute and are committed to deliver high quality consultancy for the RBS and external clients. Although the systems developed within Operations Support are small, there still needs to be an appropriate and consistent methodology used to support the quality management systems in place. The methodology adopted follows fairly traditional lines involving prototyping and an emphasis on user involvement and gaining user commitment to the project. A significant element of the methodology is the understanding that system development and change management should run in parallel. The process of project development used by the Operations Support team is described below:

Initial contact and specification: The client may approach Operations Support in terms of a specific development project. The client is encouraged to produce a 'brief' or detailed specification to demonstrate that the overall business requirement has been examined and considered objectively. The specification will include what the new system is going to achieve, how it will be interfaced with the rest of the business, any input and output requirements, and what the dependencies will be in terms of on-going service and maintenance from Operations Support.

The client is encouraged to go away and think through its requirements, and to ensure that the system is sufficiently flexible to allow further development in the light of any changing business needs. Largely, Operations Support encourages clients to develop their own specifications although help is available to focus on specific issues if required. No standard format for the specification is requested although advice is given when needed.

Timescales and resourcing: The client is encouraged to consider the repercussions of any changes to the specification at a later stage during or following development. Milestones are agreed with the client, and it is emphasised that changes to the specification will result in timescales for delivery being affected. At this early stage the client is encouraged to consider the practical business and organisational issues resulting from the proposed project. The finished specification is received from the client. This may be subject to final polishing by negotiation before the terms of reference are agreed which will incorporate the responsibilities of the client and Operations Support. At this stage Operations Support determine the resourcing requirements of such a project and evaluate their capability for such a task. Following this phase, costs are calculated, the project start date is agreed and the project can be launched.

Design and development phase: User involvement is regarded as critical to the success of the programme. John Kerr offers an analogy: 'It is like an old-fashioned tailor. The customer goes back a number of times to check the fitting of his suit, before final delivery. The more times that he goes back, the better the final fit will be.' Dialogue is kept in place throughout the project. This continuous communication is used as part of the validation process and formally in the acceptance phase at each predetermined milestone in the project.

A prototyping approach is adopted in the sense that the systems will evolve over time. Operations Support never subscribe to the attitude that a project is completely finished and the users left on their own. The project team is there to provide continuing support, upgrade, revise, and maintain the systems in conjunction with comments from the users.

Implementation and maintenance: The Operations Support team provides on-going support in the maintenance of systems. They also provide assistance in the management of change prior to the implementation phase. For instance, it is stressed that there are likely to be required changes within the client's area including management control and working practices. The human issues such as the effect on working conditions are considered to be vitally important.

Again John Kerr comments 'It's the people that you are involving, rather than simply the box or document. It's very much the relationship (between the client and Operations Support) that is important.' An attempt is made to eradicate problems of user resistance to the new systems. The Operations Support team communicate with all appropriate levels within the client organisation, including the managers who have provided the initial specification and the people who are actually going to use the systems in place. It has often been found that the users at the operational level give an added dimension to the client's requirements in terms of generating new ideas, and suggesting additional features which can benefit the development.

■ Cultural changes

Operations Support have been involved in a major review of the network of branches in the RBS. One aspect of this review was to consider the culture of the workplace. In particular, this involved a number of primary attributes such as analysing how the management structure operated and consideration of the locations of staff within the organisation. Furthermore, a range of relatively intangible areas were analysed such as a review of the self-worth of employees, and the views of staff on their working environment and overall impressions of the atmosphere in the work-place.

An early section of this project required the construction of an information database involving the collection of data via questionnaires, individual and group interviews. In order to build up the confidence of staff, groups of employees were briefed on the project and assured on issues such as the confidentiality of information and that results would be treated with the utmost discretion. In this way, from the outset, a relationship was built up between the staff and those involved in the project. As John Kerr commented, 'If you have an arm's length approach to people then you will get an arm's length response.' Thus the slow, methodical and empathic approach to the project ensured that data collected was accurate and the overall results realistic. This type of approach has been used successfully in many projects resulting in organisational and cultural changes including the Columbus programme described in the following section.

■ The Columbus Programme

The Columbus Programme incorporates a five-year plan for rebuilding of processes in the RBS in order to improve the level of service offered to customers. This has involved a wide-reaching review of the bank's services and implementation of the New Branch project which includes the redefinition and design of information systems in the branches. The management of branches has been restructured. For instance, traditionally a separate manager would control the operations at each branch. Following the restructuring each manager may control a number of branches, and the back-room processes have been removed from many branches to a central area office. Thus, the customer interface has remained relatively unchanged, with major changes occurring in the transaction processing and management levels. The RBS recognised the importance of the human factor and that to achieve and sustain a successful change it was essential that existing behavioural skills be identified.

As part of this massive change programme the Aberdeen city centre branches were reorganised. The geographical location of this group of branches was ideal for piloting the reorganisation. Paper processing could be removed from each branch and merged into a single central location which could be relatively close to all branches. There were a number of problems associated with such a change and the RBS learnt some important lessons from this reorganisation which assisted continued implementation of the change programme. The following highlight a range of issues raised:-

1. A number of employees were relocated from the branches to the central processing site. A common theme became apparent in that the poorer performers were often the ones who were designated to move to the new site.
2. The employees who were relocated were not held in high esteem by the remaining staff in the Branches and consequently there was a lack of empathy between the two groups. The central staff were considered to be simply processing paper and their skills were not highly regarded.
3. The logistics of the new location were poor. Documents were held in inappropriate areas resulting in unnecessary time wasting. For instance, files located in the basement were most needed by staff housed on the fourth floor of the building.
4. The majority of staff only had contact with central staff via the telephone and consequently had little knowledge of the conditions that their colleagues were working under, or the specific work that was being undertaken.
5. The central site was an easy target as a source for floating staff. If there was a staff shortage at one of the branches then staff from the central site were requested to step in at short notice resulting in disruption of the processes at the central location.

A team from Operations Support was invited to analyse the problems and suggest solutions to improve the situation. As John Kerr stated, 'Everything that you can think of that might lead to cultural deterioration took place there.' Operations Support could take an objective, independent view of the whole situation, including a consideration of the centre and its relationship with the whole network. A number of issues were identified and considered, including:

- Working relationships between the centre and branches needed to be resolved.
- Management needed to be improved and the management structures redefined.
- Reporting lines were confused.

Following the review conducted by Operations Support new business practices were introduced and the central site was relocated to a preferred location. Other developments included facilitating visits from branch staff to the centre to view the work that was taking place and the environment in which the centre staff were working. The branch staff came to realise the pressure that the centre staff were working under and a camaraderie built up between the two groups. These changes had a major effect on the working environment of staff in the centre and on their feeling of self-worth. The morale and motivation of the centre staff was enhanced to the point where there was a sense of pride in their work. Now the central site is held in high regard and is considered as a centre of excellence for processing and supporting the branches. It is now a quality environment incorporating a refurbishment and the implementation of new information systems. This has supported and enhanced the work undertaken resulting in its improved quality and in the level of customer service. There have been many financial benefits resulting from these changes including the virtual eradication of on-call and overtime working at the central site.

The assistance of Operations Support was vital in managing these changes at the RBS. Their degree of flexibility, objectivity and primary concern with people ensured that the change process was smoother than is often the case with reorganisations on this scale. As John Kerr has said, 'IT has often been regarded as a failure, partly because the management of change has not been given its rightful place. There is a need to anticipate potential problems,. . . and the business (not the technology) should be the initiator for change.'

■ Further developments in Operations Support

The Operations Support department in RBS continues to plan for further diversification. Originally considered as an organisation and methods section, they have shrugged off their image of carrying stop-watches and are now more concerned with helping the strategic development of the organisation. Their primary concern is to support the business objectives of their clients, both RBS and external, and assist in the achievement of such objectives. They have been engaged in the forefront of change initiatives and ask questions such as: Where is the business going? What is the organisations strategy? How can we support this strategy? There is a general view in RBS that managers cannot be expected to take on change alone, and that there will always be a role for an independent and objective viewpoint.

Operations Support have become increasingly pro-active rather than simply reacting to the demands of clients. Furthermore they have a vision to allow their business to flourish by supporting the operations of the RBS, and develop by exposing it to outside organisations. There is an understanding that an organisation which is too inward looking is likely to stifle innovation and restrict change. The extra dimension of external experience can be incorporated into much of the work undertaken within the RBS adding greater credibility to the work of Operations Support and an improvement in the overall service offered. Furthermore, Operations Support are developing long-term links with outside organisations through their consultancy work which will have an impact on the banking profile for the RBS. Clearly, there is an important emphasis on the provision of a top quality consultancy service, partly because of the resulting impact on the RBS as a whole if anything less than professional is delivered.

■ Drivers for Change

The RBS management team are well aware of the important relationship between the users and those whose primary role is to develop and maintain the systems. In many organisations this relationship is not considered or at best ignored. In the early 1990s the systems in use at RBS were rapidly developing and it was paramount that the staff should be actively involved and take 'ownership' of these changes. This was of particular concern in the Technology department at RBS which was involved in the development, operation and maintenance of the large-scale computer systems within the RBS. The Renaissance project started in 1994 had the specific objective of achieving necessary cultural changes in the organisation and shifts in attitudes of the stakeholders in order to facilitate further advances in the use of technology. To achieve these objectives the project, managed from within the Technology department, incorporated a number of features including the 'Partnership', 'Framework' and 'Team' programmes as briefly described below:

☐ 1 Partnership programme

IT projects are necessarily partnerships between Technology and the RBS businesses (users). Value for money, excellent service and improved project deliveries are required by the users. A working group was set up to consider the issues raised by customers and a number of problems were addressed, including:

(i) **Customer support:** A review of the coordination of the interfaces between customers, Technology and the support services.

(ii) **Delivery times:** An effort has been made to improve the delivery times of products though Technology had a reasonable record on this delivering over 70 per cent of projects on time and to budget. However, it was recognised that further improvements could be made in a number of areas such as:

- agreements on customers needs and expectations
- careful monitoring and reporting based on these expectations
- the need for a lateral approach to potential solutions
- improved planning and control

(iii) **Added value:** The Technology department provides a wide range of services to customers related to the design, development, implementation and maintenance of information systems. To provide added value to customers a number of areas have been considered, including:

- Regular customer surveys to ascertain the type of service and the levels required
- Effective tracking and reporting mechanisms to measure performance on quality compared with the requirements specification and additional documentation for development projects, and service level agreements for operational or support services.

The Partnership programme is at the centre of the Renaissance project and is an effort to work closely with customers to understand and facilitate their needs.

☐ 2 Framework programme

This programme is designed to clarify the variety of services provided by Technology and to inform the customer on the technical aspects of this provision. For instance, the software tools and project life cycle methodology used by Technology should be defined and explained to customers. Those involved in the Framework programme include systems development teams, IT Services within Technology and the customers (RBS departments or external organisations). Project development methods have been reviewed and clarified, and a multi-disciplinary approach is used in all developments.

☐ 3 Team programme

This addresses the people and teamwork issues of Renaissance. It provides management training and development, career planning and appraisal processes to motivate staff towards the improvement of Technology services and products. The Team programme is largely the human resource management element of Renaissance and is arguably the most difficult and yet most important element of the whole project. As George Mathewson, Chief Executive of the RBS, has argued, 'People management is the hardest task of management . . . it is a task that is often shirked at all levels.' Essentially the Team programme is involved in facilitating a change in the behaviour of staff. Figure 4.4 shows its elements where culture, job and key result areas (KRAs) combine to influence the behaviour of individuals. Enhancement of this behaviour has a positive effect on the customer service provided.

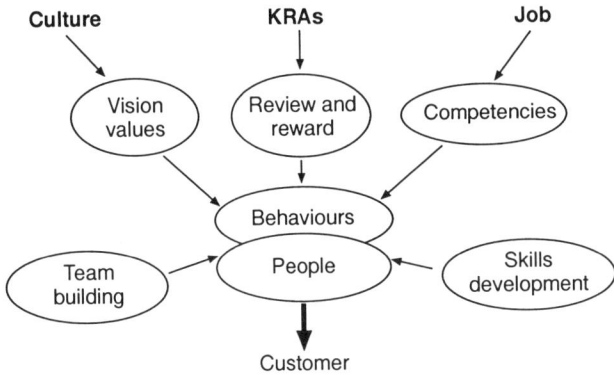

Figure 4.4 The Team theme

The interrelationship between the three primary themes 'Partnership', 'Framework' and 'Team' has been carefully monitored and reviewed since the inception of the Renaissance programme. A major aspect of the change programme has been identified as the need to change the culture of the organisation and the behaviour of individuals. It is recognised that no significant change can take place in the organisations systems without a fundamental change in these elements. One of the major vehicles to facilitate such change has been the performance monitoring process for senior management levels. Managers are given key result areas incorporating targets on delivery, cost management, internal management and service levels. Feedback is given using a ratings scale of 1 to 10 from a range of stakeholders including customers (internal Technology customers, or RBS departments), financial controls, and staff. This performance scheme has made the whole Renaissance programme more coherent and benefits in terms of improved output are starting to emerge.

For Technology staff various schemes are being implemented such as the Quality Initiative programme to encourage new, innovative ideas from them. A range of proposals is considered including those aimed at increasing production, reducing customer costs, and streamlining processes. Participating staff are rewarded in various ways including additional pay and the communication of best practice. Quality Initiative (QI) workshops are organised to brainstorm new ideas, consider the technical aspects and feasibility of proposed methods, and formulate strategies for further work. Some QI projects are funded by Technology to help bring them to fruition.

The Team Excellence reward is another scheme to encourage improved output from staff. A team can suggest various areas of improvement that it feels can be achieved such as people management or business results. A consultancy group from within Technology would then be asked to identify elements that could be improved within the areas specified, and levels of performance are agreed on a short time-scale (typically three to six months). At the end of the agreed period an evaluation takes place on the improvements that have been achieved within the team and a suitable reward (possibly financial) is given.

Currently the middle management group have been largely excluded from these initiatives although there a number of benefits from work already undertaken. Firstly, the middle managers usually act as sponsors for the Team Excellence reward and consequently will be involved in the success of any changes. Furthermore, there is a positive effect from the performance monitoring of the senior management group. There is a trickle-down effect which encourages improved performance of managers in this group. Other schemes involving the middle management group include the development of a Management Forum which incorporates a mixture of social and pure development programmes to enhance motivation.

After a slow start the Renaissance programme is steadily showing signs of improvements. At the outset there were problems with a lack of acceptance by staff of the need or usefulness of such a project. Since Martin Webb (Head of Technology) took over the role of heading the Renaissance programme it has been made more of a priority and is now firmly on the agenda at the RBS. The combination of these two roles has meant that Technology has real ownership of the change programme and its importance has been enhanced in the eyes of managers. The RBS continues to expand and develop its use of technology in information systems and has implemented a range of projects that will surely promote and accelerate this progress in the years to come.

■ 4.8 Conclusions

This chapter has described a two-way relationship between information systems and the organisation; changes in the organisation require corresponding modifications in information systems. Technology can often be the catalyst for change for a business. The introduction of new information systems into an organisation can revolutionise its working processes, and potentially lead to a change in the scope and range of services offered to customers and clients. Furthermore, new systems can facilitate radical changes in the fabric of the organisation; changing the communication flows, management structures, and ultimately the organisation's strategic goals.

The approach used in changing information systems in an organisation is vitally important. The standard methodologies such as those utilising development life-cycles are fundamentally satisfactory, provided that they are used in the correct way. It has been suggested that the relationship between organisation, culture, people, and objectives plays a vital role in the change process, and any implementation must consider all of these elements. In particular an important element in the development process is the human factor. A range of stakeholders in an organisation should be involved at all stages of a new system development in order to facilitate the change and ensure that a successful outcome is achieved.

■ Questions for discussion

1. (i) 'It is much easier to implement a new management information system in an organisation with a traditional hierarchical management structure than in one with a more open fluid structure.' Discuss this statement and comment on the suitability of information systems in specific organisational structures.
   (ii) There is often resistance to change in an organisation and this is particularly highlighted in the introduction of new technology. Critically analyse the problems that can develop during the installation of a new system, and how an organisation can attempt to overcome such problems.
2. (i) Evaluate the systems development methodology adopted by the RBS. Comment on the suitability of such an approach.
   (ii) There seems to be a strong emphasis on the 'people' aspects of any new development in the RBS. Comment on how this is achieved and any benefits that are gained from this strategy.
3. Operations Support and Technology are two distinct departments in the Operations Division at the RBS.
   (i) Analyse the differences in the work of these two departments in relation to information systems development.
   (ii) In what ways do these departments assist the change process in the RBS?
4. (i) In general, information systems development should not be solely the responsibility of technical specialists. Discuss other specialists who should be involved in any development. Describe how the RBS have approached this problem.
   (ii) Change involves consideration of a range of elements in the organisation including people, technology, structure and objectives. Discuss how technology and information systems can be used as a catalyst for change. Analyse the circumstances that can occur when information systems are a barrier to change.
5. (i) The Renaissance programme at the RBS has been used an instrument for change. Critically discuss the methods used in this programme.
   (ii) The RBS management consider that the culture of the organisation is an important attribute in the process of change.
   (a) Describe some aspects of culture, and how these can affect the ability of an organisation to change.

(b) Discuss the use of information systems as a catalyst for change in culture.

(c) How are the RBS attempting to change the culture of the organisation? Discuss whether these methods are likely to be successful in the long term.

■ Bibliography

Adams, C. and Thomas, R., 'Computer Failure – The Need for a "Future" View', *IRIS '96 Conference*, Gothenberg, Sweden, August 1996.

Dhammi, K., 'Is Your IT Project Risky?', *Business & Technology Magazine*, Cromwell Media, London, Nov. 1994, pp. 13–14.

Drucker, P., 'The Coming of the New Organisation', *Harvard Business Review*, Jan/Feb 1988.

Johnson, G. and Scholes, K., *Exploring Corporate Strategy: Text and Cases* (London: Prentice-Hall International, 1989).

Keen, P., *Shaping the Future: Business Design through Information Technology* (Harvard: Harvard Business School, 1991).

Laudon, K. C. and Laudon, J. P., *Management Information Systems – Organization and Technology* (New Jersey, USA: Prentice-Hall International, 1996).

Laudon, K. C. and Marr, K. L., *Information Technology and Occupational Structure*, Centre for Research on Information Systems (New York: New York University, 1995).

Leavitt, H. J., *Applying Organisational Change in Industry: Structural, Technological and Humanistic Approaches, Handbook of Organisations*, ed. J. G. March (Chicago: Rand McNally, 1965).

O'Brien, J. A., *Management Information Systems: A Managerial End User Perspective* (London: Richard Irwin, 1993).

Pliskin, N., Romm, T., Lee, A. S. and Weber, Y., 'Presumed versus Actual Organizational Culture: Managerial Implications for Implementation of Information Systems', *The Computer Journal* vol. 36, no. 2 (1993).

Porter, M.E., *Competitive Strategy: Techniques for Analysing Industries and Competitors* (New York: Free Press, 1980).

Porter, M. E., *Competitive Advantage: Creating and Sustaining Superior Performance* (New York: Free Press, 1985).

Sathe, V., *Culture and Related Corporate Realities* (London: Richard Irwin, 1985).

Scott-Morton, M. (ed.), *The Corporation of the 1990's: Information Technology and Organisational Transformation* (Oxford: Oxford University Press, 1991).

Thomas, R. and Ballard, M., *Business Information – Technologies and Strategies* (Cheltenham: Stanley Thornes Publishers, 1995).

Tom, P. L., *Managing Information as a Corporate Resource* (New York: Harper Collins Publishers, 1991).

Weber, Y., *The Effect of Top Management Culture Clashes on the Implementation of Mergers and Acquisitions* (South Carolina: University of South Carolina, 1988).

CHAPTER 5

The marketing conundrum

Ashok Ranchhod

■ 5.1 Introduction

Marketing is a complex and ill-defined discipline. However, the general idea is one of transaction or exchange between two individuals or organisations. Marketing has, for a long time, been subjected to analysis by utilising an essentially simple concept, that of the four P's – product, place, price and promotion (see also Chapter 1.8). Most ancient civilisations and traders fitted into this concept. The way of trading determined the emphasis placed on these parameters. In the modern marketing of products and services, some of these parameters may have become less important. For instance direct marketing techniques employed by the larger catalogue companies account for a substantial amount of consumer trade. The emphases have shifted away from place to speed of delivery, promotion and product characteristics. Companies can be located anywhere, either nationally or internationally.

This chapter will explore the history of marketing, from initial fragmentation, to mass marketing and, now, to global marketing via the Internet. It then discusses the impact of the new information technologies and their effect on marketing within businesses. The case study 'Direct footwear' illustrates the impact of the new technologies on marketing. The new dilemmas faced by the growth of the Internet are discussed at length in the latter part of the chapter.

■ 5.2 What is marketing?

Marketing, as a discipline, has no clear home, unlike some of the defined sciences. It draws its knowledge base and inspiration from many different fields such as mathematics, science, psychology, etc. (see Figure 5.1). In this sense marketing is a truly eclectic area of study. Below, are a few examples of the use of various disciplines from which marketing borrows, and which illustrate the diverse nature of marketing practice.

The UK's Chartered Institute of Marketing (CIM) defines marketing in the following manner:

'Marketing is the management process responsible for identifying, anticipating and satisfying consumers' requirements profitably.'

A broader, and perhaps more encompassing, definition is provided by the American Marketing Association (AMA), which argues:

'Marketing is the process of planning and executing the concept, pricing, promotion, and distribution of ideas, goods and services to create exchanges that satisfy individual and organisational goals.'

The absence of 'profitability' in the American definition shows that the concept is applicable to both profit and non-profit organisations. Indeed the past decade has seen a tremendous growth in the use of marketing techniques by charities and non-profit organisations such as the World Wildlife Fund (Medley 1988).

Currently, however, the discipline of marketing is facing a mid-life crisis. As we know, marketing is influenced by many disciplines (see Figure 5.1) and it lacks an agreed or defined core. Its boundaries are somewhat ill-defined and the current inexorable movement towards the greater use of technology, in what is threatening to become a global market for small and large businesses alike, seems to have thrown the subject into some disarray. According to Brown

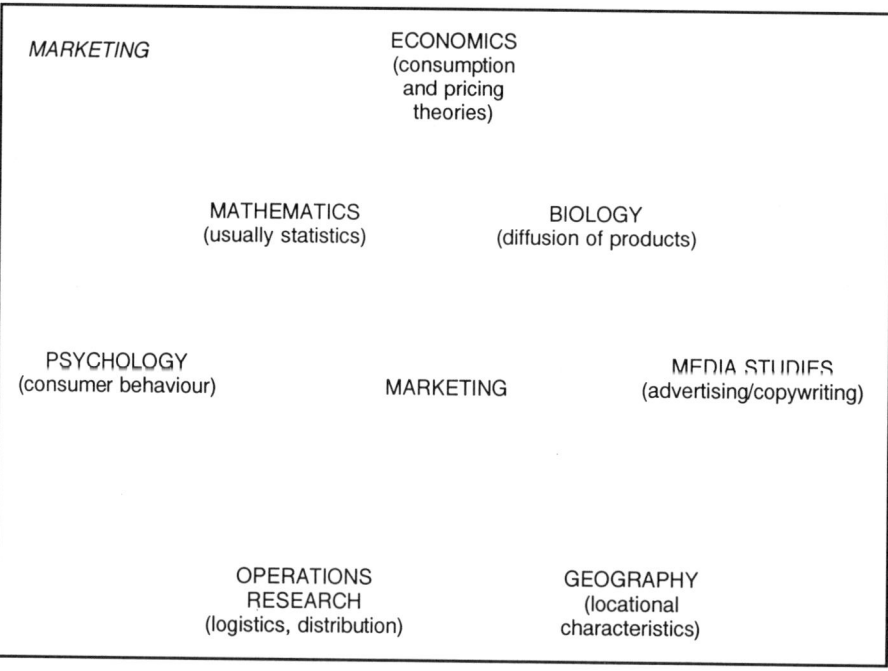

Figure 5.1   Influences on marketing

(1995), in his excellent book on Postmodern Marketing, he argues that many prominent practitioners, consultants and academics are concerned that the marketing field in its modernist concept is facing a crisis of representation. He outlines this with the following points from prominent academics:-

- Piercy (1992) maintains that the traditional marketing concept 'assumes and relies on the existence of world which is alien and unrecognisable to many of the executives who actually have to manage marketing for real'.
- Gummesson (1987) states that ' the present marketing concept . . . is unrealistic and needs to be replaced'. He then outlines the rationale for relationship marketing.
- Thomas (1993), one of the most respected academics in marketing, has raised serious doubts about the efficacy of the conventional marketing message.
- Brownlie and Saren (1992) argue that 'it is questionable whether the marketing concept as it has been propagated can provide the basis for successful business at the end of the twentieth century'.

Brown goes on to argue later in his book that, 'Marketing scholarship, in short, became increasingly divorced from "reality" and this has been followed by the fragmentation of the discipline into a multiplicity of hostile factions, retrenchment and the search for a new guiding paradigm. In short a crisis of representation.'

There are many discussions as to where marketing is heading, and the debate centres around where its role is in the so-called Post-Modern world. Venkatesh *et al.* (1993) have produced a table which looks at the relative cultural and technological emphases in Modernism and Post-Modernism (Table 5.1). The postmodern view considers symbolism, fragmentation in markets, digital/communicative technology and the relentless move towards globalisation as features of the current and near future emphases within societies. Writers such as Mueller-Heumann (1992), Thomas (1993) and Lansley (1994) consider the disintegration of mass markets and the growing enthusisasm for micro-marketing, database marketing and one-to-one marketing, where consumer interests are paramount. Strangely, the whole notion of marketing, through the growth of information technology and the Internet, is potentially closing the circle which began with fragmented markets up to the 1850s. The next section considers how marketing has evolved to its present state.

■ 5.3 Marketing history

Business subjects are often studied as current disciplines and many organisations and academics ignore historical research at their peril. History helps to trace the development of business issues.

A well-developed study by Tedlow (1993) seeks to understand the evolution of mass marketing within the USA and then apply the model to various case histories within segments such as whisky, British cars, retailing and pharmaceuticals, to name a few. His main argument is that markets within the USA went through four distinct phases before they reached their current state. Marketing strategies were often limited by the lack of development of technology. Technology facilitated the development of mass marketing. The main marketing phases designated are the following:

■ Fragmentation – phase 1

Marketing strategy played a small part in this phase which was characterised by high margin, low volume goods, for example localised flour production or localised shoe production. The market size was restricted due to logistics involving high transfer costs and lack of market feedback information. For any product to achieve national distribution it had to have a very favourable ratio of weight and bulk to value. Most products, therefore, were sold in very localised areas.

Table 5.1   Relative emphases in modernism and postmodernism

MODERN EMPHASIS	POSTMODERN EMPHASIS
Object	Image, symbol
Cartesian subject	Symbolic subject
Cognitive subject	Semiotic subject
Unified subject	Fragmented subject
Centred subject	Decentred subject
Signified	Signifier
Objectification	Symbolisation
Representation	Signification
Truth (objective)	Truth (constructed)
Real	Hyperreal
Universalism	Localism, particularism
Society as a structure	Society as a spectacle
Logocentric reason	Hermeneutic reason
Knowing	Communicating
Economy	Culture
Capitalism	Late capitalism
Economic systems	Symbolic systems
Production	Consumption
Shift from use value to exchange value	Shift from exchange value to sign value
Science/Technology	Science/Technology?
Mechanical technology	Digital/communicative technology
Harnessing nature	Working with nature*
Sciences	Humanities
Euro-American centrism	Globalism
Phallocentrism	Feminism/genderism
Orientalism, colonisation	Multiculturalism/globalism
Fragmentation	*Holism**

* Author's additions

■ Unification (1880s to 1950s) – phase 2

The major change during this period was the notion of marketing on a national basis. Companies began branding goods and began to market nationally at low margins. Many of these brands still survive today. Brands such as Heinz, Coca Cola and Beechams are etched in people's minds.

Three main factors brought about this remarkable change from local manufacture to mass production and mass marketing. The railroad was the most important innovation, opening up the country to the new manufacturing companies and making national marketing a possibility for the first time. The invention of the telegraph was also a critical factor, allowing companies to access vital marketing information, direct the sales force and react quickly to changes in the market place. Accompanying the rail and communications revolution was the development of advanced machinery and manufacturing processes which made it possible to produce a standard product in large volume and, where needed, in small packages (see also Chapters 6.2 and 7.1). The early part of the twentieth century saw these revolutions impacting on Europe. For instance, Sloan (1967) understood the idea of market research and design issues and incorporated these into the design of cars at General Motors during the 1940s and 1950s: 'I am sure we all realise how much appearance has to do with sales; with all cars fairly good mechanically, it is a dominating proposition and in a product such as ours, the individual appeal is so great, it means a tremendous influence on our future prosperity . . . beauty of design, harmony of lines, attractiveness of colour schemes and general contour of the whole piece of apparatus [were seen to be equally as important as] soundness of workmanship and other elements of a mechanical value.'

This concept was translated into the development of a fully fledged design department with accompanying mass production systems. According to the analysis carried out by Church (1993), the British industry failed to develop an organisational capacity for the design of mass-produced vehicles, the missing dimension (fourth) from the mass marketing of motor cars in Britain during the first half of the twentieth century. The fourth dimension refers to aspects of design, the other three being advertising, credit facilities and pricing strategies for cars.

Also, during this phase, as companies began producing and packaging at their plants, they began to put their own names on the packages and advertise nationally. This began the relentless move towards branded products. The Phase 2 products were standardised and uniform with little attempt at segmentation. They were designed to appeal to the wider set of consumers.

■ Segmentation (1950s to 1990s) – phase 3

The introduction of mass communication media, such as television and radio, were as important in Phase 3 as the railroad and telegraph had been in Phase 2. Advertising through radio and television brought a company's selling messages directly into households with unprecedented impact. It soon became apparent that certain programmes attracted certain types of viewers, and the possibility of segmenting markets by demographics and psychographics was enhanced.

Segmentation was explained by Kotler (1995) who stated that: 'markets vary in their degree of heterogeneity. At one extreme, there are markets made up of buyers who are very similar in their wants, product requirements and responses to marketing influences. At the other extreme are markets made up of buyers seeking substantially different product qualities and/or quantities.'

A key factor during Phase 3 was the growth of the 'baby boomer' generation in the USA which was looking for badges of belonging which could serve to link them to similar minded within their age group and to differentiate them from their elders (Tedlow, 1988). This resulted in the mass market that had dominated since the 1880s splitting apart into innumerable product categories from soft drinks to expensive cars as marketers attempted to reconfigure and exploit the latest consumer interests.

■ Micromarketing (1990 to 1995?) – phase 4

The advent of information technology (see Chapter 4) and computer-collected and analysed information has permitted the development of just-in-time or flexible manufacturing systems using techniques such as Materials Resource Planning (see also Chapter 1.2 and 7.1). This permits the manufacture of a wide range of goods in short runs while still benefiting from economies of scope and excellent stock control of components,using Just-In-Time techniques. The development of databases allows marketers to build a more complete picture of their target customers' lifestyle, behaviour and buying patterns. Greater quantities of information can be analysed, sometimes using entire populations.

As consumers are becoming more demanding, so marketers are competing to satisfy their needs, which creates even more expectation and so intensifies the situation. This major change has again been aided by technological developments which have not been instigated by marketers. Phase 1 has been described (Tedlow 1988) as taking one more step closer to every marketer's dream – to sell the potential customer precisely what he or she wants. This combination of technology and desire for direct customer communication has led to the belief that the future of marketing lies in interactive technology where on-line communications via either a TV or a PC can provide personalised advertising messages as well as a means of ordering and paying on-line.

There is now the possibility of a move to Phase 5 which could be called Refined Micro-Marketing – 1996 onwards. This is due to the rapid developments in electronic selling systems such as interactive TV (iTV) and the Internet, showing that radical change may once again involve technological factors outside the normal dimensions of product marketers. It is possible, with the amount of detail that can be captured on a single customer, that segmentation can be refined even further.

■ 5.4 The growth of direct marketing

As the section above showed, technology has played, and will always play, a large part in the marketer's arsenal. The biggest impact seems to be the amazing way in which products can be moved about and communicated about, revolutionising the somewhat static view of the 4P concept. The use of database technology has enabled the enormous growth experienced in direct marketing. There is hardly a consumer in the developed world who is not bombarded with direct mail literature offering products ranging from cars to wines to financial services. Direct marketing is defined by the American Direct Marketing Association as 'an interactive system of marketing which uses one or more advertising media to effect a measurable response and/or transaction at any location.'

The foundations of direct marketing were built in the nineteenth century in America with the birth of the US mail order industry, which was needed to supply all the remote locations in which people had settled in (Stone *et al.* 1995). By the 1980s and 1990s the remote location idea had been translated into general direct marketing to different market segments nationally. Technology has enabled companies to become more cost effective, at the same time pinpointing and developing relationships with individuals.

Another reason for direct marketing's growth could be the realisation that by increasing customer loyalty a company increases profits. The use and manipulation of databases and the growth in the power of computing enables this to happen quite effectively.

Currently, in Britain, one of the biggest growth areas has been home shopping and mail order, as is shown in Table 5.2.

Even so, 65 per cent of households never use mail order as many people still desire personal service, human interaction and tailored mechanisms for selecting the appropriate product. This shows the potential impact that a more interactive service could have on direct marketing.

Table 5.2 Mail order and home shopping's share of total retail sales 1988–93 (£ billion)

	1988	1989	1990	1991	1992
Mail order and home shopping sales	3.48	3.55	3.7	3.77	3.92
Total retail sales	113.29	120.91	129.32	135.4	140.32
% share of all retail sales	3.09	2.94	2.86	2.78	2.79

Source: Euro-monitor from *Catalogue Sales Orders* and *Business Monitor Retailing.*

Currently, according to Stone (1988), direct marketing has the following characteristics:

- Interactivity – it offers one-to-one communication between marketer and prospect/customer.
- Multiplicity of advertising media – direct marketing is not restricted to any one media. Direct marketers have actually discovered synergism between media. A combination of media is often used for maximum productivity.
- Measurable response – measurability is the hallmark of direct marketing. Everything is measurable, both in terms of spending and the returns obtained.
- Transactions can take place at any location – a global presence is possible and transactions can take place by phone, at a kiosk, by mail, or by personal visit. The direct marketing chart in Figure 5.2 elaborates this flow quite effectively.

Direct Mail, House Shopping via Catalogues and Telemarketing are probably the methods that are most easily identified by people as Direct Marketing methods. This may be supplemented by direct response advertising where our immediate response is required together with a coupon or a freephone number. The *Reader's Digest* has perfected direct mail and the magazine has the second largest circulation in the UK, after the AA magazine. Avon Cosmetics and Eissmann freezer foods are recognised users of door-to-door selling.

■ 5.5 The future for direct marketing

'Companies are moving from dealing with a faceless mass market to direct interaction with known prospects and customers.'

(Rapp and Collins 1994)

As mentioned above, target marketing through increasingly sophisticated databases will enable the one-to-one future to come to fruition. Some supermarkets are already trialling their EPOS systems (see Chapter 2) to develop relational databases for each customer. This increasing level of sophistication means that companies no longer have to waste money on prospective non-users of their products or services. For insurance the launch of the TESCO loyalty card demonstrates the amount of data available on each customer. Each individual within a socio-economic group can now be targeted with their own mix of favoured foods and wines or tailored financial packages!

■ 5.6 Technology and marketing

The previous section alluded to the growth of the potential power of relational databases. Companies with processing power equivalent to the large mainframe IBM computers which existed ten years ago are now within easy reach of most individuals. It is expected that the power of computers will nearly double every

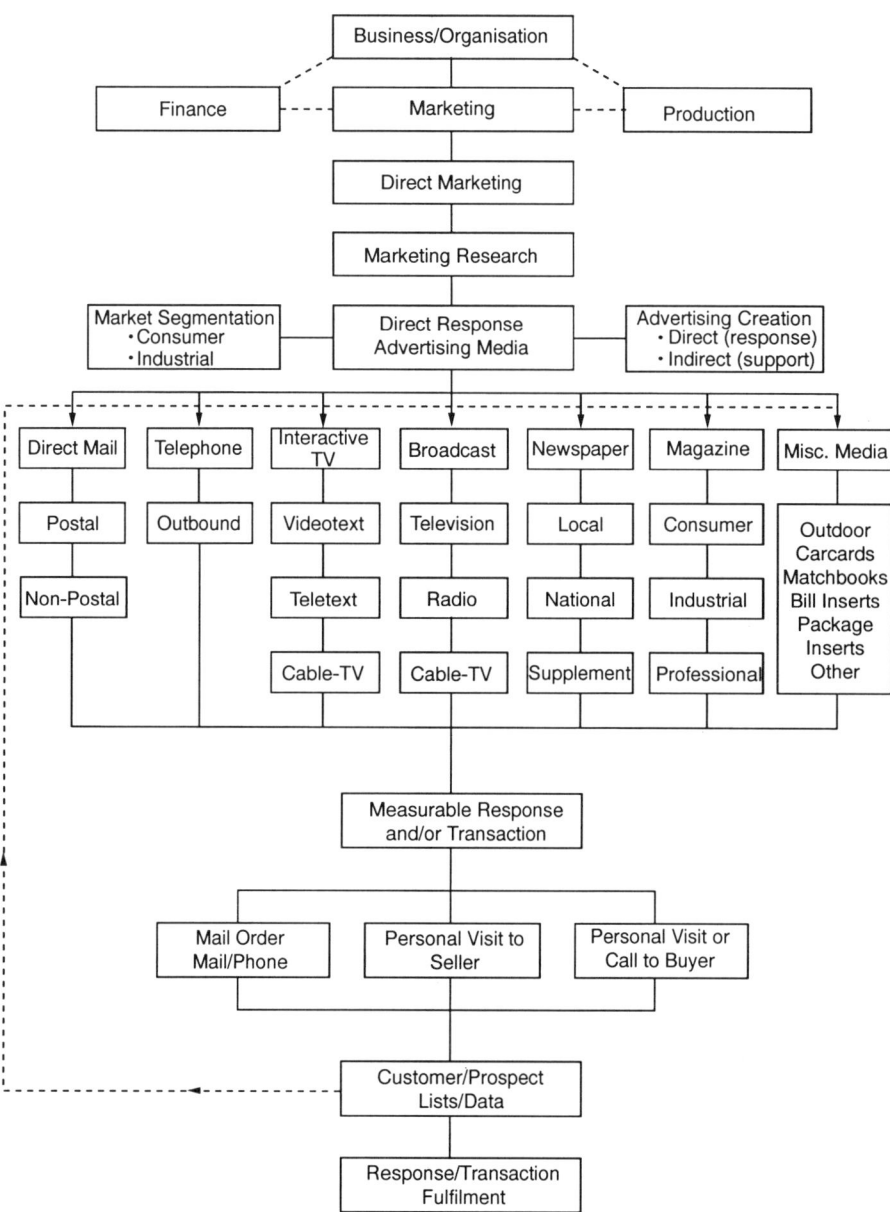

Figure 5.2   Direct Marketing chart
Source: Stone, *Successful Direct Marketing Methods*, NTC Business Books, 1988.

year. The development in the foreseeable future of a sophisticated database is therefore within reach of many small companies. For instance, according to Patron (1996), computer processing costs halve every eighteen months. However, he goes on to say that sadly this does not translate itself into the halving of computing costs; but it does enable organisations to process twice as much data for the same money. It is now a thousand times cheaper to keep a customer's name and address on a computer than it was twenty years ago, or for the same money it is possible to maintain one thousand times more customer information.

According to Patron currently most companies use their marketing databases to improve customer acquisition and retention via direct mail. In the future, this is likely to be a sufficiently strong marketing tool on its own. It is likely that marketing databases will then have to become more integrated marketing information systems (see Figure 5.3). Many companies are already making moves to create these integrated and sophisticated systems to develop strong marketing strategies. As can be seen in Figure 5.5, much statistical data can be gathered leading to both market research facilities and also to an external market intelligence overlay on to general trends within an organisation. Not only is this possible but the detailed access allows site evaluation and sales forecasting. The system can be used to drive shelf-planning, inventory control and the development of communication strategies. For manufacturers it can be extremely useful to access such systems or import data into their systems for mutual retailer/manufacturer benefit. In fact, data connections are becoming as important as data collections. Cowe (1996), illustrates this by the links that Lord's Mushrooms have developed with Asda Superstores. This 'inclusive approach', advocated by the Royal Society for Arts, envisages businesses working more closely with suppliers and customers. This means good data connections and also the possibility of the EPOS system connections, in this case mushroom sales to be linked to this key supplier.

Apart from these links and the possibility of integrated market intelligence systems, the growth of technology is also fostering lateral developments which are having a greater impact on marketing. These are now discussed below.

■ The concept of the real virtual factory

In their thought-provoking paper, Upton and McAfee (1996) discuss the idea of a community of dozens if not hundreds of factories, each focused on what it does best, all linked by an electronic network, enabling them to operate as one – flexibly and inexpensively – regardless of their location. They go on to elaborate three basic demands on such a network, if it is to work at all:

1. The network must be able to accommodate other members whose IT sophistication varies a great deal. It should therefore be inclusive, from the small machine shop with a single PC in the office, to the large site that boasts an array of engineering workstations and mainframes.

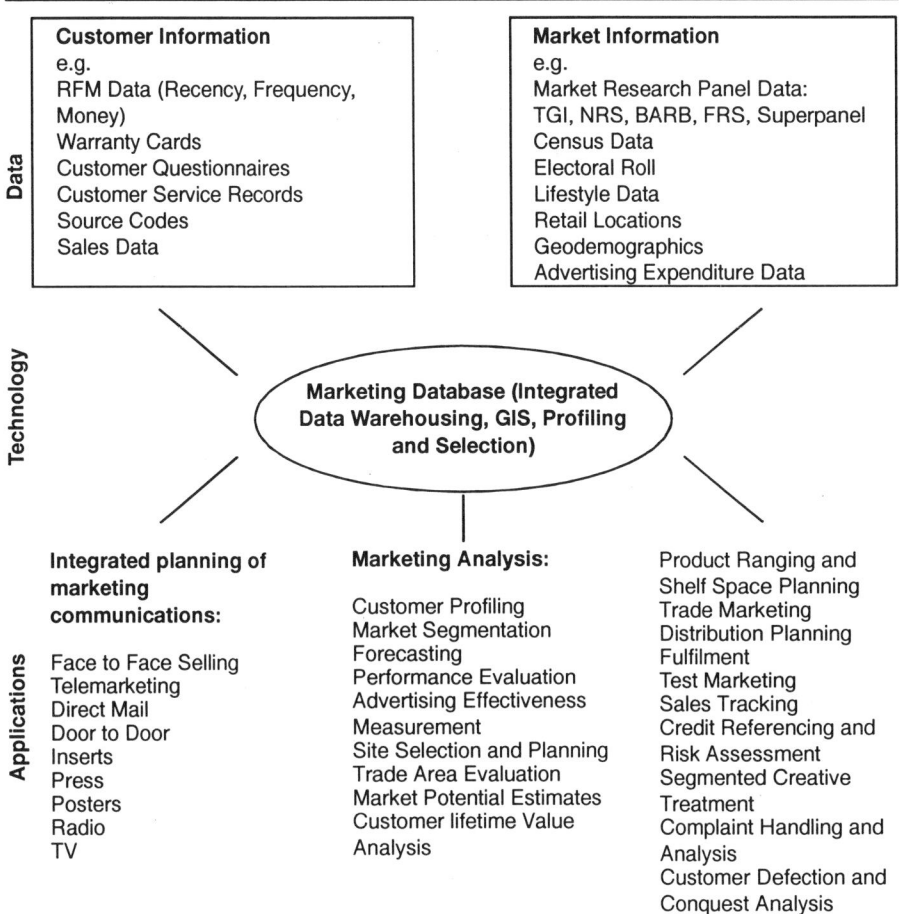

Figure 5.3 Integrated marketing information systems

2. The network should have a higher level of security and be able to cope with a constantly changing pool of suppliers and customers whose relationships vary enormously in intimacy and scope.
3. The network needs to give its members a great deal of functionality, including the capacity to transfer files between computers, the power to access common pools of information, and the capability to access and utilise all the programmes on a computer located at a distant site.

At present, these wide area networks do not satisfy all the above characteristics. There is a need to have open standards. These open standards are now becoming easier to install and use. The one commonly used for intercompany links is Lotus Notes. The other open standards are available though the Internet's World Wide Web.

These factors determine the ease of information sharing and the needs of a virtual factory. (See Figure 5.4.)

In many cases brokered networks may be formed so that security and quality exchange can be maintained.

This section of the discussion has looked at the issues surrounding the possibility of establishing large virtual factory networks in the future. The next section considers another lateral use of technology for mining existing data for ultra-sophisticated target marketing.

■ Data-mining

Some companies are now using technology to further their knowledge of customers and to find lateral limits which were impossible to discuss with previous computing power. Data acquisition is the starting point for data-mining. According to Ramprasad (1996), effective acquisition involves learning

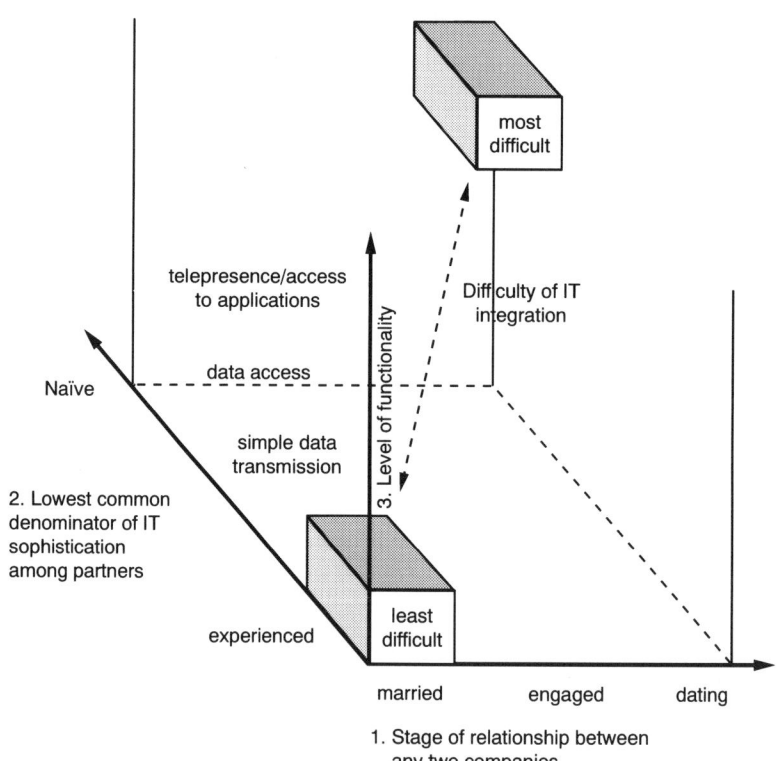

Figure 5.4   Three factors determining the ease of information sharing
Source: Upton and McAfee, 'The Virtual Factory', *Harvard Business Review*', July–August 1996.

and it evolves with each cycle of prospecting and extraction. The concept of data-mining needs three key stages:

☐ 1 Data acquisition

The storage of data from both internal and external sources. The data needs to be well documented.

☐ 2 Data integration

Data from many sources and on different media has to be integrated into a coherent data file for further analysis. This is data integration. Some statistical pruning may be necessary here.

☐ 3 Data mining

Data mining is the process of extracting valuable information from the integrated data files. The commonly used tools for such work are statistical analysis, artificial neural networks, rule induction, genetic algorithms, artificial intelligence and fuzzy logic. These techniques can be applied singly or in combination. Extracting insights and validating these insights are critical aspects of data mining. Constant prospecting and extracting cycles refine the data for constructive use in marketing. As Ramprasad (1996) says, systematic data mining is an innovation and it will take time to diffuse into organisations. Matthews (1996), writing in the *New Scientist*, says that nowadays nearly every organisation from supermarkets to the police can boast a vast mine of electronic data. Separating the gold from the dross is the real challenge. He illustrates the problems surrounding data mining by giving this example:

> 'Just rummage through your customer data and find out who chose prawn cocktail and steak and chips, but eschewed the black forest gateau in favour of apricot tart. But what if there are five starters, ten main courses and eight desserts? That's 400 combinations for a start. Then there are different permutations of age groups, social classes and income levels. It's called the "curse of dimensionality"; the way in which a handful of variables can produce a colossal number of permutations. Multiply it by the size of the customer base – which can easily be hundreds of thousands; even millions – and finding a trend starts to look impossible.'

Data miners, using powerful computers and mathematical tools, are now happy to tackle such daunting tasks.

This section has taken a close look at the impact that technology is having on the development of marketing and the powerful tools and ideas at the disposal of the marketer. The next section considers the impact of the Internet on marketing and whether this new medium, coupled with new technological breakthroughs, is indeed likely to change the face of marketing.

■ 5.7 The growth of the Internet and its implications for marketing

In the previous section some of the concepts of connectivity between computers, data acquisition and transfer were considered. These links are critical in both teaching a mass audience and interacting with them. Inter-connectivity with simple and powerful computers theoretically offers each of us the freedom to link with anyone on a global basis with the use of a modem. The open software written by companies such as Netscape enable access to information concerning companies, individuals, marketing data, brochures, pictures, science, specific discussion groups, music, sports, politics and a host of other sources. The last three to four years have seen an explosive growth of the number of people using the Internet. The current worldwide usage is estimated to be around 35 million, though in a rapidly growing medium figures can be somewhat suspect.

■ The Internet – what is it?

The Internet is an interconnected system of more than 7,500 individual computer networks. Although estimates vary, it is generally thought to connect over 2 million computers representing more than 30 million individual users.

The Internet's origin came with ARPA, the Advanced Research Project Agency, a US government agency working for the Department of Defense through the early 1970s. They developed a computer network that would be able to withstand a nuclear attack. If part of the network went down, information would be routed around the damaged part and communications lines would be secure. The need for academics involved in the project to communicate was the impetus behind the growth of a research network known as the ARPANET. The US government then funded its extension to colleges and universities, thus initiating the National Research and Education network, which until very recently, represented the Internet's core.

In the 1980s, developments in computing were responsible for the Internet's continued expansion. One of the key developments was the emergence of the workstation/server system, linked by the Ethernet Local Area Network, as the standard for linking computers within an organisation. It was used principally for communication by e-mail but its growth has mushroomed since the introduction of the World Wide Web and the launch of Net browsers such as Netscape software. The Internet was opened up to commercial traffic in the early 1990s and was essentially a network of computer networks, all of which had agreed to speak the same language (TCP/IP) which can be installed on various makes of computer such as IBMs, Apple Macintosh, Acorn, etc.

No one is technically in charge of the Internet, and because the Internet is a global network there is no possibility for one particular government to control what is on it. It is, however, now being scrutinised more closely by libel lawyers and worried governments but only minor action has so far been taken.

Part of the reason for the Internet's rapid rise in recent years is the growth in sales of personal computers for use in the home, and the introduction of the World Wide Web. Developed in Switzerland, the World Wide Web provides a more ordered structure to the provision of information on the Internet. Information is stored in 'pages' and separate pieces of information on these 'pages' have the facility to be linked. Each page is filled with 'hypertext' which can consist of text, pictures, sounds, and links to other hypertext pages. By clicking on these hypertext links, the user can jump between pages and thus travel around the Internet. The web browser software has been a major reason for the rapid growth in Internet usage. For the purpose of this dissertation, the Internet will refer to the Web and will exclude the non-Web Internet because it is inaccessible to most consumers and does not carry much commercial activity.

■ The current situation

Modahl and Eischler (1995) tell us that men dominate the Internet with women representing 22 per cent and children 4 per cent of the Internet population. They also found that the largest sector of economic activity, by far, was access provided by commercial on-line services. Areas like business information services, home banking, financial services and business-to-business sales of materials and components have nil revenues to date. They claim that real economic development is hindered by lack of government, unreliable payment systems (covered in detail in a later section), and a weak infrastructure with low-speed connections for consumers (see Cable TV).

A slightly different view is provided by Computer Intelligence Infocorp's latest study (1996) which shows that 2.7 million people used the Internet for shopping or to obtain commercial services such as banking or travel information. Neilsen Media Research (1996) confirms that more than 2.5 million people have purchase products and services over the Web with the most popular of Web site categories being music. It is claimed that the top five music distribution sites are selling more than 25,000 CDs every day. In addition, Thalheimer (1996) of Sharper Image comments: 'We're already selling on the Web. We don't think there's a security problem, and apparently our customers don't either. Our sales have tripled in the last three months and we're going to be making from $2 to $5 million this year on Web sales.'

Booz and Hamilton, part of Boston Consulting Group, predict that in ten years as much as 20 per cent of all household expenditures will be funnelled through the Internet. Two forecasts of the actual Internet revenue by the year 2000 are shown in Table 5.3 and Figure 5.5.

Table 5.3   Revenue projections for the Internet industry

	1995 (US$m)	2000 (US$m)	CHANGE IN MARKET SIZE
Equipment	500	2,500	× 5
Network services	300	5,000	× 17
Software	260	4,000	× 15
Enabling services	20	1,000	× 50
Expertise	50	700	× 14
Content and activity	50	10,000	× 200
Total	1,180	23,200	× 20

Source: 'GVU4 Internet User Survey', *Cyber Atlas 'Agents' Interstellar*, 22 April 1996.

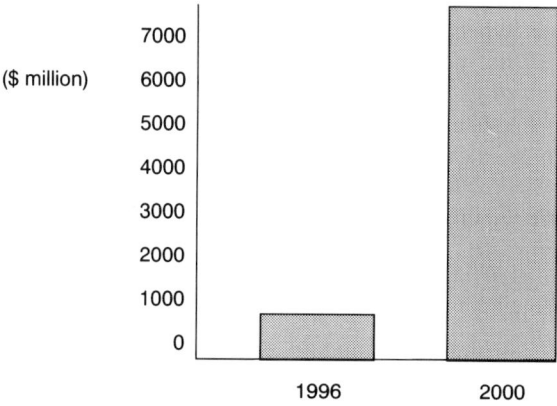

Figure 5.5   Online retailing revenue forecast
Source: 'GVU4 Internet User Survey', *Cyber Atlas 'Agents' Interstellar*, 22 April 1996.

■ Internet problems

The Internet and its World Wide Web application is now generally agreed by those at the top of other IT sectors to be the basis of the future of interactive services. Meanwhile, the Internet has many problems to contend with. Scales (1996) commenting on Internet Access Providers (IAP) (technology driven computer companies) says:

'To them, Internet access provision is a computer application with the added annoyance of a lot of technically incompetent remote users logging onto it. In more cases than not, their service levels are appalling and their customers hate them. If you were compiling a case study on how not to provide a network service, you'd hesitate to use the IAP community as an example because it defies credibility.'

These problems are compounded by the inherent and growing delays in Internet traffic. This has caused some cable operators to consider 'overbuilding the Internet' by building additional backbones while at the same time maintaining full Internet connectivity. Zavistovich (1996) comments: 'The current public Internet is incapable of handling the amount of traffic that will be generated by widely available high-speed Internet access.' And Levy (1995) adds:

'The present day reality is baffling to install, requires a love of staring at hourglass-shaped cursors and maybe lets you buy Monty Python jokes with an insecure credit card transaction. Travelling the Net in these pioneer days is like a journey to a rugged, exotic destination – the pleasures are exquisite but you need some stamina.'

It is clear that companies must update information and graphics on Web sites on a regular basis in order to give people a reason to come back again and again. In addition to useful content a site must be easy to navigate, because if users cannot find what they want, or the navigation is too obscure, they will not revisit.

A report by GVU4 (1996) into Internet problems found that most Web users report the following problems as shown in Figure 5.6, while on-line.

Another study by FIND/SVP (1995) found evidence that 34 per cent of Web users turn off graphics in order to speed up browsing – a major cause of concern to companies who may spend a great deal of money on graphics in order to

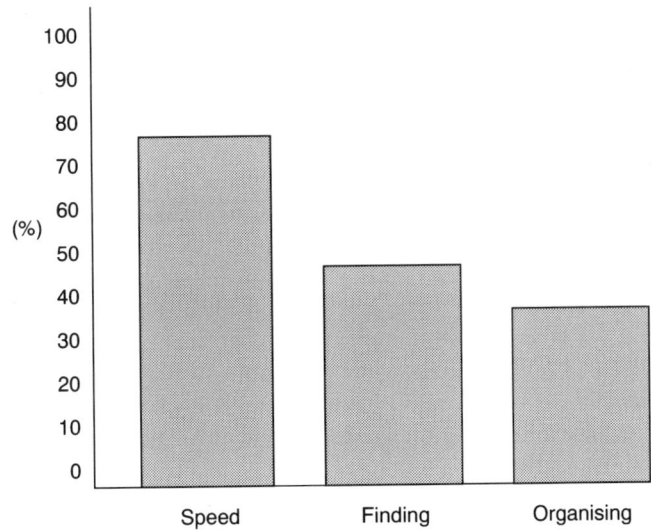

Figure 5.6   Common problems using the Web
Source: 'GVU4 Internet User Survey', *Cyber Atlas 'Agents' Interstellar*, 22 April 1996.

entice as many users as possible to their Web sites. FIND/SVP also found that search engines are no longer effective in a vast majority of searches and that only 16 per cent of users are satisfied with their ability to find information on the Web.

A particular worry to companies hoping to do business on the Web is the finding by FIND/SVP that 60 per cent of users visit fewer than ten sites regularly (once a month or more). In comparison, the average US adult reads ten magazines per month. They claim that their results show that a small group of heavy users disproportionately influence Web statistics.

Even given these problems, the rush to market on the Internet is on and some companies are moving towards the concepts of E-money and Web-crawlers.

■ E-money

In his seminal article on electronic money, Kleiner (1995) argues that the prize for developing digital or electronic cash, that is usable by individuals all over the world, is enormous. He argues that sitting around the world are millions of Internet users all of whom might like to buy something straight from the seller. It is a vast market worth billions, but, more importantly, it is a whole electronic economy in the making. Banks and businesses are obviously showing a keen interest in developing these systems (see Chapter 2.2). Currently, the biggest problems are security and some sort of equable currency transfer between different countries. There is also a danger that the E-money could be used for tax evasion, drug transactions and other criminal activities.

The very arguments used for the development of data-mining can perhaps be levelled against the use of E-money. Imagine the files that can be built up on an individual. The inter-transfer of data between retailers could be possible, if they co-operate, enabling a picture to be built up of detailed accounts of an individual's spending habits. It is really a question of how much individuals would tolerate such an invasion into their privacy.

Currently, Baird (1996) reports that this vision of shopping on the Internet has moved a stage closer. Microsoft have linked up with Verifone to form the Microsoft Merchant system to help companies advertise on the Internet and obtain customers' credit card details in a way that keeps them secret. The problems of security are still being investigated by the Department of Trade and Industry who want to license the encryption services to 'trusted third parties' such as banks and telephone network operators to provide other companies – such as financial services organisations – with encryption services. Further issues surrounding marketing on the Internet will be discussed in the Summary and Conclusions section.

■ Web crawlers

There is a view amongst scientists that a second wave of companies, owing their existence to the Internet, are readying themselves to go public (Moody 1996).

The dozen or so companies that offer search services, such as Lycos, Infoseek and Open Text, employ search engines – programs that scan the Net, record everything they find, and salt it away in gigantic databases. These can then be used by individuals to search for topics or products. However, vast lists are produced which are pretty useless to someone who wishes to access information quickly but at the same time wishes to have useful information in order to enact a dialogue with the seller of a particular item. These companies which can keep track of traffic on the Net with details of the individuals who use the sites would provide marketers with a goldmine of information in order to sell products and services.

■ 5.8 Case study: direct footwear

■ Introduction

In July 1994, David Price, the Managing Director of Cosyfeet, sat down with Nick Carter, his part-time financial and legal executive, to review the past year and to consider what strategies the company should adopt over the next three to five years. Three years ago, David had purchased Cosyfeet from John and Masie Rex in a complex financial and operational agreement. The ensuing three years had seen business, technical and financial success in Cosyfeet's currently defined market. The business environment had been turbulent over the last five years. In spite of this, the year-on-year turnover of Cosyfeet had increased by 20 per cent.

Cosyfeet was established by John Rex in 1984 to provide specialist slippers for persons with difficult or disabled feet. Such people need different slipper structures and also especially wide fittings which were not available through normal retail outlets. Initially, the business was run from home with a mail order catalogue. All production was undertaken on a contractual basis with a manufacturing company in Lancashire.

The business was run by John and Masie Rex. After the takeover of the company by David Price the organisation expanded to employ a flexible workforce of ten to twelve people. To accommodate the increased size of the operation Price took up leases on two factory units covering 5,000 square feet from an estate belonging to Clarks. The company had the potential to take a substantial market share in the elderly footcare market.

David was aware that the company was serving the current market sector very well and that the company had evolved with the market. However as the year 2000 loomed nearer, some strategic thinking and planning was needed as the business continued to expand. In the summer of 1994 David embarked upon a series of consultations and meetings with his key staff in order to develop a comprehensive five-year plan. In his own words, 'the business has now reached a stage where many people are involved and I have a social and ethical responsibility to them'.

■ Background: company history post-1991

David Price was a Clarks manager and recognised a niche in the footwear market in the same way as John Rex. Clarks owned a DIY shoe kit design called Simple Way and in January 1983 David left Clarks, having bought the Simple Way design from Clarks, and set up his own business with his wife Annette.

The Simple Way design comprised polyurethane moulded soles and all-leather factory-cut pieces which were sent to the customer as a shoe kit, complete with needles and thread, for the customer to make the shoes for himself. The shoes were very comfortable for difficult or swollen feet and even badly deformed feet could be catered for with leather being cut to match the customer's foot outline drawn on a piece of paper and sent in.

The business, trading throughout using the name Simple Way, started as Seaton & Price Ltd. Later the company name was changed to Footshop Ltd, since by that time the business included other foot comfort products and the company name was changed to suit its new image.

During 1983 the business moved out of the Price house into a factory unit and later into a small trading estate called The Tanyard where it occupied one unit, and eventually four units. The heart of the business was always mail order but accounts built up for customers who made up the kits and supplied their own customers.

The turnover figures for the years 1983 to 1990 indicated steady growth (350,000 in 1990), but, in 1991, turnover declined. David instinctively felt during 1989 and 1990 that the business needed another activity grafted on to it if it was to survive. It was never certain whether it had a natural business ceiling, which had been reached, or whether the business depended on David's personal injection of creativity and business energy which, after 7 years, he wanted to put to wider use and a different challenge.

In 1990, Cosyfeet, a very compatible product, came on the market and David bought it out of revenue with very little call on the bank for support. By very thorough pre-planning and using a new combined catalogue immediately after the acquisition of Cosyfeet the merger was a success, with a positive cashflow from the beginning.

The Simple Way turnover declined further in 1992 and 1993, but the Cosyfeet income improved steadily starting with an increase of 25 per cent in the first trading year. It became obvious then that Simple Way should be sold in order to give it a new lease of life with a new owner and to free David to concentrate all his energies on Cosyfeet. This was done in April 1994. (See Figure 5.7 for David's core business responsiblities.)

SIMPLE WAY (Kit Shoes)

JOHN LOCKE (Made to Measure)

MASS PRODUCTION
Speciality for Export

Figure 5.7:   David Price's core business responsibilities at Clarks

■ David Price's personal background

David Price left school with 'A' Levels and joined Clarks' management training programme. Clarks sponsored him for a one-year Diploma in Business Administration at Bath University. At the age of 21 David decided to move to America where he worked for a shoe company. He also worked for a company in the City where he experienced the joys and pitfalls of running small to medium enterprises as each section was left to run these businesses as they saw fit. The variety of experience he gained was immense. He left the City to rejoin Clarks as a retail consultant in the late 1970s. This post entailed offering independent retail advice to shoe shops based mainly in outer London and Anglia. He left this position to take up an appointment in Street, the 'home' of the shoe industry. The post entailed running peripheral businesses for Clarks.

These were three small businesses that David was running for the prestigious Clarks company. However these were peripheral businesses and at some stage perhaps it was inevitable that they would be closed down. Nevertheless, David Price kept the Simple Way shoe business going and bought it after redundancy.

David has always been fascinated by strategy, but stresses the importance of personal circumstances in dictating business. At the same time he recognised a limit to the potential growth of Simple Way and would always be trying new ventures. One of the most important developments was the diversification into foot comfort products. The company name was changed to Footshop Ltd to encompass this change.

The most significant initiative in the search for new markets was ironically a failure. He bought 3,000 pairs of slippers with a velcro fastening to sell through postal advertisements in newspapers. David had seen advertisements for a company called 'Cosyfeet' in the weekend newspapers and tried copycat advertising. What worked for Cosyfeet did not work for David. This also illustrated the importance of correct data and datamining for target marketing.

■ Cosyfeet

As Handy (1991) suggests when extolling the virtues of lifelong learning, getting it wrong is part of getting it right (negative capability). David Price was keen not to miss the opportunity of learning from his setback with the slippers!

David was keen to learn from John Rex. Mr Rex had a flair for shoe design and had built up an enviable little business, following his experience at Tuf shoes. In the end, David Price came to an amicable arrangement to buy the business as Mr Rex was nearing retirement.

The business continued to expand out of its own revenues. There were cashflow crises in the early stages which were managed because of the tight control procedures adopted by David. He was determined to develop the business into a larger viable entity. To this end he set about improving the mail order catalogue and developing the response systems for mail order. He also understood the need actively to nurture his key stakeholders and he began regular scheduled visits to the factory manufacturing the slippers.

■ The market

David is aware that the market he serves is not clearly defined and he is constantly updating his notions of what market he is serving. The market for his products is defined as 'Footwear for people with wide and swollen feet'. The segmentation of this so-called 'Grey or Elderly' market is not clear. Some of the greys are too young to perceive themselves as grey whilst many are people who find it difficult to get to a shop. These are often the customer types that Cosyfeet would be serving. The wearers of the product are usually elderly, but could be anywhere between 55 and 100! The need for specialist footwear is not confined to any particular strata of society. The mail order advertisements therefore go out to a range of different newspapers and magazines. The favourite seems to be the *Daily Mirror*. The market needs to be constantly trawled for new customers, as some of the existing ones meet an early death! In some cases the products are returned as the prospective wearer has sadly passed away before getting a chance to wear the product. This obviously impacts on the marketing strategy as the search for new customers has to be an ongoing exercise.

The target for the products are the carers of the elderly. These could range from close relatives to chiropodists, physiotherapists and the care professionals.

What David wants to impart, through his catalogues, is a 'caring' image. He is genuinely concerned that the right value for money is received by the customer. To this end, the operations are tightly managed so that 'next day delivery' can be effected. The European and American markets have not been explored.

■ Developing the marketing and operations

The company has a great potential for growth and this has led David to reconsider the way he does business. In terms of modern linkages and computerisation he appears to be in the vanguard. He has the following links :

- A computer link to his house to prevent loss of data.
- A link with the manufacturers in Lancashire, with whom there is data exchange on orders and sometimes of designs as well.
- A new Internet presence.
- E-mail facilities.

This move towards the increasing use of technology has made David wonder whether he should consider outsourcing the following:

- Telephone reception.
- Warehousing.
- Developing modem links with hospitals and nursing homes, so that a catalogue service with added items could be provided. This would also speed up the order/delivery cycle.
- Developing marketing via the Internet.
- Expanding into marketing on a more international basis.

The operations management of such an organisation and speed of delivery are vital. Also important are the timing of advertisements and the need to keep sensible stock control and forward ordering schedules from the factory in Lancashire. The planning systems for this type of enterprise are unique and they have been devised by Nick Delgarno who is the stock controller for the whole enterprise. As indicated above, the quality issues are tackled directly with the manufacturers with both Nick and David frequently making trips to Lancashire. The moulds, knives and equipment at the factory have been bought by Cosyfeet. The company is at present establishing modem links with the factory to enable production plans to be updated on a regular basis. Mail order by its very nature requires discipline and tight systems. So Cosyfeet is constantly striving for improvements to enable speedier responses to customer needs.

■ Human resource management

At the present stage in the company's development human resource management (HRM) is considered to be very important (see also Chapter 6). There is now a good knowledge base in the company but this needs to be built on and used. In the past, employment of individuals to meet needs was the main basis of HRM. Many of the tasks are simple and as long as workers are fit and reasonably motivated in the majority of cases this sufficed.

The business has, until recently, employed a flexible workforce of associated friends, family and students who learned the work quickly. Their priority was not necessarily security of employment. However David Price now sees a small core workforce becoming established. He realises that he needs to invest in these people and recognise the contribution of their skills to business success now and in the future.

One vision that David Price has is of farming out all the warehousing side of the business to his manufacturers. He already has good links with the manufacturers in Lancashire. To assure a quality partnership David Price owns all the moulds, machines, etc.; the manufacturers' workforce know that he could take it all away. David Price talks directly to the workforce at the factory from time to time so that they see the whole picture and understand quality requirements.

■ New product development

Given his skills and knowledge of the shoe trade, David has been undertaking new product development for Cosyfeet. His redesigns have included better Velcro fasteners and also the production of moulded footwear. The new product, which is moulded footwear, has been designed by him. This has meant that Cosyfeet has control of the mould ownership and the machine used in the manufacturing of these newer, more flexible slippers. About £2,000 has been spent on new product development so far, including 'Sweat equity' as David mentioned. The new moulds will cost around £20,000 and will be purchased in 1995. These designs can now be forwarded directly to Lancashire through the computer links.

■ Financial management

This small organisation is very tightly managed. David is very aware of the problems small businesses face when they are trading. He therefore keeps a tight control on the cashflow within the enterprise. Just as cash comes in quickly, owing to the mail order aspects of the business, it can drain out just as easily to pay the manufacturers and the ongoing requirements of the business. The enterprise has begun to produce cashflow forecasts and profit/loss projections. It has also adopted a policy of paying its creditors within 10 days wherever possible. This not only keeps its many stakeholders happy but also willing to support them in moments of crisis. This method of early payment also produces a spin-off for the company in the form of discounts. David takes the social responsibility role very seriously and felt quite unnerved when he realised that Cosyfeet was ranked as the number three buyer from the factory in Lancashire, after Clarks and another major company. This made him realise that many livelihoods depended on his business, apart from the small operation in Street.

■ Cosmic decorations

When the business was going through a bad patch, David decided to call in a Feng Shui expert. Each time this expert was called the business prospered. The staff are also now less sceptical of this issue. Feng Shui, the ancient art of divining energy – known as chi or qi – within a room is now becoming popular in the West. Feng Shui is about eliminating stress within a room. This stress removal can be effected by a consultation with a Feng Shui expert who works out the organisation of the room and the desirable plants, colours and paintings for the room. The changes are effected during an auspicious occasion. If there are human problems these could also be helped by the organisation of the room and the requisite decor accompanied by a change of responsibilities. Throughout the Cosyfeet factory unit are paintings, crystals and stripes on the toilet doors, to stop money being flushed down the toilet! Mr Price has also undertaken regular meditation to accompany the Feng Shui changes. This has helped with the roller-coaster effects of the business. He feels that he can understand what is going on with a more detached eye. Mr Price comes from a Quaker background which instilled in him the idea of 'service to the community'. The empathy with Feng Shui, meditation and Krishna reinforces this notion. In this context, it is important to note that Feng Shui has become an accepted form of thinking in some business quarters in the City. A recent major example of a company that has taken advice from a Feng Shui practitioner is The Hong Kong and Shanghai Bank, arguably one of the biggest banks in the world.

■ The future

The nature of the responsibility above and the future of the business has made David think about planning for the future. The strategic development of the business is important to Cosyfeet. With the new technology in place and with the potential it offers, David is considering how 'virtual' his organisation can become. There is a chance to subcontract much of the work and just concentrate on developing new markets and new marketing links via the Internet. The organisation is small and flat, and the market is growing. There is also an existing database. This is the marketing conundrum he is battling with at present. (An organisation chart for the company is shown in Figure 5.8.)

ORGANISATION CHART

David Price

Nick Carter

| Claire Banwell | Erika Howell | Mark Gristock | Nik Dalgarno | Dominic Sorensen | Wendy Merry | Betty Richards |

Span of work

David Price	Director
Annette Price	(Non-executive director) and early mail receiver (home based)
Nick Carter	Self-employed, legal, book-keeping, cashflow formulator, administration and planning (confidante for David Price)
Claire Banwell	Processes orders, debtor control (has been line forewoman) and knows the business thoroughly
Erika Howell	Orders and telephone work
Mark Gristock	Computer network, advertising, customer database
Nik Dalgarno	Stock control
Dominic Sorensen	Packing, despatch, Desktop publishing
Wendy Merry	Shop
Tyson Evans	Warehouse and general maintenance
Elisa Young	(leaving) Customer complaints, enquiries, refunds
Betty Richards	Outwork
Wendy Brine	Order processing (part-time)
Sally Fayter	Order processing

Figure 5.8   Organisation chart: Cosyfeet

■ 5.9 Summary and conclusions

■ Introduction

The evolution of marketing has been traced from the early phases of mass marketing to the current vogue for ultra micro-marketing fuelled by the advances in computer technology. The changes are also exacerbated by the growth of the Internet. So how much is the Internet living up to its promise?

For any new marketing stance to be productive in this area, it is important that the enabling technology is well diffused throughout the population. This is true of media such as radio and television. Advertising on these mediums came of age once television and radio sets were well diffused throughout 50 per cent of the population. True interactivity on the Internet is still some way off as the technology is not fully developed to offer this. Currently most users are 'active', in that they conduct the search for sellers of goods or services through their PCs via modems linked to servers. At the moment the Web is passive and people are doing all the work. User benefit is derived only in relation to the amount of time spent searching. When machines are put into the loop and computer power is used to filter and search for information, then the Web will begin to fulfil its potential. It is anticipated (Steinberg 1996) that this will happen in three stages.

The first stage will involve making the client and server smarter. On the server side, this means linking Web sites to information stored in local databases and spreadsheets. On the client side, it requires making every application (not just browsers) able to access the Web. In the second stage, the client and server will begin to exchange not just data but programmes called 'applets', allowing new and more powerful kinds of interaction. In this way, an architect's site may provide a front end allowing one to experience a 3-D walk through a planned building. In the final stage, both clients and server send 'applets' back and forth and some of those 'applets' may live partly on the Net. Applets will begin to resemble agents – nomadic programmes sent out to find and gather information. At this stage, the Web will become fully animated and truly interactive.

■ Consumer attitudes

The attitude of customers will play a great part in the development of interactive selling through the use of technology. Current trials using cable television, satellite links and video on demand have been somewhat mixed. Sharrock (1996) writing about the VOD (Video-on-Demand) trials in particular says:

'The great white hope of video-on-demand has turned into a spectre. Trials have been plagued by technical difficulties and more importantly, have failed to provide sound commercial justification for the introduction of video-on-demand. Whilst many US trials of VOD have reported significant viewer uptake, most trialists admit that consumers are unwilling to pay for such services at a level that would make them economically attractive to the operator.'

This leaves PC technology as the next most important potential source of interactivity. See Table 5.4.

Table 5.4 Relative penetration of PCs compared with televisions, 1994–5

COUNTRY	HOUSEHOLD (MILLIONS)	% WITH PCs	% WITH CABLE TV	% WITH SATELLITE TV
UK	22	17	5	11

Cable operators have found that children are now viewing less television because they are migrating to the Internet. It is therefore hoped that a combined TV/Internet access platform will entice them back to television.

■ Diffusion of PC technology

As can be seen above, consumers are still unsure of the interactive medium for buying and selling. It is therefore fair to assume that consumer uptake of interactive technology will be gradual.

'There is no reason to believe that interactive applications will display anything other than the standard product life cycle trend. Early adopters will be the first to enter the market. Uptake will occur slowly in the early part of the cycle before the mass market consciousness, and price range is breached and the product takes off.' (Samways 1995)

This fits in neatly with Rogers (1962) who found that, in general, innovators think for themselves and try new things where relevant; the early adopters, who have status in society, are opinion leaders and they adopt successful products, making them acceptable and respectable; the early majority, who are more conservative and have slightly above average status, are more deliberate and only adopt products that have social approval; the late majority, who are below average status and sceptical, adopt products much later; the laggards, with low status and income are the last to adopt products. In his current treatise, Rogers (1995) also mentions the attributes of innovations and their rates of adoption.

Rogers has picked out the five perceived attributes of innovations.

□ 1 Relative advantage

This is a function of how much better an idea is compared to that which it replaces.

□ 2 Economic factors

Aspects of status and incentives can add to an innovator's perceived relative advantage.

□ 3 Comparability

The innovation must have some comparability with the current values and beliefs in society. Its needs and the way previous innovations are adopted generally influence the rate of adoption positively. For instance, videos are currently used by the majority of the population. Any innovation such as better picture quality, or longer taping times, have to fit in with the current technology. In other words, it is better to have incremental innovation. This has been illustrated by the way in which the general population is unwilling to change from the tape format to the video-disc format even though the latter offers a better quality of pictures. Gradual upgrading is also often preferable to drastic change in the use of software on personal computers.

□ 4 Complexity

The complexity of an innovation is often negatively related to an innovation's rate of adoption.

□ 5 Trialability and observability

The ability to be able to trial a particular innovation, such as the Internet, is of particular importance to early adopters as they do not usually have peers to ask for advice, and with the medium being interactive, observability is not an issue. However, observability may be important when a complex product such as a new combine harvester is launched on to the market.

If previous examples are anything to go by, broad adoption may be decades off. According to government statistics, in 1976 only 50 per cent of households had a telephone – 100 years after it was invented. By 1992, the telephone was a fixture in 89 per cent of UK homes.

This seems to be supported by the current Mintel (1996) report *Multimedia – The Domestic Market Forecast.*

This penetration seems rather slow, particularly with high level of sales. According to Mintel, with obsolescence rates high compared to other durables, the replacement market is very important in the sector. Some computers are still a minority interest, and only 42 per cent of the population are at least interested in the technology (Table 5.5). The Technocrats are ABC1s and often have the funds to purchase computers. Still, eight million households amount to a third of the household population.

■ The move towards globalisation

The above discussion underlines the importance of globalisation of *certain segments* of the market at a low cost via the Internet. Many business decisions taken within organisations in the 1990s have to be taken with the view that

Table 5.5 Household ownership of home computers, 1995–9

	1995	1996	1997	1998	1999
Household (millions)	26.0	27.0	29.0	30.0	31.0
Household Owned (millions)	24.6	24.8	25.0	25.1	25.3
Households Owning Computers (millions)	6.4	6.7	7.3	7.5	7.8

companies are indeed competing in a world without borders. The ease of communications and the promise of speed in the future renders the world borderless. Currently the large multinationals have been truly global in their search for large and mass markets. The new age threatens fragmentation. Conversely for the larger multinationals, the speed of information processing allows a global approach to the provision of services. Segal-Horn (1993) shows the potential for scale and scope economies in different service sectors aiming to be players on an international arena (see Figure 5.9).

In the 'softer' sectors where information transference is important, i.e. most of the services in the right-hand side of the diagram, there is also great potential for economies of scope. For instance, professional service firms such as accountants, surveyors or software programmers could have shared teams of expertise across national offices. For hotel chains or airlines, however, world-wide reservation systems allow flexibility for the consumer and instant information access for the companies. Much of the 'back-office' work in services therefore can now be located anywhere in the world. The provision of large databases also allows the potential for tracking individual customers, as discussed earlier in the chapter (the reader is also referred to Chapter 9 where intellectual property rights are discussed in this context).

In order to exploit the notion of economies of scope (see also Chapter 2.8), it may be worthwhile considering an IT Adjacency map produced by Houghton *et al.* (1996) (see Figure 5.10). They argue that the proposed map represents a development of existing classification schemes in that it accommodates both commodity and industry based classification systems. They feel that the

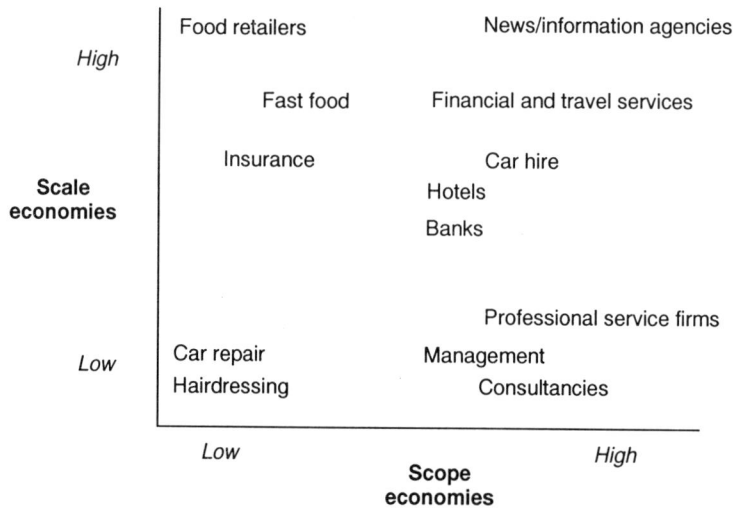

Figure 5.9   Potential for scale and scope economies in different service businesses

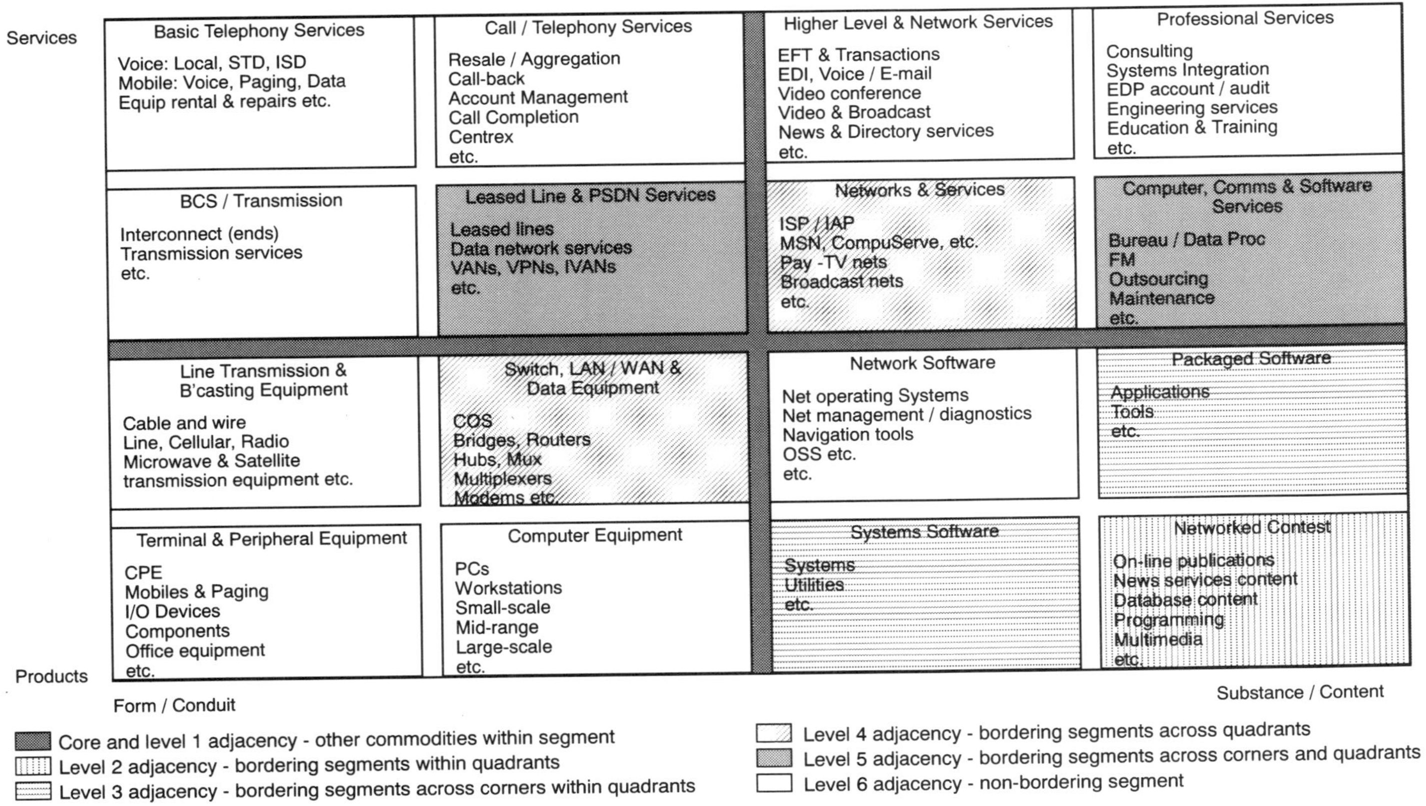

Services

Basic Telephony Services	Call / Telephony Services	Higher Level & Network Services	Professional Services
Voice: Local, STD, ISD Mobile: Voice, Paging, Data Equip rental & repairs etc.	Resale / Aggregation Call-back Account Management Call Completion Centrex etc.	EFT & Transactions EDI, Voice / E-mail Video conference Video & Broadcast News & Directory services etc.	Consulting Systems Integration EDP account / audit Engineering services Education & Training etc.

BCS / Transmission	Leased Line & PSDN Services	Networks & Services	Computer, Comms & Software Services
Interconnect (ends) Transmission services etc.	Leased lines Data network services VANs, VPNs, IVANs etc.	ISP / IAP MSN, CompuServe, etc. Pay -TV nets Broadcast nets etc.	Bureau / Data Proc FM Outsourcing Maintenance etc.

Line Transmission & B'casting Equipment	Switch, LAN / WAN & Data Equipment	Network Software	Packaged Software
Cable and wire Line, Cellular, Radio Microwave & Satellite transmission equipment etc.	COS Bridges, Routers Hubs, Mux Multiplexers Modems etc.	Net operating Systems Net management / diagnostics Navigation tools OSS etc. etc.	Applications Tools etc.

Terminal & Peripheral Equipment	Computer Equipment	Systems Software	Networked Content
CPE Mobiles & Paging I/O Devices Components Office equipment etc.	PCs Workstations Small-scale Mid-range Large-scale etc.	Systems Utilities etc.	On-line publications News services content Database content Programming Multimedia etc.

Products

Form / Conduit — Substance / Content

Core and level 1 adjacency - other commodities within segment
Level 2 adjacency - bordering segments within quadrants
Level 3 adjacency - bordering segments across corners within quadrants
Level 4 adjacency - bordering segments across quadrants
Level 5 adjacency - bordering segments across corners and quadrants
Level 6 adjacency - non-bordering segment

Figure 5.10 IT product/service map
Source: Houghton *et al.*, 'Mapping Information Technology', *Futures*, vol. 28, no. 10, 1996.

proposed map is two-dimensional and opens up the possibility of exploring relationships between products and services, market segments and industries. For example it is possible to explore 'convergence' in terms of economies of scope. These economies may derive from process or product similarities. In so far as the structure of the IT map embraces the continuum between process and commodity criteria for industrial and commodity classification, it is able to accommodate this range of sources of scope economies. Figure 5.9 shows where the closest overlap is, in offering the greatest potential for economies of scope. This proposed map transcends simple, one-dimensional hierarchical classification schemes and provides unique opportunities to explore interrelationships between products and services, market segments and industries. The complexity and, at the same time, simplicity of this approach, shows that many markets are now evolving along an information-led pathway, fuelled by the underlying IT framework shown above. Companies such as British Airways and some of the bigger software houses subcontract much of their information-based work to smaller companies in India. In *The Age of Discontinuity*, Drucker (1969) developed the idea of *knowledge work*. He considered that knowledge was emerging as the critical resource in many economies. Nearly thirty years later, the new technologies are helping to redefine market structures for knowledge-based activity on a global scale. This intensification of global activity in *both* manufacturing and services is creating innovative and unusual openings for differing types of marketing strategies.

■ Where next?

In the light of the discussions above, it is difficult to predict how the marketing environment will evolve over the next ten years. It is clear, however, that the standardised ways of buying and selling are going to change considerably, and closer thought is going to have to be paid by companies to becoming global and at the same time developing relationship marketing skills. The first attempts on the Internet by many companies have not exactly been a roaring success. Note Friar (1996), writing in the *Daily Express*:

> 'Natwest, like Barclays before them, have been seduced by the shimmering surf on the superhighway. Today, the bank opens Buckingham Gate, a virtual shopping mall with posh logo, coat of arms and a hat-full of high-class tenants including Natwest's own classy Coutt's division. Good luck to them. But a successful presence on the Net needs more than a pretty home page and a razzmatazz launch. It must be nurtured and tended, just like a conventional shop. Among the retailers in Barclay Square is Victoria Wine. Yesterday it was still making the same special offer as four months ago: 'Spicy wines to keep out the winter chill'. In the real world, the temperature was 22 deg.F. This, alas, is typical. The motto of the superhighway seems to be 'Launch it and forget it.'

Hoffman and Novak (1996) mention that the Internet, because of its 'open architecture' system, is more inclusive and offers numerous advantages over private networks. None of these mechanisms for facilitating commerce electronically has the same far-reaching scope and potential for the transformation of the business function as does the Worldwide Web.

They go on to produce a comprehensive diagram showing the dynamic/static and impersonal/personal links between different types of media. Figure 5.11 shows this.

They conclude by saying that much of the commercial success of the Internet will depend on the consumers' ability to achieve flow, i.e. visiting sites, repeated behaviour, scanning, etc. The author believes that the next stage of marketing is likely to involve the consumer to an unprecedented degree, mainly because technology will improve and offer this facility. However, marketers may face a challenge where markets are defined along two main segments:

1. The technology-literate populace who have access to PCs
2. The conventional majority

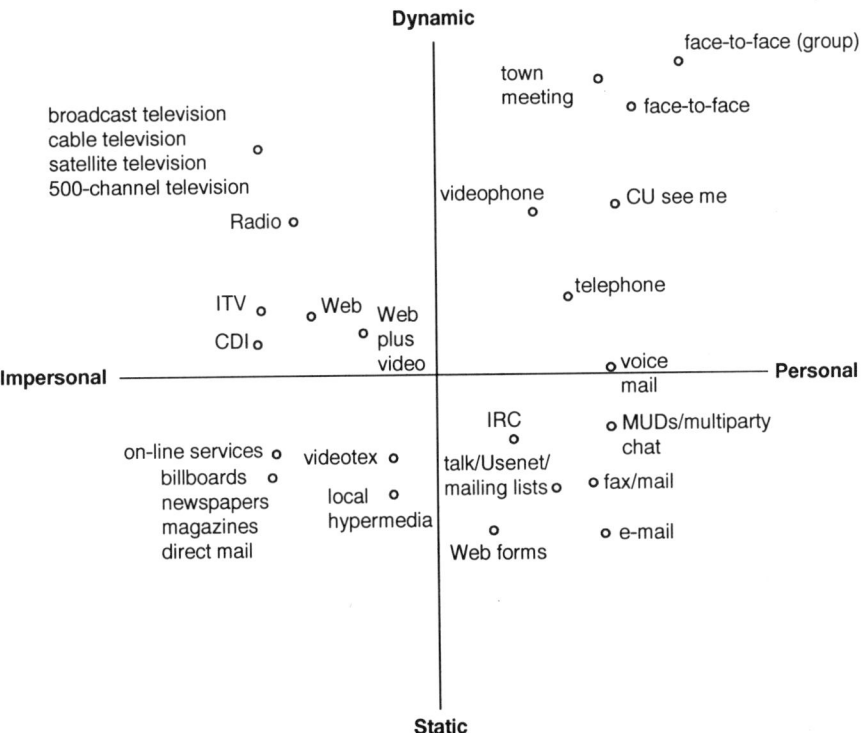

Figure 5.11   Media typology based on objective characteristics
Source: Hoffman and Novak, 'Marketing in Hypermedia, Computer-Mediated Environment: Conceptual Foundations', *Journal of Marketing*, vol. 60, July 1996.

For the technology-literate populace the model consumer and firm interaction as proposed by Hoffman and Novak (1996) based on Steuer's model (1992) is the likely outcome. The big change is the interactivity with the medium (the machine) and *through* the medium (i.e. person interactivity). See Figure 5.12.

This is a fundamental shift from the concept of the Four P's and the current views of market planning and control. In the future it is likely that place may be unimportant as consumers roam the Internet looking for bargains. Price, promotion and product strategies may have to be drastically altered if consumer interactivity is allowed. Currently, complaints about products are made to the retailer and manufacturer in person or by letter. Consider the implications of a one-to-many communication via the mailing system on the Internet!

It is likely that, for the conventional majority, the conventional marketing approaches will suffice well into the next century. Until consumers are happy with, and able to enter, a virtual world the new age of marketing is unlikely to touch the general population. The brave new interactive marketing world will only appear once the Internet is freely accessible, is easy to use, the infrastructure offers speed of access and interactivity and it is affordable by the majority of the world's population.The move towards market fragmenta-

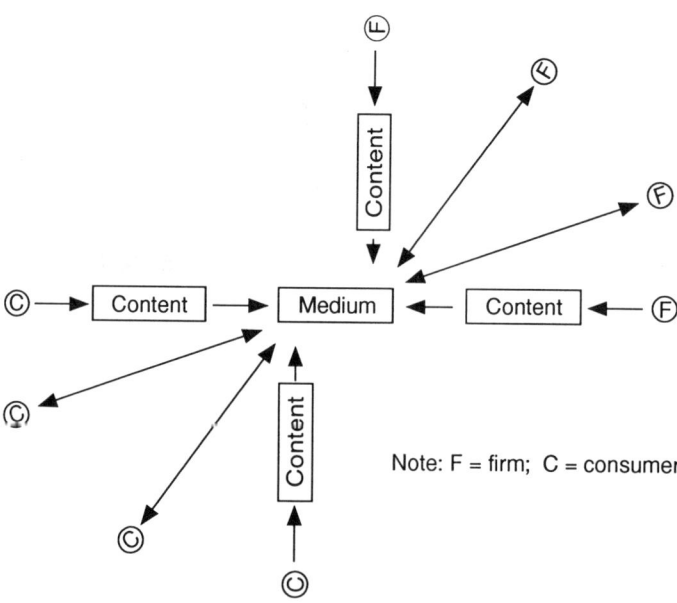

Figure 5.12   A model of marketing communications in a hypermedia CME
Source: Hoffman and Novak, 'Marketing in Hypermedia, Computer-Mediated Environment: Conceptual Foundations', *Journal of Marketing*, vol. 60, July 1996.

tion and globalisation, nonetheless, is inevitable. The simple fact is that there are no easy answers for the marketer. He or she has to be vigilant and embrace the new postmodern world of marketing where certainties no longer exist and be aware of the marketing possibilities on offer, without compromising years of achievement through conventional marketing strategies. 'Ask not what marketing can do for you, but what you can do for marketing!'

(Ashok Ranchhod would like to acknowledge the help given to him in the compilation of this chapter by Mike Jubb and Adam Palmer.)

■ 5.10 Questions for discussion

1. How has direct marketing contributed to the growth of the business?
2. What possibilities does the informational database offer to David Price?
3. Consider the marketing strategies that David Price could follow in the future through the Internet.
4. What possible advantages would interactive marketing offer traditional insurance companies?
5. 'Marketing means communication'. Discuss.

■ Bibliography

Baird, R., 'Surf See and Sound in a Shopping Dream', *The Guardian*, 10 August 1996.
Booz and Hamilton 1996 in *Cyber Atlas* 'Agents' Interstellar [http://www.cyberatlas.com/agentsd.html].
Brown, S., *Postmodern Marketing* (London and New York: Routledge, 1995).
Brownlie, D. and Saren, M., 'The Four Ps of the Marketing Concept: Prescriptive, Polemical, Permanent and Problematical', *European Journal of Marketing*, vol. 26, no. 4 (1992) pp. 34–47.
Church, R., 'Mass Marketing Motor Cars in Britain before 1950', in *The Rise and Fall of Mass Marketing*, edited by Tedlow, R. S. and Jones, G. (London: Routledge, 1993).
'Computer Intelligence Infocorp', in *Cyber Atlas*, Electronic Commerce I/PRO, June 1996 [http://www.cyberatlas.com/emoney.html].
Cowe, R., 'The Shrinking Suppliers in the Strategy for Growth', *The Guardian* 27 August 1996.
Drucker, P., *The Age of Discontinuity* (New York: Harper Row, 1969).
'FIND/SVP (1995) Study' in *Cyber Atlas* 'Agents' Interstellar, 22 April 1996 [http://www.cyberatlas.com/agents.html]. [FIND/SVP = telephone consultancy].
Friar, B., 'Barclays Discovers Virtual Reality Bytes', *Daily Express*, 27 March 1996, p. 47.
Gummesson, E., 'The New Marketing – Developing Long-Term Interactive Relationships', *Long Range Planning*, vol. 20, no. 4 (1987) pp. 10–20.
'GVU4 Internet User Survey', in *Cyber Atlas* 'Agents' Interstellar, 22 April 1996 [http://www.cyberatlas.com/agents.html] [GVU4 = Graphics, Visualization Users 4th Survey].

Handy, C., *The Age of Unreason*, (London: Business Books, 1991).
Hoffman, D. L., and Novak, P. K., 'Marketing in Hypermedia, Computer-Mediated Environments. Conceptual Foundations', *Journal of Marketing*, vol. 60 (July 1996), pp. 50–68.
Houghton, J. W., Pucar, M. and Knox, C., 'Mapping Information Technology' *Futures*, vol. 28, no. 10 (1996) pp. 903–17.
Kleiner, K., 'Banking on Electronic Money', *New Scientist*, vol. 146, no. 1992, 8 April 1996.
Kotler, P., *Marketing Management: Analysis, Planning and Control* (Englewood Cliffs, N.J: Prentice-Hall Inc., 1995).
Lansley, S., '*After the Goldrush. The Trouble with Affluence: 'Consumer Capitalism' and the Way Forward* (London: Century, 1994).
Levy, S., 'The Year of the Internet', *Newsweek*, 25 Dec. 1995 /1 Jan. 1996, pp. 22–26.
Matthews, R., 'Panning for Data Gold', *New Scientist*, vol. 150, no. 2031 (1996) pp. 30–3.
Medley, G. J., 'Strategic Planning for the World Wildlife Fund', *Long Range Planning*, vol. 21, no. 1 (1988) pp. 46–54.
Mintel Report (1996) 'Computer Retailing' (Forecast), 1 May 1996.
Modahl, M. A. and Eischler, S. H., 'People and Technology Strategies', *The Forrester Report*, vol. 2, no. 5 (1995) pp. 1–11.
Moody, G., 'Searching the Web for Gigabucks', *New Scientist*, vol. 150, no. 2024, 6 April 1996.
Mueller-Heumann, G., 'Marketing and Technology Shifts in the 1990's: Market Fragmentation and Mass Customisation', *Journal of Marketing Management*, vol. 8, no. 4 (1992) pp. 303–14.
Neilson Media, in *Cyber Atlas 'Agents' Interstellar*, 22 April 1996.
Patron, M., Editorial: 'The Future of Marketing Databases', *The Journal of Database Marketing*, vol. 4, no. 1 (1996) pp. 6–10.
Piercy, N., *Market-Led Strategic Change* (Oxford: Butterworth-Heinemann, 1992).
Ramprasad, A., 'A Methodology for Data Mining', *The Journal of Database Marketing*, vol. 4, no. 1 (1996) pp. 65–75.
Rapp, S. and Collins, T. L., *Beyond Maximarketing: The New Power of Caring and Daring* (New York: McGraw-Hill, 1994).
Rogers, E. M., *Diffusion of Innovations*, (New York: The Free Press, 1962).
Rogers, E. M., *Diffusion of Innovations*, 4th edn (New York and London: The Free Press, 1995).
Samways, A., *Interactive Advertising* (London: F.T. Telecoms and Media Publishing, 1995).
Scales, I., 'Surely Some Mistake?', *Communications International*, 9 February 1996, p. 44.
Segal-Horn, S., 'The Internationalisation of Service Firms', *Advances in Strategic Management*, vol. 9 (1993) pp. 31–55.
Sharrock, S., 'The Confused World of Cable', *Voice*, vol. 3, no. 4 (1996) pp. 26–8.
Sloan, A. P. Jnr, *My Life with General Motors* (London: Pan Books, 1967).
Steinberg, S. G., 'Get Ready for Web Objects', *Wired*, February 1996, pp. 52–5.
Steuer, J., 'Defining Virtual Reality: Dimensions Determining Telepresence', *Journal of Communication*, vol. 42, no. 4 (1992) pp. 73–9.
Stone, B., *Successful Direct Marketing Methods* (Lincolnwood, Illinois, USA: NTC Business Books, 1988).
Stone, M., Davies, D. and Bond, A., *Direct Hit: Winning Direct Marketing Campaigns* (London: Pitman, 1995).
Tedlow, R., *New and Improved: The Story of Mass Marketing in America* (New York: Basic Books; Oxford: Heinemann, 1988).
Tedlow, R., 'The Fourth Phase of Marketing', in *The Rise and Fall of Mass Marketing*, edited by Tedlow, R. S. and Jones, G. (London: Routledge, 1993).
Thalheimer, P., in Cyber Atlas Interstellar, 22 April 1996.
Thomas, M. J. 'Marketing – in Chaos or Transition?', in D. Brownlie *et al.* (eds), *Rethinking Marketing* (Coventry: Warwick Business School Research Bureau, 1993).

Upton, D. M. and McAfee, A., 'The Virtual Factory', *Harvard Business Review*, July–August 1996, pp. 123–33.

Venkatesh, A., Sherry, J. F. and Firat, A. F., 'Postmodernism and the Marketing Imaginary', *International Journal of Research in Marketing*, vol. 10, no. 3 (1993) pp. 215–23.

Weisman, D. E., Trevino, V. B. and Sweet, S. R., 'Money and Technology Strategies', *The Forrester Report*, vol. 1, no. 7 (1996) pp. 1-11.

Zavistovich, A., 'In Cable Modems: The Race for Your PC Gains Speed – Part 2', *International Cable*, 9 April 1996, p. 54.

CHAPTER 6

The human impact of organisational change

Brian Thornton

■ 6.1 Introduction: 'May you live in interesting times'

To the ancient Chinese, living in 'interesting times' was something to be avoided at all costs. For interesting times bring change, and change, in a feudal society, brings danger. To be cursed with living in interesting times was a terrifying prospect.

Few would disagree with the statement that the times in which we now live are 'interesting' and filled with challenge and uncertainty. Never before has the pace of change been so constant, unremitting or all-pervading. We now confidently challenge the traditional values and beliefs our parents and grandparents held dear and the structure and fabric of our society reflects these changing attitudes. With marriage on the decline and divorce becoming more common, the resulting single parents must find new ways to combine work with raising children and innovative working patterns have emerged to accommodate them. Computer technology now affects all aspects of our lives. But while technology has improved the world in which we live, it has not been without cost. Many workers have faced redundancy and long-term unemployment as their jobs have been replaced by robotised and computerised systems. As Western countries move from manufacturing to service economies, so trades union membership has declined and with it union power and influence. Political changes have opened up new business opportunities in the former Eastern Bloc and the European Union now provides a huge single market of consumers whose numbers will continue to increase as more countries join.

But what impact are these interesting times having in the workplace? How has work, and in particular employer and employee relationships and attitudes to work, changed in recent years? To appreciate the true nature and extent of these changes one must first understand the historical and social context within which work has evolved. This chapter opens by briefly considering the development of management theory and its influence on the way people are treated at work. It then discusses the development of the personnel function, whose traditional role has long been to act as an intermediary between management and the workforce, and traces its evolution into human resource management within this theoretical framework. External pressures for change are then discussed together with the responses that organisations are taking as they strive to achieve 'flexibility' in their employment practices and to survive in these turbulent times. The chapter concludes with a discussion of the human impact of these changes, a case study and review questions.

■ 6.2 Management theories and their evolution

Because so little was written about management practice and theory before the early 1900s, it is tempting to think that management is a relatively modern concept. However, the logistical and human problems inherent in the management of people were as familiar to the pharaohs who built the pyramids as they are to today's production or personnel managers. Management is not new but analysing and studying it is.

■ The classical school

Classical theorists, of whom Fayol, Taylor and Urwick are typical, working during the early years of the twentieth century, sought universal principles or 'rules' of management practice that could be applied to good effect within any organisation. They argued that through a clear understanding of an organisation's purpose, objectives could be set that would clarify duties and responsibilities at all levels within a hierarchy of formal relationships. While such general principles gave guidance on the structuring of organisations, they failed to view employees as independent and variable elements in the system, nor did they take account of the different technologies and types of production system in use.

Frederick Winslow Taylor's contribution to management was aimed at improving productivity through breaking down complex tasks into separate components each of which could then be analysed to find the most efficient method of carrying it out. A believer in the rational-economic needs theory of motivation, Taylor advocated enhanced financial rewards for increased production. Taylor's methods proved very successful at increasing productivity but his main failing was his lack of understanding of human behaviour at work and the social aspects of employment.

Henry Ford applied Taylorist 'scientific management' principles to great effect at his huge River Rouge factory in Detroit. Ford de-skilled the work of craftsmen by breaking down their jobs into separate stages, each of which could be carried out by an unskilled worker using a specially designed, single-purpose machine. Obsessed with the need to control the pace at which his employees worked, Ford then revolutionised manufacture by introducing the moving assembly line to dictate the speed of their labour. However, in a similar response to that which met Taylor's new methods of working, his employees' reaction to the tyranny of the assembly line was to seek more satisfying employment elsewhere. Faced with unacceptably high employee turnover, Ford eventually had to double his rates of pay in order to attract workers back to his factory (see also Chapters 5.3 and 7.1).

■ The human relations school

The main preoccupation of the classical school of writers lay in organisational structures and methods of controlling workers. It was during the 1920s that researchers began to look at the social aspects of the working environment and at how people behave when they are at work. The best known research into these fields was carried out from 1927 to 1937 at Western Electric's Hawthorne Works in Chicago by a team led by Elton Mayo, an Australian-born associate professor of industrial research at Harvard University.

What the Hawthorne experiments showed was that the employees selected for the studies responded to the interest that was being shown in them by management, perceiving themselves to be members of a team of individuals as opposed to being mere 'cogs in the machine'. Consequently, their output rose irrespective of changes made to their working conditions leading Mayo to become highly critical of Taylor's principles of scientific management based on worker self-interest. Perhaps his main contribution to management debate was to demonstrate how sound principles of management–worker communication and the motivation of individuals can have a significant impact upon an organisation's performance. This theme of linking management and employee behaviour to 'bottom-line' performance is one to which we shall return when we consider the emergence of human resource management.

■ Neo-human relations

Since the Hawthorne conclusions were published, a more psychological approach has been taken to individual worker motivation and adjustment within the workplace. The best known of these later contributions came from Maslow (1943) who suggested that everyone is driven to satisfy a 'hierarchy of needs'. Once basic physiological needs such as warmth, food, and a safe environment have been satisfied, the higher needs of love, esteem and realising one's optimum potential are released. Drucker (1974) suggests, however, that as a need is satisfied, ever-increasing incentives are required to maintain the same level of satisfaction. Thus any additional financial rewards paid to employees will eventually be viewed as rights and entitlements and no longer serve to motivate.

Peters and Waterman (1982) showed that many low-status workers, treated by their employers as capable of performing only menial and low-paid jobs, nevertheless take on high levels of responsibility and achieve remarkable goals in their hobbies and leisure-time activities. They argue that, by changing their management styles, employers can tap into the latent talent within their existing work force and use it to the greater benefit of the organisation.

■ 6.3 Personnel management and the emergence of human resourcing

■ The development of the personnel function

The Institute of Personnel and Development defines the personnel profession as having as its principal aim the task of ensuring the optimum use of human resources to the mutual benefit of the enterprise, each person and the community at large (Armstrong 1991). Torrington and Hall (1995) view personnel management as 'a series of activities which first enable working people and the business which uses their skills to agree about the objectives and nature of their working relationship and, secondly, ensures that the agreement is fulfilled'.

To achieve these aims personnel specialists assist organisations in recruiting, selecting, developing and motivating workers, and advise them on the creation and maintenance of appropriate structures and cultures within which people can work together with a high level of commitment towards clearly communicated organisational objectives. Employees must also be assessed and developed to make the best use of their skills and talents within a complex legal framework governing the employment relationship and the quality and safety of working life.

Until the 1980s, the role of the personnel function was mainly administrative and advisory, dealing with employee welfare, consultation and employment legislation. With the growth of the 'enterprise culture' and the market economy in the 1980s, personnel managers began to make a more strategic contribution to the development of their organisations. Managers looked towards Japanese management methods and philosophies for their inspiration, and writers such as Peters (1989) stressed the importance of creating positive corporate cultures that thrived on, rather than felt threatened by, change. It was during this period that the concept of human resource management (HRM) first emerged in the UK.

■ Human resource management

The term 'human resource management' (HRM) came into common usage during the 1980s and is used to describe a shift of emphasis or change in direction of personnel practice. Storey (1995), who also wrote the first British book on HRM, defines it as 'a distinctive approach to employment management which seeks to achieve competitive advantage through the strategic deployment of a highly committed and capable workforce, using an integrated array of cultural, structural and personnel techniques'. Storey describes HRM as enshrining the basic belief that it is the people in a successful organisation that differentiate it from its competitors. As such they should be nurtured so as to increase their commitment to the organisational objectives. In view of the importance of achieving competitive advantage through people, the HR specialist, if not actually sitting on the board, should at least contribute to the strategic direction of the organisation and manage cultural change with a view to achieving unity of purpose and a more flexible workforce.

Beardwell and Holden (1994) trace the roots of HRM to United States businesses in the 1950s, pre-dating its emergence in the UK by 30 years. They see international competition during the recession of the early 1980s and the need to increase American workers' productivity mainly against that of their Japanese counterparts, as encouraging its growth. Closely associated with this was the need to reduce conflict in the workplace and to motivate both employers and employees towards the common purpose of achieving organisational objectives. In the UK, government intervention in labour relations during the Thatcher years gave further impetus to the development of more employer-focused employment policies and two major reports that were highly critical of UK companies' record on management training and development focused directors' attention on to human resourcing issues (Handy 1987, and Constable and McCormick 1987). Although the validity of many of Peters and Waterman's (1982) conclusions regarding 'excellence' can now be challenged, there is no denying the effect they had in changing managers' attitudes towards worker involvement and commitment and in encouraging the fashion for 'leaner, fitter organisations' with 'empowered' employees. This trend towards flatter, less bureaucratic structures (in which employees who deal directly with the customer or end-user of the service provided have the authority to make important decisions without referring them upwards through successive layers of management) is aimed at speeding response times to problems and thus improving customer care.

In larger organisations in particular, the activities of personnel practitioners have thus become more closely identified with strategic objectives and with the creation and management of appropriate cultures and structures for their achievement. At the same time there is a far greater emphasis upon the 'bottom line', financial contribution that personnel policy and procedure can make.

For our purposes, then, HRM can perhaps best be seen as a logical development of personnel management in response to changes in the environment in which organisations now operate. Whatever one's personal standpoint on the personnel management versus HRM issue, the debate has stimulated a much needed reappraisal of the employment relationship and its effect upon employee commitment and motivation.

■ 6.4 External pressures for organisational change

Having discussed how the HRM approach arose in response to changing conditions in the business environments in both the USA and in Britain, we can now consider the effect environmental factors are having on human resourcing in organisations.

The PEST analytical model (introduced in Chapter 2.2) is often modified by human resourcing specialists to 'PESTLE' so as to ensure that important Legal and Ecological/Ethical factors are not overlooked. This framework can now be used to look at some examples of the external pressures for change that affect organisations (see also Chapters 1.3 and 1.8).

■ Political and legal factors

Governments are elected to achieve political, social and economic objectives based upon their particular ideologies. In the pursuit of these they can exercise a unique influence over the way in which organisations are run.

At a local government level, council policies made within political, administrative, financial and legal constraints imposed by central government, can substantially affect employment within their areas. A town centre bypass, for example, while greatly improving the quality of life of local residents may take away the passing trade upon which local businesses depend.

In the UK successive industrial relations legislation has, since 1979, greatly reduced the power and influence of the trades union movement giving managers greater freedom to exercise 'macho' management styles over a largely cowed and submissive workforce. Much of this intervention has been aimed at removing barriers to competition and efficiency. By abolishing the Wages Councils, for example, which set minimum wages for many low-paid jobs particularly in the catering and clothing industries, the government allowed market forces to prevail giving free rein for unscrupulous employers to take advantage of unemployed people desperate for work at any price.

Government control of privatised utilities such as British Telecom and British Gas has increased in recent years with the appointment of regulatory bodies that can influence pricing policy, control 'unfair' competition and determine the structure of the industry. When the Ofgas regulator reduced the price of transmission of competitors' gas in mains owned by British Gas TransCo in 1996, the immediate reaction of British Gas was to talk of the 10,000 redundancies that would result from the decision to curtail its profits.

European restrictions on the volume of Japanese imports have led to inward investment by Japanese motor and electronics companies. These new factories have created thousands of new, high-technology jobs in the former industrial heartlands that were particularly badly hit by the closure of traditional industries such as shipbuilding and steel manufacture (see Chapter 10).

Decisions of the smaller courts can also send shock-waves through the most powerful and established industries even though they do not set a precedent. When a jury in Florida in August 1996 awarded a retired air traffic controller $750,000 damages for lung cancer against BAT, the manufacturers of the 'Lucky Strike' cigarettes he had smoked throughout his adult life, billions of dollars were wiped off tobacco company share values overnight in New York and London. The size of the award was of little significance to a company that made a profit of £1.6 billion from the sale of tobacco products in 1995 and which spends £50 million each year fighting such court actions. The important issue was the message given to the industry that it was no longer invincible.

■ Economic factors

The previous section showed how government policy can affect economic activity and exert an important influence on the economic environment in which an organisation operates. At a more local level, an organisation's physical location can have a major impact on its fortunes. With vastly improved transportation systems and telecommunications networks, location close to sources of raw materials is not now so important for many businesses, particularly those in the service sector. Groupings of industries nevertheless still occur, as, for example, with the high-technology industries that have sprung up in Silicon Valley, Palo Alto, California, the Sophia Antipolis business park near Nice in the South of France and along the M4 corridor in the UK. These thriving areas enjoy the benefit of higher wage levels, which in turn give local consumers higher levels of disposable income. Other, more traditional 'metal bashing' industries have been attracted into areas of high unemployment and urban decay such as the north-east of England and South Wales, by the availability of development grants, green-field sites with planning consent and plentiful supplies of cheap, skilled and reliable labour.

Organisations have no direct control over national economic factors such as economic growth, unemployment levels, demographic trends, the balance of payments deficit and levels of taxation. During periods of high unemployment it is tempting for companies to become more relaxed about recruitment and selection, but a surplus of job applicants does not necessarily mean that people with the required skills and potential will be available for hire. Fluctuations in exchange rates can have a major impact on company profitability as exports become either cheaper or more expensive in foreign markets.

As companies increasingly become globalised in their outlook, so they become more susceptible to world economic trends. International economic communities such as the European Union and economic accords like the former General Agreement on Trade and Tariffs (GATT) (see Chapters 3.1 and 9.3), now replaced by the World Trade Organisation (WTO), must figure in the plans of organisations operating within their ambit. Companies with expatriate employees and overseas subsidiaries must take account of levels of personal and corporate taxation in the countries within which they operate. As demand for goods increases, producers must identify the demand and exploit it. In times of recession companies will aim to survive through greater cost-effectiveness and competition.

■ Sociological factors

The mid-1980s saw a great deal of debate among personnel professionals and academics about the demographic changes taking place in Britain and the impact they would have on the nation's economy. Demographics is the study of population trends using statistics on factors such as births and deaths, age structures of populations and ethnic groups within communities. The much-predicted 'demographic time bomb' refers to the combined effects on society of a reduction in the number of young people coming on to the employment market with the required skills together with a rise in the average age of the working population.

Beardwell and Holden (1994) point out that current European statistics predict a decline of 1.7 per cent per annum in the supply of labour in the age group 20–30 throughout Western Europe. This can be demonstrated by an analysis of the median age of the UK population which has increased from 34.6 in 1980 to 35.9 in 1990 with a predicted rise to 37.7 in 2000. The explanation given is that the increasing proportion of retirements has not been compensated for by an equivalent number of young people entering the labour market. The implication of all this is that employers will increasingly be obliged to seek new, more innovative and 'flexible' ways of staffing their organisations if they are to match the supply of labour to the demand. Typical employer responses have been to increase the recruitment of part-timers and to retain women in the labour force.

Advances in medicine during the twentieth century have increased the life expectancy of the population. With a static or falling population the effect of this is that the proportion of retired people will increase and the proportion of productive or working people will decrease. The working population must, therefore, bear an extra burden through increased taxation of their incomes to provide for old age pensions, health services and care of the elderly and education of the young. As children reach working age they will, if they can find employment, contribute to the nation's wealth. Those who remain unemployed or, as is increasingly the case throughout Europe, opt to remain within further and higher education, only add to the burden of those who are in work.

■ Technological factors

The main problem facing organisations today is not simply the fact that technological change is taking place but rather the rate at which this change is occurring. Adapting the organisation to meet and exploit the technological challenge is a constant headache for human resource managers. Some organisations are better able to adapt than others depending on the environment in which they operate. Thus new technological developments will be more easily assimilated into a high-tech manufacturing company, where change tends to be incremental, than they will in local government or the civil service, for example, where they might involve major organisational responses and/or the adoption of new working methods. Some of the effects of technological change are:

- **The development of new products and services.** Obvious examples include personal computers, mobile telephones, satellite television and telecommunications, fibre optics and software for computer networks. Technological advances in one area can often spin-off into others as was the case with developments in armaments that led to non-stick coatings for frying pans and the networks of US defence computer systems that spawned the Internet.
- **New manufacturing methods.** Manufacturers have been quick to take advantage of new design and production techniques in order to reduce the number of employees, and consequently their wages bills (thus remaining competitive in a global marketplace) and also to improve the quality of their products to keep up with advances made in the Far East. Car production plants today are much more efficient and cost-effective than those in Henry Ford's time. Computerised design and manufacture (CAD/CAM), 'just-in-time' components delivery and robotised assembly have all helped to reduce the time it takes to develop a new model, build a better product and create a safer and more pleasant working environment.
- **New ways of providing services.** Advances in computerised systems and telecommunications have revolutionised retailing and banking. New 'direct banking' services have also appeared which carry out all transactions over the telephone (see Chapters 2 and 4). These services can be situated anywhere, thus relieving the service provider of the need to pay high property charges for prime, high street locations. It can be argued that workers with computers and modems can operate just as effectively from home as from an office and be freed from monotonous, repetitive tasks thus providing new opportunities for more creative working.

It is important that organisations keep up-to-date with technological developments within their industry otherwise they will fall behind their competitors and eventually be forced to modernise or risk going out of business. For new technology to be implemented effectively, new skills will be required within the workforce (see Chapter 4). But how will these new skills be obtained? One option is to develop the company's own employees through a programme of in-service training and education (the so-called 'gamekeeper' approach). The alternative is to attract people who are already suitably qualified and experienced from other organisations (the 'poacher' approach). Both have their merits. The former, more strategic option, has the benefit of developing what has come to be known as a 'learning organisation' that can better respond to organisational change. It is, of course, expensive and time-consuming to implement. The latter option is cheaper and provides a more immediate solution to the problem but without the associated, long-term organisational benefits. Once organisations start poaching their competitor's staff it leads to an inflationary wages spiral with current employers offering improved remuneration packages in an attempt to retain their staff and prospective employers becoming ever more generous as they try to tempt them away.

■ Ecological and ethical factors

One of the most important changes in public attitudes in recent years has been the growing awareness, especially among young people, of the damage being done to the environment by man's activities. People are also becoming more concerned and knowledgeable about business ethics in their roles as employees, investors and customers. Many investors now withdraw their money from institutions which invest in countries with a poor human rights record. Others are prepared to take direct action in an attempt to prevent activities with which they profoundly disagree. Such was the case when quite ordinary people, with no previous involvement in campaigning, blockaded Channel ports in 1995 in an attempt to prevent what they considered to be the unacceptably cruel, live export of farm animals to the Continent.

One thing is clear: organisations, and particularly those operating internationally, can no longer afford to ignore public concerns about the ethics and environmental impact of their activities. Powerful lobbying organisations such as Greenpeace and Friends of the Earth can be relied upon to take very public issue with even the largest multinational companies and, as they demonstrated in the case of French nuclear testing in the South Pacific, will confront and embarrass governments. The potential impact of such adverse publicity upon sales, profitability or tourism revenues is incalculable.

While some companies are no doubt guilty of cynically exploiting the 'green' revolution through the use of spurious or misleading claims, others, which have managed to convince the public of the sincerity of their commitment to reduce pollution or to help Third World communities, have been rewarded with massive sales and huge profits. The trade-off for prospective employees of such companies is the likelihood of their being expected to conform totally to the proprietor's ideology, a role that many find themselves obliged to act out in return for the security of employment in such benevolent dictatorships.

The practical implications of all this are that if organisations seek to prosper in a modern business environment, they must be prepared not only to invest in the latest design and production technologies with a view to minimising waste and energy consumption but also to review the public acceptability of their products, their services and their investment strategies (see Chapter 8).

■ 6.5 The pursuit of flexibility

In 1984, John Atkinson, a research fellow at the Institute of Manpower Studies, published his research into the pressures then influencing the employment plans of UK firms. His paper 'Manpower strategies for flexible organisations' which appeared in the August 1984 edition of *Personnel Management* identified 'core' and 'peripheral' workforces and first coined the expression 'the flexible firm'. Atkinson identified several important common themes influencing the employment plans of UK firms including market stagnation, job loss, uncertainty, technological change and working time.

Atkinson realised that a combination of factors had resulted in firms seeking more effective ways of staffing their organisations. Most importantly he saw that there was a growing need for a workforce that could adapt to unforeseen changes, that could contract as smoothly as it could expand, in which worked time precisely matched job requirements and where unit labour costs could be kept to a minimum. He concluded that firms were actually looking for what he called functional, numerical and financial flexibility (see Figure 6.1).

Atkinson acknowledged that while none of these aspirations was new, there had emerged a growing trend for firms explicitly to seek all three forms of flexibility at the same time, mainly through a change in the ways in which work was organised. This was leading to a new model of employment in which hierarchical structures were being broken up so that different employment policies could be pursued for different groups of workers. The old distinction between 'blue collar' manual and 'white collar' managerial workers was being replaced by a new emphasis on those with 'firm-specific' and those with 'generalist' skills. Firm-specific skills include the sort of jobs that are vital to the organisation and which are difficult to replace from the external labour market. Examples include production managers and maintenance engineers in factories using specialised processes. Generalist skills are those which can more easily be replaced, for example heavy goods vehicle drivers and word processor operators.

Atkinson's now familiar model of these new organisational structures comprises what he calls 'core' and 'peripheral' groups of employees. Core group workers are the full-time, permanent, career employees such as managers, designers, and technicians who, in return for job security and enhanced terms and conditions, accept both short- and long-term functional flexibility. This means that they are expected to perform a wide range of often unrelated tasks according to the demands of the job, to forget the old barriers of demarcation and to work as members of multi-disciplinary project teams. In the longer term they may be expected to undertake retraining or even to abandon existing careers and begin new ones. In short, the firm intends to retain the services of these especially valuable employees by treating them differently from its peripheral workers thereby separating them from the external labour market.

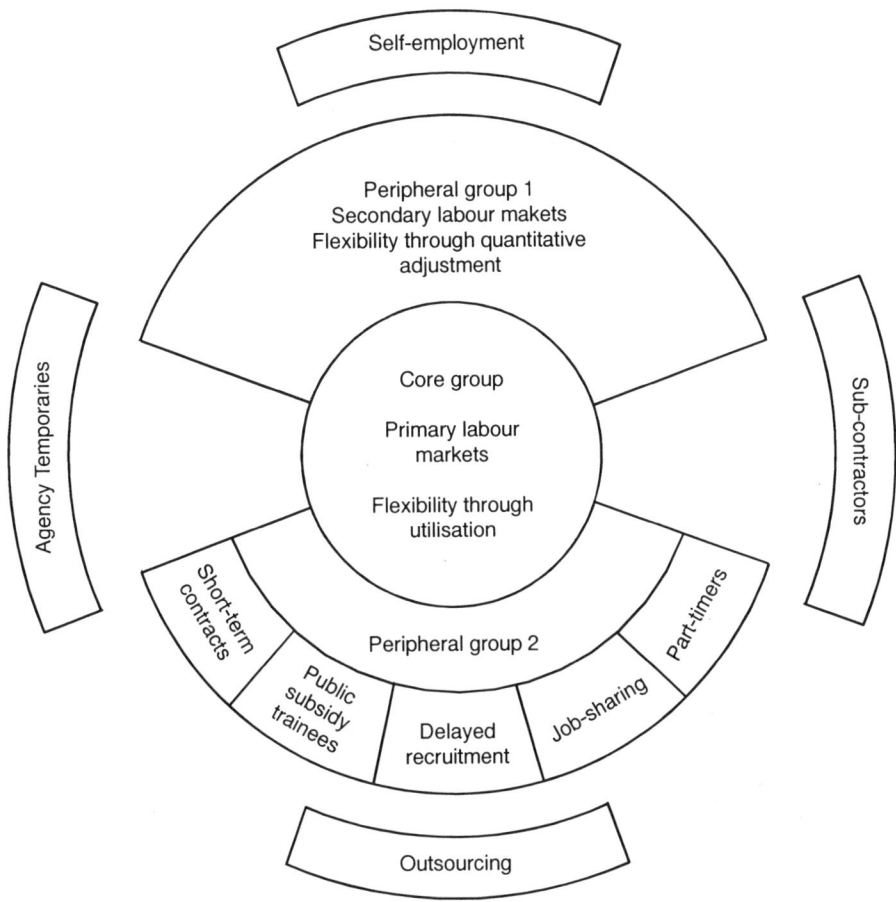

Figure 6.2 **Labour market flexibility in Britain: full and part time employment.**

By contrast, the further away from the core group that the remaining employees fit into the model, the less favourable will be their conditions of employment and job security. At the periphery, workers have jobs and not careers with the company. Their work is non-firm-specific and consequently can be carried out by anyone with the required, more generalised skills within the external labour market.

While the importance of Atkinson's work cannot be denied, it has nevertheless been criticised (notably by Pollert 1988) on the grounds that the pursuit of flexibility, far from being a deliberate strategic thrust underpinned by documented policy, is no more than an *ad hoc* response on the part of employers to changing work circumstances. Despite these criticisms, flexibility is now very much the watchword of British employment practice which many politicians and industrialists claim provides much needed competitive advantage over our European partners with their strong trades unions and high social costs. It can also be argued that the current enthusiasm for flexibility at all costs is simply a result of attempts to introduce Japanese management practices to the UK as the flexible use of labour is a key factor in the global success of Japanese corporations. When British industry was being crippled by successive and bitter strikes over demarcation issues, Japanese workers were being trained to carry out their own tool changes, repairs and statistical process control. For the worker at least, flexibility is a matter of attitude and employers are increasingly keen to recruit workers who are adaptable, open-minded and both willing and able to learn new skills. Employers' attempts to create a multi-skilled workforce within a working culture free from the traditional craft boundaries is evident from job descriptions which increasingly embody generic rather than specific, narrowly-defined duties and responsibilities. It clearly makes more sense, and is considerably less expensive, to employ one multi-skilled maintenance engineer who can be kept fully occupied than to recruit separate electrical, mechanical and hydraulic engineers who will spend much of their time idle.

The extent to which Japanese working practices are being incorporated into British companies is difficult to assess. Whereas in Japan practices such as employee involvement, quality circles, just-in-time manufacture and single-status workforce are elements of an integrated approach to human resource and production management, in the UK a specific technique is more likely to be adopted by a company in an attempt to resolve a particular problem (McKenna 1988). The success of Japanese working practices has to be seen against a national culture which encourages co-operation, working towards a common goal and giving extensive feedback to earlier stages in the production process. It is unrealistic, therefore, to look to the adoption of Japanese methods by British companies as some form of industrial panacea.

■ 6.6 Organisational changes and their human impact

■ Downsizing

One of the criteria for assessing managers' comparative status among their peers used to be the number of staff that they managed. Empire-building was thus a principal concern of management. The oil crisis of the early 1970s, which brought about a fourfold rise in fuel prices, soon made it clear even to casual observers that major changes were imminent in our traditional industries. Devastating as these changes undoubtedly were, most workers understood that they were the unavoidable consequence of global economic circumstances and international competition.

Downsizing (also known as delayering, rightsizing, rationalising, restructuring and a host of other euphemisms for sacking people) is different. Downsizing is based on the belief that the quickest and best way to reduce an organisation's costs is to reduce its payroll. As wages account for approximately 65 per cent of an organisation's costs, shedding staff shows an immediate impact upon its financial performance, provided of course that the work formerly done by these people can be redistributed among the remaining employees. Employers have been quick to take advantage of the fact that during a period of recession when good jobs are difficult to find and when the power of the trades unions has been drastically reduced, most workers will readily agree to take on more duties and responsibilities for no extra pay rather than risk dismissal.

It can be argued that this macho-management trend towards 'flatter, leaner structures at all costs' is largely due to the eagerness of gullible senior managers to implement the latest ideas of fashionable management gurus without thinking through the long-term consequences for their own organisations. In May 1996, Stephen Roach, chief economist at one of America's leading investment banks and a major proponent of downsizing, wrote to his clients, 'I must confess I am now having second thoughts. . ..Tactics of open-ended downsizing and real wage compression are ultimately recipes for industrial extinction.' In an article in *The Sunday Times*, 19 May 1996, journalist David Smith pointed out that the cutting of more than 3 million jobs in British factories since 1979 has apparently achieved a productivity miracle. 'Output per head has risen by 80 per cent. Overall output, however, has barely risen, up by only 8 per cent since mid-1979. British industry is producing roughly the same amount with far fewer workers. However, there is no evidence that those sectors that have pushed through the biggest job cuts have turned in the best productivity.' He concluded that downsizing is not, therefore, the way to achieve greater productivity.

When a company reduces its workforce it takes a number of risks. First it risks losing the trust of the remaining workforce. Employees who have seen the harsh psychological effect of redundancy on their colleagues cannot help feeling demoralised by the experience. Some may be so traumatised that they will seek to leave the organisation as soon as possible to avoid suffering a similar fate. Among those with little option but to remain, some will do their utmost to avoid drawing attention to themselves by keeping a low profile in the hope that any further job cuts will pass them by. Others will do the opposite, displaying what has become known as 'presenteeism' by working excessive hours in an attempt to demonstrate their total commitment to the firm. This has led to increased stress levels, physical illness and broken personal relationships. Risk-taking, innovation and the entrepreneurial attitudes so highly valued by modern employers inevitably suffer and may disappear completely with potentially disastrous consequences for the organisation. And who could blame such employees for developing a cynical mistrust of anything the company tells them in the future?

The other main risk that organisations take with over-enthusiastic downsizing is the loss of experienced employees. The better employers try to avoid making compulsory redundancies wherever possible, preferring to shed staff by 'natural wastage', that is by not recruiting replacements when jobs become vacant due to retirements, resignations and deaths in service. When natural wastage has failed to achieve the required reductions, organisations usually invite voluntary redundancies and early retirements from older employees rather than implement the now old-fashioned 'last in, first out' (LIFO) system. The danger here is that the young, high-flyers who are confident of their ability to secure alternative employment, and the senior, more financially secure employees with years of experience in the job, will be lost. The workers who remain in organisations that have arbitrarily cut out certain levels and jobs are unlikely to be the ones best suited to taking them forward in an uncertain marketplace. This was brought home to an incredulous nation when, in February 1997, South West Trains was forced to cancel trains due to a 'shortage of drivers'. In its enthusiasm to reduce costs the newly formed company had encouraged too many experienced employees to take early retirement and found itself with insufficient drivers to maintain its schedules.

The wholesale redundancies of recent years have given rise to a new workplace phenomenon, the so-called 'survivor syndrome' (in which those fortunate enough to have kept their jobs exhibit decreased motivation, morale and loyalty to the organisation and increased stress levels). Employees who have survived redundancy need to undergo a period of readjustment. Research suggests that survivors seek reassurance that the redundancy programme has ended, clarification of the new skills and behaviours expected of them in the changed organisational culture and confirmation that those who left have received reasonable assistance in finding new employment.

One should be careful, however, not to paint too universally black a picture of the effects of downsizing as, for some people at least, redundancy can provide new and exciting opportunities. For those fortunate enough to receive a generous compensation package, self-employment can be an attractive option. As firms become more flexible they are more likely to buy-in services that previously were provided in-house and this can provide lucrative opportunities for ex-employees to contract their services back to their former employers on a consultancy basis. For others, redundancy has provided the impetus needed to make career or lifestyle changes that previously they could only dream of.

■ New patterns of working

With the return to full employment after the Second World War, the individual's 'right' to permanent, full-time work became enshrined within our culture. A typical working week for a white collar worker was 0900 to 1700 from Monday to Friday with blue-collar workers starting and finishing work slightly earlier. This traditional form of employment is costly and often inconvenient both for employers and employees. New patterns of working have emerged as employers seek the flexibility to take on staff when they need them and to release them when they are no longer required. At the same time employees, who now have far more leisure time, want greater autonomy in the way their work and social lives are integrated.

Traditionally the only alternative to full-time, 'nine to five' working was part-time and/or shift work but over the past few years more and more employers have been offering flexible options to the five-day working week. Originally, such arrangements were rare and restricted to exceptional employees who were unable to conform to traditional patterns of employment. Now, flexible and innovative methods are being used to recruit target groups such as women returners and older workers (See Figures 6.2 and 6.4).

☐ 1 Part-time working

Part-time working has long been viewed as a low-status, secondary form of employment largely because most part-timers are women and pay and conditions have been less favourable than those enjoyed by full-time employees. This perception is changing and on 3 March 1994 the House of Lords ruled that the law on unfair dismissal and redundancy (Employment Protection (Consolidation) Act 1978), discriminated against part-time workers and was in breach of European equality laws. The main reason for this was that, as most

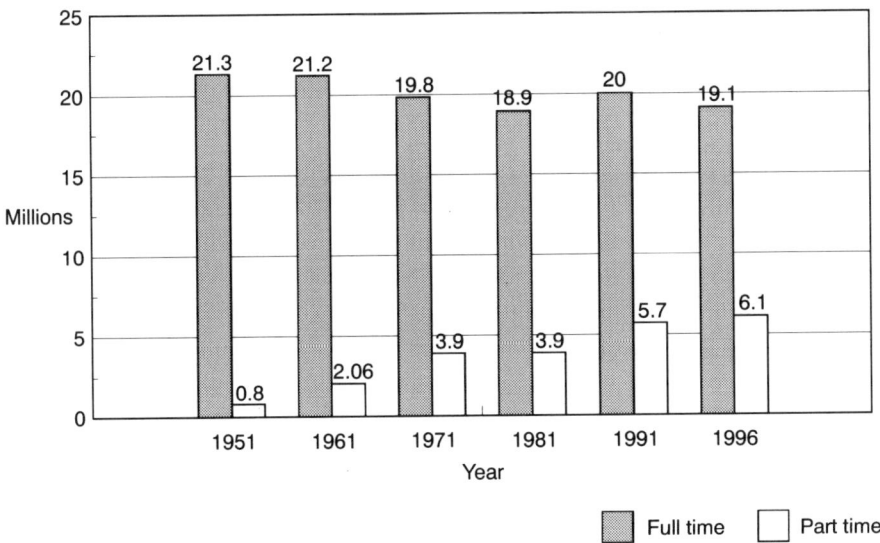

Figure 6.3   Temporary employment 1996

part-time employees are women (approximately 90 per cent), anything that discriminates against part-timers is automatically *indirect discrimination* against women and thus illegal. Part-time employment allows employers to cover absences and peak business hours more easily and to reduce overtime hours worked. Trained part-time employees also provide a pool from which employers can recruit as full-time vacancies become available. Part-time working is particularly attractive to women, students, disabled and older people.

☐ 2 Job sharing

This is a way of working in which usually two people share one full-time job between them, each carrying out half of the duties and receiving half the pay, holidays and other benefits. Job sharing potentially gives access to higher-status, better-paid jobs than are usually available to part-time workers. The way in which a job is shared depends on its particular requirements, the needs of other workers that the job-sharers must satisfy and the personal circumstances of the sharers themselves. This is because different types of job need different amounts of information to be exchanged during the hand-over period. Some may require a few hours per week while others need only a telephone call or a brief note. Common arrangements for sharing include each person working two and a half days per week, one working mornings and the other afternoons and working alternate weeks or months. The advantages claimed for the employer include reduced absenteeism, continuity of cover during holidays and sick leave, a wider range of skills and experience brought to the job and promotion of the image of a 'caring employer'. Against this employers considering introducing job-sharing must consider the increased recruitment and administration costs which they will incur and the additional supervision that will be required. From the employee's perspective this form of working has the advantage of providing a flexible alternative to full-time employment that provides the opportunity to pursue a career while raising a family. Shared jobs, unlike part-time ones, have full-time status and promotion prospects. They are also a possible route to full-time employment should one of the sharers decide to leave.

☐ 3 Flexible work patterns

Flexible work patterns that allow hours to be considered on a daily, weekly or annual basis, enable employers to alter work schedules to meet production or business requirements. The idea of flexible hours was first tried in the UK in the early 1970s and has proved very popular both with employers and employees. 'Flexitime' schemes do away with the requirement that all employees must work a standard 'nine to five' working day allowing individuals to exercise choice over their start and finish times. Each employee is contracted to work a specified number of hours, usually on a monthly basis, and can then attend work within limits set down by the employer.

One typical scheme (see figure 6.5) requires each employee to work 37 hours per week or 148 hours per four-week 'settlement period'. The employer also specifies the 'bandwidth' between which work must be carried out, from 0800 to 1600. Within these limits each worker must be at work during 'core time' (1000 to 1200 and 1400 to 1600) but may choose to start and leave work from 0800 to 1000 and 1600 to 1800 respectively. Each employee must take a minimum half hour for lunch but may take up to two hours. At the end of each settlement period, deficit or credit hours below or above the required 148 are calculated. Any deficit must be made up during the next four-week period and if a minimum of seven credit hours have been amassed, the employee can take a day's 'flexileave'. Any hours credited in excess of ten are forfeited by the employee.

Flexible working hour schemes are of course open to abuse by employees 'working the system'. To prevent this they require careful monitoring and staff may occasionally have to be reminded that the original purpose of the scheme was to permit greater flexibility for the organisation allowing it to remain open over the lunchtime period, for example, and not to give everyone an extra 13 days holiday per year. For this reason, and to avoid any suggestions of favouritism or shirking, rigorous time-recording systems are usually a feature of such schemes.

☐ 4 Compressed working weeks

These allow working time to be compressed into fewer and longer periods during the week. Examples include the 10-hour day, the 4½-day week and the 9-day fortnight. The actual hours worked in the period are not reduced. Reasons for introducing such schemes include improving employee morale, productivity and recruitment, reducing absenteeism, savings on overhead costs and reduced overtime payments.

☐ 5 Annualised hours schemes

Annualised hours schemes contract the employee to work not the 38 hours per week or 148 hours per month of a typical flexible working hours scheme but 1,732 hours or thereabouts per year. This permits flexible working schedules to be devised that allow manufacturers to make the fullest use of expensive or continuous process machinery. The full potential of annual hours can only be realised where the industry has a seasonal or cyclical dimension (such as leisure or tourism). When this is the case, more hours can be rostered during busy periods and less when business is slack. The RAC has put the system to good use to cover its port services operations during holiday periods and an annualised scheme has been introduced for Channel Tunnel workers.

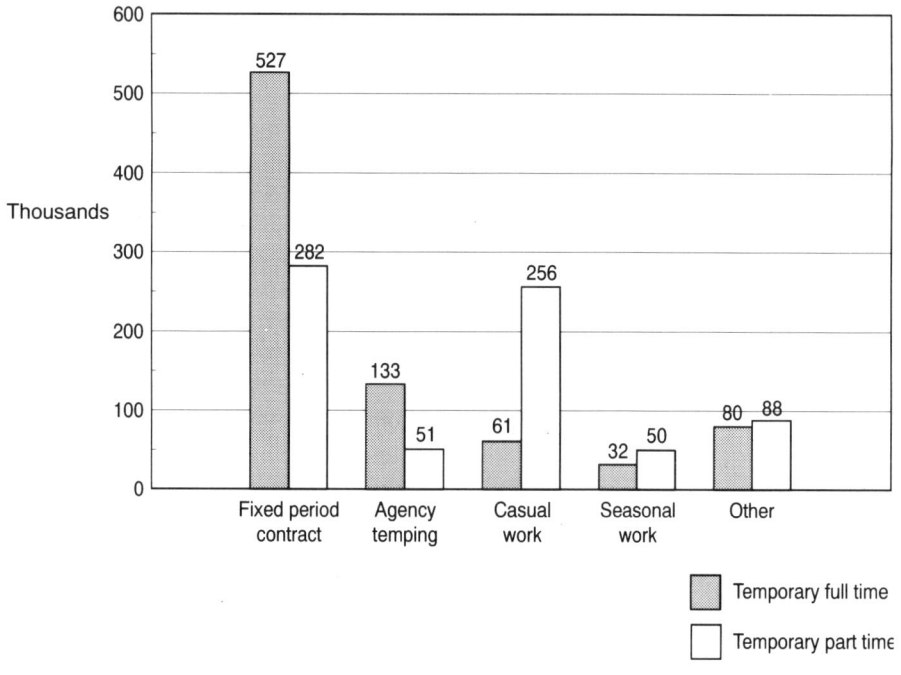

Figure 6.4   A typical flexible working day

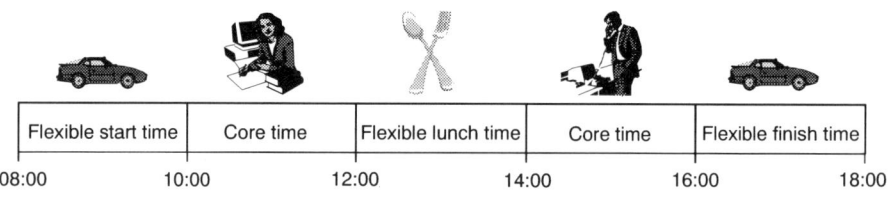

☐ **6 Zero-hours contracts**

These are the most controversial extension of the flexible working philosophy. These arrangements provide the employee with no guarantee of hours that will be worked nor of pay that will be earned. Employees taken on stay at home until they are called in to work, often at very little or no notice. Although previously restricted to high street shops, there are indications that the practice is spreading to other sectors. The advantage to the employer of zero-hours contracts is obvious: people need only be paid when they are actually working. To opponents of these contracts the disadvantages for employees are equally clear: they exploit people already in the most vulnerable employment position. In 1995 a major fast-food chain abandoned zero-hours contracts following extensive media coverage and public condemnation. Staff employed in the company's restaurants had been required to clock off during slack periods thus earning a pittance despite having been on the premises for long hours. The company had to pay significant compensation to the employees involved.

□ 7 Term-time working

Under these arrangements, employees are given unpaid leave of absence during school holidays while retaining the same conditions of service of full-time and part-time staff. The Alliance and Leicester Building Society introduced the scheme in 1989 to encourage women with older children to return to work. Under such schemes, parents of children aged 5 to 14 can work during the term time only and have ten weeks unpaid leave each year to take during the school holidays. On top of this they are expected to take at least four weeks of their paid leave during school holidays. During the holiday periods the company reschedules work and takes on casual labour. Many of these schemes have been taken up by working fathers.

□ 8 Career breaks

Career breaks allow an employee to take an unpaid break from work of two to five years while remaining in touch with the organisation through training courses, newsletters and short working periods. On returning to work the employee is guaranteed a job at the same level as the one previously held. Take-up of career breaks has not been as high as predicted, due perhaps to the legal and financial implications of having a break in continuous service that affects redundancy and pension entitlements.

□ 9 Sabbaticals

Sabbaticals are extended periods of paid or unpaid leave (granted as a reward for long service) to allow travel, education or pursuit of outside interests. The idea originated in the USA where one in six employers offers them. At present they are rare in the UK.

□ 10 Homeworking

More than two million UK workers are now estimated to work from home but only around 6 per cent are true 'teleworkers' linked to their company computer systems via modems. Homeworking schemes require close supervision and effective communications if they are to be successful. Homeworking is claimed to improve job satisfaction and to increase productivity by around 20 per cent.

It widens the pool of labour to include homebound workers, such as the disabled, people caring for elderly relatives and parents who otherwise might not be able to earn an income. The main advantage for employers is the substantial reduction in overheads that can be gained by not having to provide office space for their homeworkers. However, working from home does not suit everyone and, to be successful, homeworkers must be psychologically suited to and prepared for their role. They must have the necessary technical knowledge and skills, be self-motivated and be able to manage their time effectively. Above all they must be able to cope with isolation. Homeworkers are often uneasy about being marginalised from the social and political life of the office and fear that their promotion prospects will be jeopardised through their being 'out of sight and out of mind'. Their managers too must adapt their previous hands-on management styles to permit the autonomy and flexibility their workers need to achieve results in their own way and at their own pace. They must be able to delegate and to agree realistic objectives and targets. They must also be able to assess individual performance from the results received. This does not always come naturally.

■ Japanisation

Extensive inward investment by Japanese companies particularly in the fields of motor and electrical goods manufacture has revolutionised traditional Western approaches toward production methods and labour relations (see Chapter 7). Central to the Japanese philosophy is the concept of 'shared destiny' between workforce and management through greater participation and the overriding pursuit of quality. The success of this was confirmed in February 1997 when Nissan Primeras built in Sunderland bearing a distinctive Union Jack motif and prominent 'Made in Britain' badge were sold out within hours of being displayed in Tokyo, thus giving a new twist to the expression 'carrying coals to Newcastle'. Japanese companies operating within the UK typically place great emphasis on flexible teamworking and the expectations they have of their relationships with trades unions. These might include single union recognition, a no-strike agreement and single-status working conditions. Managers have wide spans of control, are responsible for their own personnel issues and may be expected to work at desks actually on the shop floor and wear the standard company uniform. Stocks of raw materials and work in progress are kept to a minimum in accordance with just-in-time principles and the emphasis is on high levels of production of quality assured goods. Each work team has strict targets to achieve and quality failures are traced back to individual employees who are held accountable to their team leader whose responsibility it is to counsel and, where necessary, discipline them. Much emphasis is placed on communication through daily team briefings and regular presentations to the whole workforce by management. The success of Japanese production methods is most evident in the revitalising effect it has had on the British car industry. Component suppliers such as Hardy-Spicer and Lucas, who were obliged to raise quality in order to secure long-term contracts with Japanese companies, now supply components to other car manufacturers on a global basis.

However, the constant exhortations for improvement can be difficult for workers to take when in reality their jobs requires little skill other than manual dexterity and an ability to keep up with the line speed. For this reason, many workers faced with the unremitting drudgery of assembly work find it hard to accept the cultural straitjacket of the workplace and feel little inclination to participate in company suggestion schemes and quality circle initiatives, much to the bewilderment of their new employers.

■ The shifting employer/employee relationship

One of the most difficult things that employees have had to come to terms with in recent years has been the disappearance of 'jobs for life'. While no one's right to a job has ever been sacrosanct, most workers in the 1960s and 70s nevertheless had a realistic expectation that if they continued to attend regularly and do their work conscientiously, their employment would be secure. Indeed, as they gained experience and qualifications so might they expect to be rewarded with increased salaries, senior positions and higher status. It was perfectly legitimate, for example, for a 16-year-old who joined a high street bank straight from school to aspire one day to manage his own branch and eventually to retire with a generous company pension. Some companies like IBM once prided themselves on their unofficial no-redundancies policies. Those days are gone. The search for leaner, fitter structures, flexibility and market responsiveness has led not only to a vastly reduced workforce but also to the emergence of an implicit shorter-term, 'contractor' employment relationship.

Schein (1980) suggests that an important element arising from the employee/employer relationship is the unwritten series of mutual expectations and satisfactions of needs that governs people's behaviour. He called this the 'psychological contract'. According to Schein, these expectations, which differ between individuals, are additional to the written and legally enforceable contractual obligations. Typically, employees might expect their employers to make all reasonable efforts to provide job security, to provide interesting and challenging work, to have fair personnel policies and to treat employees with consideration and respect. Conversely, employers might expect their employees to accept the ideology and culture of the organisation, be conscientious and diligent, promote the organisation's good image and be loyal.

Gerard Egan, writing in *Management Today*, January 1994, identified changing provisions in the employment relationship which include a move to a short-term contractor relationship, an expectation that employees will constantly seek to add value to the business and develop new competencies in exchange for longer job-tenure. Employees must accept, he argued, that in flatter organisational structures promotions will be very scarce and that they will be moved laterally from time to time and paid according to their performance. Lifetime careers will no longer be the norm and when the 'fit' between the organisation and the individual is no longer right, they will part. In a paper to the Institute of Personnel and Development (IPD) conference in 1995, John Baillie, an IPD researcher, stated that 42 per cent of respondents in a survey on job satisfaction said that they either had little enthusiasm for going to work or actually disliked it. He added that, 'People increasingly realise their loyalty is not being reciprocated with the careers and job security they are still expecting. . .Much as organisations may be saying that their employees are their most valuable asset, the levels of trust, job satisfaction and loyalty shown to the employer are depressingly low.' There is a gap, he concluded, between what employers are actually doing and what their employees perceive them to be doing. According to Baillie, the challenge now facing employees is that they must take responsibility for their own careers by constantly updating their skills at a time when employers can no longer be relied upon to provide continuity.

■ 6.7 Case study

Sheila Bassett came out of her manager's office in tears. Never since her school days had she felt so angry and humiliated. And being old enough to be her new boss's mother had only made things worse. As she walked back to her workstation the office manager appeared in the doorway to his office and bellowed, 'Mrs Williams. Get yourself in here. Now!' and slammed the door behind him. No one looked up as Eileen Williams walked past, white faced. They were used to Sean Baker's dictatorial management style and did not want to risk incurring his wrath if they were caught 'slacking', for they knew from previous experience that that was how he would view any expressions of sympathy to a co-worker. Sheila sat down at her desk, dried her eyes and put on her headset. With a sigh she pressed a key and mechanically began to recite her greeting. 'Good afternoon. Thank you for calling Midheath Financial Services. My name is Sheila. How may I help you?'

Sheila, who was in her forties, had left grammar school at 16 with five O levels and had started work in the wages office at the local clothing factory. Not finding this work to her taste she had left and quickly found a job typing ships' manifests and bills of lading in a local shipping office. She had loved working at Glover's with its pleasant, old-fashioned office atmosphere. Sheila had really fitted in there and had quickly made lots of new friends. Harold Leetham, the manager, was one of the old school. He expected hard work from his employees but was always courteous and quick to give praise wherever it was due. Once, when Sheila was taking Mr Leetham his morning tea, he had asked her to sit down and had then congratulated her on what he called her 'excellent telephone manner'. Apparently, quite a few of the firm's clients had commented upon Sheila's friendly way of chatting to them when they called. 'Keep up the good work, Miss Jenkins,' said Mr Leetham as she left the office. Sheila still remembered how proud she had been that day.

When she was 21, Sheila married Dave, her childhood sweetheart and, after a year with two wages coming in, had left Glover's to have a baby. Dave had completed his engineering apprenticeship just before Laura was born and had been put on craftsman's rates at Meteor Motorcycles where he worked as a turner-fitter. Dave took immense pride in being a time-served tradesman and Sheila recalled his proud boast to her father that 'No wife of mine will ever have to go out to work.' Being naturally careful with money, the couple had soon saved enough from Dave's regular overtime to raise a mortgage on a new bungalow and a little later had traded in Dave's Meteor for a second-hand Mini. Over the next few years they had two more children and Sheila was in her element as housewife and mother. Dave had become active in his trades union and had been elected as shop steward. Yes, life had been good in those early years together. And then everything had started to fall apart.

Meteor Motorcycles had been forced to cut back on overtime and Dave's wages fell drastically. He would come home and sit in front of the television all night hardly speaking to anyone. A normally placid man, he had become quite short-tempered and regularly railed against the government and the bosses who he blamed for the state of the country.

'It's the factory, Sheila,' Dave confessed one evening after a particularly unpleasant row. 'I haven't said anything before because I didn't want to worry you but Meteor sales are at an all time low. Nobody seems to want to buy British bikes any more. I went to look at a Honda in Jordan's last Saturday. I thought they would be cheap and nasty like Japanese toys used to be when we were kids, but they're not. They are really up to date and the quality is as good as anything I've ever seen. What's worse, the road testers are giving them rave reviews after their race wins so the young lads are all buying them. Jordans can sell all they can get their hands on.' Dave had gone quiet for a minute and then went on, 'We had an emergency meeting at work last week. The board are rushing us into producing a new model to try to compete but we're just not ready. I told them that the new engine hasn't been fully developed yet but the managers wouldn't listen. "Just do it" they told us. I'm telling you, Sheila, if this new 'bike doesn't sell, we're finished. I'm really scared.'

Her husband's worst fears had soon been realised. The new motor cycle was a disaster. Customers complained of unreliability, high fuel consumption and constant oil leaks. Not even the most pessimistic sales targets had been met.

It seemed such a long time now since the factory had closed and Dave had had his 'fifteen minutes of fame' on local television berating a government that 'was intent on destroying the working class' and a company that 'had failed to invest in the future of the industry'. As a tradesman Dave had confidently expected to find work but when he had gone for interviews he had been unprepared for the questions about computer-controlled machines. He had ended up arguing with the production managers about all these 'new-fangled machines' and incompetent management putting craftsmen like him out of work. Not surprisingly they had not taken him on. When Sheila had tactfully suggested that he go to the local college to do a course on computer numerical control systems he had stormed out of the house shouting that he was a tradesman and he wasn't going back to school for anybody.

Dave did manage to find occasional short-term jobs none of which made use of his skills or had the status of his previous job. And then even these jobs had disappeared as the recession bit deeper and Dave became long-term unemployed. How they had rowed when Sheila said she was going to look for a job!

When the Job Centre clerk had asked about her qualifications and work experience Sheila's initial high hopes were shattered. She did not even know what a 'WP' was let alone how to use one, and the clerk had looked at her blankly when she said she knew how to cut wax stencils for a Roneo machine. And then she had remembered Mr Leetham's comments about her telephone skills, and that was how, after dozens of interviews, she had landed her job in telesales working for Sean Baker. True, the money was not very good and the job was only on a six-month contract, but 'beggars can't be choosers' as her mother always said, and she was desperate.

At first Sheila was afraid to use the computer but Jean, her supervisor, had quickly reassured her and taught her the basics. In fact Sheila seemed to have a natural flair for the system. Her job involved answering telephone responses to press and radio advertisements and selling insurance to the callers. Everything she did was prompted and controlled by the computer. When a call was allocated to her workstation she had to greet the caller in the prescribed manner, ask a series of questions and input responses to generate quotations. At certain points in the conversation she was expected to try to 'close the deal' and make a definite sale.

On the wall in front of the 30 workstations in the office was an electronic display that constantly updated information about the number of calls being processed per hour, the number of callers on hold at any one time, the average response times of the operatives and the cumulative value of sales for the shift. It was not so much the constant pressure that Sheila minded but the mechanistic, robot-like conversations with customers. She longed to personalise the transactions and to sound less like a speaking clock. But the company rules were quite strict. Paragraph 27 (c) of the staff manual read, 'Under no circumstances may sales operatives deviate from the procedures specified by the company.'

On her way home one evening Sheila mentioned this to Eileen who sat at the next workstation. 'You don't want to worry about that, love,' Eileen had said. 'You don't have to say the exact words that come up on the screen. Of course you can change things . . . provided you sell the policies.' The next day, Sheila had logged-on as usual and then started to take calls. The changes she made to the script were only minor but they seemed to be appreciated by the customers and Sheila really enjoyed the new, more relaxed conversations.

Then, just after lunch, she had been called to Sean Baker's office where he immediately started shouting at her about 'breaking company's rules'. When Sheila protested, Baker had produced a computer-generated analysis of her performance ratios and played a tape recording of her conversations with a series of customers. He was furious that Sheila had taken it upon herself to stray from the standard responses. 'Cleverer people than you have analysed thousands of transactions to find the best way of selling insurance over the telephone,' he shouted. 'Who the hell do you think you are to change the system?' When he had calmed down a bit, Sheila explained that she had only been trying to be pleasant, and in any case she had been told that it was in order to make minor changes to the conversation. At this Sean Baker went wild. 'Who told you that you could do that?' he shouted, coming from behind his desk and standing over her. 'Either you tell me who it was or you can get out now and not bother coming back!'

Sean Baker was oblivious to the tears that by now were rolling down her cheeks. 'I'll wait all day if I have to,' he threatened, and eventually, after much pleading, Sheila had blurted out Eileen's name. 'Right,' he said, 'now get back to work and don't let me catch you messing about again, because if I do, lady, you'll be out of here so fast your feet won't touch the ground.'

■ 6.8 Conclusion

Job security, now that jobs for life are a thing of the past, will depend not so much on actually having a job but on being employable. That is, possessing the qualifications, experience, skills and flexible attitudes for which potential employers are prepared to pay. As the contractual relationship becomes looser so will employers become less inclined to provide education and developmental opportunities for peripheral employees, other than those specifically required to do the current job. For many workers, managing their career is thus likely to become more a personal responsibility, to be pursued largely in their own time and at their own expense, than part of the employment package. Such privileges will increasingly become the reserve of the core employee.

Fear of change is a normal human reaction. Most people, given the choice, would prefer the comfort of familiar working methods and habits to the challenge and uncertainty of new ways of doing things. People are naturally concerned at having to learn new skills and worry about how they will cope with new working methods and altered relationships. But the need to compete in global markets means that we must constantly question traditional attitudes to work and seek new, more efficient ways of doing things. As people are a major cost it is inevitable that employers will seek to reduce their headcounts by adopting flexible employment policies aimed at more closely matching the labour available to the amount of work to be done. However, as flexible firms decrease their commitment to their workers and pursue hard HRM policies, they should not be surprised when their employees reciprocate by doing the minimum that is expected of them at work and use what creative energies they possess in the pursuit of their own hobbies and interests. Weakened trades unions, high unemployment and the lack of minimum wage legislation in the UK have encouraged many employers to exercise their managerial prerogative and return to dictatorial management styles redolent of a past age. As jobs continue to be de-skilled and the pride and satisfaction that workers once derived from doing their jobs in their own distinctive way is denied them, so will they become more demotivated and alienated from the workplace. As we have seen, Taylor's scientific management methods raised productivity but robbed workers of job-satisfaction with disastrous results. Our current preoccupation with efficiency and productivity at all costs risks repeating the mistakes made by previous generations of managers but where they could claim ignorance of the psychological needs of the workforce we have no such excuse.

■ Questions for discussion

1. To what extent was Sheila Bassett justified in seeking to change the telesales procedure? If you were Sean Baker, how would you have handled the interview?
2. Why did Dave Bassett find it so difficult to obtain a decent job following his redundancy? What advice would you give to him to improve his chances?
3. Using the PESTLE framework, analyse the environmental factors that led to Meteor Motorcycles' closure. Assuming that the company had had a free hand to implement change, what actions might they have taken to remain in production?
4. 'Taylor's principles of scientific management are outdated and have no place in a modern organisation.' Discuss this statement in relation to the above case study.
5. How effective do you think Harold Leetham and Sean Baker would be if they were to exchange roles within their two companies? What factors might contribute to their respective success or failure?

■ Bibliography

Armstrong, M., 'Human Resource Management: A Case of the Emperor's New Clothes?', *Personnel Management*, vol. 19, no. 8 (1987).

Armstrong, M., *A Handbook of Personnel Management Practice*, 4th edn (London: Kogan Page, 1991).

Atkinson, J., 'Manpower Strategies for Flexible Organisations', *Personnel Management*, vol. 16, no. 8 (1984).

Bassett, P., 'Price of Workplace Flexibility May Be Rising Job Insecurity', *The Times*, 11 June 1996.

Beardwell, I. and Holden, L. (eds) *Human Resource Management – A Contemporary Perspective* (London: Pitman, 1994).

Constable, J. and McCormick, R., *The Making of British Managers* (London: British Institute of Management, 1987).

Doherty, N. and Horsted, J., 'Helping Survivors to Stay on Board', *People Management*, vol. 1, no. 1 (1995).

Drucker, P. F., *Management: Tasks, Responsibilities, Practices* (London: Heinemann, 1974).

Egan, G., 'What's in Store for Employee Contracts: Hard Times' *Management Today*, January 1994.

Fayol, H., trans. Constance Storrs, *General and Industrial Management* (London: Pitman, 1949).

Handy, C., 'The Making of Managers', *Report on Management Education, Training and Development in the United States, West Germany, France, Japan and the UK* (London: NEDO, 1987).

Hayward, S., 'Search for the Feelgood Factor', *The Sunday Times*, 29 October 1995.

Institute of Manpower Studies report, *Changing Working Patterns – How Companies Achieve Flexibility to Meet New Needs* (NEDO, 1986).

Maslow, A. H., 'A Theory of Human Motivation', *Psychological Review*, vol. 0, July 1943, pp. 370–96.

Mayo, E., *The Human Problems of an Industrial Civilization* (London: Macmillan, 1933).

McGregor, D., *The Human Side of Enterprise* (New York: McGraw-Hill, 1960).

McKenna, S., 'Japanization and Recent Developments in Britain', *Employee Relations*, vol. 10, no. 4 (1988) pp. 6–12.

Peters, T., *Thriving on Chaos* (London: Macmillan, 1989).

Peters, T. J. and Waterman, R. H., *In Search Of Excellence* (New York: Harper and Row, 1982).

Pollert, A., 'The flexible firm – fixation or fact?', *Work, Employment and Society*, vol. 2, no. 3 (1988) pp. 281–316.

Schein, E. H., *Organisational Psychology*, 3rd edn (New Jersey: Prentice-Hall, 1980).

Smith, D., 'The Jobs Axe That Fell But Failed', *The Sunday Times*, 19 May 1996.

Storey, J., *Human Resource Management – A Critical Text* (London: Routledge, 1995).

Taylor, F. W., *Scientific Management* (New York: Harper & Row, 1947).

Torrington, D. and Hall, L., *Personnel Management – HRM in Action*, 3rd edn (Hemel Hempstead: Prentice-Hall, 1995).

CHAPTER 7

Lean production is only for the large?

Heather Stewart

■ 7.1 Introduction: What is lean production?

Lean Production is a term used initially in the late 1980s by John Krafcik, a researcher for the International Motor Vehicle Program (IMVP) at Massachusetts Institute of Technology. The term is used to describe the production methods involved in world class manufacturing as typified in the Toyota Company of Japan.

Originally all production was craft based. This resulted in fairly time-consuming low production levels. As consumer demand increased in the United States of America with the introduction of the Ford Model T in 1908 alternative production methods were sought. In the West there was a tendency to move to mass production as typified by the Ford Motor Company in the United States. However, Toyota was, for a variety of reasons, unable to move to mass production at the same time and therefore created its own, rather different, production methods which have enabled it to produce high quality output at exceptionally competitive prices.

The West has, since then, been trying to catch up by attempting to copy Toyota's success. Vehicle production prior to the introduction of the Ford Model T and the idea of a production line involved highly skilled labour using comparatively simple tools manufacturing one item at a time. The product was often made to meet a customer's special requirements. The market for these products was small because the high price charged deterred demand. However, European and American manufacturers realised that a lower price would unleash considerable demand and they moved towards higher production levels during the period following the introduction of the Ford Model T, which enabled them to reduce costs and prices. They aimed to offer an affordable alternative and moved relentlessly toward mass production.

Mass production was exemplified by the motor industry in the US. Huge plants were created in the 1920s in Chicago, Detroit, etc. where unskilled or semi-skilled labour tended expensive single purpose machines that had to be in continuous operation to achieve the necessary economies of scale. The mass-producers' output was a narrow range of standard products for which the life-cycle was extended for long periods because the costs of developing and producing new products was so high and the time-scale so long.

It was normal practice to keep large stocks of materials, to employ extra labour and to provide extra space in order to cope with problems and to ensure smooth production. Large stocks of finished goods were also kept to meet peaks of consumer demand. Stocks acted as a buffer which tended to hide the real problems of manufacture. The result was that consumers were offered a comparatively low-cost product with limited choice. Each employee carried out limited and undemanding repetitive tasks. The workforce were not motivated and absenteeism was high which meant that extra labour had to be employed to ensure that the plant could be manned and that there was no disruption to production flow (see also Chapters 5.3 and 6.2).

The mass producer simply wanted to manufacture a product which was 'good enough'. A certain level of defects was considered acceptable. These defects may have been identified during production but were not corrected at that time because that may have meant halting production flow. Instead defects were allowed to continue to flow down the production line and on completion were extracted and sent to a rework area for rectification. This meant that certain defects became exceedingly difficult to correct. In fact, although the production line did not stop for defects to be extracted, or the cause corrected, it did stop because of material supply and production scheduling co-ordination problems. A yield of 90 per cent for the automobile industry was considered good (Womack, Jones and Roos 1990).

In comparison to mass production, lean production uses less of everything – it halves the labour effort in the factory and new product development time, it reduces inventory and it reduces the number of defects while increasing the range of product variety. Lean production is a unique management strategy that gives organisations a distinct competitive edge in terms of cost, quality and service. In an article in the *Independent*, on a visit by the Confederation of German Industry (BDI) to four companies in Britain to learn about their experiences with lean production, the leader of the German delegation was quoted as saying that 'lean production was not a technical process but a management philosophy based on trust and the delegation of responsibility'. 'What the visitors found when visiting Nissan in Sunderland, Bosch in Cardiff, Komatsu in Durham and ITT Tever in Ebbw Vale was the implementation of Japanese practices balanced, in the case of Bosch, with the best of German methods' (*Independent*, 5 December 1993).

Lean production was developed at Toyota, in Japan, over a period of thirty years, because of a combination of Japanese cultural effects together with considerable resource limitations during and after the Second World War.

Japan was identified as 'different' long ago. This was documented by Vehblen in 1915 when he looked at Japan from an organisational point of view. He argued that it was 'An overcrowded and impoverished land – Japan has to import all its raw materials. Its one principal resource is the dedication of its people' (Vehblen 1915).

The founding family of Toyota were Sakichi Toyoda, Kiichiro Toyoda and Eiji Toyoda. Initially they invented and developed an automatic power loom; on the sale of the patent the proceeds were used to help finance the personal goal of developing a car. With Taiichi Ohno, the Chief Production Engineer, the Toyoda family studied mass production in the United States. However, for a number of reasons, they concluded that mass production could not be recreated in Japan. These reasons included that:

- Japan had a tiny domestic market that required a wide range of products
- The Japanese are alleged to choose group needs over personal desires
- There was no source of cheap immigrant labour
- Women had a limited role in the economy
- The economy was starved of capital and foreign exchange and was, therefore, unable to import Western technology unless some liaison with an overseas firm was established.

The rest of the industrialised world wanted to set up in Japan but foreign investment became prohibited in the motor industry. In 1936 the Automobile Manufacture Enterprise Law was passed concerning manufacture of motor vehicles. It recognised and established Japan's automobile industry. The law required those with output of more than three thousand units to be licensed and licences could only be issued to companies with 50 per cent outstanding shares and with positions on the Board of Directors held by Japanese citizens. Only three companies were given licences at this time and of these Toyoda Automatic Loom Works and Nissan represented 85 per cent of production. This legislation gave the government the opportunity to experiment with promotional and protectionist strategies which included:

- elimination of complete vehicle imports
- elimination of local assembly by foreign companies
- elimination of overseas investment
- encouragement to acquire foreign technology and invest in plant and equipment.

These import barriers encouraged more Japanese companies to enter the motor vehicle industry. These barriers to trade created, and still create, tension with the rest of the world with reference to inward trade and investment. The Japanese government wanted to merge companies and to encourage mass production but the manufacturers defied the government and each continued with its chosen range. Craft methods were unrealistic for the volume concerned and mass production was not ideal given the capital investment limitations.

- The workforce were able to negotiate better terms of employment hence raising production costs

- Government and industry were closely related
- Transport was expensive. For exports to be successful they needed a high value to weight ratio.

Toyota's success has resulted from a series of circumstances with the right people, in the right place at the right time. It has involved the outstanding efforts of individuals, with a vision of the future automobile manufacturing industry in Japan, with the ability, flexibility and drive to develop new and better ways of producing superb quality products at very competitive prices.

'Cars are the precious metal of industrial culture. Demand for them is an indicator of economic well-being. The ability to manufacture them at a profit is the surest sign of technological competence, the quality of their design is cruelly revealing evidence of the intellectual fitness of a nation. Japanese cars have never been in greater demand and sales in Europe are held back only by quotas'. (*Sunday Times Magazine*, 9 October 1993)

One of the Japanese reactions to quotas was to make the most of the quota by producing a premium priced product with high profit margins, hence the Toyota Lexus range. The Lexus was designed in a way that means faults are virtually eliminated at the conceptual stage. It is almost impossible for errors to be made in its assembly. The Japanese now design and manufacture cars so that quality is planned, incorporated and inevitable.

Just-In-Time is synonymous with Lean Production. It is a management 'philosophy and not simply a toolbox of techniques' (Cobb 1991). However, the term Just-In-Time is frequently applied simply to the supply of materials and production to meet consumer demand. This is too simplistic; the philosophies of Just-In-Time and Lean Production apply to both the whole organisation and the whole production cycle (see Chapters 1.2 and 5.3 also). Specific characteristics of a Lean Production organisation are identified later in this chapter.

'A survey of the motor vehicle industry in 1984 revealed a cost advantage to Japanese manufacturing relative to the United States of $2203 per unit. 25 per cent of this advantage came from using Just-In-Time production, 15 per cent from quality control systems, 2 per cent from material handling, 22 per cent from other productivity improvements, 25 per cent from wages and benefits, 4 per cent from absenteeism, 4 per cent from relief systems and allowances and 3 per cent from technology'. (Smith 1989)

It is clear from this that Japanese supremacy does not come from a more advanced technological standing but from factors associated with non-value adding activities.

The characteristics of Lean Production are summarised in Table 7.1.

Table 7.1   The major characteristics of lean production

NEW PRODUCT DESIGN
Product range growing
Product designed for easy manufacture
Design stage input from all functions
Team exists for project life
Target costing used
Speed from idea to sale accelerating

SUPPLY
Low inventory held
Parts delivered to meet production requirements
Delivery to production line
Inventory expressed in terms of production time
Long term supplier relationships
Exclusive or semi-exclusive supplier agreements
Few suppliers
Large volume order, small batch delivery
Low prices
Involvement in supplier profit margins
Quality assured suppliers
Simplified invoicing
Open supplier relationship

MANUFACTURE
Flexible automated machines
Few indirect workers
Low set up times
Ideal of a batch of one
Customisation possible
Minimal stocks of work-in-progress and finished goods
Space savings achieved
Low rejection rates
Zero defect aim
Little rework
Low cost
High volume
Elimination of waste
Idle times expected
Employees have problem solving skills
Responsibility delegated to the factory floor
Changes made incrementally
Cell manufacture
Teamwork
Production scheduling to meet known demand
Production may be halted in response to a problem
Finished goods are distributed directly from production
Use is made of computer aided design and manufacture

SALES AND DISTRIBUTION
Comprehensive customer database maintained
Demand forecast and adjusted for actual demand
Customers consulted about new products

RESEARCH AND DISTRIBUTION
Takes place within the organisation and is not isolated
Directed at some specific objective

EMPLOYEES
Lifetime employment
Staff turnover low
Pay be seniority
Bonuses (typically 30% of pay)
Overtime (typically 10% of pay)
Good working conditions
Flexible workforce
Multiskilled
Promotes the company
Trained
Geographical exchanges encouraged
Increased job satisfaction

INFLUENCES ON SUCCESS
Culture

■ 7.2 Lean production: product design, development and engineering

These areas require a very broad range of skills and hence large numbers of employees are involved. In many organisations the hoped for synergy from this meeting of minds is frequently not achieved because of communication and co-ordination problems. In a Lean Production organisation teams are set up containing all the relevant expertise. Rewards go to the team rather than to any individual. This results in increased productivity and quality and a willingness to respond to the demands of change. There is a designated project leader who is very powerful and needs to be creative in his direction of the skills necessary to create complex manufactured products. His role is one involving technical, social and organisational skills. All necessary resources are under his control. He selects his team from the functional departments and they remain with him for the life of the product or project.

In the past this was a lengthy period of time but as the time from the initial idea to production is rapidly decreasing it is a very realistic proposition. The average development time for a new Japanese car is 46.2 months, in the United States 60.4 and in Europe 57.3 months. The average team size for Japanese automobile manufacture is 485 compared with 903 for the United States of America and 904 for Europe (Fujimoto 1987).

Although the Japanese team size is smaller, there is significantly less staff turnover then in the United States or Europe. Outside Japan team members are constantly being called back to their functional divisions or departments whereas in Japan once on the project team that is their task and no other. They are not called back to their functional departments although they maintain close links with them to ensure coordination with other projects. Japanese teams rapidly identify any critical path tasks and ensure that these are dealt with at a sufficiently early stage to avoid a delay affecting other stages.

One of the major critical factors in automobile manufacture is the production of the dye and in Japan a typical dye development time is 13.8 months compared with 25 months in the United States and 28 months in Europe (ibid 1987). This is achieved by ensuring that the dye designers and the body designers are in direct contact at the earliest possible stage so that the dye designer can begin the necessary preparatory work ready for the release of the final panel designs when final cutting can take place. Any conflict arising within the group is dealt with at the time and not put off until later when it may be extremely difficult, if not, impossible to correct. Products are designed with ease of manufacture and quality in mind using standard components and parts wherever possible. 'The Japanese consider themselves to be long-term players on the global game board, so quality is aggressively pursued. It is designed into their products and manufacturing processes' (McMann and Nanni 1995).

Ease of manufacture should also consider the future implications of materials used and the activities involved to ensure that efficient use will be made of support facilities once production commences. Companies operating in an advanced manufacturing environment typically find 90 per cent of production costs are determined during the early stages of a product's life cycle (Berliner and Brimson 1988). It is expensive to make changes to design and production after these early stages making it important to be thorough at the design stage. 'Focusing on costs after the product enters production results in only a small proportion of life-cycle costs being manageable. This has created a need to ensure that the tightest controls are at the design stage, because most costs are committed or "locked in" at this point in time' (Drury 1996). Another Japanese idea is that of target costing which was developed at Toyota in the 1960s: 'A revenue estimate is provided by the price-volume point where the new product's target market penetration is achieved. These estimates are, in turn, obtained via a market analysis based on the product's attributes and features' (McMann and Nanni 1995). The desired profit is deducted from this revenue estimate leaving an allowable amount for which the product must be produced. 'Given a set of desired features and an allowable cost, designers and engineers attempt to design the product and its production process under the allowable cost' (McMann and Nanni 1995).

Toyota has a formal quality control programme which was introduced in 1961. Design quality and quality assurance already had a long history in the company because initial production was of unacceptably poor quality and unsuitable for the proposed markets. Errors were made in market research when exporting to the United States where the different requirements of the market were not identified and hence led to poor sales.

Between 1954 and 1960 quality control was largely ignored as a separate function and was devoted to managing production operations. In order to ensure smooth production components underwent 100 per cent testing rather than sampling because of the high rate of defects.

It was at this time that production employees were asked to do their own inspection. Toyota eventually realised that very valuable publicity could be obtained by producing high quality products and launched a quality programme that combined processing, design and cost controls which involved self-inspection, the use of control charts and sampling techniques. An in-house quality control manual associated with internal training was produced with the intention of improving inspection methods, standardisation and process controls. An independent committee was set up to oversee quality control and an office established to deal with customer complaints, design and prototype manufacture. The programme was extended to include sub-contractors and suppliers. Toyota gained the reputation of having the most effective quality programme in the Japanese automobile industry.

■ 7.3 Lean production: supply

Mass production in the United States was typified by vast in-house production within vertically integrated companies. Those items that were not produced internally were offered for tender from drawings and a defect allowance was included. There was little or no contact with the supplier and certainly no chance offered for the supplier to suggest improvements in what was, after all, their own specialist area. The whole approach was masked in secrecy and there was limited information flow. This ultimately resulted in the need for high stocks to be held by manufacturers in order to avoid both supply problems and rejection rates due to defective or possibly unsuitable parts.

The Toyota–Supplier relationship is very significant. Initially the supply infrastructure in Japan was extremely poor in terms of both quality and volume. Consequently Toyota was forced to produce some important items in-house to ensure that quality improved to some extent. However, the supply infrastructure expanded in close proximity to the manufacturing plants. When demand soared Toyota found it cheaper, safer and faster to recruit suppliers than to hire employees and/or invest in equipment. The advantages were that fixed costs were lower, less operating capital was required, less warehousing space was needed, it was simpler to cut production levels and any over-capacity risks were passed on. Toyota even began to sub-contract final assembly.

It was anticipated that companies, even small ones, could specialise and reduce costs so Toyota risked time rather than money to help suppliers. The company lent executive expertise, gave technological assistance, offered loans of equipment and money and arranged contracts to purchase all, or almost all, output for an extended period. This enabled the suppliers to automate, have better production engineering, cost accounting, production management and quality control. In return, quality supplies were guaranteed. Some suppliers actually became subsidiaries of Toyota (Toyota Motor Corporation 1987).

In Lean Production the aim is both to reduce cost and improve quality. 'The Japanese see no trade-off between cost and quality. Over the long-term, better quality will always result in less waste and, therefore, lower cost' (McMann and Nanni 1995). Japanese companies tend to select a limited number of suppliers at the outset of product development. Normally there will be a number of suppliers for each item so the company is not reliant on one supplier. However, it is not unusual for a single supplier to be selected for an item on the grounds of specialisation and past performance.

Suppliers are encouraged to liaise and to improve the design. As such, a supplier representative is assigned to the development team. There is a free flow interchange of information about company costs and profitability. A quote will typically include:

- Specification
- Operation details
- Scrap details
- Overhead charges
- Direct labour and direct material costs
- Profit
- Transport and packing

Anything less is considered inadequate. Initially suppliers resisted the provision of such detailed information but the Japanese are prepared to offer suggestions to solve any problems and suggestions for cost reduction and increased efficiency. Value analysis and value engineering help to identify areas for cost reduction and both the buyer and supplier are interested in reducing costs. The supplier is rewarded with a reasonable profit margin. If he can reduce costs further any additional profit is his reward.

'The effects of the presence of Japanese manufacturing investment in the UK go far beyond the direct employment created. Several studies have outlined that there have been and will be beneficial effects on suppliers, subcontractors and even third level companies due to the so called "demonstration effect" '(Smith 1989). Suppliers included in the surveys indicated that all suppliers had experienced difficulties in the new arrangements in part due to pricing and costing. The surveys made it clear that in some cases the financial consequences of supplying the Japanese had not been fully thought out. The main financial problems were the:

1. significance of the quoted price
2. Japanese interest in the supplier's cost structure
3. strain of complying with just-in-time delivery.

The supplier expected the price he quoted to be stable for the period of its use. He also expected to be able to pass on any price increases. However, the Japanese expected the price to reduce because they anticipated economies of scale as volumes increased and for the learning curve to have some effect. The Japanese viewed price increases as sufficient reason to look for supply elsewhere. As suppliers became aware of the Japanese views on price they were able to set a price which allowed them to offer reductions in the future. Unwanted business can be politely refused by setting a high price although this ploy becomes increasingly unnecessary as suppliers become dependent on supplying the Japanese firms.

'Suppliers are expected to deliver parts, components and sub-assemblies as production requires' (*Daily Telegraph*, 19 October 1992). Synchronous supply may be required where the supplier/manufacturer relationship requires supplies to be delivered to the production line in the order determined by the production flow. This is becoming increasingly important as products become more differentiated and virtually customised cars are required. A signal (Kanban) indicates that parts are needed on the production line. This should generate delivery. The production line, therefore, holds no stock. It is argued that the supplier has to hold stock instead which causes his costs to rise unless he too operates a 'lean enterprise'. Problems are likely to arise with just-in-time delivery when definite requirements are only available in the very short term. Frequently economic batch run sizes are much larger than the short-term requirements. The result is that the supplier may hold buffer stocks to ensure they maintain the use of their economic batch quantity but at the same time ensure supply to the Japanese manufacturer. This, in turn, causes increases in the supplier's working capital requirements which can have a significant effect on the cash requirements and may cause cash flow problems.

Suppliers in the UK have undergone a considerable learning process and are beginning to realise that a good return can be achieved by allowing the Japanese to take a very real interest in their companies and by achieving a very close supplier/buyer relationship (Munday 1990).

■ 7.4 Lean production: manufacture

After the Second World War, Japanese automobile producers were required to register with the government. There were shortages of materials, operating capital and credit; inflation was extremely high which meant that cost reduction was not possible and estimating future costs was an impossible task. However, production needed to increase to provide employment for those returning to work from the armed forces. Private sector demand was low because inflation had destroyed the value of any savings. However, the majority of vehicles in circulation were no longer operational and General

Headquarters (Occupying Forces) (GHQ) sold surplus military vehicles to the Japanese. Truck production was encouraged from 1945. This, however, did nothing to increase demand.

Deflationary measures in 1949 further depressed demand for automobiles. During the post-war period trade union activity increased with the setting up of independent unions (Sanbetsu) which were not industrial and tended to be dominated by communist members. Sanbetsu eventually became the All Japanese Automobile Industry Labour Union (Zenji) which was dissolved in 1954 after a series of major strikes. Nissan and Toyota developed their own unions. In the case of Toyota the 'Toyota Motor Koromo Labour Union' was formed. The main demands were for wage increases and employment guarantees in return for which co-operation for cost reduction and productivity was offered. The Japanese Automobile Manufacturers' Association tried in 1948 to get GHQ to modify its policies on automobile manufacture. This evolved into a lobbying and public relations exercise for the industry which wanted continued protectionism, low cost loans and export quotas. It was at this time that Toyota stopped volume production that maximised the use of the available resources and instead produced to meet actual demand. This was the commencement of a fifteen-year period of incremental change to extract maximum added value from the manufacturing system and the employees and the beginning of lean production.

A financial crisis in 1949 caused bank investors to insist on reductions in inventory held by Toyota. This meant large batches were no longer possible and economies of scale disappeared. The early days of target costing had arrived. Between 1948 and 1953 worker flexibility therefore increased dramatically.

The objectives of lean production manufacture are the elimination of wasted effort, wasted time and wasted materials. The characteristics of such production are:

- Continuous reductions in costs
- Very few indirect workers are used
- Significant reductions in space utilised are achieved
- No space is available for stocks of work-in-progress or raw materials
- Employees work in teams in work cells
- A motivated multi-skilled workforce is developed
- The use of highly flexible, increasingly automated, machines
- A batch size of one (customisation)
- High volume production
- Production runs smoothly and is well balanced
- Any defective parts or production problems undergo the '5 Whys' to isolate the underlying cause (IMVP World Assembly Plant Survey 1990).
- Any employee can stop the production line
- Zero defects ('Because any acceptable defect level is a commitment to produce defects' (Crosby 1979))
- There is virtually no reworking
- Products go directly to the distribution network from the production line
- No buffer stocks are held

- No parts warehouses are maintained
- Parts are delivered at intervals to suit the production line
- Inventory can be expressed in terms of minutes of production
- Endless variety is available for customers

One of the first steps taken by Toyota was to identify those employees who did not work on the production process and, by definition, did not add any value to production. The tasks carried out by these employees were delegated to the production line workers who because of their direct input had an intimate knowledge of the production line. Toyota then experimented in incremental steps. Initially assembly employees were grouped into teams. One of the team members was designated as leader and would fill in for any absentees. The actual assembly was broken down into a series of steps. Each individual had a 'piece of the line' but the team as a whole were to decide on the best way for tasks to be performed. Once this had been established minor repairs and quality checks were delegated to the team. Once the line was running smoothly time was set aside to allow the team to consider how the process could be improved.

This practice ultimately led to the adoption of quality circles in the West. Any member of the team could 'stop the line' at a sign of a problem which could not be easily and immediately rectified. The team would then gather together and discuss the problem and by asking 'Why?' many times were able to isolate the underlying cause and, by correction, the problem was eliminated permanently. At first there were many stoppages but as problems were solved the stoppages became infrequent and quality improved. The objective of zero defects was becoming reality. Fewer defects resulted in less rework and additional space savings were achieved.

Today Toyota has the lowest defect rate of any car manufacturer. They have very little factory space designated for rework areas whereas mass-producers have typically set aside 20 per cent of their plant area for rework and 25 per cent of the total hours worked are used in error rectification (IMVP World Assembly Plant Survey 1990). The introduction of the highly flexible automated machines together with very rapid set-up times, meant that customisation became possible. The customer could now have the exact model, colour, trim, etc. he or she desired.

■ 7.5 Lean production: selling and distribution

Consumers are increasingly demanding non-standard reliable products with greater sophistication (see economies of scope, Chapters 2.8; 6.9). There are many product segments within the overall vehicle market, e.g. passenger cars, buses, industrial vehicles and trucks. Each of these segments can be broken down further. These superior products command premium prices.

One of the aims of lean production is that of a batch size of one which lends itself to supplying the consumer with a product that meets their demands whilst achieving efficiently low costs. The batch of one carries with it little or no cost penalty. Lean production has been shown to reduce the time and effort taken for product change and model specification to be half that of the mass producer. Another term for this is the 'agile producer' (Womack, Jones and Roos 1990).

Toyota have been involved with the selling and distribution of their products since the 1930s when they initially copied the networks set up by General Motors and Ford in Japan (one main dealer with several outlets and lots of models).

Consumers tend to be under the illusion that Japan simply produces very high volume standard products. This stems from the Japanese practice of distributing a limited number of product categories to each export market. However, the illusion is merely transitory. The Japanese have a broad product portfolio and are still steadily increasing the range offered in the world market. Each product tends to have a much shorter life-cycle than an equivalent product from mass production simply because the Japanese are able to introduce new products on to the market so much faster than the West (*The Economist*, 5 December 1992). Lean production is therefore well placed to attack and gain strong holds in niche markets.

It is vital that production meets the consumers' needs or a company will achieve no sales and production will go into stock utilising vital space and capital investment in working capital. Mass production achieves this by limiting product variety and in the case of cars allows dealers to create demand rather than the consumer. The consumer has to be content with what the dealer offers.

Within lean production Toyota considers production to have a strong relationship with the 'dealer' and for the customer to have a strong relationship with product development. Toyota has a very effective sales force who establish a very close relationship with their customers. The customer is expected to be a repeat purchaser and this relationship provides data for a very large information base on Japanese households and their preferences. The company has a very extensive system of surveys. The twice-yearly survey covers a very large proportion of the population and together with other smaller surveys an annual production plan can be produced (Delbridge and Olner 1991). This is reviewed at two-month, one-month, ten-day and four-day intervals prior to manufacture when the model mix is programmed to meet demand and to avoid stockpiling. The survey questionnaires are followed up by a direct approach from the dealer with regard to style, model, colour and price, etc.

Because of this system, virtually all cars in Japan are made to a specific customer order (Cusumano 1985). The production line cannot physically wait for an order to come in before planning production but the database and experience enable smooth and efficient production scheduling to take place.

Surges, troughs or shifts in demand cause problems but then all sales efforts are targeted on those most likely to purchase the scheduled products using the database for information. In planning new products the customers are always consulted.

Ideally supply, production and sale should be located in the same geographical area. In Japan this was feasible because of the small area involved. However, as Japanese manufacturers moved into North America, Europe and Eastern Asia to avoid anticipated trade blocs they found that there were further advantages to this strategy.

Initially it enabled them to avoid trade barriers but they subsequently discovered that it enabled them to be impervious to exchange rate problems which could otherwise be quite devastating. Because different geographical areas required different products it became easy to gear production to meet the local market needs. This provided the volume production required while allowing export of the product to niche markets at volume cost. The wide variety of geographical locations allowed more exchange of management which, while being seen as a 'reward', also allowed employees to gain experience and fulfilment. By operating in a wide range of markets throughout the world any problems arising from the business cycle generally have only a limited effect. Any risk can be spread over the wide-ranging geographical areas which are unlikely to all suffer at the same time.

■ 7.6 Lean production: research and development

Usually research and development (R&D) takes place in an isolated environment which means that communication and co-ordination become much more difficult. Within the lean production organisation any research and development has a time scale within which the problem must be solved, because it is anticipated that some other part of the organisation will require the solution in order to continue their own work. R&D usually requires input from all the functions of the organisation. Specific objectives are often tied to market requirements.

All engineers start work at the production line level to ensure that they have a full understanding of the implications arising from any future decisions. It is usual for employees to be assigned to some other functional department for some period each year which ensures that they are kept up-to-date. The engineers rotate to other functional departments, for example marketing and engineering. They are finally assigned to their true task which may be, for example, part of a new project development. During the life of the project their contact with their functional department will be limited to routine tasks until completion, after which they return to their functional department. The more promising are then trained further and will be selected to work on longer-term advanced projects which will involve liaison with outside specialists.

With this approach Japan has been consistently able to beat the West in bringing patented innovation to the market. As markets become saturated product development must move into new areas rather than simply adapting present technological ideas. Manufacturers will have to respond to the requirements of a more sophisticated market and will, therefore, have to invest heavily in the research and development of new technology.

Cash-rich Toyota are inevitably involved in significant expenditure on research and development and frequently advertise this aspect of their work. However, the company must be involved in research and development simply to maintain its leadership position. The design of Japanese cars leads the world (Bayley 1993). For example, a major competitor, Honda, uses the discipline of motor cycle racing and, more recently, Grand Prix motor racing to train its engineers as part of its research and development programme because components used in these sports must be designed to operate to extraordinary tolerances (ibid). However, problems associated with the recession have indicated an overall fall in research and development expenditure by Japanese companies (Garth 1993).

'In 1992 Toyota spent £1.9 billion in cash on research and development (equivalent to 5 per cent of the next year's sales). Development costs constitute a huge part of the car industry's overheads and any kind of cooperation can mean big savings. Toyota is not under pressure to cooperate in this way but has set up a joint venture company in America with General Motors and has a deal for the production of its pick-up at the Volkswagen plant in Hanover'. (ibid)

Areas of particular interest are those of mechanical efficiency, materials science, reliability and handling. The product life-cycles of Japanese cars may be 24 months compared with other European companies, e.g. Volkswagen, with eight years (Bayley 1993).

Change is no longer slow. There are many environmental problems that involve the automobile, e.g. pollution, health, global warming, recyclability, alternative fuels and the more efficient use of fuel. It is no longer socially acceptable to ignore these problems and investment is seen as socially desirable.

■ 7.7 Lean production: the employees

Toyota is often quoted as being the company for lifetime employment and this was, and to a great extent still is, the case. Between 1948 and 1950 Toyota held down wage costs and reduced the number of employees because of large operating losses. These dismissals convinced union leaders that management was not interested in full employment and, therefore, the union leaders wanted to act to protect the remaining jobs. The unions called on Nissan, Toyota and Isuzu employees to present a united front by setting up shop committees and mounting a joint strike as a protest against the dismissals.

Despite these protests the shop committees generally failed to organise the united front required and in the summer of 1950 Toyota dismissed 2,000 employees. The remainder desperately wanted to keep their jobs and accepted pay cuts. The unions settled for guarantees of employment, wage increases for permanent staff and co-operation with regard to cost reduction and productivity. Lifetime employment, for which Toyota is famed, was therefore simply a way of avoiding conflict and any problems it presented were overcome by using non-permanent employees. In July 1952 there were several major strikes and in May 1953 wage negotiations agreed a sliding scale based on seniority with guarantees to new employees that their wages would rise with years of service until a maximum was reached after 20 years.

Lifetime employment and the sliding scale of pay encouraged the workforce to remain with the company. To move elsewhere would mean starting at the bottom. This in turn encouraged the company to invest in training their employees thereby increasing their knowledge and experience.

After 1953 wages and benefits fell, in real terms, and did not increase, in real terms, until the 1970s when production expansion enabled large wage rises, relative to other major manufacturing sectors, to be given. By 1983 wages were approximately equal to those paid in the electronics and electrical equipment industries, more than shipbuilding but less than other industries. Toyota paid 17 per cent above the average within the automobile industry. Currently salaries and wages in the Japanese automobile industry are no longer low; in fact they are higher than those in the United Kingdom which must have provided an additional incentive for the Japanese when seeking a foothold within Europe. Japanese companies have been remarkably successful in setting up their production and supply networks in the United Kingdom which is a country previously notorious for strikes although the striking power of the unions has been substantially weakened over the last 15 years.

Toyota had a distinct advantage over other Japanese automobile manufacturers because its rural location and position as a large, local employer carried with it a special sense of loyalty and community. The only other employment was in farming or with Toyota suppliers. Initially Toyota had been forced to employ local labour because nothing else was available and thus Toyota was the mainstay of the area's economy.

By 1960 employees were having their aptitude evaluated for particular jobs or promotion. Opinions from fellow workers and supervisors were sought and a report produced which stated objectives for the year ahead and whether those of the previous year had been met. These reports were sent to the individual's family. Japanese culture required good reports so employees conformed to the company's requirements. It seems surprising that such pressure was required if lean production gave employees the additional responsibility to motivate themselves to achieve high performance levels.

There is divided opinion on whether or not employees find their work fulfilling under lean production. The United Automobile Workers in the United States say lean production is worse than the boredom of the one tiny repetitive task of mass production because it is 'management by stress' where pressure is continuously applied to identify and eliminate slack. The Udevalla Volvo plant in Sweden uses teams of ten workers assembling a vehicle – it is argued that this is simply mass production with an extended cycle time. Each team is expected to produce four vehicles a day. Others argue that this is as good as lean production but better for the employee.

Those siding with lean production agree that the elimination of slack is fundamental but that it provides employees with the skills needed to control their environment and meet the challenges offered. The move to lean production is a move away from the 'mind-numbing stress' of manual work to the 'creative tension' of thinking. However, lean production must offer job security or the creative thinking applied to slack elimination will be avoided because it may merely result in the achievement of lost jobs.

In essence, lean production eliminates waste from every process, every machine and every worker. However, there are critics of the system. Toyota have been accused of treating employees as human transfer machines where eight to ten hours a day were spent in an area of one square yard with only a short break for lunch. There was no time to speak or to understand the part being played. Toyota has been compared with other Japanese automobile manufacturers and it has been shown that the pace of work has led to a higher than average level of major accidents, leading to 4 or more days' absence, and a high number of blue-collar suicides.

Despite this, Toyota does have a flexible, multi-skilled, highly experienced workforce who are able to self-inspect their work at every stage of the manufacturing process. The ideal of lean production is that employees are highly skilled problem-solvers who are offered challenges and potential fulfilment and this does seem to be achieved. Another view is that mass production is simply lean production run by the rule book so that no one takes the initiative and responsibility to continually improve the system.

Lean production offers a career of solving problems. Following success at one level a career move will offer the challenge of increasingly complicated problems. Pay traditionally increases with seniority but this is overcome to some extent by the payment of performance bonuses. Even though an employee's title may not change his self-esteem can increase because of his performance. Another form of promotion or reward is for managers to hold key posts in supplier companies or for senior and middle management to rotate between geographical locations. Both of these rewards allow a network of relationships and contacts to be created which in turn enables the philosophy of lean production to be passed on (Oliver and Wilkinson 1988).

■ 7.8 Case Study of lean production: Johnson and Johnson Orthopaedics

■ Introduction

Johnson & Johnson was founded by Robert Wood Johnson and incorporated in 1887 during a period when the United States, which had been lagging behind European standards of healthcare, began to take an interest in hospital care. Together with two younger brothers, Robert founded a medical production company in New Brunswick, New Jersey, a busy inland port midway between New York and Philadelphia. There were excellent transport links by road, rail and sea with access via the Raritan river. The company expanded rapidly to meet ever more increasing demand. After the First World War, and the replenishment of supplies, demand fell and new growth opportunities were required. The company was convinced that international manufacturing units should be set up commencing with Slough, England in 1924.

Overseas policy was that initially new products were placed with agents, then international affiliates were formed which were managed by nationals of the country concerned. Most of these grew rapidly and by 1956 there were 25 such affiliates. The pharmaceutical aspect of health care was considered 'risky' and entry was resisted until 1958 when the President of the company, George F Smith, considered that the area offered long-term growth potential and several acquisitions were made. The company structure was becoming unwieldy and changes were introduced that set the scene for the decentralised organisation structure which exists today (Foster 1986).

Johnson & Johnson has 168 companies in 53 countries. It manufactures in 194 locations in 48 countries and markets its products in 158 countries. It also employs 5,800 scientists in 60 laboratories worldwide. The company employs approximately 84,900 people (Johnson & Johnson 1992). It is the largest most diversified health care company in the world and is the only company to serve all medical specialities. It is a highly decentralised organisation with each individual company having its own identity and name. The company has three major divisions, Pharmaceutical, Professional Products and Health Related Consumer Products.

'The Professional segment includes suture and mechanical wound closure products, less invasive surgical instruments, dental products, diagnostic products, medical equipment and devices, ophthalmic products, surgical instruments, joint replacements and products for wound management and infection prevention. These products are used principally in the professional fields by physicians, dentists, nurses, therapists, hospitals, diagnostic laboratories and clinics. Distribution to these markets is done either directly or through surgical supply and other dealers. Johnson & Johnson

Orthopaedics was one of five companies achieving very high sales volume gains in the United States and abroad.' (Johnson & Johnson (1) 1992)

The Professional segment began with the founding of the company and has always had a strong and sound relationship with physicians, nurses and hospitals. During the 1970s health care costs escalated whilst advances in scientific approaches and technology became evident. The company retained its competitive edge and during the late 1970s emphasis was placed on new products and improved product investment by research and acquisition. During the period 1976–85 thirty acquisitions were made which added to the product range. Johnson & Johnson Hospital Services was formed which complemented the decentralised companies by improving distribution and marketing to the providers of health care (Johnson & Johnson (1) 1992).

Johnson & Johnson Orthopaedics Limited was originally the fracture management group of the Patient Care Division of Johnson & Johnson in the late 1870s. It was based in Gargrave, North Yorkshire, with a sales and marketing office in Slough. As this division expanded and with Johnson & Johnson's policy of decentralisation the group became a division. It was, however, only involved with certain goods. The implants market beckoned as a way of expansion and a suitable acquisition was sought. A company which was already manufacturing and selling implants to the Health Service was considered ideal and after some searching Derek Howse & Company was acquired in 1982.

In 1984 the company moved into purpose-built accommodation at New Milton, Hampshire, and became a limited liability company. The New Milton site was mainly a manufacturing and research and development facility with the administration being dealt with at the head office which was then in Slough. Further decentralisation took place in 1987 and Johnson & Johnson Orthopaedics became responsible for its own administrative functions. Today Johnson & Johnson Orthopaedics is the only UK orthopaedic operating unit within the company. Considerable expansion has taken place at the New Milton facility and more is planned.

A study was made of Johnson & Johnson Orthopaedics in 1993 comparing the characteristics of lean production at Toyota with attempts to introduce world class manufacturing to the New Milton facility (Stewart 1994). The results of this study are outlined below. Many of the facts and figures were obtained by personal interview with Johnson & Johnson staff.

■ Design

Johnson & Johnson Orthopaedics hip and knee products tend to have a rather long-life cycle. Surgeons become used to, have success with and hence faith in a particular product and, despite redesign and development, are unwilling to change their procedures. Because of this, it is unlikely that the company could set up a design and development team to last for the life of the product.

However, the design task force is made up of a multi-functional team containing product engineers, bioengineers, quality assurance staff, design draughtsmen, technicians, purchasing staff and shop floor employees. The engineers also work with research and development. The opinions and views of suppliers are sought and the senior buyer is now included on new product introductions. 'Hips' are designed in the United Kingdom whilst 'Knees' are designed in the United States.

A great deal of emphasis is placed on designs which will allow easy and efficient manufacture as well as the very high quality specification demanded by the company and expected by the consumer. This compares well with the lean production emphasis on manufacturability.

There are many new products within the company's portfolio and the company has found that it has been able to increase the speed with which a product moves from simply being an idea to actual production. New products are frequently clinical improvements or technological developments to existing products based on clinical experience. The 'Ultima Hip Range' is no exception.

The range has been developed by working in co-operation with clinicians. The range has been developed from the original 'Howse I' stainless steel total hip replacement whose six and ten year clinical results showed it to be an excellent hip replacement with few post-operative problems. The replacement of stainless steel with a titanium alloy led to the 'Howse II Range' and further research led to developments which offered reduced wear and hence a longer life. Further advances have led to the introduction of cementless implants and standardisation of both techniques and instrumentation. In 1991 the 'Ultima' range was introduced which incorporated ceramics. This range should meet all needs and offers both a variety of materials which optimise the properties of the various alloys used and a rationalisation of instrumentation provided in a tray system which offers numerous advantages over isolated instruments (Johnson & Johnson (2)). A total package including all instruments to ensure efficient and effective use of the products is supplied. Surgeons provide a very valuable source of feedback for change and improvement.

■ Supply

Johnson & Johnson Orthopaedics produce a very high quality, premium priced product. Unlike the automobile industry the overall production volume is very small. The company, therefore, requires comparatively low volume purchases of raw materials and components which means the company has little leverage with its suppliers and in some cases supply is a 'goodwill' relationship by companies which predominantly produce for the aerospace industry. Supplying a company with the scope and reputation of Johnson & Johnson adds a certain prestige and impression of social awareness to any external reporting. Among the purchases made is that of forgings. There are two main suppliers, one providing 90 per cent of the forgings required for hip and knee replacement products the other providing the balance. These forgings are made from cobalt-chrome and titanium which are both commodities quoted on the world market. They are very price sensitive and it is almost impossible to control the prices of these purchases. Suppliers have, however, been very co-operative in keeping prices low.

All raw materials must be quality validated. It is difficult for suppliers to obtain such validation and Johnson & Johnson insist that quality is imperative and much more important than price. Both statistical process control and total quality management are expected at the supplier level. It is necessary for products to be lot traceable back to the supplier so that simply monthly invoicing and delivery straight to the production line are not possible. All deliveries must go through the store which is, therefore, treated as the first part of the production process and initiates the necessary documentation. It is interesting to note that documents must be stored for the life of a patient. This ensures traceability should any problem arise and should help to back up clinical trials if this is required. In a way this is similar to the procedure for automobiles where, if a defect is found, all owners can be notified and corrective action taken. In a similar way all finished goods go through the store which is the final part of the overall process and ensures that the necessary documentation is undertaken. The Department of Health requires all documentation to be kept.

Johnson & Johnson Orthopaedics operate a batch/job production mode where demand is predicted using an integrated forecasting package and production is in response to a pre-planned production level rather than a demand forecast. It is therefore a 'push' system rather than the 'pull' system of lean production where actual demand 'pulls' production through its various processes. The comparatively low production volume operation causes some problems with raw material supplies which are determined using a computer software package. This package is based on the economic order quantity model which identifies the order quantity that minimises the total cost of stock holding and ordering. Frequently stock holding costs, in particular, are likely to be understated causing higher than necessary stocks due to high order quantities. Raw material stocks are equivalent to three months' production which is exceptionally high when compared with Toyota's average inventory of parts equal to two hours' production. However, some suppliers are prepared to accept large volume orders to be followed up by small batch delivery as required. It is inevitable that if the manufacturer is not in a powerful position over the supplier then the manufacturer will be the stockholder.

Johnson & Johnson Orthopaedic employ an integrated forecasting package, Logol, which uses information on advance orders and trends in demand to produce a production forecast. This is then linked to the supply software and the material requirements to meet production are determined.

To a great extent Johnson & Johnson Orthopaedic have exclusive or semi-exclusive agreements with a few suppliers per item or group of items. There seems to be a fairly open relationship between the company and its suppliers and plant visits are encouraged both to and from major suppliers.

■ Manufacture

Johnson & Johnson Orthopaedic aim to provide not only exceptionally high quality products but also an exceptional service. By 1987 the company was expanding, new products were being developed and produced and sales increased. Despite investment in technologically advanced equipment the company could not cope with demand. Inventories and back-order levels were high because the company produced high volume batches and a product lead time of six to eight weeks was not unusual. The company's commitment is to fulfil orders within 24 hours (Stewart 1994). A major performance indicator used is that of percentage orders fulfilled within that 24-hour period. In 1993 the company achieved a rate of 97 per cent; however, the target is 99.9 per cent. With a minimum production cycle of two weeks including five days' irradiation it is impossible to meet orders within this 24-hour time slot unless they are supplied from stock. Therefore large stocks of finished goods are held.

Irradiation is confirmed by an indicator on the packaging which changes colour on treatment and packages are labelled with the appropriate language. The irradiation process, which takes between 3.5 and 5 hours, is contracted out to a company in Swindon (approximately 60 miles away) and is essential because it ensures sterility. The company is therefore to a great extent at conflict with itself. It wants to move totally to the concept of lean production where the company would only manufacture to meet customer orders but wants to be able to offer the ultimate in service. However, whether or not the company wishes to hold stocks, produced in response to demand forecasts predicted by its forecasting model, it can still apply the majority of lean production principles. Where necessary it will compromise in order to achieve the competitive edge that will enable it to establish itself as the major implant manufacturing site in Europe.

The company's strategic plan (see also Chapter 1) emphasises the need to continually decrease inventory levels whilst manufacturing to order rather than for stock, and decreasing manufacturing lead time to ten days including the five-day irradiation period (Stewart 1994). However, there are further problems as demand is not steady throughout the year. There are three peak periods, the first being at the end of March which is the end of the financial year for organisations within the National Health Service. If funds are available at this time of the year it is most probable that budget holders will want to use up all of their remaining money. In order to do this they must, at present, both order and physically receive the products. The health organisations are not able to order in bulk but require delivery on request. In the same way once the end of March has passed and a new budget is set money will be available and so orders are placed.

This actually presents a very interesting point in that if such organisations can be provided with their annual supplies at one particular point in time then the competition is immediately excluded for the following year! Inventory tends to build during the summer when demand falls. Other peak periods are at the end of June and December when mid and end-year bonuses are paid to salesmen who make extra efforts prior to these points in time. A change in the bonus system for salesmen is being considered at present. Demand is therefore very erratic which causes considerable problems when trying to schedule production.

Another problem arises with the introduction of new, improved products. Surgeons become used to, and have success with, particular models. They frequently wish to continue using these models and are reluctant to change. Johnson & Johnson try to accommodate requests for old models provided a minimum number are ordered; but a point will come where customisation is a better option. However, customisation does not meet the next-day-delivery target and is more likely to be ten days and at considerable extra cost. Therefore a much higher price is charged. Customisation uses computer aided design and is specific to individual patients and their surgeon. It provides a very profitable source of income mainly from Germany and the Middle East and not only covers older models but also products designed specifically for an individual patient's use where a suitable product from the range is not appropriate.

Encouragement is given to surgeons to change to new models in the form of empirical surgical evidence. They are asked to carry out trials and are invited to become involved at the design stage. The product may even be named after them. However, the company frequently approaches the younger surgeons because they tend to be more adaptable and will use the product for their career hence extending its life-cycle.

Other factors that affect demand are funding for the National Health Service and the potential political expedient of reducing waiting lists.

It is likely that production will continue to be shared out evenly throughout the year based on the sophisticated forecasting model which produces weekly production schedules based on demand data for 35 countries. This must mean that stocks of finished goods are likely to remain at a fairly high level although they have been reduced hugely over the last few years from a high of 15.4 months and £13 million in July 1991 (when Mecron, a German subsidiary, merged with United Kingdom operations and all production was transferred to the New Milton site) to the current level of 5.4 months and £6.4 million in June 1993. It is anticipated that this will fall further and new targets have been set accordingly.

The manufacturing facility is dedicated to reduce set-up and throughput times by using quick change tooling. Typically set-up times of 1.5 hours have been reduced to a matter of minutes and batch sizes average 20 units. The facility is highly automated and the craftsmen who worked on the early hip and knee replacements are still highly skilled but in a different way. They are increasingly computer literate and much of the highly automated facility is now computer controlled. There are two very impressive robotic machines in use for abrading part finished products to very specific tolerances. With the use of unmanned machines the level of maintenance is increasing, with some of the machines able to run all night.

'The thrust of cellular manufacturing at Johnson & Johnson Orthopaedic, Raynham Massachusetts, focused on cycle time reduction whilst product and process improvements became integrated into the manufacturing process allowing us to meet other critical factors such as cost reduction and an increase in quality' (Johnson & Johnson (4)). New Milton followed this example and an implementation team was set up including engineering, quality systems, facilities, planning and production packaging. The team drafted a detailed implementation plan which, after they explained the reasons for the changes and the anticipated effects, was implemented incrementally, where possible during evenings and weekends. The employees were suspicious at first and thought the idea 'American and Glitzy' which was not an unreasonable reaction. Skill was needed to sell the idea to the work force who eventually accepted it and have since found that change was for the better.

'There is a greater degree of flexibility within the cell, working at other stations within the cell provides a change of pace and decreased the boredom associated with repetition. The rotation has also been a good team builder' (Johnson & Johnson (4)) (see also Chapter 6.6).

Workers are generally flexible but only the knee cell has totally multi-skilled workforce flexibility. There are very few indirect workers. Those that exist are supervisors, some of whom can carry out operations, with the exception of the cell leaders and cleaning staff. Significant space savings have been made in the raw materials store. Minimal work-in-progress is held in the cell. To achieve a dramatic improvement in stock-holdings of finished goods it will be necessary for the main purchasers to even out their demand over the year rather than the present emphasis on expenditure early in the year when a new budget is set and expenditure late in the year when budgets balances must be spent in order to achieve full spending and avoid the accusation of over-estimation. This is typically dysfunctional behaviour.

The plant at New Milton operates at high capacity. Overtime is frequently worked. One of the ten cells, the Clean and Pack Cell, is a bottleneck and a night shift operates. Shift allowances are paid typically at overtime plus 10 per cent and overtime represents between 14 per cent and 23 per cent of salary earned. Rates of pay are good although by no means the highest in the industry. Profits are shared on a flat-rate basis at present although a change was at the discussion stage at the time of this study.

There is an employee money saving suggestion scheme. There is also a Total Employee Involvement Programme with an employee committee representative which meets every six weeks.

There is no laid-down career path apart from internal training and an excellent apprentice scheme. Idle time is no more than 5 per cent and is used for maintenance and training. Scrap levels are comparatively small and work to be scrapped tends to be identified early in the manufacturing process and is frequently due to some plastic related problems which are acceptable in the United States but not in the United Kingdom. A scrap report is produced regularly and has identified scrap as accounting for between 1.5 and 2 per cent of units produced.

Responsibility has been delegated to the very experienced and capable employees on the factory floor. These self-inspecting operators decide whether rectification is possible and if so it takes place immediately. Previously defects would be found very late in the production process.

■ Sales and Distribution

Of total sales approximately 50 per cent are domestic and the remainder are exports. Despite, or perhaps because of, the premium price the products are in demand throughout the world but especially in Europe. The European market offers significant growth opportunities but competition is becoming increasingly international with a particular focus on Europe. More stringent European regulatory controls have made things difficult for the small manufacturer who may well leave the market allowing the larger firms to expand by merger or acquisition. Growth in Europe is anticipated at approximately 4 per cent per annum and Johnson & Johnson's 5.2 per cent share of the European market makes it clear that a well-developed sales infrastructure from which products can be promoted has become increasingly important (Johnson & Johnson (3)).

One of Johnson & Johnson's key strategic objectives is to concentrate on the major market segments of hips and knees which represent 54 per cent of the total supply of products related to the repair and rehabilitation of the musculoskeletal system. The strategic plan indicates that investment in the sales infrastructure in Europe must continue with the provision of a rapid delivery service from a centralised warehouse. Investment in sales personnel has increased from 28 employees in 1990 to 43 in 1993. Further growth in this area is anticipated. Johnson & Johnson control their own distribution. The two market leaders, Howmedica and Zimmer, have both moved away from the use of distributors. Further centralisation would enable the company to become a major supplier particularly in Belgium, France and Spain (Johnson & Johnson (3)). Johnson & Johnson is currently eighth in the world but number one in the United Kingdom.

An alternative, or additional, strategy for growth towards a leader in the field would be to acquire some of the competition. For example, Depuy (part of Boehinger Mannheim), Stryker, Richards, Smith and Nephew, Zimmer, Biomet and Howmedica are potential acquisitions but there are problems such as excessive costs or outstanding or potential anti-trust issues.

■ Research and development

Johnson & Johnson continually updates its products and searches for new and better materials that will improve the quality and length of implant life. It is researching into high mobility, shoulder, elbow and back joints and the stresses and strains placed on joints to help in the search for solutions to present operational problems. For growing children research is being undertaken into expanding bone and joint replacement. In both the United Kingdom and the United States, Smith & Nephew, a major competitor, has links with university research where particular efforts are also concentrated on extending the life of a replacement joint. The life depends on a number of factors but in particular age and the level of activity. Research into nuclear fusion has had some interesting spin-offs in this field and a life of forty years for a replacement joint has been mentioned which is significantly longer than that of present models.

Other areas of research in the industry are:

- 'A new superglue, designed to replace surgical stitching, which is fast acting, able to reach otherwise inaccessible body areas and does not leave scars' (*Daily Mail*).
- 'Scientists in America have discovered that the way oysters create their shells can be copied to help provide stronger artificial joints. The joint rarely wears out but the "cement" leads to bits of bone flaking off causing pain and inflammation . . ... Something was needed that was a more natural interface with metal, plastic and bone to prevent this weakening. In essence it involves building layers of ceramic material on metal surfaces' (*Daily Mail*).

Johnson & Johnson are working in particular on cements with United States backing, and Arthroscopy (keyhole surgery) which will require backing. Johnson & Johnson's knee design in the United States and hip design in the United Kingdom encourages the free flow of ideas and joint ventures between the two parts of the company. Conference attendance is encouraged.

New product appraisals are analysed on the basis of their return on capital employed. The method used is not particularly sophisticated and, in fact, because costs may all be charged in the first year, it is perhaps more an adaptation of the very simple payback method of capital investment appraisal which ignores the time value of money and is considered, academically, to be rather crude. It is not clear whether this method is effective because no post-audit procedure is carried out. Normally fairly rapid returns are anticipated which will cover the research and development costs. If a project is likely to be particularly expensive it goes to the Brussels office for approval. The availability of research grants and the importance of patent law is realised in this context.

■ Employee conditions

Johnson & Johnson offer excellent working conditions but do not, by their own admission, pay premium rates. However, staff turnover is very low. Employees are reluctant to leave and the introduction of lean production, despite initial resistance to change, has not resulted in any increase in turnover. The flexible multi-skilled workforce includes highly experienced employees who are of great value to the company. Internal training is maximised and a number of apprenticeships are offered although there is no career path policy. Lifetime employment is not guaranteed but unacceptable behaviour would initially result in an enquiry, further training and ultimately dismissal (see also Chapter 6.6).

Pay is increased for inflation, not seniority. Additional payments are performance related and year-end annual bonuses or share bonus plans where 2 per cent of annual salary can be paid into an independent trust to purchase Johnson & Johnson shares. A move to a more 'individual-based' scheme was under discussion during 1993 which has resulted in a range of bonus payments with a proportion based on individual performance. Overtime is paid at time and a half with the exception of Sundays and public holidays when double time is paid. Annual leave entitlements increase with seniority. However, plant shutdowns must be treated as holiday entitlement and are usually one week in duration during the summer period when most production is for stock. After five years all employees have an entitlement to private health insurance. In fact, middle and senior management receive this on joining the company and other grades can pay a reduced rate prior to completion of the five-year qualifying period. There are long service awards to employees after 5, 10, 15, 20 and 25 years. During the last year of employment, prior to retirement, a phased reduction in hours with no loss of salary can be arranged. There are numerous other employee benefits.

■ 7.9 Conclusions

Toyota provided the characteristics of lean production which Johnson & Johnson Orthopaedics proceeded to apply in their move toward world class manufacturing. They have successfully moved from a situation of huge stocks, poor production scheduling, high backlogs of orders and poor performance to one of very high performance by introducing lean production based on production cells. Despite initial scepticism of cellular manufacture the workforce has rapidly become multi skilled and flexible giving improvements in quality, cycle times and customer service. Because of this sales are forecast to increase dramatically in the future. As Walter Hak (International Vice President) stated, 'What they have accomplished is really significant and positions the plant beautifully for the future. As we grow, this business, these accomplishments will continue to pay off handsomely' (Johnson & Johnson Operations Institute (4)). It can be seen, from the above, that Johnson & Johnson have adopted many aspects of lean production but are hampered by the production cycle length together with their 24-hour delivery promise, their lack of purchasing power with their suppliers and peak demand periods due to inflexible budgeting constraints within the National Health Service, one of their major customers.

It is clear, therefore, that lean production characteristics can be adapted to meet the requirements of comparatively small organisations and is not only applicable to the large producer. However, production volume levels of standardised products hardly need the degree of sophistication that lean production provides, and as Johnson & Johnson Orthopaedic's production volume increases cell manufacture many no longer be appropriate.

Table 7.2 lists the major characteristics of lean production at Johnson and Johnson.

Table 7.2   The major characteristics of lean production at Johnson & Johnson

	J & J
NEW PRODUCT DESIGN	
Product range growing	1
Products designed for easy manufacture	1
Design stage input from all functions	1
Team exists for project life	2
Target costing used	2
Speed from idea to sale accelerating	1
SUPPLY	
Low inventory held	2
Parts delivered to meet production requirements	2
Delivery to production line	2
Inventory expressed in terms of production time	1
Long term supplier relationships	1
Exclusive or semi-exclusive supplier agreements	1
Few suppliers	1
Large volume order, small batch delivery	3
Low prices	1
Involvement in supplier profit margins	2
Quality assured suppliers	1
Simplified invoicing	2
Open supplier relationship	1
MANUFACTURE	
Flexible automated machines	1
Few indirect workers	1
Low set up times	1
Ideal of a batch of one	2
Customisation possible	1
Minimal stocks of work-in-progress and finished goods	2
Space savings achieved	1
Low rejection rates	1
Zero defect aim	1
Little rework	1
Low cost	1
High volume	2
Elimination of waste	1
Idle times expected	2

Table 7.2 (cont.)

Employees have problem solving skills	1
Responsibility delegated to the factory floor	1
Changes made incrementally	1
Cell manufacture	1
Teamwork	1
Production scheduling to meet known demand	2
Production may be halted in response to a problem	1
Finished goods are distributed directly from production	2
Use is made of computer aided design and manufacture	1
SALES AND DISTRIBUTION	
Comprehensive customer database maintained	2
Demand forecast and adjusted for actual demand	2
Customers consulted about new products	1
RESEARCH AND DISTRIBUTION	
Takes place within the organisation and is not isolated	1
Directed at some specific objective	1
EMPLOYEES	
Lifetime employment	2
Staff turnover low	1
Pay be seniority	2
Bonuses (typically 30% of pay)	1
Overtime (typically 10% of pay)	1
Good working conditions	1
Flexible workforce	1
Multiskilled	1
Promotes the company	1
Trained	1
Geographical exchanges encouraged	3
Increased job satisfaction	1
INFLUENCES ON SUCCESS	
Culture	1

Key: 1 Adopted, 2 Not Adopted, 3 Partial Adoption

■ Questions for discussion

1. Many of the benefits gained from the mechanisation required for lean production involve very high levels of capital expenditure. Any proposal for such expenditure must be supported by a capital investment appraisal. However, many of the benefits resulting from this mechanisation are unquantifiable which may result in the proposal being rejected. How can organisations overcome this problem?
2. How can Johnson & Johnson overcome the fundamental problems that prevent it from being a completely lean company?

3. What is so special about Japan that allowed the philosophy of lean production to evolve whilst the West was still mastering mass production?
4. Will Western manufacturers always try to 'mimic' successful Eastern practices or can they take the initiative and move ahead? If so, what changes to manufacturing practices can you envisage for the future?
5. Japanese manufacturers are obsessive about quality. They believe improved quality is desirable with little regard to cost. Do you think this is a wise move or will it enable Western manufacturers to obtain a cost advantage over the Japanese?

■ Bibliography

Bayley, Stephen, 'Zen and the Cycle of Motor Art', *Sunday Times Magazine*, 19 September 1993.
Berliner, C., and Brimson, J. A., *Cost Management for Today's Advanced Manufacturing* (Harvard: Harvard Business School Press, 1988).
Cobb, Ian, 'Understanding and Working with Just-In-Time', *Management Accounting*, February 1991.
Crosby, Philip B., *Zero Defects. Quality is Free. The Art of Making Certain* (New York: McGraw-Hill, 1979).
Cusumano, Michael A., *The Japanese Automobile Industry. Technology and Management at Nissan and Toyota* (Council on East Asia Studies, 1985).
Daily Mail, 'Stitches are out – Stick to Glue', *Daily Mail*, 26 April 1994.
Delbridge, R. and Olner, N., 'Just-In-Time or Just-The-Same', *Logistics Information Management*, MCB University Press, vol. , no. 3 (1991).
Drury, C., *Management and Cost Accouting*, 4th edn (Thomson Business Press, 1996).
Economist, The 'The Race to Survive', *The Economist*, 5 December 1992.
Eisenhammer, J., 'British Work Impresses German Firms', *Independent*, 5 December 1993.
Foster, Laurence G., *A Company That Cares. One Hundred Years Illustrated History of Johnson & Johnson* (Johnson & Johnson, 1986).
Fujimoto, Takahiro, 'Organisation for the Effective Product Development Case of the Global Motor Industry', *Brookings Papers on Economic Activity* no. 3, 1987.
Garth, Alexander, 'Japanese Invaders Change Lanes', *Sunday Times*, 12 September 1993.
Garth, Alexander, 'Crisis in Japan', *Sunday Times*, 19 September 1993.
Halle, Martyn, 'Scientists Are Copying Nature to Help Ease the Pain of Hip Operations', *Daily Mail*, 12 April 1994.
International Motor Vehicle Program World Assembly Plant Survey 1990.
Johnson & Johnson (1), *Annual Report. 1992. Growth in World Markets*.
Johnson & Johnson (2), *Ultima Hip System Brochure and Specification*.
Johnson & Johnson (3), *Strategic Plan 1995–2000*.
Johnson & Johnson (4), *Voice of World Class*.
Johnson & Johnson (5), *Employee Handbook*.
Krafcik, J.F. and MacDuffie, J.P., 'Explaining High Performance Manufacturing – The International Automobile Assembly Plant Study', Paper presented to the *IMVP International Policy Forum. Acapulco*, 7–10 May 1989.
McMann, P. J. and Nanni, A. J. Jr, 'Means versus Ends: A Review of the Literature on Japanese Management Accounting', *Management Accounting Research*, CIMA, vol. 6, no. 4 (December 1995).

Munday, Max, 'Financial Consequences of Linkages with Japanese Manufacturers', *Management Accounting*, July/August 1990.

Oliver, N. and Wilkinson, B., *The Japanisation of British Industry* (Oxford: Blackwell, 1988).

Smith, Malcolm, 'Towards Decision Useful Management Accounting', *Management Accounting*, September 1989.

Stewart, H. M., 'Lean Production', MBA Dissertation submitted to Brunel University, 1994.

Toyota Motor Corporation, *Toyota: A History of the First 50 years* (TMC: 1987).

Vehblen, T., *The Opportunity of Japan. Easy in Our Changing Order*, (New York Press: 1954) (Reprinted from *Journal of Race Development*, 1915).

Womack, J.P., Jones, D.T. and Roos, D., *The Machine that Changed the World. The Triumph of Lean Production* (New York: Rawson Macmillan, 1990).

CHAPTER 8

EU environmental policy and business

Adrian Webb

■ 8.1 Introduction

This chapter analyses the relationship of European Union (EU) environmental policy and business with the particular example of the packaging directive and its impact on the Swedish paper firm, Korsnäs AB of Gävle, as its case study. For the discussion to be meaningful, however, it must unpick a much wider network of relationships which impinge on the main argument and determine its whole character. Those other relationships, moreover, are themselves multi-dimensional and by no means necessarily internally consistent. The final section of this chapter will be devoted to a review of some unresolved questions.

The relationships impinging on the main discussion are essentially five in number. The first is that between EU environmental policy and EU policy as a whole. The nature of that relationship is constantly evolving and has at least three dimensions of its own:

- the ongoing tension between economic and environmental objectives which has been absorbed in theory, but not necessarily in practice, by the adoption of the concept of sustainable development
- the impact on that tension of the wider pressures for the globalisation of trade characterised by the successful conclusion of the Uruguay round and the establishment of the World Trade Organisation (WTO)
- the interplay of those wider pressures with others emanating from within the EU itself for subsidiarity and deregulation but also the maintenance of higher environmental standards by the newer entrants to EU membership in particular, but also encompassing Denmark.

That interplay is also associated with the constant struggle for influence between the EU's own institutions. This is reflected in the arguments over the desirability of environmental taxation and its proper role in influencing behaviour. That third dimension above also links back to the first, in that environmental taxation has to be national to be practicable but any effective national structure is almost by definition a barrier to the free movement of goods within the single market.

The second relationship is that between EU environmental policy as a whole and its approach to waste management generally and to packaging waste in particular. That relationship has been shaped in the past by intense lobbying by industry and by environmental Non-Governmental Organisations (NGOs) and is virtually certain to continue to be so. It is a relationship on which NGOs have exercised a great deal of successful influence, notably persuading the Commission that waste should not be regarded as a commodity to be bought and sold on the open market, but something to be reduced to the absolute minimum and disposed of as near to source as possible. An integral part of this relationship is the established hierarchy of waste avoidance, reconditioning, and disposal, with the latter only as a last resort. Finally there is the particular issue of packaging waste.

The third relationship is that between packaging legislation and the beverage cartons industry in particular, and the pressures it exercises, not least through its Brussels based representative organisation, to promote recycling rather than re-use. This relationship relates back to the first one above with its tension between the goals of free trade and environmental improvement and the constraints which that may impose on the freedom of national governments to implement distinctive policies.

Within this third relationship, the paper board suppliers occupy a particular position because of the positive contribution which the industry can make to the environment through the adoption of sustainable forestry policies.

The fourth relationship is that between the EU's packaging directive and Scandinavia in particular. The impact is wide-ranging from the potentially adverse effect on public opinion of any approach which runs counter to the traditionally high Scandinavian respect for the environment, to contradicting the traditional appreciation of the forest and of wood as the most environmentally friendly and natural of products of which the nation should make maximum sustainable use.

The fifth relationship is complex in that it relates the preceding four to the dilemmas faced by the Swedish firm Korsnäs AB, the subject of our case study, and that firm's attempts to resolve the tensions experienced by adopting a sustainable approach to forestry as the source of its raw material, and also to production and to marketing.

The chapter finishes, as we have already noted, with an assessment of some of the ongoing controversies to which it has drawn attention. That assessment can only be subjective, but is none the less valid for that.

■ 8.2 The relationship between environmental policy and policy as a whole in the EU

■ The evolution of EU environmental policy

The inspiration of the 1957 Treaty of Rome, which established the European Economic Community, was both idealistic and prosaic. Perhaps that is why it succeeded. The ideal of bringing the peoples of the six founder states into an ever closer association to banish for ever the spectre of war, was to be achieved by the integration of their economies within a common market. That common market was conceived in essentially capitalist terms, and was accordingly rejected by many on the left of the political spectrum. Its goal of 'continuous and balanced expansion' of economic activity certainly reflected the aspirations of business and indeed of the ordinary citizen for whom the shortage of many goods, often including food, was a far from distant memory. Much has changed in the ensuing forty years, but the almost religious faith in the centrality to the European ideal of the free movement of goods within a single market has not.

It is a framework within which the environment has never fitted entirely comfortably. The growth in environmental concern which mushroomed during the 1960s led the Commission to decide that environmental concern was implicit in the Treaty of Rome, and its first communication on Community environmental policy appeared in 1971. It was followed by a series of directives and regulations laying down quality standards for products and processes which had a considerable impact on national administrative and legal practices, and formed an important cornerstone of a competitive level playing field within the single market (Haigh 1984). Differing environmental standards between countries could, after all, easily be interpreted as conferring unfair advantage on businesses located in, or deliberately relocating to, less demanding member states. The extent to which this level playing field may be jeopardised by any repatriation of policy under the guise of subsidiarity is a question which will be returned to. A number of other environmental directives and regulations laid down standards on matters much closer to the concerns of the EU citizen, such as drinking-water and bathing-water quality. Although they had to wait for some 10–15 years before they exercised their full effect, these were to become far better known than their more technical cousins.

The force for change was to be the public relations skills employed by the environmental NGOs and the EU environment commissioner of the time, Carlo Ripa di Meana, who jointly succeeded in making EU environmental policy genuinely popular. Indeed it could be persuasively argued that the bathing-water directive enjoyed more direct political legitimacy than any other single piece of EU legislation. Less controversially, but of wider relevance to our present purpose, EU environmental policy has had a much greater level of success and acceptability than EU initiatives in most other sectors.

It may seem contradictory in such circumstances to describe environmental policy as fitting uncomfortably into the EU framework, but it remains the case that the original Treaty of Rome was a very single-minded document and the specific inclusion of environmental protection within the EU's duties and competences under the Single European Act and the Maastricht Treaty has not yet led to the integration of the two (see also Chapters 1.2 and 2.3 for reference to the single market). This is a very live political issue closely tied up with the comparative influence within the Commission of the respective commissioners, and the draft Treaty agreed at Amsterdam in June 1997 gives them an even more sensitive role. It is also a battleground between business interests, which in general are seeking to assert the primacy of the single market, and the NGOs together with influential voices within the European Parliament, not least in its Environment Committee, who are championing the environmental cause. The struggle over beverage cartons is just one campaign in this much larger battle. It is arguably an ill-conceived battle because many of those involved appreciate that environmental compatibility is actually a prerequisite of effective competition within the single market, not to mention of such modern management concepts as Total Quality Management (see also Chapters 1.2 and 7.1). Nevertheless that is not how some of the current protagonists actually see it.

The concept of sustainable development should indicate the way out of this dilemma, but as Haigh (1996) has pointed out, even the renderings of the term vary between the different languages and the Treaties, and in many cases mean little more than sustained growth, a formula which John Major himself used and which does not resolve the dilemma at all. In the German case, only one of the four formal renderings corresponds to the literal translation of 'nachhaltige Entwicklung' routinely used by the environment ministry.

■ The tension between environmental and single market objectives

The current field of battle is the role of environmental taxation, but before turning to that it is necessary to underline the extent to which environmental standards are challenged not just by the EU's single market philosophy but also by the trend towards the globalisation of trade.

This has an impact on two interrelated fronts. On the one hand there is the thrust towards global standardisation at levels lower than those endorsed by the EU, which is particularly associated with America and the developing world. That has taken the form for example of pressing for the adoption of International Standards Organisation (ISO) standards to qualify for Environmental Management and Audit Scheme (EMAS) registration – a proposal which many would see as making EMAS much less stringent (ENDS Report 252, January 1996).

Secondly, there is concern that pressures for the free movement of goods will whittle down environmental standards generally. The extent to which developed countries have the right, or alternatively the duty, to impose environmental or social obligations on developing countries is a highly contentious moral and practical issue, but one is on safer ground if one merely points out that it will be widely interpreted in the developing world as protectionism. The current wisdom is that would be wrong. Be that as it may, global trade and environmental protection may prove uncomfortable bedfellows. Friends of the Earth have argued that the new World Trade Organisation needs to be counterbalanced by a new international environmental body and the concept was favoured by almost every group to give evidence to the Inquiry into Trade and the Environment by the UK House of Commons Environment Committee in the spring of 1996 (*European Trends*, 2nd quarter 1996). The European Commission itself and most OECD governments would, however, prefer to develop the role of the United Nations Environment Programme (ibid). The Commission is arguably excessively relaxed over the issue. When she presented a joint communication on trade and the environment with the trade commissioner, Sir Leon Brittan, in February 1996, the environment commissioner, Ritt Bjerregaard, declared in typically forthright language that, 'There are those who feel that the relationship between trade and the environment is like the relationship between virtue and sin. I do not share that view.' Sir Leon added, 'Not only are they compatible but they can be mutually supportive.' The communication argued that trade did not have to be environmentally damaging and that fears that environmental regulation would damage European competitiveness were largely unfounded as the normal additional burden on production was only some 1–2 per cent. It also repeated the Commission's established view that it saw no virtue in levying eco-duties on imported products which had been manufactured under substandard environmental conditions (*Europe Environment*, 7 March 1996). This is the key question, but the Commission does not appear to have any real answer. From an environmental perspective that is not reassuring.

It is not, however, totally surprising considering the strength of the related tensions within the EU itself. Those are focused on the drive for subsidiarity and for deregulation; on the pressure from the newer members for EU environmental standards to be brought up to their generally higher level for environmental reasons and the countervailing pressures for them to be brought down to the EU norm for single market reasons; and last but by no means least the potential impasse over the introduction of environmental taxation.

■ The impact of subsidiarity and deregulation

Subsidiarity is in essence the philosophy that issues should be decided at the lowest level consonant with the efficient discharge of associated functions. To put it in its traditional form, the parish pump should be the concern of the parish council and the army the concern of parliament and the crown. Expressed like that it is hardly controversial but in the context of EU environmental policy it is much more so. This is to no small degree because there are two complementary forces at work which are actually quite separate, but which some interests are ready to confuse. The first is the force towards 'technical' subsidiarity, and away from all-encompassing legislation with comprehensive blanket provisions. It is seen in the growing tendency towards framework sectoral directives for air quality, integrated pollution prevention and control, waste, water, and the like, and subordinate or 'daughter' directives dealing with precise problems and giving more scope for local considerations to be taken into account. It is a change in emphasis justified by greater scientific knowledge permitting a more discriminating approach to, say, trace pollutants and the reality that environmental conditions vary in a Europe stretching from the north of Finland to Crete in a way that was not the case in the original Europe of the six.

'Technical' subsidiarity is, however, essentially separate from the 'political' subsidiarity which is concerned with decisions being taken at the lowest effective level. In practice their operation is widely confused because all tiers of government are anxious to retain and extend the powers which they already enjoy, or at least think they enjoy, and a doctrine like subsidiarity lends itself to selective interpretation. A UK national government which often seemed to be almost at war with its own local authorities saw nothing incongruous in claiming powers back from Brussels under the guise of subsidiarity – to prevent it from 'delving into the nooks and crannies of British life', to quote Douglas Hurd's celebrated phrase. The practical consequence is that arguments over the level of discretion necessary to achieve an environmental result are overlaid or undermined by fears that the real objective is the repatriation of policy for political reasons with little regard to the environmental implications. These considerations are, as we shall see, as relevant to waste and packaging as to any other environmental sector, and in a further complication they are closely associated with the pressures we have already noted for deregulation of trade generally. Governments like those of the United Kingdom, which have been firmly wedded to free trade principles, have had a strong philosophical predisposition in favour of minimum regulation, and have seen subsidiarity as a means to avoid being constrained by what they perceived as the overly regulated approaches of many of their Continental partners. Similarly their enthusiasm for the earliest possible admission of the applicants from Eastern Europe has been motivated to no small degree by the belief that the Europe resulting could only function on a highly decentralised, deregulated basis. This is as true of the environment as of any other field, and one possible consequence is that future environmental legislation will have to be set at a very modest level if there is to be any pretence of compliance at a pan-European level.

Pressures to deregulate or to repatriate environmental policy are, however, shot through with contradictions of their own. Common environmental obligations within states have long been seen as a precondition of fair competition within the national territory, and a single market without comparable environmental standards between member states hardly represents the competitive level playing field which all see as the cornerstone of that same single market. Pressures for higher environmental standards applicable only in those countries where environmental concern is greater are open to the same type of objection, with countries such as Greece or Spain readily interpreting them as protectionism and hence by definition incompatible with the single market. A parallel can be drawn with the contemporary moves towards economic and monetary union, where those unwilling or unable to participate fear the creation of a two-tier Europe with unequal benefits and ultimate dissolution of the whole.

On the other hand, ignoring those pressures for higher environmental standards is equally unsatisfactory. The most recent states to join the EU – Austria, Finland and Sweden – brought with them environmental standards which were generally higher than those applicable in the EU, and the conditions of accession included a four-year transition period throughout which those higher standards would remain compatible with EU law. There is little doubt that the European Commission was hoping that significant progress could be made in the interim towards raising the EU's standards to the higher level of those of the new member states. In practice the requirements of the free market and the pressures for subsidiarity which have already been discussed have made that outcome increasingly unlikely (*Europe Environment*, 9 July 1996). Indeed the Commission has already opened infringement proceedings against Austria for doubling its toll charges for lorries using the Brenner Pass transalpine motorway between Germany and Italy. The corollary is that public support for EU membership in the countries concerned is slipping and is likely to slip appreciably further if standards are demonstrably relaxed.

If such a web of contradictions and competing objectives were not enough, it is exacerbated by the tensions between and within the European institutions themselves. It is perhaps not surprising that there should be jockeying for influence between the Directorates-General within the Commission responsible for trade policy and for the environment, and between the respective Commissioners, but it was less objectively predictable that the environment should have such a high profile in the permanent tug-of-war for influence between the Council, the Commission and the European Parliament. The environment has unquestionably become a European Parliamentary cause with environmental issues being called on to justify enhanced influence in European counsels. This is explained in part by the environment's nature as a natural trans-boundary issue and by the reality that the Parliament can only progress on the basis of broad coalitions in which Green and more general environmental votes count. Most of all, however, it is attributable to the influence of the Parliament's Environment Committee and its highly energetic and long-serving chairman, Ken Collins MEP. It is totally in keeping that he is a major protagonist of environmental taxation, the arguments over which encompass all the conflicting threads which have been discussed above. All member states agree in broad terms that further progress on environmental protection is essential, and that the way forward is through the internalisation of costs realised through environmental taxation. The Fifth Environmental Action Programme encourages such taxation. At the same time, member states regard taxation as a national prerogative, which means that eco taxes can only be levied on a national basis. National taxes, however, will almost certainly differ in conception and as a corollary almost certainly act as a barrier to trade within the single market. As such, they will run the risk of being illegal under European law.

■ The Commission's communication on 'environmental taxes and charges in the single market'

The European Commission has attempted to cut through this Gordian knot by drawing a distinction between those environmental taxes which are in accordance with European law and those which are not. It suggests that member states have room for manoeuvre in implementing national green taxes in that a variation in the competitive position of different products does not of itself impinge on EU legislation unless there is a measure of trade discrimination, and that green taxation can be applied to imported goods for which there is no national equivalent, provided there is no impediment to the free movement of goods. Moreover a national environmental tax which happens to have a greater effect on imported products is still permissible provided that the justification is sufficiently strong and the market impact observes the rules of proportionality. A recycling levy and a deposit refund scheme may thus both be acceptable, as may a levy to fund the collection and disposal of hazardous substances, provided that basic commercial approaches otherwise apply (*Europe Environment*, 14 May 1996 and 11 February 1997). That approach by the Commission clearly holds out the possibility of accommodation with some of the more controversial national approaches to waste and packaging waste in particular which will be discussed below, but it remains far from clear how it will be interpreted in practice. The commissioner with responsibility for taxation and the single market, Mario Monti, was equivocal at a conference in Rome in early June 1996 when he gave his full backing to the use of fiscal measures, including energy taxes, to remedy environmental problems, but also maintained that 'the increasing interdependence of economies within the single market means that member states cannot be left entirely free to introduce fiscal measures designed to achieve environmental goals' (*Europe Environment*, 11 June 1996).

Business is less ambiguous. The Union of Industrial and Employers Confederations of Europe (UNICE) which is the European employers' confederation, lobbied hard for the Commission communication to rule quite specifically that any obstacle to the free movement of goods was contrary to EU law. There is also little doubt that UNICE is concerned that environmental taxation will prove more restrictive to business than the traditional regulatory approach (*European Policy Analyst*, 3rd quarter 1996). Its scope to lobby in the particular case of applying the directive (94/62) on packaging and packaging waste is, however, to some extent limited by the provision in the directive itself that national environmental levies are possible (the reader is also referred to Chapters 1.3 and 1.8, and 6.4).

It is therefore apposite to turn now to a review of the EU approach to waste and packaging waste in particular in the light of the foregoing interplay of relationships.

■ 8.3 The EU approach to waste and the case of the packaging directive

The EU's first instinct was to treat waste as a commodity which could and should be freely traded like any other within the emerging single market. In what is arguably, however, the Green movement's greatest success to date, the Commission accepted the reverse proposition. This is that waste should be disposed of as close to source as possible, and that waste disposal should in any event be a last resort, following observance of a hierarchy of initial waste avoidance, reconditioning, and finally disposal.

The provisions that waste production should be minimised, and that waste should be disposed of as near as possible to source, have been absorbed into the ethos of mainstream business where they are consonant in any event with such concepts as Total Quality Management. The respective positions within reconditioning of re-use and recycling have remained much more controversial.

The reasons for this encompass the political and the practical, but are ultimately philosophical. The thrust of environmental thinking generally is towards the definition of producer responsibility for manufactured goods and their packaging and towards what Germany has christened the 'Kreislauf-wirtschaft'. This is best rendered into English, perhaps, as the 'circular economy'. Its 'circular economy and waste law' for example, which came into force on 7 October 1996, has as its basic long-term goal the conversion of Germany from a 'throw-away' society to a society with a circular economy in which waste from production and consumption is ultimately brought down to nil. The German law therefore firmly places the responsibility for avoidance, reconditioning and environmentally compatible disposal on the commercial waste producer. Equally it firmly moves away from the approach of the repealed waste law, whereby the economy produced and local authorities undertook disposal at the expense of the wider community (*Business Europe*, 23 October 1996). This does not, of itself, demote the concept of recycling which , in many fields, will be the only way in which the concept of a circular economy can be put into practice. The whole ethos of a circular economy with producer responsibility will be against the production of what might be characterised as anonymous recyclable material. In such a context the slightly esoteric arguments, which will be returned to, about whether, for example, the returnable UK glass milk bottle has more or less impact on the environment than a one-way paper or plastic carton, are a little misleading. The real questions are rather whether the environmental advantages across the board of applying the principle of producer responsibility outweigh any possible injustice to particular business sectors, as environmental NGOs and the European Commission's environmental Directorate-General argue, or whether the shared responsibility strongly urged by industry is to be endorsed instead. If producer responsibility is to be preferred, how is it best accommodated within the single market? In no circumstance have those arguments been fiercer than in the case of the EU packaging directive 94/62, which produced a lobbying effort described by Anne van Goethem as 'without precedent in the history of the Common Market' (van Goethem 1996). The reasons were clear. Packaging waste was a prime concern for all parties. For the environmentalist its inexorable increase represented the rape of scarce natural resources with a severe impact on environments some of which, such as the Amazonian rainforest, were of global concern. For governments, local and national, many of which were in any event strongly influenced by environmental thinking, the waste mountain represented at the very least an insatiable demand for ever more tipping spaces, and for expensive transportation. For business it represented expensive changes of approach and, in some cases, a threat to long established markets.

The resulting text accordingly attempts to balance the principles which were discussed in section 8.1 of this chapter, and the Objectives set out as Article 1, paragraph 1, read:

'This Directive aims to harmonise national measures concerning the management of packaging and packaging waste in order, on the one hand, to prevent any impact thereof on the environment of all Member States as well as of third countries or to reduce such impact, thus providing a high level of environmental protection, and, on the other hand, to ensure the functioning of the internal market and to avoid obstacles to trade and distortion and restriction of competition within the Community.'

Paragraph 2 of Article 1 then goes on to say

'To this end this Directive lays down measures aimed, as a first priority, at preventing the production of packaging waste and, as additional fundamental principles, at re-using packaging, at recycling and other forms of recovering packaging waste and, hence, at reducing the final disposal of such waste.'

It will be readily appreciated that this poses rather than answers two key questions: first the comparative weighting to be given to environmental protection and to the single market, and secondly the comparative weighting to be given to the different forms of waste recovery. The waters are then thoroughly muddied by certain further clauses in what was, it must be remembered, a compromise text which took two years to pass through the EU institutions. Article 5 thus states that 'Member States may encourage re-use systems of packaging, which can be re-used in an environmentally sound manner, in conformity with the Treaty.' Unfortunately, conformity with the Treaty begs the question because Article 100a(4) of the Rome Treaty as amended by the Single European Act of 1987 allows a Member State to derogate in certain circumstances from the principle of the free movement of goods in the interests of environmental protection or public health. The only real answer is to clarify the Treaty, but that is highly unlikely except in the very long term. That leaves the European Court of Justice as the arbiter but its findings have so far been tentative, which is hardly surprising when the legislation it has to interpret is inherently contradictory. The clearest guidance to appear to date is that any derogation from the principle of the free movement of goods should respect the principle of proportionality, or in other words that the size of the environmental benefit should bear a clear relationship to the negative impact on the operation of the single market. Any such judgement, however, is bound to be subjective.

Similarly, the directive does not establish any clear guidance on the comparative merits of the different forms of waste recovery, notably re-use and recycling. As we have already noted, Article 5 permits the national encouragement of re-use systems, but the preamble to the directive notes both that 'from an environmental point of view recycling should be regarded as an important part of recovery' and that 'life cycle assessments should be completed as soon as possible to justify a clear hierarchy between re-usable, recyclable and recoverable packaging'. It has been argued that re-use is an integral part of waste avoidance and therefore by definition superior to recycling in the hierarchy of approaches to waste, but it is not an interpretation which has commanded general support (EIS 1996).

The directive and the targets it sets are an important milestone on the path to a more sustainable approach to waste in the EU, and the directive deserves respect accordingly. However it must also be said that it represents many of the worst features of any compromise. It alarms industry but fails to satisfy environmentalists, and gives disproportionate employment to lawyers and lobbyists. That was not the intention. Environmental NGOs, the Greens in the European Parliament and the governments of Belgium, Denmark, Germany, Luxembourg and the Netherlands, for example, all wanted a strict hierarchy in which re-use would be preferred to recycling. They lost, though, to the majority who preferred national flexibility.

The result in practice has been unremitting pressure on those member states favouring re-use from an alliance of those for whom the single market is more important than environmental protection and those for whom recycling is a commercial interest. Their particular targets have been Denmark and Germany, where national legislation already existed favouring the re-use option and where beverage containers were a particularly sensitive issue.

■ 8.4 The packaging directive and the beverage cartons industry

The reader may be tempted to sense a descent from the sublime to the ridiculous in changing the focus of the discussion from the philosophy of the single market and international diplomacy in Brussels to the level of the common milk carton or disposable coffee cup. The reader would, however, be wrong because it is the fact that regulatory changes decided upon in Brussels can affect the nature of such mundane articles as the beverage cartons used by up to 350 million consumers in the EU from Lappland to Andalucia and from County Cork to Brandenburg, and in due course perhaps as far as Ruthenia, which makes the single market so significant. It is significant for the consumer, but even more so for the manufacturer whose potential area of operations is that same single market.

It is for this simple reason that the pressure placed on Denmark and Germany was so intense. For environmental reasons Denmark had introduced a domestic ban on the marketing of tin or aluminium drinks containers as long ago as 1984. Some always argued that this was hypocritical because Denmark continued to export annually 400 million metal drinks containers, notably for beer, and they interpreted the ban as protection of the domestic market. The Danish government continued to enforce the ban, however, but soon found after the enactment of the packaging directive that its provisions were to be used against it. The producers' association BCME (Beverage Can Makers Europe) together with the Danish retail trade association, Dansk Handel og Service, and the European associations representing tin-plate and aluminium manufacturers, APEAL (Association Professionnelle des Producteurs Européens d'Aciers pour Emballages) and EAA (European Aluminium Association), jointly called on it to repeal the ban. They argued that it was contrary to Article 18 of the directive which placed a duty on member states 'not to impede the placing on the market of their territory of packaging which satisfies the provisions of this directive', and continued that any discriminatory national eco-tax on recyclable packaging would be equally unacceptable. Moreover, 'the can prohibition cannot be justified as a necessary element of the Danish drinks distribution system as there are equally effective alternatives for a high environmental protection which allow free trade and competition.' Moreover, the government should demonstrate which particular environmental circumstances justified more stringent measures than foreseen in the [packaging] directive (*Europe Environment*, 28 November 1995).

BCME has similarly complained to the European Commission about the introduction of a Finnish eco-tax on aluminium beverage cans, although it is only in the form of a deposit of Fmk1 per recyclable can. It is instructive that the association is opposing the principle of a national eco-tax as a barrier to trade within the single market. A similar proposal by Luxembourg is producing comparable responses, which all underline the extent to which the principle of subsidiarity, in the form of the power to levy national eco-taxation, and the ability to maintain more demanding environmental standards are being placed under immense strain by the philosophy of the single market (*Europe Environment*, 16 April 1996).

The Danish government has continued to insist that the ban will stay, but it has met its opponents half way over the packaging of non-carbonated drinks. Although carbonated drinks will still have to be sold in refillable packaging, beverages such as ice tea can now be sold in single use packaging, namely cartons. The change in policy was implemented on the day on which the packaging directive came into force and it is noteworthy that the motivation was free competition. As one observer said, 'It is a victory for a competitive environment unhindered by artificial trade restraints' (*Alliance Information*, October 1996). It can perhaps be added, without entering into the merits or otherwise of the particular case, that virtually any environmental obligation can be interpreted as an artificial trade restraint.

The European Commission, itself, initiated the legal infringement procedure against Germany in December 1995 alleging that its 1991 packaging ordinance, the so-called Töpfer ordinance, was a barrier to the free movement of goods within the single market. The basis of the Commission's case was that the German requirement for a minimum of 72 per cent of beverages to be marketed in refillable containers and for tinned drinks in other packaging to be subject to a high compulsory deposit places foreign competitors at a disadvantage, because they do not have the same infrastructure for collecting the returned containers, normally bottles. There was reason to believe in mid-1996 that Germany might prove willing to bend to this pressure and reduce or drop the quotas for foreign producers (*Business Europe*, 28 August 1996).

The Commission's move against Germany was endorsed almost immediately by the producers' association BCME, which argued that it would be a major contribution 'to bringing common sense back to the present German discussions on packaging policies'. The association considered that the Commission's legal examination should help to establish what the association saw as a fairer balance between the interests of environmental protection on the one hand and of innovation and competitiveness on the other. It accordingly threw its weight behind the market commissioner, Mario Monti, and his expressed desire at the preceding Internal Market Council, to reinforce the rules of the single market and to guarantee a level competitive playing field through faster and more transparent infringement procedures. The association also alleges that the directive establishes that environmental protection and free competition are equally valid objectives and argues in addition that the equal validity of re-usable and recyclable packaging should be guaranteed across the EU (*Agence Europe*, 11 January 1996).

German industry also is unsympathetic to the constraints imposed on them by the 'Töpfer' ordinance but their position is, to some extent, weakened by the evidence that the federal government's approach to packaging waste is effective.

Following an annual increase of 3 per cent between 1988 and 1991, the total for the domestic and small business markets fell from 7.6 million tons in 1991 to 6.7 million tons in 1995. That corresponds to a fall in per person usage of 13kg over the same period. There is every reason to believe that that favourable trend is continuing (German Environment Ministry press release 27/96).

It has to be repeated, though, that these pressures from business to push the case for recycling reflect the enormous concern of the paper and board industries that the packaging directive might irreversibly diminish their market share. Their lobbying is, by definition, self-interested, which in no way invalidates it, but it does tend to deflect attention from the arguments for producer responsibility. The lobbying by NGOs such as Friends of the Earth is equally vociferous, if less well funded, but inevitably is less concerned with the impact of its arguments for re-use and producer responsibility on any particular business sector. The chosen field of battle is the comparative environmental impact of re-usable and recyclable packaging and successive studies are called in aid by each side to support its arguments. It is in no way to decry science to remark that such arguments about the respective impact of the carton and the glass or plastic bottle can seem a shade reminiscent of those interminable Cold War negotiations between East and West over nuclear disarmament. If a position already exists, scientific arguments in its favour can almost always be found, which then stimulate the search for scientific counter-facts. Perhaps such an observation is ungenerous, but the debate often seems to be conducted in a very narrow context.

Lobbying on the beverage cartons issue has been led by the Alliance for Beverage Cartons and the Environment (ACE), a lobbying organisation based in Brussels and established in 1990 which represents the three main beverage carton manufacturers – Tetra Pak, PKL, and Elopak – and nine major suppliers to them of paper board – Assi Domän Frövi, Champion, Potlatch, Korsnäs, International Paper, Stora Billerud, Enso Gutzeit, Westvaco and Weyerhaeuser. The general objectives of ACE are to emphasise the benefits of the carton for packaging foodstuffs and its strong environmental credentials in a world looking for more sustainable forms of production and consumption.

Its priorities with reference to the packaging directive are naturally more specific. First is to stress the provision of the directive that recycling and energy recovery are both legitimate means of packaging waste management, and to underline the provision of Article 18 that 'Member states shall not impede the placing on the market of packaging which satisfies the provisions of this Directive'. The Alliance's great fear is that other member states will follow the German precedent of introducing quota systems which favour re-usable packaging, most obviously bottles, and thus restrict the market share available for recyclable and other forms of packaging. Quota systems are alleged to be contrary to Article 30 of the EU Treaty, which prohibits quantitative restrictions on trade between member states or measures having an equivalent effect, and thereby to Article 5 of the directive itself.

The second priority is to put over the argument that the beverage carton is one of the few packaging materials which fulfils the requirements of all approaches to waste management. It can be recycled in a variety of ways with the high quality paper fibres being repulped for re-use in other paper products or being recycled into trade-mark products. Another option is to exploit its high energy content by incineration to generate energy or by use with other waste as a source of fuel. A quite different possibility is to exploit the fact that the carton is three-quarters paper board manufactured from wood, and to use it as compost. (See Table 8.1.)

The third priority is to underline the extent to which the carton industry had steadily improved its recycling performance from a period well before the adoption of the packaging directive in December 1994. In Germany, as just one example, a recycling rate of 47 per cent had been achieved by 1995. Research was also being funded by ACE into automatic sorting equipment which could separate beverage cartons out from the general waste stream, a development which could give it a greater claim to producer responsibility (ACE publicity). ACE also inevitably draws attention to research the results of which endorse its own position. The Fraunhofer Institute, a leading food technology and packaging research centre based in Munich, has recently updated its 1993 report on milk packaging and come to the conclusion that neither returnable systems nor cartons have a clear across-the-board advantage. Nevertheless ACE records with satisfaction the advice of Dr Wolfgang Holley of the Institute that 'there are market segments in which . . . non-returnable milk cartons have a clear advantage . . . Cartons . . . which can be transported highly efficiently compared with refillable systems, enjoy a clear advantage [in terms of emissions].' It can be accepted that, on those terms, the longer the transportation distance, the greater the advantage. The Institute has doubled its presumed transportation distance from 100km to 200km, with Dr Holley declaring that 'It is now perfectly obvious that these [100km] distances are too short.' ACE concludes with satisfaction that 'Regulatory preferences which favour refillable packaging have been further discredited by authoritative research findings recently published in Germany' (*Alliance Information*, October 1996).

Table 8.1 Energy content of the carton (calorific value)

	MJ/kg
Oil	41.0
Coal	26.0
Beverage cartons	20.5
Wood chips	8.3
Municipal solid waste	6.0–8.0

Source: Korsnäs.

That conclusion is completely legitimate within its own terms of reference, but the difficulty with all scientific studies of this kind is that the conclusions are conditioned by the initial questions, whether set by government, industry or environmental NGO. They tell you about the effect within the present status quo rather than the benefits or disbenefits of an alternative approach. Is a transportation distance of 200km, for example, truly appropriate for milk? Many environmentalists would say no, and point out that increasing distances for distribution of all kinds is one of the most negative environmental effects of the single market. We have returned yet again to that troubled relationship. A parallel may perhaps be drawn with the Brent Spar affair where arguments by the UK government that sea disposal was the best available environmental option fell on deaf ears because continental Europe had simply decided that the sea was no longer available to be an option.

Be that as it may, the Fraunhofer report was on less contentious ground when it drew attention to the radical improvement in the rate of recycling for beverage cartons. Estimated to be 12 per cent in 1993, it had now risen to between 55 and 60 per cent. Dr Holley's conclusion that 'you cannot go to Brussels and say that there is any justification for a quota for refillable systems because the figures contradict this' was music in ACE's ears (*Alliance Information*, October 1996).

Distinctions can never be absolute but, if the arguments put forward by ACE on behalf of the industry could be characterised as intensive, then those by the environmental NGOs tend to be extensive. Friends of the Earth, for example, in their briefing sheet, 'Bring Back the "Bring Back"', lay particular stress on the importance of cradle to grave life-cycle analysis, and draw attention to environmental damage caused across the world by the extraction of raw material for packaging, including, for the specific subject matter of this chapter, the draining and cutting of globally significant Finnish peat bogs to provide land for conifer plantations from which paper is ultimately derived. It is a particular strength of their broad approach that they also take into account the impacts on the much wider global environment of the developed world's thirst for packaging. They go on to argue that the environmental impact of refining the raw materials and of manufacturing the product must be taken into account as must the energy used in the extraction and transport of raw materials and in product manufacture, distribution, use and disposal (Friends of the Earth 1992). Much of that approach is common ground between the two sides, but a strength of the stance of the Friends of the Earth is that it incorporates the possibility of behavioural change. It argues, for example, that supermarkets are mistaken in believing that the widespread establishment of re-usable packaging systems is no longer practicable. Perhaps Friends of the Earth underestimate the difficulties, but surely they are right to imply that practicability is partly a question of public will?

As already noted, Friends of the Earth are like ACE in having scientific data to support their case. Some inherent limitations of such data have already been discussed, but it also has to be said that utilising their conclusions is a subjective issue.

The same ACE newsletter as publicised the revised Fraunhofer findings also drew attention to a conference speech by Tetra Pak's development manager in China explaining:

'how the traditional Chinese custom of putting old waste to new uses had been used to encourage a highly unusual yet pragmatic attitude to waste reduction. He described how professional "scavengers" collected and sold "high value" waste items for profit, creating a market for secondary raw materials. The system benefits from China's lack of recycling laws and from the fact that most initiatives are based on economic rather than environmental motives. The Chinese example underlines the most illuminating fact to emerge from the conference, namely that the more successful waste reduction systems tend to be voluntary. It's a fact of which ACE members have been aware for some time.' (*Alliance Information*, October 1996)

This is a very questionable assertion even as a tendency in view of Germany's successful government initiatives to reduce waste production, although no system will work without public involvement. Indeed it is the unforeseen level of public enthusiasm for separating waste for recycling which has caused the German green dot scheme its greatest difficulties. It also implies, perhaps unintentionally, that ACE's real aim is to reverse the whole thrust of EU waste policy initiatives – to go back to the concept of waste as a commodity, to deregulate, and to reduce the role of government and that of the whole concept of public policy, so as to move almost into a 'post-democratic' phase. It is doubtful whether many Europeans would agree that either the communist world that was or the developing world that is should act as models for the foundation of environmental policy.

■ 8.5 The implications for Scandanavia and its paper industry

It goes without saying that such issues are of 'life and death' significance to those branches of the paper industry with a particular interest in the manufacture of beverage cartons. Levels of investment to date are extremely high, and reduced sales are a serious threat to the return on that investment. Beverage cartons are obviously not the sole product – sanitary towels, nappies, hospital bedding and the like are another large field – but new product directions are not straightforward and a subject on which the industry is reluctant to show its hand. Paper clothes might be one possibility. The industry is though anxious to stress the versatility of its product.

The introduction to this chapter noted that it was all about relationships and, so far, a pattern of relationships which has been discussed which is essentially reactive. Concern over waste levels in the more densely populated parts of the EU, not least from Germany which lost its ability to send its waste to the East in 1990, together with the dominant single market philosophy of the EU core, led to the enactment of a packaging directive which put the paper industries of the new Scandinavian member states, Finland and Sweden, in a more vulnerable position than they had perhaps anticipated.

This is partly a matter of psychology, with Sweden, on which this chapter will focus, seeing the forest which is the prime source of paper as part of its natural inheritance and its conservation almost as a moral duty. This is not without its problems when it leads to the return of predators, such as the bear and the wolf, to centres of human settlement even including Stockholm. However it remains the case that Swedes find the suggestion that, say, the returnable bottle might be considered more environmentally friendly than the natural produce of their renewable forests difficult to understand at the emotional as much as at the intellectual level. There are also the strictly practical considerations that timber is one of the nation's largest natural resources and paper one of its most significant exports. Not least the entry into EU membership of Finland and Sweden has increased the EU's forest area by almost 50 per cent, and increased its political significance accordingly.

One outcome is that Sweden will place great emphasis in EU circles on the importance of sustainable forestry, from which it has everything to gain. It protects its own natural resources for commercial exploitation as well as for cultural and environmental reasons and it gives Sweden a pro-active diplomatic role in environmental councils. It must always be remembered that the EU's environmental action programme, currently under review, is actually entitled 'Towards Sustainability'. The current position can certainly be improved upon. Although forests in the EU cover some 130 million acres, and the importance of forests to the global eco-system is recognised more clearly than ever before, particularly in the context of global warming (see Figure 8.1), the EU Treaties neither deal with it specifically nor integrate it within the Common Agricultural Policy. Some observers would add that one of the culprits is the doctrine of subsidiarity which is used, or misused, to maintain national discretion in a context where it is no longer appropriate. The EU agriculture commissioner, Franz Fischler, has also pointed out that the costs of sustainable patterns of forest management are on the increase, and that the forestry industry will need to be highly flexible if resources are to be preserved. Picking up a theme which has been a leitmotiv of this chapter, the commissioner notes that any public support would have to be in accordance

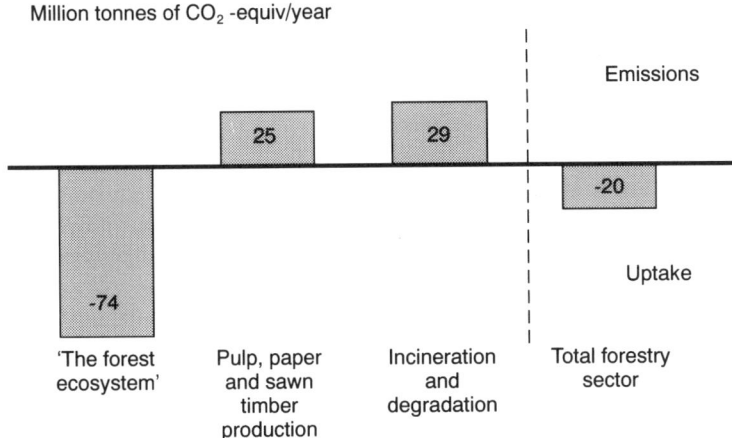

Figure 8.1   **Emissions and uptake of greenhouse gases in the Swedish forestry sector**
Source: Korsnäs.

with World Trade Organisation rules and that in consequence the initiative will be primarily dependent on the sector itself (*Europe Environment*, 5 November 1996).

It is now appropriate to turn to our case study of the paper firm, Korsnäs AB of Gävle, Sweden, to explore how it has responded to all the complex pressures which have been described. Before so doing, however, a paradox has to be recognised. Korsnäs, both in its own right and as a member of ACE, is currently mounting an international public relations exercise to emphasise the environmental friendliness of modern paper production and of one of its major applications, the beverage carton. It is fighting as hard as it can against those strands in EU environmental policy, notably producer responsibility and preference for re-use over recycling, which it fears will damage its commercial interests. In so doing it is employing many arguments such as those favouring the primacy of the single market and shared responsibility for waste which stand in an ambiguous relationship to environmental objectives. The whole thrust of its case, however, is that its product meets the most demanding environmental and sustainability criteria, and indeed goes beyond them. The relationship with both EU environmental policy and the packaging directive is, therefore, complex rather than direct. The tactics, if not the strategy, reflect the same cleavages as were described at the beginning of this chapter between EU environment policy as a whole and the single mindedness of the Treaty of Rome.

■ 8.6 The paper industry response: a case history of Korsnäs AB, Gävle

■ The company

Korsnäs is by any standards a large paper company, although by no means the biggest in Sweden. Originally founded as a sawmill in the village of Korsnäs near Falun in central Sweden in 1855, it moved to Gävle on the coast at the turn of the century, where a pulp mill was built in 1910 to be followed by paper production in 1925. By 1996 the output from its sulphate pulp mill had reached 650,000 tonnes and from its paper mill 550,000 tonnes. The company is organised in four divisions: Korsnäs Forestry, Korsnäs Timber, Korsnäs Board Paper Pulp and Korsnäs Packaging.

Korsnäs Forestry is one of the largest owners of forest in Sweden with total holdings of 666,000 hectares and over 516,000 hectares of productive forest land. Nevertheless it supplies only about 50 per cent of the company's needs. Korsnäs Timber has an annual sawmill output of 160,000m³ (see Figure 8.2). Korsnäs Board Paper Pulp, the largest of the four divisions and concentrated in a single complex at Gävle, produces white kraft board, liquid packaging board, sack and kraft paper, and fluff pulp for a range of hygiene products. The company is one of Europe's principal producers in those specific areas. Much of the sack paper produced is converted by the fourth and last division, Korsnäs Packaging, which also has plant in Germany and the UK.

Only 3,164 people are employed by the Korsnäs Group, 2,416 of them in Sweden, in what is now a highly automated and mechanised production process.

Although paper may be made from a range of materials, the commonest source is timber, a raw material with which Sweden has been liberally endowed.

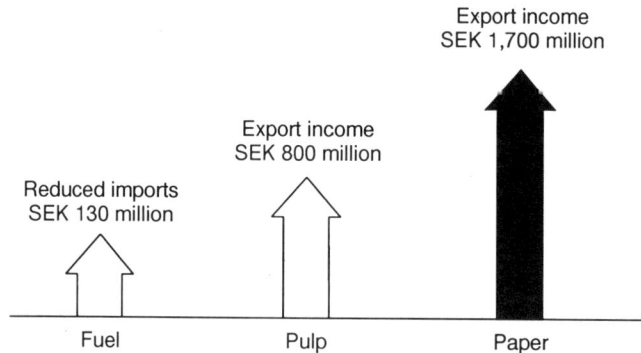

Figure 8.2   This is how one million cubic metres of wood can be used
Source: Korsnäs

It is therefore hardly surprising that paper has grown into one of the country's most characteristic industries and that great tracts of forest are owned and managed by the large paper companies of which Korsnäs is only one.

■ Korsnäs and forestry

Despite Sweden's real attachment to tree and forest, its past forestry practices were by no means irreproachable. The advent firstly of the iron industry and its need for charcoal several hundred years ago and then of large sawmills about 150 years ago seriously depleted almost all Swedish forests with the result, which will be unexpected to most outsiders, that there is very little virgin forest left. The choice of the largest and best trees for felling because it gave the best financial return was particularly damaging, and was one of the major stimuli to the world's first forest management law passed in 1903 whereby every Swedish forest owner has to plant as many trees as he or she fells.

That law left open however the question as to whether trees should just be thinned or clear-felled whereby a whole area is totally felled. Selective thinning worked well in Germany but was less suited to the cold of Scandinavia, where young pines, deciduous trees and other plants need the protection afforded by the mixed forest. On the other hand, clear felling permitted the introduction of mechanisation and with it greatly improved living standards for forestry workers. However, for all its advantages of operational simplicity and cheapness it was aesthetically insensitive, injurious to wildlife and encouraged replacement by characterless plantations.

The current philosophy, therefore, as practised by Korsnäs since the mid-1980s, is to seek to achieve a sustainable pattern of forestry management by imitating nature's own cycles. It is appreciated, for example, that forest fires are a frequent natural phenomenon and that many plants and animals obtain the space they require in that way. At the absolute extreme, there are insects which lay eggs in trees that are still burning, with the sooty black wood-borer beetle being able to seek out fires from afar. Tree clearance is, therefore, now similarly untidy with the areas being irregular in shape, the retention of some old trees, living and dead, and the abandonment of twigs and branches to rot down. Some smaller areas are even deliberately burned. Wetland forest areas are left undisturbed as they are the least exposed to natural fires and protect disproportionately high quantities of wildlife. In another reversal of approach, deciduous trees which would all have been eliminated as encroaching on commercial conifers are retained to protect them as it is now recognised that they improve the quality of the spruce in particular. Moreover, technical advance means that birch as well as pine can be used as a raw material for pulp production.

This new pattern of sustainable forestry works at the three levels of ecological countryside planning, regeneration management, and attention to detail. Ecological countryside planning relates to the overall long-term planning of large continuous areas of forest of from 5,000 to 25,000 hectares and seeks to recreate their natural condition. Regeneration management is concerned with the indigenous habitat groupings within that area, and attention to detail is literally what it says. It requires the forester to identify and retain those trees and stumps which may be able to make a particular contribution to natural regeneration and the forest as natural habitat.

Care does, however, need to be taken in assessing these changes. The 'natural' forest which is being restored is not in one sense natural at all. It remains a cultivated forest to which many, though not all, species have adapted with advantage and which is accessible to human beings in a way that a truly virgin forest will never be ('The New Genesis', Korsnäs 1995).

That philosophical objection aside, the question does have to be posed of precisely what forces caused Korsnäs as a major forest owner to make such a radical change of policy. It was obviously not the packaging directive in itself which only dates from 1994, although the pressures for re-use and its particular implications for the Swedish paper industry would have been known long before, as the establishment of ACE in 1990 testifies. Entry into the EU in January 1995 was likewise too late although it enabled Sweden for the first time to participate directly in the EU waste debate. It must also be acknowledged that the Scandinavian countries in general have a deeper environmental strand in their culture than most, perhaps all, other Europeans. Mrs Brundtland of neighbouring Norway was hardly a lone Scandinavian voice.

The answer can only be a complex of interrelated factors. The warnings of environmental experts on the dangers to biodiversity and eco-systems generally of industrial approaches to forestry increasingly attracted the attention of both management and public opinion as the 1980s advanced. It is perhaps worth noting that there is less cleavage between the two in a firm like Korsnäs than is sometimes the case in more exclusively industrial environments. It is conspicuous that many employees remain with the company for life, as do successive generations of employees, and that the company has an organic relationship with the town and the surrounding countryside. In no sense is Korsnäs an absentee landlord.

The changing climate of public opinion was inevitably reflected in changing national legislation. The former forest policy, which only dated back to 1979, subordinated the forest environment to timber production and gave a considerable role to state intervention and to subsidies for forestry investment. The new forest policy, however, approved by the Swedish parliament in May 1993 and operative from 1 January 1994, reflects the wider moves in Swedish life towards deregulation and reduced state intervention in the economy, by placing greater direct responsibility on owners, from both an economic and management point of view. That is balanced, however, by the new law's establishing equal priority for its twin goals of forest environment protection and timber production (Skogsstyrelsen 1994). In other words, and in a development which would have been foreseen, the approach already adopted voluntarily by Korsnäs has become legally enforceable.

There was also growing concern over the threat to Sweden's forests posed by acidification of its naturally thin soils by industry at home and abroad, but particularly abroad. Prior to the dissolution of the Soviet bloc there was little which Sweden could do about the severe consequences of transboundary pollution from states such as Poland and East Germany. However, EU membership did hold out the possibility of greater bargaining power with countries such as the UK which had been conspicuously reluctant to acknowledge any responsibility. It was unlikely, however, that the results of such bargaining would be rapid, and there was an urgent need to increase the forest's own ability to survive through the enrichment of its own bio-diversity.

There was also the highly important perception that high environmental standards would give as much of a competitive edge to timber exports as to the more familiar industrial exports. The new Swedish forestry policy specifically recognises that a weakness of its predecessor was the failure to promote the growth of sufficient quantities of high quality timber. Principles, criteria and standards are currently being developed for a Swedish environmental marking system to be used in forestry, which will be compatible with those of the international Forest Stewardship Council and thus facilitate the international trade in forestry products. It is an integral feature of the system that a firm's operations be certified by an international certification organisation, in a manner similar to that of the EU Environmental Management and Audit Scheme (EMAS), and Korsnäs forestry is increasingly under such certification ('Forest Ecology Audit', Korsnäs 1995). Like so many other environmental measures, however, it has been attacked as a barrier to trade (ENDS Report, May 1996).

Lastly, although the change in policy had significant revenue implications, its capital expenditure impact was comparatively modest, particularly when set against that incurred on improving the production process which is described below.

■ The production process

Although, then, the packaging directive had little direct impact on Swedish forest practice, management had long recognised that Korsnäs would be vulnerable in the competition with suppliers of other forms of packaging in the impending single market if its own products did not perform well in any cradle-to-grave analysis (see also Chapter 1 for a detailed discussion of business strategy relevant to this analysis). It will also be remembered that the Friends of the Earth laid a great deal of emphasis on the environmental impact of the initial extraction of raw materials. In the sense that the packaging directive was the culmination of an anticipated regulatory process, its indirect impact on the forestry management policies pursued by Korsnäs has been significant. This largely explains the paradox that, although the packaging directive played no direct part in the formulation of Sweden's current forest management policies, those policies are one of the most significant planks in the case presented by ACE and by Korsnäs against the re-use provisions of the directive.

Similar comments could be made about the improved production styles adopted by Korsnäs over the last 20 years, which are a second major plank of its current case. Paper is hardly the fruit of the forest in the sense that the apple is the fruit of an orchard, and traditionally its manufacture has required the use of a number of agents, some far from environmentally friendly. Korsnäs claims to have invested Skr1 million per day for the last 22 years in new technology which will also improve the environment – an enormous sum by any standards which fully explains the company's concern not to suffer as a result of the application of the packaging directive. The raw timber is brought to the factory by rail because it has less environmental impact than by road, and in normal circumstances the factory is self-sufficient in energy as it uses the extracted lignin, the glue which holds the wood fibres together, as fuel for the whole process. Indeed, there is sufficient surplus to heat 20,000 households in Gävle, a substantial proportion for a town of 90,000 people. A high premium is placed on operational efficiency with the level of heat extraction from the exhaust gases in the soda furnace being such that the temperature of 1,200°C in the furnace is just 20°C by the top of the chimney ('The New Genesis', Korsnäs 1995). Similarly, emission standards to air and water have been greatly improved in recent years.

These are just illustrations of a designedly three-dimensional management and auditing system in which profitability is the fruit of equal attention to the environment, to quality and to economy. Korsnäs is implementing its own environmental safety system, ISO 14001, which will be complementary to the monitoring of emissions by the authorities and run in parallel with quality system ISO 9001.

The initiative for change came, as Korsnäs readily admits, from the authorities who were anxious to improve the local environment, and who reflected a climate of public opinion in which the paper industry had a comparatively poor image. A system was introduced under the 1969 Swedish Environmental Protection Law granting a 10-year permission period for each mill and giving the authorities regular opportunities to introduce new solutions and to press for ever tougher regulations (Nordin 1995). Important improvements were made accordingly at that time, notably the provision of an aerated lagoon, the dredging of accumulated fibre from the sea bed near the mill and the installation of more effective equipment for burning off discharges of ill-smelling gas. Sensitivity to public opinion remains high. The company's environmental results are regularly published in a full-page spread in the regional newspaper (*Gefle Dagblad*, 6 May 1996). It must be said that similar improvements were being made under similar pressures to a number of mills in Western Europe in the same period of time.

What was different in the case of Korsnäs from that of some of its competitors was that when the time came for production line modernisation in the mid-1980s, the highest environmental standards were envisaged because it was accepted that customer and regulatory requirements as well as long-term competitiveness all pointed in the same direction. The contrast with the aggressively negative approach to quite modest environmental improvements adopted by the very well-known owners of one UK paper mill known to the author is stark. Korsnäs thus estimates that of the nearly Skr5,000 million invested in mill equipment between 1983 and 1995, some Skr1000 million or 20 per cent was spent on environmental improvements. In one of its clearest advances on regulatory minimum standards, the legal obligation to reduce the limits for the emission of organic chlorine compounds to 1.5kg AOX per ton of pulp by 1991 was pre-empted in 1990 by Korsnäs becoming the first mill in the world to eliminate the use of chlorine gas from the bleaching process (see Figures 8.3 and 8.4).

Similarly the biological oxygen demand of emissions into Gävle Bay is now lower than it was in 1915 despite a ten-fold increase in production and emissions of sulphur dioxide have been reduced by 80 per cent since 1980 and thus already meet the authorities' target for the year 2000. The company's Environmental Policy Statement ('Korsnäs Environment Policy', 1995) includes one really quite remarkable clause, 'Over and above what is laid down in the relevant laws, ordinances and conditions in the environmental field, any new opportunities to improve the environment that are ecologically justifiable, technically possible and financially reasonable shall also be taken.' It will be noted that there is no requirement for them to be commercially justifiable.

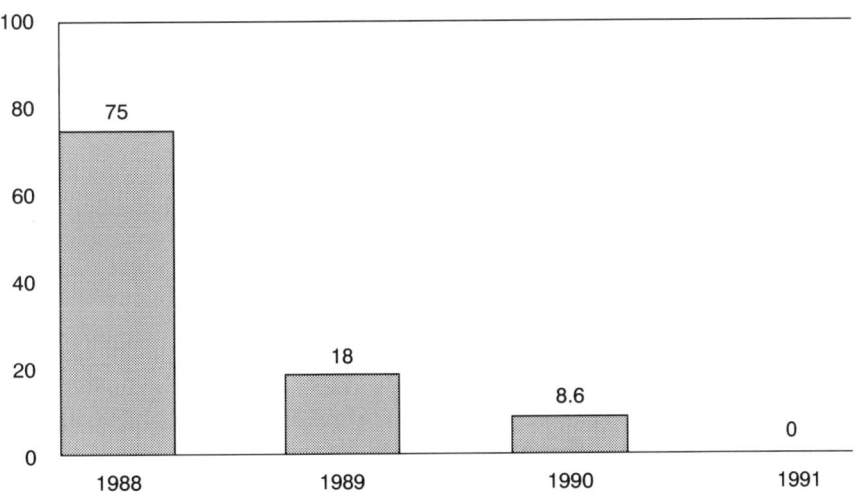

(Kilograms per ton of bleached pulp)

Figure 8.3   Chlorine consumption in the Korsnäs bleaching process
Source: Korsnäs

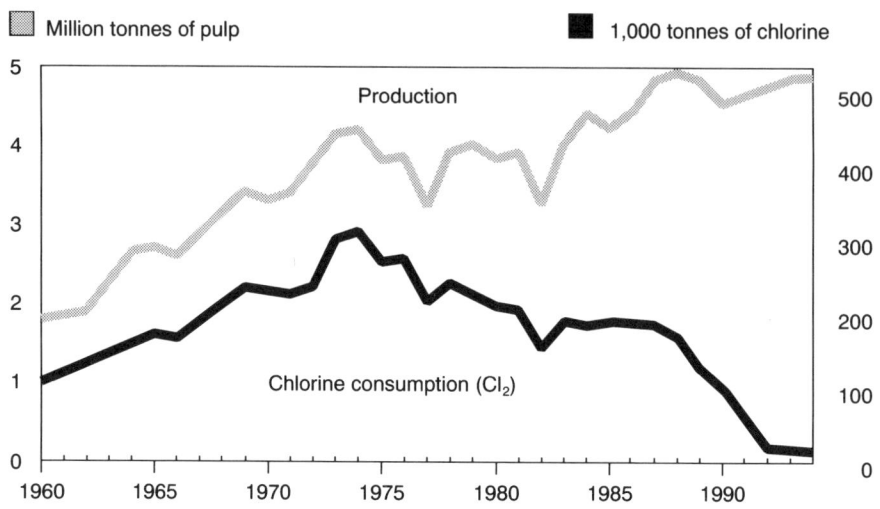

Figure 8.4   Chlorine consumption down to zero
Source: Korsnäs

Although the packaging directive clearly did not provoke these changes in a direct sense, it is inspired by the same combination of factors. As one Korsnäs report states, 'The packaging directive from the European Commission concentrates on ecobalance. The market has also already begun to demand such studies and data. This means that our emissions have a direct effect on business through laws, regulations and business practice. A new pattern can be discerned within commerce'('Korsnäs and the Environment: A Report', 1996). The same report then quotes the following draft definition of ecological sustainability within the UN environmental conservation strategy:

'- the preservation of vital ecosystems and biodiversity;
- making sure that the use of renewable resources is sustainable and that the consumption of non-renewable resources is minimised;
and
- staying within the overload limits applicable to vital ecosystems.'

The report draws the following robust conclusion:

'The pulp, paper and paperboard industry should be able to achieve these aims more easily than any other industry, since the raw materials base is renewable and the manufacturing process generates bioenergy. The technology for keeping environmental parameters under control is either already in place or accessible. The waste from each product can be used as raw material for other fibre-based products in the production chain or as a source of energy.'

Lastly, there is the challenge of improving product quality, and on this count the relevance of the packaging directive both directly and indirectly is high indeed. Korsnäs is arguing vigorously not only that any discrimination against its product is without justification in the EU single market, but also that the newer cartons for which it supplies the paper have much greater potential than re-usables world-wide. Amongst the more striking examples are the development of cartons with thin aluminium linings which keep milk fresh without the need for refrigeration even in the heat of Africa and Asia ('The Cardboard Journey', Korsnäs 1995) and are no less useful in more remote European locations. Technical improvements also have been significant. The carton of today weighs only about 28g and can contain the juice of 8kg of oranges. Ninety-five per cent of the volume transported in cartons is produce compared with 60 per cent in other containers. Such advances are more persuasive than the comparative statistics on which both ACE and Korsnäs itself lay so much stress. There is also little doubt that the packaging directive has been a powerful catalyst to change and thoroughly benign in its effects in this direction. It must also be said, though, that even with such advances the problem of producer responsibility is still not directly addressed. The thrust of Korsnäs publicity is effectively that it does not matter. Other countries, particularly those without forests of their own, can use waste paper and cartons as the raw material for building board, for example, or even as compost. In Sweden itself, the cartons which are not used for such purposes are burned with other domestic rubbish in high-efficiency incinerators powering district heating plants. The proponents of re-use will not find this totally satisfactory. They will argue that the problem of the waste mountain is not being addressed at source, that composting does not encompass the small percentage of plastic in every milk carton, and, perhaps, that the incineration of general domestic waste generates noxious emissions overall, regardless of the carton component.

It has been the purpose of this chapter to explore the network of relationships on which the packaging directive has had an impact, with Korsnäs as its case study, and it has been shown that there is what can almost be described as an underlying culture clash between the philosophies of re-use and recycling. It has also been noted that that culture clash is being fought out in the much wider context of an EU whose future shape is far from certain.

There is, though a more nebulous, though not necessarily less important, overreaching relationship between Korsnäs and the evolving EU. Korsnäs is a highly confident company with sales in 1995 of Skr5,092 million, an increase of 13 per cent over the previous year, and an operating profit after depreciation but before transfer to the employees' profit sharing plan of Skr1,304 million, an improvement of 34 per cent. The return on capital employed was 15.5 per cent. That level of success is rooted in structural changes dating from the mid-1980s, which saw the business change from being a traditional forestry company to a niche enterprise whose goal is to make each product unique in its field. Its workforce, which was reduced without redundancies in the earlier 1990s by about 1000, is a highly skilled team of specialists ('Korsnäs Annual Report 1995'). The management of Korsnäs is clearly attuned to the challenge of the single market and is confident that it is an environment in which it can succeed. There is an awareness amongst individuals of the more pro-active role open to Sweden as a result of its entry with Finland into EU membership and of the withdrawal of Soviet influence from Finland and Soviet control from the Baltic States. In an interesting aside to the author, one Korsnäs vice-president drew a clear distinction between his own outward-looking country and its neighbour Norway which in his view had the wealth and the will to remain an inward-looking society meeting its own needs on its own terms. Time alone can test the truth of that perception, but it is another aspect of the relationship between the packaging directive and Korsnäs which should not be overlooked.

■ 8.7 Conclusions

This chapter has looked progressively at the relationship between EU environmental policy and EU policy as a whole, at approaches to waste and at the way in which these approaches are reflected in the EU packaging directive. In particular, it has drawn attention to the underlying tension at every level between economic and environmental objectives. The chapter then focused on the implications of that directive for the beverage cartons industry and in particular for the suppliers of the paper board from which the cartons are made. The paper company Korsnäs AB of Gävle, Sweden was chosen as the subject of the case study.

The case revealed, however, an element of paradox. The firm had over many years invested very substantial sums in more environmentally friendly styles of production and manufacture but its present high level of performance could be attributed directly neither to EU environmental policy in general nor to the packaging directive in particular. Korsnäs has, in practice, pursued a parallel path motivated by considerations of long-term self-interest, seeing eco-balance as much as a commercial as an environmental imperative. The practical result is somewhat ambiguous. On the one hand the packaging directive requires high environmental standards of all firms in the industry, ensuring Korsnäs is competing on a level playing field within the EU. On the other hand, however, Korsnäs is extremely apprehensive that any encouragement of reusable packaging over recyclable packaging under the terms of the directive will seriously affect its market share. It is, therefore, being associated with lobbying which emphasises the single market rather than the environmental elements of EU legislation, although at the same time laying particular stress on its own environmental credentials. The key question is whether that dichotomy will not finish by undermining the company culture, not least in the circumstances of a takeover. The author hopes not, but fears otherwise.

■ Questions for discussion

1. To what extent does the community have the right or perhaps the duty to place a business at a commercial disadvantage in the interests of a philosophy which may later prove to be mistaken? If it does, should there be some right to compensation, or should it be interpreted as a commercial risk like any other and even as a beneficial spur to competitiveness?
2. Can EU single market and environmental objectives be reconciled and, if so, on what terms? Would any reconciliation be vulnerable to WTO pressures?
3. Are EU single market values inimical to any concept of company culture? Is the concept of company culture in any event economically out moded?
4. What is the proper role of commercial lobbying? To what extent can it, or should it, be regulated?
5. Are commercial pressures a threat to a democratic EU environmental policy? How much influence should business have on the formulation of policy?

■ Bibliography

ACE publicity.

Agence Europe, 11 January 1996 (Brussels).

Anon, 'European Industry Launches Assault on Danish Can Ban', *Europe Environment*, 28 November 1995 (Brussels: European Information Service).

Anon, 'EIS, Trade and the Environment Can Be Reconciled Says the Commission', *Europe Environment*, 7 March 1996, p. 1, 18 (Brussels: European Information Service).

Anon, 'Finnish Eco-Tax on Drinks Cans Annoys Aluminium Industry', *Europe Environment*, 16 April 1996, p. II, 1 (Brussels: European Information Service).

Anon, Guidelines on "Green" Taxes Compatible with the Treaty', *Europe Environment*, 14 May 1996, p. 1, 5 (Brussels: European Information Service).

Anon, 'Timber Merchants Attack "Sustainable Forestry" Scheme' (ENDS Report 256, May 1996) p. 25.

Anon, 'Mario Monti Puts Member States on Their Guard', *Europe Environment*, 11 June 1996 (Brussels: European Information Service), p. I, 20.

Anon, Europe Environment, 'New Member States Legislation Under Threat', *Europe Environment*, 9 July 1996, p. 1, 6 (Brussels: European Information Service).

Anon, *Alliance Information*, October 1996 (Brussels).

Anon, 'Commission Calls for Sustainable Forest Management', *Europe Environment*, 5 November 1996, p. 1, 2 (Brussels: European Information Service).

Business Europe

Economist Intelligence Unit, 'Environment Report' (London: *European Trends*, 2nd quarter, 1996) p. 53.

Economist Intelligence Unit, 'Environment Report', *European Policy Analyst*, 3rd Quarter 1996, p. 51 (London: EIU).

Economist Intelligence Unit, 'New German Waste Law', *Business Europe*, 23 October 1996, p. 8 (London: EIU).

ENDS (Environmental Data Services) Report 252, (January 1996), p. 41, 'EC Steps Nearer to Bridging Gap between EMAS and ISO 14001'.

Friends of the Earth, 'Bring Back the "Bring Back"' (London: Friends of the Earth, London, 1992).

Gefle Dagblad, 6 May, 1996.

German Environment Ministry, press release 27/96, '5 Jahre Verpackungsverordnung'.

Haigh, Nigel, *EEC Environmental Policy and Britain* (London: ENDS, 1984) pp. 27–36.

Haigh, Nigel, *Sustainable Development in the EU Treaties* (Hanover: International Environmental Affairs, University Press of New England, 1996).

Kornsäs, 'The New Genesis' (Korsnäs, 1995).

Korsnäs, 'Forest Ecology Audit', p. 12 (Korsnäs, 1995).

Korsnäs, 'Korsnäs Environment Policy' (Korsnäs 1995).

Korsnäs, 'The Cardboard Journey', p. 15 (Korsnäs, 1995).

Korsnäs, 'Korsnäs Annual Report 1995' (Korsnäs 1995).

Korsnäs, 'Korsnäs and the Environment: A Report' (Korsnäs, 1996).

Nordin, Bengt, 'Korsnäs and the Environment' (Korsnäs, 1995).

Skogsstyrelsen, *Sweden's New Forest Policy* (Jönköping, 1994).

van Goethem, Anne, *Environmental Protection versus Internal Market: Packaging Waste Directive Case Study*, p. 1 (Brussels: European Information Service, 1996).

CHAPTER 9

Intellectual property law: providing protection for intangible business assets

Mark Wing

■ 9.1 Introduction: what is intellectual property?

Intellectual property rights often comprise some of the most valuable assets of a modern business. Intellectual property law is the legal control and protection of the use of intellectual property rights. Intellectual property may be contrasted with what is commonly understood to be real or personal property. With *real* or *personal* property something tangible is owned. This may be land, buildings, plant, machinery or stock in the context of a business, or houses, cars, household goods in a domestic context. With intellectual property nothing as tangible is evident. Instead intellectual property is the protection of ideas, works of authorship, designs, business goodwill and reputation, confidential information and others.

An industrialised society needs intellectual property law to encourage its members to create and innovate. Imagine the situation where a pharmaceutical company spends many years and millions of pounds developing a cure for a previously incurable disease. It then puts the drug on the market and its competitors immediately obtain samples, find out how the drug is made and then put their own, cheaper equivalent on the market (it will be cheaper because they have not spent millions in research developing the drug). Without intellectual property laws this would be a frequent occurrence, and no organisation would be encouraged to invent because their investment in research would not get an adequate return.

In the terminology of the intellectual property lawyer the broad heads of protection are given effect by the following areas of law:

- Copyright
- Trade Marks
- Patents

- Design Law
- Plant Breeders Rights
- Confidentiality
- Trade Secrets
- Trade Libel
- Rights in Performances

This chapter will concentrate on the first three areas, as these areas are the major ones which a business may invoke to protect itself from unfair activities by competitors. This chapter discusses change and the modern business from two intellectual property law perspectives – changes in the law affecting the modern business, and a suggested beneficial change in practice for the modern business.

■ 9.2 Changes in intellectual property law affecting the modern business

This field of law is extremely complex, which offers those who practice it a varied and challenging workload. To add to this area of law's complexity, it is itself rapidly changing. In some areas of law a lawyer using 20-year-old books would be at no great disadvantage. In this area of law it would be extremely careless. As will discussed below, the three major fields of copyright, trade marks and patents have all undergone great changes in the last 20 years. Major changes were introduced to the UK patent system in 1977 and new copyright and new trade mark laws have been enacted in the last 10 years, with more changes expected in the near future. To analyse all these changes affecting the modern business is outside the scope of this chapter; instead a narrower time scale – since 1990 – will be detailed. The format this chapter adopts is to provide a basic outline of the law, and then discuss these recent changes.

■ Changes in practice in the modern business

It is suggested that an awareness of the availability of intellectual property rights is becoming increasingly important for those involved in the administration and management of business organisations. To have a manager or other employee with a basic understanding of intellectual property laws can be distinct advantage for the modern business should any dispute arise so that he or she can be the first 'port of call'. Further, by providing basic advice on the availability of rights, and on how to best protect them, disputes can be avoided and losses mitigated. It is often the case, however, that no such 'in house' advice is available and costly specialist lawyers are only consulted when disputes arise. This in some instances may be disadvantageous as illustrated in the case study for this chapter.

As 'in house' advisors are not common at present, the modern business could benefit from change. For how can a right be claimed and protected in ignorance of its existence ? Further, opportunities inherent in recent technological advances, particularly the 'Internet', mean that many more business organisations will begin creating and exploiting works protected by intellectual property law (see also Chapter 5). To balance against these opportunities, it is almost entirely the responsibility of a business and its legal advisors to protect its rights. It is hoped that this chapter will assist in providing useful knowledge of the scope and existence of those rights as a benefit, and perhaps even an instigator of change in the modern business.

■ 9.3 Preliminary matters: national laws and international standards

The marketplace where goods protected by intellectual property rights circulate has always been an international one. Where goods are exported, owners of intellectual property right need to feel certain that their goods are adequately protected by intellectual property laws of other states. Most of today's industrialised nations recognised this many years ago, and signed international treaties in various areas of intellectual property law. Simply put, these treaties usually have two main features:

First, they lay down internationally recognised minimum standards of protection to which all signatories to the treaties hopefully adhere. This should guarantee a national minimum level of protection.

Second, a national of one signatory to an agreement should be able to directly sue for infringement of his intellectual property in another signatory's courts. This reciprocity of protection, which basically states 'if you protect our intellectual property we will protect yours', i.e. 'tit for tat', is another feature of these international agreements.

The two main international agreements of this type are the Berne Convention (1886), which protects copyright, and related rights, and the Paris Convention (1883), which protects patents, trade marks and designs among others. Although both agreements are well over 100 years old they have been amended to take account of changing circumstances. They display the two main features of laying down minimum acceptable standards and reciprocity.

However, despite the success in terms of numbers of signatories of the various treaties, problems still existed. Although most Western industrialised nations were signatories to at least some treaties, a significant number of countries, mostly developing nations, were not signatories. This created significant problems relating to piracy of intellectual property rights in those countries. Intellectual property rights simply did not exist, or were inadequate either in terms of content or enforceability. This was a significant cause for concern for the industrialised nations of the West, whose companies were losing billions of pounds of lost revenue to piracy. Goods from these developing countries even found their ways into Western markets such as fake Lacoste shirts, Rolex watches and Chanel perfume.

To combat this international piracy, the TRIPS (Trade Related Aspects of Intellectual Property) initiative, part of the GATT (General Agreement on Tariffs and Trade) negotiations, resulted in the GATT TRIPS agreement (see also Chapter 3.1 and 6.4). The TRIPS agreement states that signatories should obey the international minimum standards in both the Berne and Paris Conventions, but also goes one step further in requiring compliance with minimum standards of its own in various areas. GATT brought countries which had been outside the previous international agreements (such as China) 'within the fold'.

But problems still remain. Nations may agree to protect intellectual property, and even pass new laws to comply with GATT; however, making laws is simply one aspect of protecting intellectual property. Ensuring that the laws are enforced by the local authorities, and that owners of intellectual property rights from other countries have adequate access to the courts, are two other aspects, and in these respects problems have emerged post-GATT. For example, China tolerated piracy after it had signed GATT which led to well-publicised trade difficulties with the United States. These were only recently resolved, with China offering a promise to the USA to protect US intellectual property in a more vigorous manner.

Having considered some important background issues relating to intellectual property we will now look at the scope of three main areas, copyright, patent and trade mark laws, and how these may be utilised to protect business activities. It is hoped the knowledge imparted of the major provisions of the law in this chapter will prove to be of assistance to those administering a business. It is impossible to give a detailed account of the law in a single chapter, so instead this chapter will have an overview of its major provisions, then consider recent important changes in the law or in circumstance that may affect business interests.

■ 9.4 Copyright law

■ Overview

Copyright protects 'original works of authorship' in the classes of literary (including computer programmes), dramatic, musical and artistic works. Generally the terminology 'Original works of authorship' usually means that the work originates from the author and has not been copied from another source. Copyright also protects the rights of individuals or organisations who utilise the above types of work in sound recordings, films, broadcasts and cable programmes and typographical arrangement in published editions. The relevant

UK authority on copyright law is the Copyright, Designs and Patents Act 1988 (CDPA).

To get copyright the work merely needs to be created and placed into a permanent form. There is no need to use the © symbol to get copyright in the UK or in most other countries although, as a matter of good practice and an assertion of copyright ownership, most publishers do use the © symbol. Copyright can protect myriad business products, including promotional material, business logos, manuals, records, books, photographs, films, drawings, sculptures, models, computer programmes and many others. It is the width of copyright, coupled with lack of formalities, which make copyright a formidable asset in the armoury of the modern business.

Several copyrights may be created by a single event. This can be illustrated by an example. Band X are a leading pop group appearing at a series of pop concerts in the UK where they perform their hit records. John and Paul are two members of the band. with John writing the lyrics of the songs and Paul the music. Band X have signed a contract with the PCA recording company who record the performances for a forthcoming album 'Band X Live' while the BBC are making a TV programme on Band X's tour. An album cover is prepared by David, an artist employed by PCA.

■ Where does copyright exist?

The lyrics of the songs will be literary works, the copyright owned by John. The music will be classed as musical works, owned by Paul. The recording by PCA will be protected as copyright in sound recordings owned by PCA. The initial videotaping by the BBC will be protected via copyright in films, while the broadcast by the BBC will also have its own copyright owned by the BBC, while the performance as a whole will have protection under the rights in performances provisions of the CDPA. This offers protection to both John and Paul and also PCA. David's artwork for the album cover will be an artistic work, but as David is an employee of PCA it is likely that the copyright will be owned by PCA for reasons outlined below.

From the above example concerning a pop group it can be seen that ownership of copyright and related rights such as these in performances confers a potentially highly lucrative ability to control commercial level copying by persons who are not authorised by the copyright owners. The question then arises, who owns the copyright, and hence may grant others permission to use it, and take punitive action against unauthorised copiers ?

The CDPA provides that the author of the work is the person who creates it and usually the author of the work also has ownership of it. The exception, as with David above, is where a work is produced by an employee in the course of his employment. The employee remains the author but the employer owns the copyright. Thus authorship and ownership are two different, though closely related, concepts. Where the work is produced by an employee, but this is not in the course of employment, then the work is owned by the author rather than the employer. Thus in the case of *Stephenson, Jordan and Harrison* v. *MacDonald and Evans* (1952) a book written by an accountant was not owned by his employer, a firm of accountants – he was employed as an accountant, not an author. However, small parts of the book which were closely based on files at work were owned by the employers. This shows the importance of establishing what exactly is 'in the course of employment'. For the modern business, knowledge of these provisions may come as a potentially very lucrative surprise!

Having established authorship and ownership this leads to what an owner of copyright may prohibit others from doing. These are the 'acts restricted by copyright'. These infringement provisions are of considerable importance, for they are the acts that may be prevented and punished by the modern business seeking to protect its copyright. The CDPA provides for five instances of what are known as primary infringement, which are:

1. Making copies of a work
2. Issuing copies of a work to the'public
3. Showing, performing or playing the work in public
4. Broadcasting the work or including it in a cable television programme
5. Making an adaptation of a work.

Most commonly, the act complained of will be copying, so only this aspect will be dealt with here. To copy a copyright work, a substantial part needs to be copied. What constitutes a substantial part is not always easy to ascertain, but from many cases it seems the issue of substantiality is one of quality rather than quantity. Thus in *Spelling Goldberg* v. *BPC Publications* (1981) a single frame from an episode of the TV programme *Starsky and Hutch* (which constituted less than a one-hundred-thousandth of an hour-long episode) was copied and made into a poster distributed by BPC publications. This constituted an infringement of Spelling Goldberg's copyright. Thus a good rule-of-thumb is, for 'substantial part' read 'recognisable part'. If a work is recognisably copied from another source then the issue of copyright infringement may well arise.

In addition certain acts may also constitute secondary infringement. Secondary infringement usually involves dealing commercially with infringing articles and can take the following forms:

● Importation into the UK of infringing copies which are not for private and domestic use
● Possession of infringing copies in the course of a business for sale, hire, or offering for sale or hire infringing copies
● Exhibiting infringing copies in public or otherwise so as to prejudicially affect the owner of copyright
● Selling articles to assist in the making of copies
● Providing premises or equipment for infringing performances.

For all acts of secondary infringement the party accused must have a certain state of mind, which is that the party must know or have reasonable cause to believe that what he possesses, sells, etc. are infringing copies. The courts assess this requirement of state of mind on a reasonable man basis – i.e. it is not whether the party accused of secondary infringement believed that he had infringing copies etc., but whether a reasonable man in the same circumstances as the accused party would have so believed.

It can be seen therefore that the Acts of secondary infringement are particularly useful in dealing with what is commonly termed to be 'piracy'.

To protect the innocent from action by over-zealous copyright owners, and provide that copyright does not provide too strong a monopoly, the following should be borne in mind. Firstly a substantial part needs to be copied – but as illustrated above this can in quantity be a very small part of the work. Each case is assessed on its facts.

Secondly it is commonly said that copyright only protects the expression of ideas, not the idea itself. Consider the Japanese film classic *Seven Samurai*. The basic plot of a lone samurai who recruits six others to help a defenceless village was later copied by the famous western *The Magnificent Seven*. No copyright in *Seven Samurai* was infringed by *The Magnificent Seven* despite the plot and character similarities. This illustrates that basic ideas and concepts may be freely copied. However to go beyond copying basic ideas is to risk an infringement. Thus, cases in England have stated that copyright law can protect detailed ideas.

In addition to the above two ways of avoiding infringement of copyright, the CDPA itself provides for what is generally known as fair dealing. There are many specific provisions in the CDPA covering areas such as copying by librarians, home video taping and computer technology which are outside the scope of this work. There are, however, three areas which are of more general importance:

1. research or private study by individuals
2. criticism or review (of other copyright works) – here an acknowledgement of the source is required
3. reporting news or current events (not photos) – again a sufficient acknowledgement of the source is also required.

Whether any one of these permitted acts will provide a defence to an infringement again depends on the facts of each individual case. For example in some cases a large proportion of a work copied in a second book has been held to be fair dealing for the purposes of criticism or review. In others a much smaller proportion has been held to be an infringement. So much would seem to depend on what an individual judge perceives to be fair!

■ Change and copyright

There have been two recent important developments that may affect the modern business. One is a legal change, while the other is a change in society.

The first legal change is in the term of copyright. Copyright lasts for a fixed duration, beyond which a work is out of copyright and may usually be freely copied; so Shakespeare's works may be freely copied and sold. However, anyone thinking of doing this needs to beware of infringing any typographical arrangement in a new edition of a Shakespeare play – this may have been produced quite recently and so could still be in copyright. The Berne convention requires its signatories to provide a term of at least the life of the author plus fifty years in the case of literary, dramatic musical and artistic works. For other rights such as those in sound recordings and films the term is generally fifty years from the date of publication, though there are exceptions to this. The UK adhered to this general 'life plus fifty' rule. The European Community, in 1993, produced a directive which requires its member states to increase the term of copyright upwards to the life of the author plus 70 years, this directive having retrospective effect. This directive was made English Law at the end of 1995 with amendments to the CDPA. This has a number of important implications. Firstly, works which have gone out of copyright in the last twenty years will go back into copyright. This is best illustrated by an example.

John writes a book in 1926, and he dies in 1940. Under the old law the copyright in John's book expired in 1990 (fifty years from his death) and beyond this period John's book could be copied. However, under the new law the copyright in John's book revives, and continues until 2010. This means many publishing companies, who take advantage of the expiry of copyright to produce their own new editions, will now have to pay fees to the representatives of long dead authors. Any persons involved in publishing need to be aware of this important change.

The second event is the beginnings of what may be a fundamental change in society, a development in which intellectual property rights in general, and copyright in particular, will assume increasing importance. If a member of the public was asked just a few years ago about the Internet most would have had to confess ignorance. Now the Internet seems to be everywhere. World Wide Web URLs (addresses) appear in advertisements and many companies have established a presence on the Internet for marketing and information purposes (see Chapter 5). This raises a number of important issues.

Firstly there is publication. The CDPA includes in the definition of publication 'made available on an electronic retrieval system'. Although there are no cases on whether this wording includes the Internet, it is submitted that it does. Thus a person or organisation who makes material available on the Internet effectively becomes a publisher even though they may have never have thought of themselves as such. This ability to publish also means that individuals or companies need to be aware of their rights to protect them. Court action by these companies so far has largely been avoided by companies in the UK through threat of proceedings, though in the face of determined infringers or infringement abroad, a spate of litigation becomes likely. Litigation in the USA is already becoming common as businesses moves on to the Internet and see their copyright infringed. Due to its flexibility and the ability to digitise many forms of copyright works such as books, pictures, photographs, sound recordings and film these works are capable of being easily copied and distributed on the Internet.

A particular problem involves those in the computer industry. The Internet and other systems, such as bulletin boards, represent the perfect medium for distributing pirated versions of their software. Pirated software is all too common due to the ease with which most programmes are copied, and the Internet, via FTP (File Transfer Protocol), offers the medium for distribution. Again there has been litigation on this issue in the USA, and this must also be expected in the UK.

In closing this brief look at copyright and changes that affect the modern business, it must be said that the Internet and the digital age represent perhaps the greatest challenge since the invention of movable type and the printing press in the fifteenth century. Changes are being discussed at national and international level to try and deal with these issues. These include changes to the Berne Convention and action by the US Government and European Community among others. Major industry figures such as Microsoft, IBM and other are investing heavily in integrating the Internet into all aspects of their products.

It is widely predicted that today's Internet will eventually develop into tomorrow's 'Information Superhighway' with features such as effective video conferencing, virtual shopping, video on demand, and other uses such as virtual reality that, at present, are science fiction. When this day arrives, and it may be just years rather than decades, all modern businesses will want to be involved, not just for marketing and information purposes as at present, but as a means of selling goods from virtual shops, and contacting and communication with clients. Many business structures may be radically altered with offices closing and teleworking from home becoming prevalent.

With all this data changing hands, much of it protected by copyright, the importance of this area of law will grow exponentially. Soon we may all be publishers!

■ 9.5 Patents

Patents are the strongest intellectual property right and are designed to protect what may be broadly called inventions of products or inventions of processes. The holder of a patent, subject to exceptions, can prevent all others using it within the territory for which it is registered. Independent creation of an invention provides no defence to a claim for patent infringement, unlike copyright where copying needs to take place. To combat this monopoly the patent law contains various safeguards and, in addition, it is more difficult to obtain a patent than any other intellectual property right. Nevertheless for business involved in research and development obtaining a patent for product can be highly lucrative,

Patents are a necessity to protect what is usually a considerable investment in time and money by individuals, or more often by large companies, in the inventive process. Patent law is extremely complex, and patent applications are usually made through patent agents. A patent agent is a legal specialist who often also has a science and/or engineering background. This combination of legal and technical knowledge is a basic necessity in being able to assess whether the legal and technical requirements of patentability are met.

■ Patents in international law

Just as copyright has the Berne Convention, so patents, trade marks and others have the Paris Convention and, as mentioned previously, this provides international minimum standards and reciprocity of treatment. However, patents in international law go much further than copyright. To be valid a patent must be registered (it will be recalled that no such requirement exists in copyright law) and the would-be holder of a patent has a number of options for international registration. These international systems are a basic necessity for a patent holder if exports of the patented products are anticipated. If one obtains a patent in the UK, solely for the UK, then tries to export goods to say Germany, and a German holds a patent for the same products or process, then the German could use his patent to prevent the import from the UK. This is hardly a satisfactory result in terms of world trade or free movement of goods in the European Community.

So, to remedy the deficiencies raised by national laws, two major systems of international patent protection exist and a third is intended to be introduced by the European Community. These systems co-exist with purely national systems.

The first international system is one which offers the opportunity for true international registration of patents. The system is known as the Patent Cooperation Treaty (PCT) of 1970, and came into force in the UK in 1978. Under the procedures laid down in the PCT preliminary searches may be made for prior conflicting patents in any of the signatory states, and, if wished, applications for patents may be made under the national laws of signatory states. Using the PCT procedure can therefore give an applicant a 'bundle' of national patents in diverse signatory states. The PCT is thus an important asset in the armoury of those who wish to obtain international protection for their inventions.

The second system is the European Patent Convention (EPC) again established in 1978. Under this system a single application is made to the European Patent Office in Munich. The Office then examines the patent to see if it complies with the basic requirements of patentability (see below) and also makes a search for prior conflicting patents. Assuming these hurdles are overcome, the application is then passed to national offices specified by the applicant, who subject the application to the requirements of their own national laws. If these requirements are satisfied the patent is granted. National laws of signatories to the EPC, were broadly harmonised to conform with the requirements of the EPC and thus the UK's main legislation on patents, the Patents Act 1977, is very similar to the EPC in many areas.

The third system, which has yet to come in effect for mainly political reasons, is the Community Patent, established by the Community Patent Convention (CPC) which was signed in 1975. When this system is established it will grant a unitary Community Patent so that with a single successful application the applicant will gain EC-wide patent protection. This differs from the EPC and PCT procedures where the applicant specifies in the application the country or countries where a patent is sought. For CPC patents EC-wide protection is the only option.

■ Obtaining a patent

Because patents confer the most powerful monopoly of all intellectual property rights a patent is also the most difficult right to obtain. To obtain one the applicant files certain documents at the patent office for the system concerned. In the UK this is the Patents Office with sites in London and, for trade marks, at Newport, Gwent. The main document filed is known as the patent specification. The patent specification can be described in basic terms as the 'blueprint' of the patent, and may consist of diagrams and written description of the patent application. It is from this document that the Patent Office decide whether the requirements of patentability are met. In addition to an examination of whether the application is capable of being a patent, the Patents Office also searches the register of patents to see if a patent has already been granted for the invention in the application. If either the requirements of patentability are not met, or a prior patent exists, then the application will be refused.

The basic requirements of patentability are found in section 1 of the Patents Act 1977. To obtain a patent it is first necessary to prove the elements of a patentable invention found in section 1(1). These are

- The invention is new (novelty)
- The invention represents an inventive step (inventiveness)
- The invention is capable of industrial application (industrial applicability).

These three basic requirements will be looked at in more detail below.

In addition, subsections (2) and (3) of section 1 provide certain matter which is not patentable. This generally relates to matter which should not be patentable for reasons of policy, and includes discoveries, scientific theories, mathematical models, aesthetic works (which are protected by copyright), computer programmes (likewise protected by copyright), and several others.

It is important to note at this stage that the requirements of registrability continue to be an issue throughout the life of a patent. It is quite common for a patent to be challenged by a third party after registration. The basis for this challenge is often that it should not have been registered initially because one of the requirements of Section 1 had allegedly not in fact been made out by the applicant. A challenge to the validity of the patent is often made by a competitor of the patent holder, who has his own product that allegedly infringes the patent. When the patent holder takes this competitor to court in patent infringement proceedings, the competitor, as a way of escaping liability, often tries to prove the patent should not have been granted in the first place.

■ Novelty

Section 1(1)(a) first requires that a patent application should disclose a new invention. 'New' is further defined by section 2 'if it does not form part of the state of the art' . 'State of the art' is defined by the rest of section 2, it stating that the invention had not been made public either through publication , or prior use, or had previously been applied for as a patent. An extremely wide definition of public availability means it is vital that details of the invention are kept secret until the patent has been applied for. Failure to do this could jeopardise the whole patent application.

An example of prior use can be illustrated by the important case of *Windsurfing International* v. *Tabur Marine* (1985). Windsurfing International applied for a patent for a windsurfing sailboard, which was duly granted in 1968. Tabur Marine started selling their own sailboards in the early 1980s (a patent lasts up to 20 years in most circumstances) and Windsurfing tried to sue Tabur Marine for patent infringement. In court, Tabur Marine contended that Windsurfing International should not have been granted a patent in the first place on the basis that, in 1958, a young boy had built a primitive sailboard which he used on his holidays on the south coast of England. The court held that the boy's primitive sailboard, used 10 years prior to the patent being awarded to Windsurfing International, did constitute prior use. Because of this lack of novelty, and other factors, Windsurfing International's patent was declared to be invalidly granted and so removed from the register.

■ Inventiveness

The issue of inventiveness is also sometimes expressed in terms relating to 'obviousness' – to be inventive an invention must not be 'obvious'. But obvious to whom ?

Section 3 of the Patent Act 1977 provides assistance which states that an inventive step is where the invention is 'not obvious to a person skilled in the art'.

Assessing obviousness is often very difficult, and is a question of fact for the court to decide. There are no set rules and it is often difficult for a lawyer to advise his client if a patent is challenged on the basis it should not have been granted because it was obvious. To assist it, the court uses a hypothetical person – the 'notional' skilled worker. The invention must not be obvious to this hypothetical person. This notional skilled worker is neither a genius nor a dunce, but a person with a good knowledge of the existing technology and state of affairs in the area for which the invention is sought. Usually this notional skilled worker is not blessed with inventive ability of his own – otherwise all inventions would be obvious. However, depending on the field, the notional skilled worker can be a very highly skilled individual with inventive faculties. So in the case of Genentech (1989), concerning a proposed biotechnological patent, the court found that the notional skilled worker would be someone akin to a research scientist.

The difficulty of assessing obviousness can be illustrated by the case of *Parks-Cramer* v. *Thornton* (1966). Here a patent was granted for what seemed to be basic scheme for cleaning underneath looms in a textile mill. This involved a vacuum cleaner, suspended underneath the machines on rails, which moved along the rails, cleaning as it went. This apparently simple (many would say obvious) scheme was indeed at first found to be obvious (and hence invalid) by the trial court. However, on appeal, the court found the patent was, in fact, valid. In looking at the question of obviousness the appeal court was heavily influenced by the fact that, despite the relative simplicity of the scheme after the fact, it was also true that prior to the grant of the patent nobody else had ever found a successful method for cleaning beneath machines in textile mills. Thus, if the patented scheme was indeed so obvious, why had nobody come up with it before? On the issue of obviousness therefore, the cleaning system met the requirements of patentability.

■ Industrial applicability

The final major requirement of basic patentability is industrial applicability. The easiest way of looking at this concept is that the invention must be of some utility in that it may either be capable of being manufactured by (or used in) industry. Methods of medical treatment are excluded by the 1977 Act from patentability, but pharmaceutical products which may be used in a scheme of treatment are not so excluded. Indeed pharmaceutical patents as an area are given extra protection because of the special circumstances surrounding their testing and use. This area will be developed further below. Industrial applicability is usually not in issue in patent cases, due to the very wide remit of what is industrially applicable. This can be contrasted with the other two more complex and demanding heads of novelty and inventiveness.

■ Dealing with patents

Assuming that a patent is valid the next issue which arises is how might the patent be utilised. In particular how is permission granted to others to use the patent (licensing) and how does the law regulate the sale of a patent (assignment)?

The 1977 Act permits the assignment or licensing of patents but such transactions need to be registered at the Patent Office. Serious consequences can occur, particularly for the holder of the licence, if it is not registered.

■ Compulsory licences

Because the patent is the strongest form of all intellectual property its abuse may also give the greatest cause for concern. A book owner who uses copyright to prevent publication of his book may cause great disappointment among literary circles but no real loss to society as a whole. A patent holder, on the other hand, who prevents the manufacture and distribution of a life-saving drug by use of his patent on the drug, is clearly another matter. Alternatively the owner of the patent on the drug might manufacture a small quantity to keep prices artificially high. By abuse of a patent, potentially ground-breaking discoveries could be suppressed. For example, Boffin, an inventor, invents a small appliance, which when fitted to a car engine enables it to run on water. Boffin obtains a patent for this invention. PetroCo, a large (fictitious) producer of petrol, fears that this product will eventually drive them out of business, and offer Boffin £1 billion pounds for the patent. Boffin, who has no means of manufacturing and hence exploiting his invention, accepts PetroCo's offer. PetroCo then use the patent to suppress manufacture of the appliance.

To combat abuses similar to those outlined above, patent law provides a compulsory licensing scheme. The Patents Act 1977 provides that if the following situations occur an application may be made for a compulsory licence:

1. If the invention is not being worked to the fullest extent reasonably practicable in the UK
2. Demand for the patented product is not being met by UK production
3. Where an invention is capable of being commercially worked in the UK and this process is being hindered by importation of the patented product
4. Where the patent holder refuses to grant licences, or refuses to grant licences on reasonable terms, and
   (a) an export market for the patented product being made in the UK is not being met or
   (b) the working or efficient working of an invention which makes a contribution to the art is hindered or
   (c) the establishment or development of commercial activities is hindered
5. Because of certain conditions imposed on the grant of licences the establishment or development of commercial or industrial activities is unfairly prejudiced.

Thus, through the system of compulsory licensing, abuse of a patent may be prevented. The example above of PetroCo using a patent to suppress Boffin's miracle invention would be unlikely to succeed. Boffins' patent specification as a public document could be inspected by any interested companies at the Patent Office, and, if PetroCo refused to allow this invention to be worked by failure to grant licences, one of the companies could apply for a compulsory licence, quoting the grounds in (1), (2), (4) and (5). At least one and possibly all of these grounds could be used.

■ Protecting patents – patent infringement.

Proving an infringement of a patent can be a difficult, expensive and frequently dangerous course of action for a patent owner. It is difficult and expensive because of the complexity of the law, and the subject-matter of the patent may require several weeks' argument, the calling of expert witnesses and the employment of highly skilled, specialist and expensive lawyers. It is dangerous because frequently the party accused of patent infringement will try to challenge the validity of the patent in order to escape liability. If this challenge is successful not only will the patent owner lose the action, but also he could lose his patent. It is often said that a rich owner of a poor patent is almost always in a better position than a poor owner of a good patent!

The Patents Act provides for four differing instances of infringement which occur when a party, without the patent owner's consent, does any of the following:

1. **for product inventions:** To make, dispose of, offer to dispose of, to use or import the product, or to keep it whether for disposal or otherwise.
2. **for process inventions:** To use the process or offer it for use in the United Kingdom where the person so using or offering for use knows, or has reasonable cause to believe, that such use is without the consent of the patent owner and would be an infringement of the Patent.
3. **for process inventions:** To dispose of, or offer to dispose of, to use, import or keep any product obtained directly by means of the process.
4. **all inventions:** To supply, or offer to supply in the UK with any of the means relating to an essential element of the invention for putting the invention into effect, knowing or having reasonable cause to believe that those means are suitable for putting, and are intended to put the invention into effect into the UK.

A major problem arises in patent infringement in assessing the scope of the patent, and hence what is protected from infringement. It will be recalled from discussions above that the scope of the patent is usually defined in the specification and the courts need to interpret this specification to find whether or not the patent has been infringed. If use is made of a similar concept, but this concept is outside the patent specification, then there will often be no infringement. It is this analysis of the scope of the patent from the specification that is one of the key elements in the patent action, and argument as to what was meant in the specification is usually one of the main bones of contention. This illustrates the absolute necessity of careful drafting of the specification to minimise these problems later on.

What is more, the owner of the patent or his legal advisors need to be extremely wary of threatening legal action for patent infringement if this is not justified. If an unjustified threat is made the party threatened can himself take action against the party making the threats.

■ Defences to a patent infringement action

A person charged with infringement may attempt to utilise a number of courses of action. He may try to argue that the patent was invalid, as outlined above. He may also choose to rely on a number of specific defences found in the Patents Act 1977 and from other sources. These include:

1. The act was done for private and non-commercial purposes
2. The act was done for experimental purposes relating to the subject-matter of the invention
3. The act consists of an extemporaneous preparation of medicine for an individual
4. The use of certain ships or aircraft temporarily passing the UK
5. The act was done in good faith before the date of filing the patent
6. The act is not one of the infringing acts outlined above.

There are several other defences which may be used, which are based on competition provisions of European law, or general principles of English law, which are outside the scope of this chapter. Suffice to say in most instances the defences found in the Patents Act 1977 will provide a satisfactory solution where a party is using a patent in some way which does not directly threaten the commercial interests of the patent owner.

■ Change and patents

A first important change, and one that is hopefully a short period of time away, is the implementation of the Community Patent Convention (CPC). This should not be confused with the European Patent Convention (EPC) since the two systems are different. As mentioned above, if a party wishes to obtain a European Patent Convention patent he will specify the countries in which he seeks registration. Once the Community Patent is established it will automatically grant Community-wide protection with a single application. At present, under the EPC, an applicant may specify all the EC member states and this then involves 15 separate national applications being made. This can be rather expensive. However, considering the extremely high value of some patents the wider protection obtained may make a community-wide EPC application economic. However, if one compares this to the proposed CPC where a single application automatically gets Community-wide protection, this will work out to be less expensive than a Community-wide EPC application and quite possibly result in a quicker grant than the EPC equivalent.

The second recent change is again European Community motivated: this relating to the complex field of pharmaceutical patents. Pharmaceutical patents are unusual in the fact that, even several years after a patent has been granted, for example a new medicine, that medicine cannot be sold because it is frequently subject to stringent testing for safety and effectiveness, both by the company producing the patented product, and by the medical authorities. Thus the usual term of protection for patents – a maximum of 20 years in UK and

European law – was seen to be deficient in terms of medicinal patents. After the expiry of the patent, a medicine, or any other matter subject to a patent, can be freely copied, and so for the patent owner the product may well lose some of its attractiveness after the patent has expired.

Two of the main competitors to the EC, Japan and the USA, both enacted laws giving enhanced protection to medicinal patents which take account of the gap between granting of a pharmaceutical patent and the ability to exploit it. Some European member states had also begun to take steps to bring out their own laws when it was realised by the European Community that it needed to take swift action to ensure any changes took effect across the Community.

A direct change to the European Patent Convention and to national laws in Europe would have taken time, and may not have been possible due to the requirement of unanimity of members of the EPC for changes to be made. Instead the European Community created a new right of a similar type to a patent known as a Supplementary Protection Certificate (SPC). An SPC can be granted to any medicinal product that is protected by a patent in a member state and is subject to an authorisation procedure. The period of the certificate is calculated by reference to how long it takes from the granting of the patent, to authorisation being granted by national authorities. This is best illustrated by an example.

In 1992 Medico-Tech apply for a patent for a drug to alleviate headaches which they call 'Neuroase'. They obtain this in 1996. They submit the drug for safety and product testing in the same year. Trials of 'Neuroase' take eight years, and the drug is finally placed on the market in 2004. The patent in Neuroase will expire at the latest in 2012 (20-year patent term). However, Medico-Tech have lost 8 years of marketing 'Neuroase' due to the authorisation process. An SPC extends the protection after the patent's expiry to provide some compensation for the lost 8 years. The term is calculated by reference to the period between the granting of the patent and first marketing, minus 5 years, so this would be 8 years, minus 5 years, equals 3 years' supplementary protection certificate. Medico-Tech would continue to be protected by an SPC till 2015, three years after the expiry of the original patent.

To take advantage of the SPC it must be applied for as soon as marketing permission is granted by the national authorities, and an SPC may last for a maximum of five years. Although an extra few years may seem like little compensation, in practical terms the SPC could provide millions, if not billions, in extra revenue from successful pharmaceutical products.

■ 9.6 Trade Mark Law

Of the three major types of intellectual property rights discussed in this chapter, trade marks are the one that has been subject to the greatest change recently, with the enactment, in the UK, of the Trade Marks Act 1994. Trade mark law is the legal protection of names or other devices which identify the origin of goods and also provide an indirect guarantee of quality. Many people buy, for example, Coca Cola because they recognise the distinctively shaped bottles, and red labelling, as denoting a high quality product with which they are familiar and which they enjoy consuming. Imagine the situation where all bottles of Cola were exactly the same – a consumer would not know what he or she was purchasing; or, imagine a worse situation, where a competitor of Coca Cola could use an identical or confusingly similar bottle for their Cola product. Coca Cola Inc. would lose sales and the consumer would be confused because the distinctive bottle and colour no longer necessarily contained his or her favourite beverage.

Trade mark law is designed to protect the manufacturer of a product or providers of a service from competitors unfairly copying a distinctive mark. It also assists consumers in identifying their favourite products. In the UK there are two separate systems protecting trade marks. The first is 'passing off', the second is registered trade marks under the Trade Marks Act 1994. Trade marks of all varieties are very important to the modern business. All businesses have consumers of their products or services, and the goodwill of those consumers can be a major asset. Goodwill could be appropriated by other businesses if the same name or other indicator of business, product or services is used. Trade mark law can prevent this.

Passing off is an area of what lawyers term the 'common law: that is, it is a law based almost entirely on past cases. Passing off requires no registration of a mark or other formalities, but instead requires that:

1. a trader or company (trader 'A') has built up goodwill in a name or other device
2. another trader (trader 'B') seeks to take advantage of this by, for example, putting goods on the market under an identical or similar name
3. the action of trader 'B' cause damage to trader 'A' because the public confuse the goods of trader 'A' and trader 'B'.

Passing off can be very useful if, for example, a registered trade mark has not been obtained, but because of its complexity, especially proving reputation, using passing off involves a lengthy and very expensive trip to the courts.

It is much better to obtain registration of a trade mark before any trouble starts so that the relatively simple and quick, and hence cheaper, registered trade mark infringement action can be brought instead of using passing off. To prove registered trade mark infringement, all that need be proved is that an infringer used a registered mark in the course of a trade, and in some, but not all, circumstances the use was likely to cause confusion. A more detailed appraisal of this is discussed below.

■ Trade marks in international law

For reasons that closely mirror those relating to patents, purely national trade marks can hinder international trade. A trade mark owner in France could use his trade mark to prevent a UK exporter importing identical or similarly marked goods. So, to remedy this situation, there are two systems of international registration which co-exist with existing national trade mark laws. The first is the Madrid Arrangement/Protocol. This system has been operative since 1893 though for various reasons the UK and other countries such as Eire did not join until 1989. The Madrid system allows an applicant to make an international trade mark application which specifies the countries in which protection is sought. The application is then forwarded to the specified national offices, who may grant or refuse registration.

The second option is to apply for a Community Trade Mark (CTM). As its name suggests, the CTM is a European Community initiative. The CTM Office in Alicante (known as the Office for Harmonisation in the Internal Market) opened on 1 April 1996 for the registration of CTMs. A CTM gives Community-wide protection with a single registration. A mark need only be used in one country, but is protected throughout the community.

For ultimate protection the CTM is particularly useful, but for smaller businesses who do not intend to market goods internationally and have no plans to do so in future, a CTM is an expensive option. For companies who only export to one or two other member states, and where funds are an issue, a Madrid Arrangement/Protocol mark, with its ability to specify countries, can work out to be less expensive than the community-wide CTM.

■ Obtaining a UK trade mark

It is important to note that the UK's Trade Marks Act 1994 is based largely on a European Directive which was passed in 1988 (Directive 89/104). All member states are required to follow this directive so the basic requirements of trade mark law are very similar throughout the European Community.

To obtain a trade mark in the UK an application is made to the trade marks registry on the prescribed forms and including the requisite fee. The application must state which classes of goods the trade mark is required to be registered in. Trade marks must be registered in specific classes of goods, of which there are 34, and seven classes of services. This system of classification is internationally recognised and is known as the Nice classification.

When the application is received the registry examines it to make sure that it conforms with the requirements of the Trade Marks Act 1994, and then makes a search of the register of trade marks to ensure there are no marks already registered which conflict with the application. Provided these requirements are met the application is advertised in the *Trade Marks Journal*, which gives the opportunity for interested parties to comment on, or even oppose, the registration of the mark. After this advertising, and assuming no opposition, the mark is entered on to the register and becomes a registered mark.

■ Initial registrability

Firstly, UK law provides that a trade mark must comply with two basic requirements:

1. It must be a sign which is capable of being represented graphically
2. It must be capable of distinguishing the goods of one undertaking from those of other undertakings

All the member states of Europe must also comply with this requirement. It is extremely wide and open-ended so nothing is automatically excluded from registration provided the basic two requirements are met. Under the 1994 Act more unusual marks which had been previously excluded from registration, such as three-dimensional shapes, place names and shades of colours, were held to be registrable.

The 1994 Act represents a major step forward in terms of initial registrability. This can be illustrated by reference to the case of Re Coca Cola (1986). Prior to the enactment of the 1994 Act the law relating to registered trade marks was found in the Trade Marks Act 1938. In 1986, while the 1938 Act was still in force, Coca Cola sought to register the shape of their famous contour bottle as a trade mark. Despite being 100 per cent distinctive, in fact, of the Coca Cola's company products, and despite being perhaps the world's most widely recognised packaging, a despite almost certainly being protected by passing off, the Coca Cola bottle was refused registration. The court said that, as a matter of policy, containers, or other three-dimensional shapes, could not be registered, otherwise undesirable monopolies could result. This decision was widely criticised.

Many aspects of the 1938 Act are no longer law, having been superseded by the 1994 Act. One of the improvements made when the 1994 Act came into force was the removal of the bar on shape registrations. Because of this change the shape of the Coca Cola bottle was one of the first new trade marks registered when the 1994 Act became law.

■ Grounds for refusal of registration

Having found that the mark applied for satisfies the two basic requirements of graphical representation and capability of distinguishing, the law states that further requirements need to be met before a mark is judged to be acceptable. The most important of these are known as the grounds for refusal of registration, and come in two main types.

The first grounds are known as the absolute grounds for registration, and the rationale for these is largely based in policy. In other words, despite the proposed mark being capable of being represented graphically and/or capable of distinguishing, there is some reason for the application to be refused. A non-exhaustive list of these grounds includes:

- The basic requirements of graphical representation and capability of distinguishing have not been made out
- Purely descriptive terms
- Terms commonplace in normal language or trade usage
- Functional shapes (for example the shape of an umbrella or a plain shaped bottle)
- The proposed mark is contrary to public policy or morality
- The proposed mark is deceptive
- The proposed mark is a specially protected emblem, such as a national flag, royal coat of arms or insignia of an international organisation (such as the EU emblem).

These absolute grounds provide a necessary foil to the wide basic criteria of graphical representation and capability of distinguishing.

The second set of grounds are known as the relative grounds, and these grounds attempt to obviate confusion among the consumers of trade-marked goods, by preventing a trade mark from being registered where a similar trade mark has already been registered.

The relative grounds apply in the following situations where existing identical or similar marks are already registered. If any of the grounds below are made out the application will be refused:

1. Where there is an identical trade mark already registered, in an identical class of goods to that applied for, the application will be refused, subject to one limited exception in the 1994 Act.
2. Where there is an identical trade mark already registered, in a similar class of goods to that applied for, or a similar trade mark is already registered for identical goods and there exists a likelihood of confusion in the minds of the public between the mark already registered and the mark applied for.
3. Where an identical mark is already registered in a dissimilar class of goods to that applied for and the mark already registered has a reputation in the UK and the use by the applicant of the mark already registered would be taking unfair advantage of, or be detrimental to, the distinctive character of the mark.

The relative grounds thus seek to protect the public from confusion by preventing identical or similar marks circulating in the same marketplace. So, if 'Whizzo' was registered in 1994 for beer, another manufacturer of beer would probably not be able to register 'Whizzo' for beer at all – it comes within situation (1) above , an identical trade mark on identical goods. If instead 'Whizzo' was already registered for beer, and another manufacturer tried to register it for vodka, the application would be refused if there was a likelihood of confusion between the two, as the situation comes within (2) (identical trade mark/similar goods). Or finally, if 'Whizzo' was registered again for beer and 'Whizzo's' beer was the UK's leading brand, and another manufacturer wished to register it for garden furniture, the application may be refused only if the facts in point (3) were made out.

Assuming that the requirements of initial registrability are made out and the grounds for refusal do not apply, the application is likely be successful. This then raises the issue of having obtained a trade mark, what may be done with it? Dealing in trade marks is often a highly lucrative activity, and is associated with the practice known as character merchandising. Most persons will be familiar with the practice even if not familiar with the terminology. Character merchandising, often involving fictional characters, is a multi-billion-pound industry. The Teenage Mutant Ninja Turtles, the Mighty Morphin' Power Rangers and their associated films, action figures, clothing, stationery, posters and seemingly any other products capable of bearing a name or image are prime examples. Soccer star Paul Gascoigne also apparently recognises how useful a trade mark can be. His nickname 'Gazza' has successfully been registered as a trade mark under the 1994 Act. A trade mark may also be successfully licensed for smaller and less high profile subject-matter.

Prior to the enactment of the 1994 Act the law relating to granting permission to use a trade mark (licensing) or the outright sale of a trade mark (assignment) was an unsatisfactory area, due to complexity and obsolescence. By contrast the 1994 Act encourages licensing and assignment by providing a modern, flexible legal foundation. To assign a trade mark the document transferring it must be in writing, and various other conditions need to be met. The granting of a licence does not have to be in writing, but it is infinitely preferable to grant a licence in writing, not only as proof of the existence of the licence, but also because a written licence gives advantages to both the persons granting and those receiving the licence. Such a licence may be registered at the trade marks registry, and such registration gives enhanced rights to both parties, but especially the person in receipt of his licence. For the first time the 1994 Act gives the person in receipt of the licence the right to take proceedings in court to protect the trade mark from piracy – something which was impossible prior to 1994.

■ Protecting trade marks – infringement

If an organisation finds that its trade mark is being used by others, in an attempt to 'cash in' on an organisation's successful products or services, then trade mark infringement proceeding may be taken. The grounds for an infringement action generally represent a widening of the grounds available prior to the enactment of the 1994 Act, and also represent a simplification of the law. Under the 1994 Act's predecessor, the 1938 Act, even senior judges had difficulty in deciphering the meaning of its infringement provisions!

The grounds for an infringement action are mostly the same as the relative grounds for refusal. Thus relative grounds (1), (2) and (3) above also provide grounds for infringement. One extra ground is provided by the 1994 Act where a trade mark is used, for example, in advertising and the use of that trade mark is otherwise than in accordance with honest practices in industrial and commercial matter and the use is taking unfair advantage of, or is detrimental to, the distinctive character of the mark. The additional ground is designed to control, among others, the practice of comparative advertising where the practice is also deemed to be unfair.

■ Defences to trade mark infringement

To prevent the monopoly conferred by a trade mark going too far, the 1994 Act provides various defences. The most probable ones are:

1. Use of a person's name or place of business.
2. Indications describing goods or services.
3. Use necessary to indicate the intended purpose of the product (particularly accessories or spare parts) – for example for video tapes 'suitable for use in a VHS video recorder' where VHS is a trade mark.
4. Use prior to registration of an unregistered mark by another in a particular locale.
5. Acquiescence by the registered mark owner for a period of five years.
6. That the owner of the registered trade mark had not used his trade mark for a period of five years, and hence the registered trade mark should be revoked.

■ 9.7 Case study: Generic Media

■ Introduction

This case study involves a fictitious organisation, Generic Media (GM), who were incorporated in the UK two years ago. The facts are, however, based on several true life cases. Generic Media are responsible for the production of children's video cassettes (mostly cartoons) and they also manufacture various goods, mostly toys based on some of the characters in the cartoons. They are based in the United Kingdom and export their videos and goods to several countries in the European Union where their products are very popular. Generic Media have not taken any previous legal advice on protection for their various products.

GM's leading products are a team of four cartoon superheros, the SupaTeenz, that have taken the UK and Europe by storm. The SupaTeenz cartoons are all produced by GM's expert team of animators headed by Rick and Dave, and are hand-drawn.

GM produce some SupaTeenz merchandise themselves, including SupaTeenz Posters and stationery. They also allow ToyCo, a UK company, to manufacture SupaTeenz dolls for a fee of £20,000 a year. GM are thinking of further merchandising schemes after being approached by several companies interested in using the SupaTeenz name or images on their products to increase sales.

GM and ToyCo have found that their sales have recently started to fall slightly, and are very concerned, as the SupaTeenz seem more popular than ever. Their suspicions are confirmed when a member of the public informs them that unauthorised SupaTeenz merchandise including posters, dolls and videos are being sold on market stalls and car boot sales. Sellers in France and Germany report similar problems. The source of illicit videos, posters and dolls imported from Taiwan is traced to three small units owned by one Bill Sykes, situated on the outskirts of London.

GM and ToyCo seek advice on the above facts, in particular how to stop the sale of the unauthorised SupaTeenz merchandise, and how to best protect their rights in the future.

■ Advice to GM: initial preventative measures

First advice to GM would be to have taken advice earlier! By doing so they may well have found preventing piracy to be significantly easier and cheaper. By waiting until problems arose, cost will certainly be increased. The reasons for this will be outlined below. By having the 'in house legal advisor' advocated at the start of this chapter costs of protection might have been significantly lowered.

■ Use of copyright law to protect GM

Copyright law offers a viable cause of action for GM. The drawings produced by Rick and Dave, which are converted into cartoons, are copyright works fitting into the artistic works category. As these drawings are produced by Rick and Dave they are to be treated as authors of the work. However it must be remembered that the concepts of authorship and ownership are different in copyright law. Although Rick and Dave are the authors of the drawings, it is likely that GM are in fact the owners of the copyright in the drawings. Where the copyright work is produced by an employee in the course of his employment copyright will be vested in the employer – subject to any agreement to the contrary. As Rick and Dave are employed by GM as cartoon artists the cartoons are indeed likely to be produced in the course of employment, and so owned by GM. The company will also own copyright in the video recordings, these being treated as films by copyright law.

Unfortunately for GM and ToyCo the dolls produced by ToyCo, and copied by Bill Sykes, are not copyright works, unless they are capable of being works of artistic craftsmanship (these types of work are a subset of artistic works). However the fact that they are mass produced by ToyCo is a factor which points against this. Finally copyright might well be vested in the SupaTeenz images, as outlined above. It will not however protect the SupaTeenz name, for it is settled law that there is no copyright in a name or fictional character. In *Conan Doyle* v. *London Mystery Magazine* an attempt was made, using copyright law, to prevent the London mystery magazine from writing new stories with the Sherlock Holmes character. However this attempt to use copyright failed; copyright does not protect names or fictional characters as they are not capable of being literary works. The policy of not using copyright to protect names is a sound one since names are protected by trade mark law.

So GM own copyright. How can this be utilised? It will be recalled from the discussion above that various acts can infringe copyright, these being either primary infringement or secondary infringement. It seems likely that Bill Sykes has not made any copies himself, nor has he done any act that can constitute primary infringement. The primary infringement in this case is being committed in Taiwan. However as Taiwan is not a member of the Berne Convention it is highly unlikely that GM will be able to prevent the manufacture of the infringing articles there. Germany and France are both members of the Berne Convention so action may be taken there to prevent primary or secondary infringements. In the UK, GM must pursue a vigorous course of action against Bill Sykes.

Bill Sykes has committed two acts of secondary infringement by importing infringing copies, and by offering for sale infringing copies. Further, it is likely that Bill Sykes knew that what he had in his possession were infringing copies, and certainly, even if Bill did not know, a reasonable man certainly would. Thus, should the matter come to trial, Bill Sykes would be in a poor position regarding the videos and the posters. Even the dolls are capable of being infringing copies because, although the dolls produced by ToyCo are not protected by copyright, GM's original drawings are and copyright is capable of being infringed by making three-dimensional copies (dolls) of a two-dimensional work (original drawings). So, in the case of *King Features* v. *Kleenan* (1941), the court held that the making of Popeye dolls was an infringement of copyright in original Popeye drawings owned by King Features. This case is similar to GM's in respect that the unauthorised SupaTeenz dolls can be infringements of GM's copyright in the drawings.

At the trial GM can claim damages for copyright infringement, and these damages are designed to compensate GM for its loss. Therefore damages equal to GM's lost profits will be payable to GM by Bill Sykes. A trial may take many months, or even years if appeals are made. GM need to take immediate action to prevent further loss and obtain evidence of infringement. This will be dealt with below.

■ Use of trade mark law to protect GM

Because of GM's failure to obtain legal advice on protecting its considerable intellectual property assets it is now unable to use registered trade mark law. As its name suggests, registration formalities need to be complied with before this area of law can be used. This leaves GM relying on passing off to prevent the use of the SupaTeenz names and images.

Proving passing off requires proof that firstly GM had goodwill/reputation (the two are used interchangeably by the courts) in the SupaTeenz name and products among customers. Secondly it requires proof that Bill Sykes's behaviour constitutes a misrepresentation to the public, in that he is selling his products in such a manner that the public think the products comes from GM or ToyCo and are confused. Finally that Bill Sykes's behaviour has caused, or is likely to cause, damage to GM. It would seem probable that GM would succeed in their action for passing off. The elements of passing off are present, and there are several cases where piracy of fictional characters in similar circumstances have amounted to passing off. One of the more recent was *Mirage Studio* v. *Counter Feat Clothing* (1991) where clothing adorned with Teenage Mutant Turtles images was held to be likely to be passing off. However, although passing off probably would work, utilising this remedy is going to involve a visit to the High Court and many thousands of pounds in legal fees proving the elements of passing off are present. It would have been easier to prove registered trade mark infringement.

■ Preventing further loss by GM and ToyCo

If legal proceedings are contemplated by GM and ToyCo, there will be a gap of at least several months before the trial is heard. In the meantime Bill Sykes must be prevented from causing further loss to GM and ToyCo. Also, in preparation for the trial GM need to obtain evidence of infringement and/or passing off.

To prevent further damage prior to the trial GM would be advised to seek an interim injunction, which is an order of the court requiring a party to desist any specified activities, pending trial. Interim injunctions are very common in intellectual property cases but, to take advantage of this, GM need to apply quickly to the court. The court will consider the weight of each party's case, and where the balance of convenience lies. After considering this the court will either decide to grant or refuse the injunction, such grant or refusal being at the court's discretion. As GM has quite a strong case for both copyright infringement and passing off it is likely the injunction will be granted in GM's favour provided that they apply for the injunction quickly. The longer GM leave an application the less likely it is to be granted. Also GM must agree, before the injunction is granted, to compensate Bill Sykes for the loss of his business should he win at the trial. If Bill Sykes does not comply with the injunction his behaviour can be treated as contempt of court, a criminal offence, and ultimately he could be committed to prison. Bill's conduct may also amount to various specific criminal acts associated with piracy found in the CDPA.

It is also very important for GM to secure as much evidence as possible of Bill Sykes's infringing activities before trial. A fairly common remedy in intellectual property action for securing evidence is the Anton Piller order, whose name comes from the case of *Anton Piller* v. *Manufacturing Processes* (1976). This is a very drastic remedy, where the party seeking the order applies for it in secret, without the infringer's knowledge. The order allows the applicant to enter the alleged infringer's premises, accompanied by a solicitor, to search and seize evidence indicating infringement. To obtain an order the applicant must show, among others, that there is a serious risk that evidence relating to infringement will be destroyed or removed before the trial, in an attempt to evade liability. We do not know if Bill Sykes has a propensity for this sort of behaviour, but an Anton Piller order is a possibility if a court can be persuaded this is the case.

■ Providing a protection framework for GM products in the future

The main priority for this is to ensure that GM make applications for registered trade marks as soon as possible. By applying the tests outlined above the SupaTeenz name and image should be registrable. It is capable of being represented graphically and is capable of distinguishing GM's and ToyCo's goods. There do not appear to be any absolute ground for refusal. It is possible, of course, that something similar to SupaTeenz has been registered before so one of the relative grounds may apply. This will not be known until the Trade Marks Registry in Newport, Gwent make a search. Assuming all goes well SupaTeenz could be registered within a year. GM and ToyCo will also want to formalise their licence agreement and register that too. Once registered the law will provide a legal framework for the relationship between GM and ToyCo, and ToyCo will receive enhanced rights, which effectively mean that ToyCo can take proceedings in their own right to protect their merchandise if GM will not do so.

Further, as others have expressed interest in merchandising SupaTeenz, a comprehensive scheme of registered licences should be introduced which could prove highly lucrative for GM.

Finally, as GM appear to market goods across the European Community, an application for a Community Trade Mark (CTM) should be seriously considered. The basic requirements of the CTM are very similar to the 1994 Act. Thus SupaTeenz should pass the initial registrability test, although there may be SupaTeenz trade mark in another member state which could cause problems at the relative grounds for refusal stage. Assuming GM are successful in their application for a CTM this gives an invaluable asset in securing Community-wide protection.

■ 9.8 Conclusions

The primary aim of this chapter has been to increase awareness of intellectual property law. An improvement in awareness of these rights is a change that could confer distinct advantages on the modern business. Bearing in mind likely future trends in technology, and increased use of the 'Information Superhighway', the modern business may do much of its advertising, sales transactions and client contact in 'cyberspace'. Intellectual property is likely to assume even greater importance in this environment and an in-house advisor starts to look increasingly important, possibly becoming a necessity.

The secondary goal of this chapter was to highlight changes in intellectual property law that may affect the modern business. As has been discussed above there have been major changes in the three major areas in the recent past, and more changes are expected. Changes such as the improvements in trade mark laws are a considerable improvement when compared to prior systems, and there may well be many businesses who are able to take advantages of these. The example of Generic Media in the case study shows their failure to take full advantage of options offered by the law can lead to greater expense should problems arise.

■ Questions for discussion

1. What are the basic conditions for copyright protection? Where a work is produced by an employee who owns the copyright?
2. How do intellectual property rights provide an incentive for creative activity by individuals and companies ?
3. Intellectual property confers what may be regarded as a form of monopoly on its owner. How does the law attempt to mitigate the severity of these monopolies
   (a) where innocent conflicts arise?
   (b) where to allow use of an Intellectual Property right would be against public policy?
4. Why is securing international protection for intellectual property important? What advantages do international systems confer?
5. What advantages do registered trade marks confer on their owners when compared with Passing Off?

■ Bibliography

Adams, John, 'Supplementary Protection Certificates: The Salt Problem', *1995 European Intellectual Property Review*, vol. 17, no. 6, pp. 277–80.

Annand, Ruth and Norman, Helen, *Blackstones Guide to the Trade Marks Act 1994* (London: Blackstone Press, 1994).

Antill, Justin and Coles, Peter, 'Copyright Duration: The European Community Adopts "Three Score Years and Ten"', *1996 European Intellectual Property Review*, vol. 18, no. 7, pp. 379–83.

Bainbridge, David, *Intellectual Property*, 3rd edn (London: Pitman Publishing, 1996).

Dworkin, Gerald and Taylor, Richard D., *Blackstones Guide to the Copyright Designs and Patents Act 1988* (London: Blackstone Press, 1989).

Holyoak, John and Torremans, Paul, *Intellectual Property Law* (London: Butterworths, 1995).

Lyons, Debrett, 'Sounds, Smells and Signs', *1994 European Intellectual Property Review*, vol. 16, no. 12, pp. 540–3.

Smith, Lesley Jane, 'Rules of Reciprocity and Non-Discrimination: National and International Copyright in a European Law Framework', *1994 European Law Review*, vol. 19, no. 4, pp. 405–12.

Vinje, Thomas, 'A Brave New World of Technical Protection Systems: Will There Still be Room for Copyright?', *1996 European Intellectual Property Review*, vol. 18, no. 8, pp. 431–40.

Vinje, Thomas, 'Harmonisation of Intellectual Property in the European Communities, Past, Present and Future', *1995 European Intellectual Property Review*, vol. 17, no. 8, pp. 361–7.

CHAPTER 10

Change in the global market: a study of UK maritime industries in transition

Mervyn Rowlinson

■ 10.1 Introduction and structure

Between the 1970s and the 1990s dramatic changes occurred in the UK's maritime industry. This chapter provides a theoretical framework with which to consider change in the three distinct, but interrelated, maritime industries – shipbuilding, ship owning and ports. The intention is to explain the change process via the utilisation of a broad-based range of economic and organisational theory. This should not only contribute to the understanding of change but also endorse the value of theory which will deepen analysis of the dynamics of restructuring and strategy in the industrial transition process.

Patterns of decline are clearly evident with reductions in investment and employment in some maritime sub-sectors. There have been accompanying shifts in management organisation, technology and labour flexibility. Conversely, there have been some areas of growth: productivity, profits and investment. Overall, the evidence of industrial change in the three maritime industries reveals an uneven pattern. Some sectors have enjoyed growth, others have rationalised or diversified, while still others have simply been submerged into the pages of economic history. Analysis of change in these related maritime industries therefore provides a rich vein of research evidence which is enhanced by the international structure and composition of the maritime industry. This lends itself to a study context drawn from two theoretical bases. Firstly there is the evolving theory of the international division of labour and globalisation (see Chapter 5.9) and, secondly, the structure of competitive advantage, as provided in Porter's seminal work, *The Competitive Advantage of Nations* (Porter 1990). Both theoretical positions provide frameworks for further analysis of the economic impact of the shock change themes of the 1980–90s –

deindustrialisation (see also Chapter 3.1), diversification, divestment and decentralisation.

The structure of this chapter allows firstly for an overview of change in the three major components of the maritime industry. By tracing industrial strategy and performance from the 1960–70s to the 1980–90s it will become evident that considerable change has taken place. The historic perspective here is very much determined by the shift away from a Keynesian demand management, full employment, economy, to a fragmented, unstable employment and market-led economy which signalled the return of economic liberalism. The focus is on the organisational and market structure factors which shape industrial change engendered by this shift in the macro economy. By acknowledging the impact of these factors on the sub-sectors of the three maritime industries it will be possible to analyse the process of industrial transition. By drawing analysis from the concept of globalisation and the new international division of labour in the maritime industries the global link up of developed nation capital with developing nation labour in particular can be established. This approach identifies the structural framework of international trade, so complementary to this process, fitting clearly into the globalisation theme. As such it can be seen as an agent of change, leading to the fragmentation of the factors of production on a worldwide scale. The use of Porter's five forces enables a focus on the structural and strategic factors that shape the fate of businesses in competitive global markets.

Finally, the changes engendered by the growing influence of economic liberalism in the 1980s and 1990s beg consideration. The maritime industries found themselves in the front line of the ensuing shock waves of deindustrialisation, diversification, disinvestment and decentralisation. During this period they felt a change process which rendered them almost unrecognisable by the 1990s. In conjunction with these themes the privatisation process has had a profound impact on selective sectors as ownership and the business ethos made the transition from public to private ownership.

In order to emphasise the impact of change, an overview of the transitions occurring in the three major maritime industries is next provided.

■ 10.2 An overview of change in the maritime industries

In the decades of the 1960s and 1970s the three industries, while not sheltered from international competition, were confident in their historically attained world market position. In the period of Keynesian full employment they were seen as an important contribution to the industrial and social infrastructure of the nation. Additionally, the Second World War was still vivid in the nation's memory; the role of the maritime industries had been endorsed as vital to the survival of the island (Hope 1990). With hindsight, the era can now be seen as shaped by the mixed economy of interventionist government, weak industrial capitalism and powerful trade unions (Lash and Urry 1987). The corporatism of this period was formed from a triangular approach towards the interests of the maritime industries and their strategic and socio-economic roles.

This involved the owners, the unions and the state in shaping the direction of the industries. The need for modernisation in the national interest was clearly recognised and is in evidence in the publications of four HM Government Committees, each of which sought to initiate technological and organisational development. The Geddes Report on shipbuilding (1965) signalled an attempt to rationalise and reorganise the shipyards into larger, more technically advanced consortia. This was deemed a necessity if UK yards were to compete with Japanese and North European yards. The restructuring was supported by the 1967 Shipbuilding Industry Act which authorised financial backing for yards participating in this restructuring (Lorenz 1991). The Pearson Report (1967) was a response to the 1966 seamen's strike in that it attempted to streamline and modernise industrial relations at sea which had been subject to the draconian provisions of the 1894 Merchant Shipping Act (Marsh and Ryan 1989). The Rochdale Report (1970) considered the competitive challenge facing the UK merchant fleet and was a major advocate of fleet modernisation, promoting a rationalisation of shipping lines into consortia to improve economic efficiency. The challenge of change in the port industry was acknowledged by the Rochdale Inquiry (1962) which sought to modernise the management and organisation of UK ports. Particular emphasis was placed on the comparison with the modern Continental ports – Antwerp, Hamburg, Rotterdam. It was widely perceived in the UK that these had much to offer as models of organisational and operational efficiency.

■ Change in the shipyards

In the shipbuilding centres of Belfast, Clydeside, the Firth of Tay, Tyneside, Teeside, Wearside and Merseyside the shock of Japanese and North European competition was challenging the once unassailable market position of the UK yards. However, the booming world market for shipping, particularly driven by the surge in oil tanker demand pre-1975, provided scope for optimism. In addition, the yards were beginning to modernise and rationalise after recognising the success stories emanating from Japan, West Germany and Sweden. Ships were getting bigger and delivery times were shortening. UK yards were still able to call upon their considerable experience and expertise to sell ships in world markets during this period. In the shipbuilding towns the boiler makers, engineers and master carpenters were still secure in their labour market role of craft elite, protected by membership of forceful trade unions.

In this era it was still inconceivable that in an island nation a significant shipbuilding industry would be allowed to fall into decline. Increasing state involvement culminating in 1977 nationalisation was seen to confirm this belief as capital investment projects were underwritten by the government. As late as 1970 the shipping trade daily, *The Journal of Commerce*, was showing confidence in the industry, claiming that 'British shipbuilding is in better shape than ever before to beat whatever the rest of the world may have to offer' (*Anon*, 1970). Within a decade, however, this optimism was to be reversed. Decline and, eventually, almost total demise proved to be the fate of the 1980s and 1990s. By 1996 only a handful of UK yards remained in the merchant shipbuilding sector, with famous British yard names such as John Brown, Harland and Wolff and Swan Hunter succumbing to overseas organisational collaborations and takeovers. The once bastion shipyards of Govan, Dundee, Newcastle, Sunderland, Middlesbrough and Birkenhead have either radically been downsized or closed, with the shipbuilding skills and tradition being relegated at worst to the chapters of industrial history, and at best to a contribution to the nation's heritage industry. Where shipbuilding has survived, the historic pride and security of elite shipbuilding skills has now been replaced by a market-enforced labour flexibility, deskilling and casualisation.

■ Change in the merchant marine

In the 1970s it was still possible to commence a sea-going career safe in the knowledge that company loyalty would be rewarded by long-term career opportunities and security. The shoreside alternatives provided by a nearly full employment economy meant that leading UK shipping lines were concerned with retaining quality crews to maintain their established prestige. In the port cities of Liverpool, Glasgow, Hull, London, Southampton, Bristol and Cardiff seafaring still provided a major source of regional employment. Many famous lines enjoyed a high level of crew loyalty as traditional allegiances and regional pride prevailed. Until this period the UK merchant marine was still regarded as the fourth arm of the nation's defence organisation (Davies 1992). By the 1990s the scene had changed dramatically: the UK fleet had suffered a massive reduction in tonnage with many lines withdrawing completely from the market and others going into receivership. Of those that survived, the flight to off-shore flag of convenience operations became an increasingly popular option. This was usually accompanied by a switch in crew supply with low-cost third world seafarers replacing UK nationals. Employment opportunities were much reduced and for those UK nationals successful in finding a seagoing career it was likely to be via the books of dedicated crewing agencies, on a short-term self-employed contract. The traditional linkages between paternalistic shipping lines and crew members loyal to their companies was severed. The demise of the UK fleet was vividly illustrated during the 1991–2 Gulf War crisis. Of the 146 vessels chartered by the Ministry of Defence only eight flew the UK flag (*Daily Telegraph*, 1993). The fourth arm and its source of dedicated seafarers had been supplanted by a globally fragmented arrangement of footloose shipping capital and labour.

■ Change in the ports

In the ports, change was engendered by a mixture of technical, political and economic forces. In the 1960s and 1970s the docks were still strongholds of trade union militancy. Employment security was enshrined in the 'jobs for life' provisions of the National Dock Labour Scheme (NDLS). The major employers were either state or local municipal/trust organisations and, as such, the politics of full employment in the Keynesian era were seen as equally important as the economics of cargo handling. There was to be no return to the inter-war 'bad old days' of the exploitive casual employment system. The first wave of change, the impact of technological shifts in shipping and cargo handling through containerisation and ro-ro shipping, was to lead to labour savings and port rationalisations. The second was politically generated in that it was the privatisation and deregulation policies of the governments of the 1980s which provided the catalyst of change. By the 1990s organisation and employment on the waterfront had been significantly downsized. Public ownership had been replaced in most ports by private ownership. Profit maximisation had become the axiom of the new wave of management while workforce rationalisation occurred as port owners withdrew from the direct employment of dock workers. Employment conditions had been deregulated and the power of the trade unions was greatly diminished. The extent of change was signalled by the reappearance of casual labour on the waterfront via the emergence of numerous employment agencies. This short overview of the considerable changes occurring in the three maritime industries provides a context for the following profile of them.

■ 10.3 A profile of the UK merchant maritime industries

As an industrial island nation the UK has developed a strong historic tradition in maritime trade. At the turn of the nineteenth century the UK possessed almost half of world tonnage and dominated world shipbuilding (Hope 1990). Although it was inevitable that this dominance would be eroded by the emergence of other maritime nations such as Germany, Japan, the USA, Norway and Greece, the UK's relative decline was somewhat shielded by continued absolute increases in shipbuilding and ship owning. The former peaked in 1965 and the latter in 1975. Whereas these two industries faced the rigours of global competition the UK ports industry was sheltered from such excesses. This is evident in the continued growth as measured by tonnage handled. It is also noticeable how changes in technology and labour flexibility (see also Chapter 6.5) have brought about an inverse relationship between tonnage handled and total employment (see Figure 10.5 below).

◼ The shipbuilding industry

The UK shipbuilding industry was the first of the maritime industries to feel the pressure of global competition, with decline becoming increasingly noticeable since 1965. Figure 10.1 shows the decline in output and employment. Between 1950 and 1995 UK output fell from 1.3m tonnes to 0.13m tonnes. During the same period employment reduced from 231,000 to an estimated 42,000.

The reasons for this early decline become particularly apparent when contrasted with Japanese growth and the continued stability of German yards until the present. Figure 10.2 shows the 2,300 per cent Japanese and 588 per cent German increase in output between 1950 and 1995.

The historic structure and organisation of British yards was to prove a hindrance to maintaining a sustainable competitive advantage. Typically, the yards had developed during the industrial revolution of the 1800s. Located in the coal mining and, in some instances, iron ore regions, the yards became an integral part of the economic infrastructure of the Belfast, Furness, Clyde, Tay, Tyne, Tees, Wear and Mersey Regions. Industrial concentration which focused

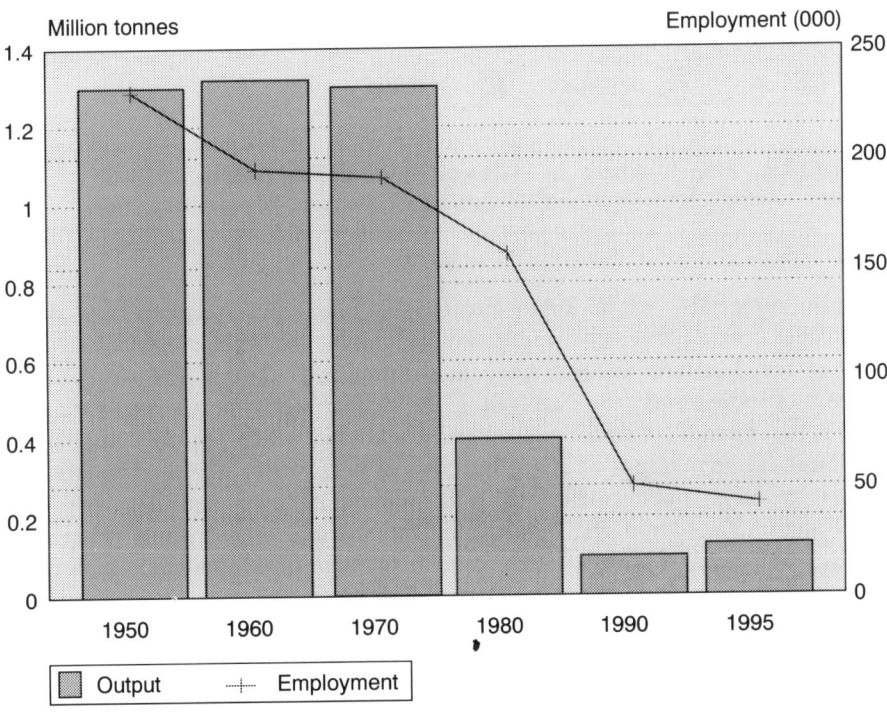

Figure 10.1   UK shipbuilding output and employment, 1950–95
Sources: CSO *Annual Abstract of Statistics*; Crown Office National Statistics; *Geddes Report* (1967).

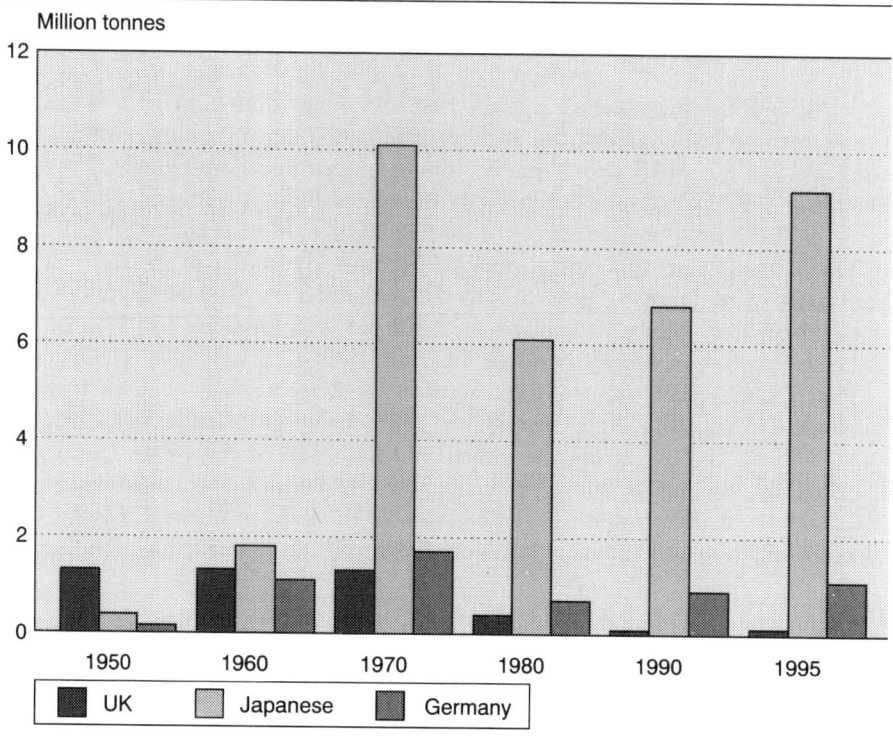

Figure 10.2   UK, Japanese and German shipbuilding output, 1950–95
Sources: Lloyd's Register Statistical Tables; ISL Bremen, *Shipping Statistics*.

on raw materials, while important to the traditional shipbuilding of the nineteenth century, became increasingly less important in the twentieth century. Part of the Japanese success story in shipbuilding, despite the almost total absence of indigenous raw materials, is the close integration between yards and steelworks. Both were developed on greenfield sites which not only emphasised the logistical advantages of space but also of deep water access. This allowed access by large bulk carriers with shipments of coal and iron ore and, additionally, facilitated the building of the world's largest ships (Hogwood 1979). Economies of scale were to result from both developments which could only enhance Japanese competitiveness.

The historic problem of UK yards was also one of composition with small units of ownership. The tradition of family-owned regionally located enterprises had continued into the post-1945 period. It can now be appreciated just how much ideas and attitudes were entrenched in the industry both at the ownership/managerial and at the workforce level (Parker 1992). The challenge facing the modernisers of the 1960s and 1970s was, therefore, one of providing a workable and co-ordinated rationalisation programme.

Continuing within the tradition of small skill-based shipbuilding businesses was clearly not an option with the rise of Far Eastern mass production based on cheap labour and North European advanced technology-based shipbuilding. This was particularly relevant given the business separation of many UK shipping companies and shipyards (Parker 1996).

This short outline of the shipbuilding industry has emphasised its historic problems. It will be seen how these were exacerbated by the growth of the global market until the present.

■ The shipping industry

Integral to an appreciation of the shipping industry is the identification of three main sub-sectors which compose it. Each has quite distinctive organisational and market structures which have influenced its change within the global context. As with the shipbuilding industry, the UK merchant fleet's world dominance was challenged in the post-1945 period by global competition. Throughout the twentieth century the UK fleet declined relatively as new maritime nations competed away its 1900s' 50 per cent share of world tonnage. However, in absolute terms, tonnage increased until 1975. Between 1950 and 1975 this was 14.9m grt; however, the period 1975–95 saw 27m grt leaving the UK register. In 1950 seafaring employment in UK shipping, including non-nationals, was 169,000; by 1995 it had fallen to an estimated 30,000. The overall trends are shown graphically in Figure 10.3.

The rapid growth of the competing fleets of Liberia and Japan until 1980 can be seen in Figure 10.4. From then the world fleet began to decline as a result of the 1979 oil price increase. Although all three fleets suffered tonnage loss after 1980, it is noticeable that the UK has by far the fastest rate of decline.

The liner sector has evolved from its fast cargo liner heritage, originally set up in response to the demands of the British Empire's overseas trade. In the 1990s this sector was dominated by the two leading conglomerates, P & O and Trafalgar House (Cunard Line). The emphasis in both groups is on high value container liner and cruise liner shipping. The dominance of these two businesses in UK shipping has been via a process of mergers, takeovers and capital concentration through larger, more technologically sophisticated vessels. Operating in the cartelised liner trades, with competition limited by the liner conference system, the emphasis has been very much on quality of service, rather than price competition (Stopford 1988). For port owners, however, the power of these liner groupings has been considerable, with the main UK ports of Felixstowe, Southampton, Tilbury, Thamesport and Liverpool in a constant state of competition with each other, as well as with their European rivals Rotterdam, Hamburg, Bremenhaven and Antwerp.

The second area of shipping organisation is that of the trampship operator. Typically, this is a low-value sector characterised by easy market entrance, over-capacity and the intense competition that this creates. The size of the

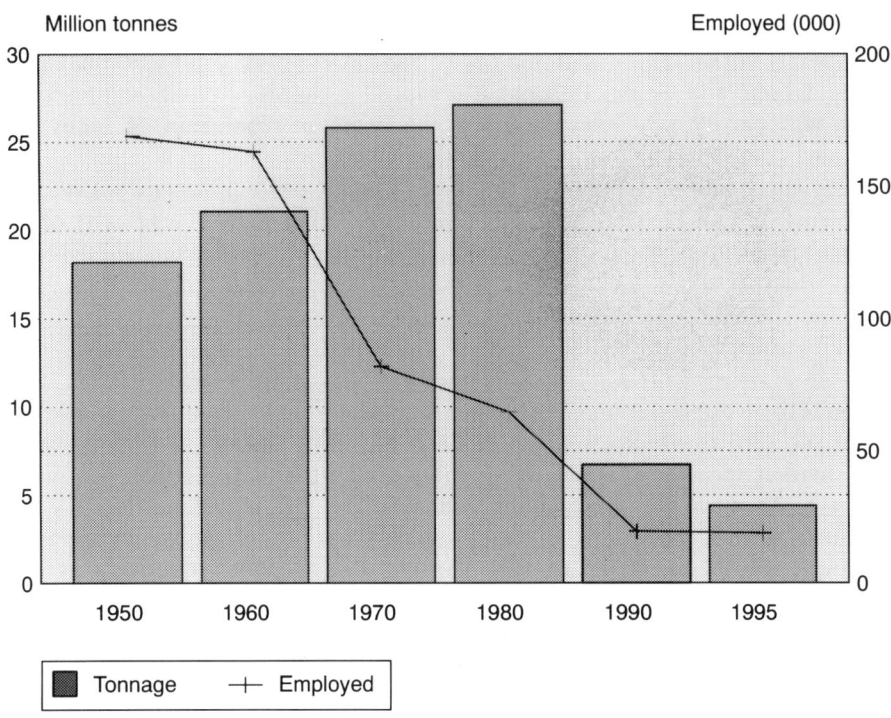

Figure 10.3   UK Fleet tonnage and seafaring employment, 1950–95
Sources: Lloyd's Register Statistical Tables; DoT Merchant Fleet Statistics; Chamber of Shipping.

companies in this market tends to be much smaller than in the liner sector. The tradition of regionally located companies in S. Wales, Tyneside, Wearside and Glasgow developed because of the coal and iron ore trades located there. Since the mid-1970s onwards this sector has suffered the highest rate of decline in the UK fleet. In 1975, 4.8m tonnes was owned by the ten largest owners; by 1990 this was 1.8m tonnes. A feature of this decline has been the retreat from an indigenous shipping organisation as virtually all remaining ships have been re-registered under flags of convenience and UK crews replaced by lower-wage third world crews.

During this period an interesting contrast has been provided by the growth recorded by trampship owners in the coastal and shortsea sectors. These companies also share a regional, family oriented lineage. Kentish based firms have diversified out of the locally derived cement industry and agricultural, river and coastal trades. The Tyne's fleets have diversified from the domestic coal trades to European bulk trades. North-western shipowners have enjoyed demand created by the local petro-chemical and nuclear industrial complexes.

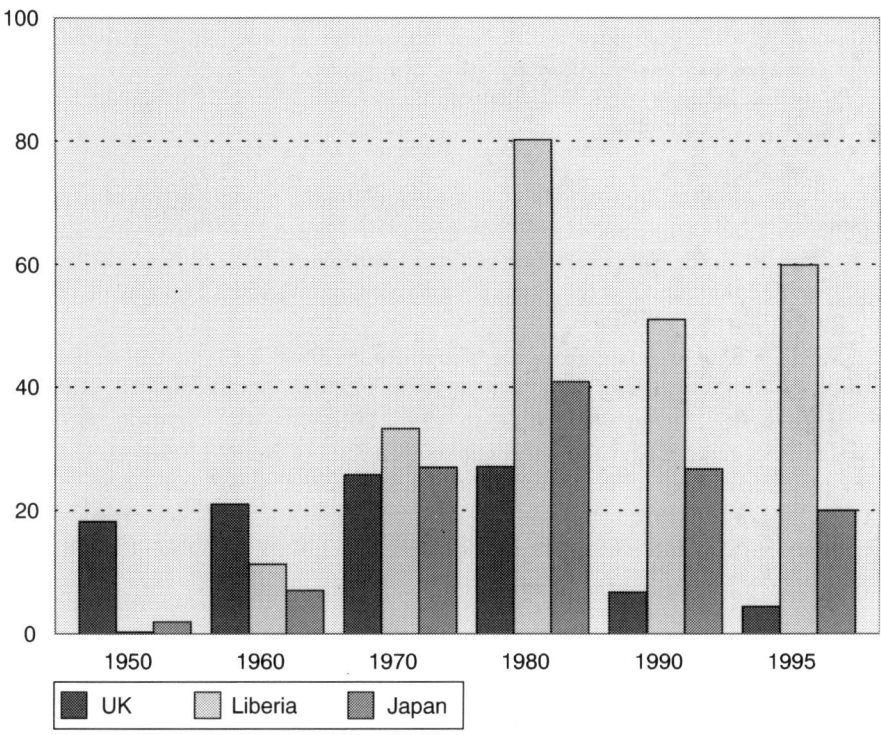

Figure 10.4   Fleet tonnages, UK, Liberia and Japan, 1950–95
Source: Lloyd's Register Statistical Tables.

Throughout the 1980–90s these firms enjoyed qualitative expansion and the mid-1990s saw them investing in new tonnage.

The third major sector of UK shipping is that of vertically integrated tonnage. This categorisation stretches from the fleets of British Rail's Sealink and British Steel's chartered bulk carrier fleets, to the massive tanker fleets built up by the oil majors in the 20-year period to 1975. Privatisation brought dramatic changes to these previously nationalised shipping fleets. No longer were they seen as an integral component of the logistics of the railway network or steel production but as cost and revenue centres within decentralised budgetary systems. The disinvestment and decentralisation of the oil majors' fleets caused the biggest impact of all on UK shipping after 1975. Between 1975 and 1990 total UK tonnage of the five majors – BP, Esso, Shell, Texaco and Mobil – dropped from 10.6m to 5.6m grt (*Lloyd's Register List of Shipowners*). The impact on the UK fleet proved even more profound as the once vertically integrated fleets were decentralised into independent, discrete business units forced to survive in the international market without the support of their oil major parent companies.

This was to lead to redundancies and rationalisations as ships changed their flags and crews in search of lower costs and taxes.

■ The port industry

Unlike the shipbuilding and ship owning industries, the port industry has enjoyed virtually continuous growth since 1950. Figure 10.5 shows that between 1950 and 1995 the total number of port employees fell from 155,000 to an estimated 28,000. During the same period, tonnage handled grew from 147,415 to 548,000 million tonnes.

The UK's biggest ports grouping stems mostly from a railway heritage. The extension of the railway to ports such as Cardiff, Southampton, Hull and Immingham led to nationalisation in 1947. Following the creation of British Rail, this occurred under the parentage of British Transport Holdings. Until the port privatisation of 1984, resulting in the creation of Associated British Ports (ABP) Plc, a mixture of nationalised, municipally controlled and smaller privatised ports and wharfers constituted the industry's organisation. The

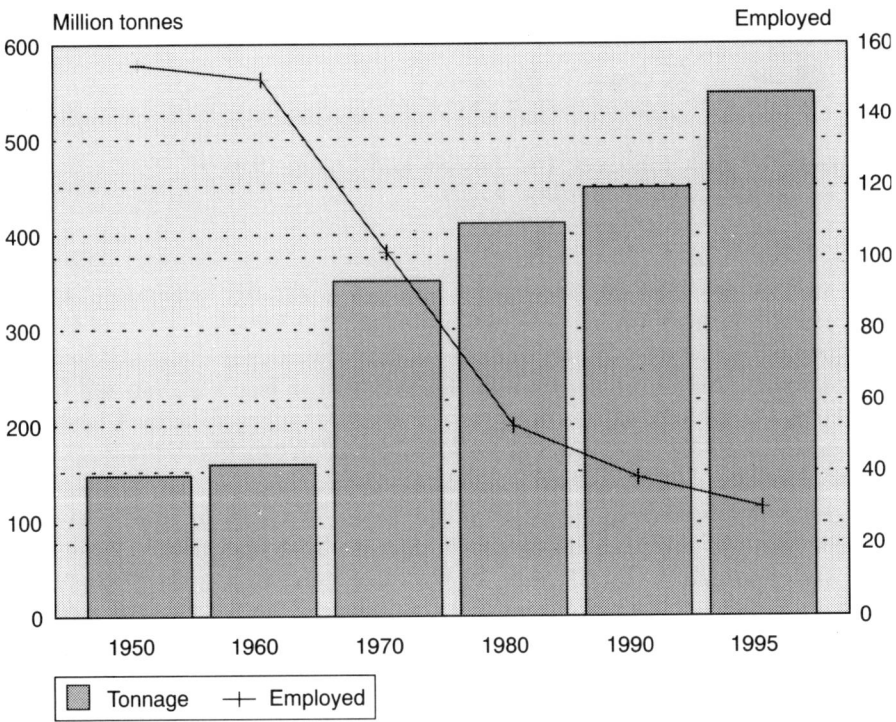

Figure 10.5   UK ports tonnage handled and employment, 1950–95.
Sources: NPC Digest, Port Statistics; BPA/DoT Port Statistics.

situation was made even more complex by the 1947 imposition of the National Dock Labour Board Scheme on the major ports, leaving the smaller ports to make their own labour arrangements. The scheme was to prove controversial in that it became a major influence on port labour. From a trade union and Labour Party perspective the scheme provided welcome stability and security against the excesses of casual labour. To port owners, shipowners and the free market politicians of the post-1979 period the scheme was seen as an unnecessary restriction on the market. Consequently it was abolished in 1991 (Evans 1993). The twin impact of privatisation and abolition of the National Dock Labour Board scheme was to have a dramatic impact on the employment and performance characteristics of UK ports. Behind the deregulation policy lay the need for them to match the performance of foreign ports.

■ 10.4 The theoretical framework

A broad range of modern economic and organisational theories have been selected to develop the analysis of change. These consist of:

1. Globalisation and the New International Division of Labour
2. Porter's contribution to understanding industrial structure and change

The synthesis of these theories provides a framework with which to consider how the central tenets of economic liberalism in the 1980–90s – deindustrialisation, diversification, disinvestment and decentralisation – have impacted on the maritime industries.

The emphasis on globalisation (see also Chapter 5.9) and the new international division of labour is explained by the global nature of the maritime industries. This theoretical position is useful in providing context for understanding changes to the structure and ownership and business behaviour of the maritime industries. Historically, the pattern of maritime globalisation has evolved around the labour–capital linkage between developing and developed nations. In its earliest form this linkage saw the combination of Indian seafarers and British ships. In the post 1945 period, however, this has spread globally, involving the capital of Japan and the new industrial economies of the Pacific Rim. More recently, the abundant labour supplies of ex-Eastern bloc seafarers have been linked with global supplies of capital. The classical theory of comparative advantage can be identified at work influencing global maritime markets; however, the historic process engendered by organisation and control calls for modifications to the theory. This is necessary if the process of developed nation capital control and developing nation labour supply is to be understood. This modification, in particular, helps to explain the changes inherent in the retreat from strongly regulated national shipping to that of deregulated flags of convenience.

Porter's contribution has been selected as it provides a comprehensive context for analysis of the link between industrial structure, performance and change. Porter's Five Forces are used as a determinant of industrial structure (see also Chapters 1.3, 1.8 and 4.4). These consist of:

- the threat of new entrants
- the threat of substitute products or services
- the bargaining power of suppliers
- the bargaining power of buyers
- rivalry among existing competitors (Porter, 1990)

The relative strengths of these is seen as a function of industrial structure and becomes a determinant of performance and thus change in the global marketplace. Specifically, the five forces provide a framework in order to explain why some maritime sectors have declined, while others have grown. Within the context of a globalised maritime market, Porter's five forces provide for analysis of the strategic business factors that are shaping dynamic change in the maritime industries. These strategic factors have obvious implications for UK shipbuilding as well as for links with UK ship owning. In particular, the rapid decline of UK shipbuilding since 1970 contrasts with the gradual decline of German shipbuilding (see Figure 10.2). It also provides a context to explain the success of such sectors as cruise shipping, while the building of new cruise ships in the UK has long ceased due to deindustrialisation and downsizing in the shipyards. Sub-sectors such as coastal shipping and the ship repair industry, have proved highly competitive in the European market at a time when industrial tanker and bulk shipping have suffered a sharp decline. Overall, the use of theory here provides an insight into the process of organisational fragmentation in the UK's maritime industries and helps to develop understanding of the erratic pattern of industrial change. Having outlined the use of theory it must be applied, firstly by considering globalisation and the new international division of labour.

■ 10.5 The new international division of labour

The thesis here is drawn from the classical models of Adam Smith and David Ricardo. Smith, in his seminal text, *An Inquiry into the Nature and Causes of the Wealth of Nations* (Smith 1776), explored the impact of the division of labour in industry. By reorganising industrial processes along the lines of specialisation – one operative concentrating on one skill process – high productivity gains were attained. This was demonstrated by the efforts of the pin factory operatives who were able to increase output several hundred per cent by implementing specialisation processes. Ricardo's work, *The Principles of Political Economy and Taxation* (1817), internationalised this process by laying down the theory of international trade and its components, the laws of absolute and comparative advantage. By pursuing a trade policy which allowed for nations to concentrate their factors of production where they had an absolute or comparative advantage, similar gains to those identified by Smith would be realised. Ricardo's conceptualisation of the trade between the UK and Portugal in the two-product model has become the foundation of modern international economics and trade. Later authors have amended the earlier foundations of Smith and Ricardo, culminating in the neoclassical model of international trade. The Heckscher–Ohlin thesis of the early twentieth century took the analysis a stage further by relating the trade model to the concepts of factor endowments and factor efficiency. Their model explains the structure of world trade within the context of the relative strengths and weaknesses that nations possess in factors of production – capital, land, labour and enterprise – and how efficiently they are employed within the context of relative capital and labour intensity (Kindleberger and Lindert 1978). This points to a rational use of economic resources on a global scale as trading nations seek the benefits of global specialisation. It follows that the more this theory is adhered to the greater the demand for trade, and hence shipping, will be. The impact on the maritime industry has proved dynamic in that it has extended far beyond the derived demand for shipping; the supply of modern shipping is just as much influenced by global specialisation.

Shipbuilding can be seen as one area where these international economic forces have come into effect. If British shipbuilding held a global competitive advantage in the Victorian era due to its strength in the factors of capital, labour and enterprise, it follows that the emergence of lower-cost labour and more innovatory enterprise in Japan would challenge British dominance. In 1959 Japanese shipbuilders' wages were reported to be 50 per cent of their British counterparts (Burton 1994). Moreover, the dynamics of Japanese yards provided an impetus for innovatory young designers and engineers who were committed to building functionally designed vessels of the future. As if Japanese competition was not bad enough for UK yards, the replica path towards industrial development pursued by Korea, and now China, could only exacerbate the decline of UK shipyards. This was confirmed when British shipowners began to sever their historical linkages. By seeking lower building costs or more technologically advanced designs UK owners were initiating a process which would inevitably lead to the decline of British shipping and seafaring. This can clearly be seen in the context of international division of labour. In the 1950–60s it had been American shipowners and their seafarers' unions who had complained about the incursions of low-wage British ships in their maritime trades (Boczek 1962); by the 1980s it was the British who were feeling the competitive threat of developing nation shipping and crews (BMCF 1988).

American shipowners, and particularly multinational commodity owners, can now be seen as early proponents of the new international division of labour

Output 1875=100

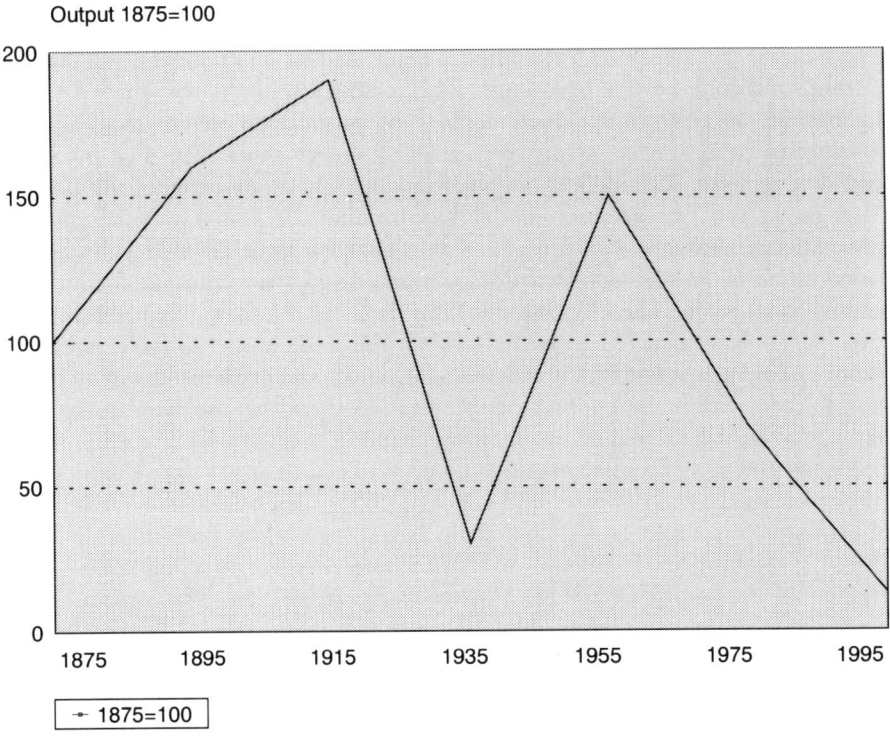

1875=100

Figure 10.6   Product life-cyle, UK shipbuilding output, 1875–1995

in shipping. Initially unable to compete in a market dominated by relatively low-wage European Shipping, they pioneered the use of Flags of Convenience (FOC). By astutely combining their capital and expertise with low-wage international labour supplies and the beneficial tax havens of Panama and Liberia, US owners were able to offset high wage costs and tax burdens to maintain a presence in world shipping. The FOC registries were to become, in the US shipowners' eyes, the flags of necessity (Carlisle 1981).

If this was the US response of the 1950–60s it was only a matter of time before the UK industry followed suit. The employment of Far Eastern 'Lascar' seamen on UK ships at low rates of pay was not uncommon from the early 1700s onwards. By the 1980s the attraction of blending the ever increasing sources of developing nation labour with the tax avoidance facilities of re-registering ships under friendly flags such as Hong Kong, Bermuda, the Cayman Islands, known as 'flagging out,' was becoming irresistible. Between 1980 and 1990 the flight from direct UK flag and crewing took place rapidly. This is illustrated in Table 10.1 which features a 392 per cent increase in UK-owned FOC tonnage, while US FOC tonnage declined by 46 per cent in the same period.

For the British shipowner this process was seen as a lifeline in the global market. Table 10.2 shows how it is possible to achieve dramatically reduced annual crew costs by flagging out.

For UK owners operating in marginal markets, where the surplus capacity of ships drove down freight rates, flagging out was the only alternative to business failure (BMCF 1988, p. 17). Even in markets less exposed to the excesses of global competition, the impact of the international division of labour was felt. The prolonged seafarers' strike in the Dover ferry industry in 1987–8 was seen by shipowners as a catalyst for achieving greater levels of crew productivity which, 'alone can preserve jobs and markets in a highly competitive world' (GCBS 1988–9, p. 8). In the following section it will be seen how well this process of globalisation fits the mood of economic liberalism during this period. The shift towards a new international division of labour was facilitated by a global approach to solving the market problems of developed nation shipping. Using the factor endowment thesis as an allocative process, global supplies of capital, labour and enterprise were blended. Although this appears to rest well with the factor endowment rationale, attention must be drawn to the dominant position of capital in this allocative process. What the new international division of labour in shipping provides is a selective choice exercised by developed nation shipowners – the controllers of capital – giving competitive advantage in the global market.

Table 10.1   UK and US beneficially owned FOC fleets 1980 and 1990

	NATION	TONNAGE (000 DWT)	FOC FLEET FOC FLEET	% DOMESTIC FLAG
US	1980	65,545	29.7	239.0
	1990	35,610	14.0	192.0
UK	1980	3,481	1.6	7.8
	1990	17,134	6.6	221.0

Sources: UNCTAD(1980); UNCTAD(1990); OECD (various years); Maritime Transport; House of Commons Transport Committee (1986/7).

Table 10.2   Annual crew cost options for UK tanker owners

FLAG	OFFICERS	RATINGS	COSTS(US$)(000)
UK	UK	UK	908
Liberia	Korean	Korean	490
Bermuda	Filipino	Filipino	480
Hong Kong	Hong Kong	Hong Kong	396

Source: House of Commons Transport Committee (1986/87).

Summarising this section it can be seen how the new international division of labour has evolved in shipbuilding and shipping. Following early inroads that Far Eastern shipbuilding made into the UK's market share, a global pattern of capital, labour and enterprise emerged. The advantage that the UK shipowners enjoyed over their US counterparts was to be eventually lost as the global process moved in search of tax havens and lower labour costs. The new international division of labour allowed UK firms to attain the goals of tax havens and low-wage developing-nation labour. This has had a fragmentary impact on the industry and sent shock waves of change through the nature and characteristics of ship owning, ship management and employment. Using the context of this overall spread of global maritime industry and organisation, it next remains to demonstrate how Porter's concentration on the five competitive forces helps to develop the analysis of change.

■ 10.6 Porter's contribution to understanding industrial structure and change

Michael Porter's major contribution to global business thinking centres around identifying the fundamentals of competitive advantage, and then developing an industrial strategy to fit. The Five Forces outlined by Porter (Porter 1990) are used here to examine the process of industrial change in the maritime industries (the reader should compare this with the Structure–Conduct–Performance methodology employed in Chapter 2). Porter recognises the importance of structural change in an industrial sector and how it provides opportunities for new entrant nations to challenge hitherto dominant industrial nations.

■ The threat of new entrants

It was perhaps inevitable that UK maritime industries would eventually lose dominance in global markets. This became the reality as new maritime nations entered the market in the twentieth century, with an inevitable destabilising impact on it. By increasing capacity and seeking market share via the acceptance of low profit margins, new entrants force established competitors into a strategic response.

Two interrelated maritime sub-sectors have been selected for consideration here: mass production shipbuilding and tramp and independent tanker shipping. Both were to represent a very real competitive threat to UK industries. Porter identifies the conditions in which a nation enjoys a sustainable competitive advantage, including high entry costs and complex technological barriers to entry. Clearly these did not apply in these two sub-sectors. Sustainable competitive advantage was only possible during the period until the mid-1950s, when Japanese shipyards began to overhaul those of the

UK. The ease of Japanese (followed by Korean) entrance was facilitated by a mixture of a dirigiste industrial policy and low capital and technology thresholds. While the Far East yards concentrated on the low-technology buildings, particularly tankers and bulk carriers, Continental and Scandinavian yards focused their technologies on the more advanced sectors of container ships, chemical and gas carriers, cruise ships and ferries. As a consequence UK competitiveness was threatened.

A shift towards more advanced production was commonly perceived to be the only possible response if UK yards were to survive. However, the problem was how to make the transition from a craft-oriented tradition to a more scientifically managed mass-production-based industry. The use of fabrication techniques and a division of labour based around a standardised production flow was the way to facilitate the effective use of systematic planning techniques (Lorenz 1991). This provided a challenge to the traditional craft approach as practised in the UK yards, however, which had enjoyed a competitive advantage in the skills available in the shipbuilding regions (Lorenz 1991). The nature of ship owning was changing and owners were more interested in the economic performance of vessels than the aesthetics of company specific designs.

An outcome of the switch to mass-production techniques was lower capital costs per vessel/tonne and an increased supply of new tonnage in the market. This proved conducive to the growth of a new wave of globally footloose shipping capital and enterprise in the period after 1960. Flag of convenience bulk and tanker shipping began to make inroads into the oil, iron ore, coal and grain markets that previously had seen a high level of UK fleet involvement. Traditional UK owners, with their British-built vessels and national crews, found it increasingly difficult to compete with new entrants.

The strategic response of both sub-sectors was to rationalise and reorganise. This resulted in a series of mergers throughout the 1970s–80s (compare with the financial services sector in the 1990s – see Chapter 2.5). The process was accelerated by state involvement and eventual ownership of the shipyards. The creation of consortia was the strategic response of the traditional tramp-ship owners. Despite the seeming efficacy of rationalisation through the pooling of capital and entrepreneurial resources, both sub-sectors can now be seen to have failed in their competitive response to new entrants. The ease of entrance into both shipbuilding and the bulk shipping market brought about an enduring over-capacity crisis during the last two decades, resulting in depressed building prices and freight rates (Davies 1992). This has exacerbated the economic difficulties of British yards and shipowners such that, by the 1990s, UK ownership in both sectors had virtually disappeared.

■ The threat of substitutes

Industrial change is measured here by the impact on the nation's transport system of the substitution effect. The threat of substitutes in maritime transport is somewhat limited by geography. In this section, however, the substitution effect of road haulage on shipping and regional ports is considered. This involves the analysis of the demise of many of the UK's West Coast ports within the context of Porter's threat of substitutes.

Competitive advantage is no longer sustainable if a substitute product offers lower prices or improved quality. For such ports as Bristol, Manchester, Preston, Greenock and Glasgow it was both of these factors which led to their demise. Until the 1970s they had enjoyed a high level of deepsea and coastal trade; by the 1990s they were either closed or surviving on much reduced trade levels. A number of explanations for their decline can be provided, notably the switch to East Coast ports as European integration intensified throughout the 1980s and 1990s. Where the impact of substitutes can be detected is in the use of overland transport from the West Coast regions to either the Channel/East Coast ports or, via ro-ro ferries or Channel Tunnel, the principal Continental ports of Antwerp, Hamburg and Rotterdam, as well as the inland ports of the Rhine, Scheldt and Seine. While British Rail's Freightliner container service has experienced some of the benefits of this process, it is the road haulage industry that has taken most trade by becoming a substitute for regional port activities. For example, exports from the Cheshire chemical industry to North America would, until the 1970s, have been loaded locally in the Manchester Ship Canal. By the 1990s the reality would more likely be a 200-mile journey by trunk road to the East Coast port of Felixstowe. The net result of this substitution is that extra tonne/miles are added to the UK's congested road network, while the West Coast ports decline, suffering serious under-utilisation of costly port assets (Rowlinson and Salveson 1991). As British liner firms either left the market or became assimilated into global container line alliances, regional affinities with West Coast ports diminished.

There is clearly a dichotomy here in that the private costs and benefits of road haulage substitution are incompatible with the social dimensions of regional employment and environmental pollution. In the competitive and deregulated transport market of the 1980–90s the substitution effect of road haulage has had a detrimental impact on UK regionally based shipping and ports.

■ The bargaining power of suppliers

The bargaining power of suppliers has an important influence on the sustainable competitive advantage of the firm. The level of costs charged by suppliers is a function of their relative market strength vis-à-vis their purchasers. As the maritime industries are essentially service providers, labour supplies have traditionally been an important cost component. The impact of change here is on the diminishing power of labour as capital intensity has developed, accompanied by a deregulated global labour market. In merchant shipping and in the ports, labour supply was very much influenced by the corporatist ethos. The Merchant Navy Establishment regulated the supply and competence of seafarers. The National Dock Labour Board had a similar role in supplying labour to ports. The global pressures of the 1980s–90s fragmented labour organisation in the maritime industries.

This has brought about an erosion of the stability and quality of working conditions and leave of UK seafarers, issues that were central to the prolonged Dover ferry strikes of 1986–7 (Marsh and Ryan 1989). The weakened position of the National Union of Seamen was one outcome of changes in maritime industrial relations, leading to the union's merger with the National Union of Railwaymen in the late 1980s. In the ports the twin impact of deregulation and privatisation had a considerable impact on the waterfront unions, to the extent that the return of casual labour has become a reality in the 1990s. While this is an outcome which is clearly contentious within the context of labour tradition and influence in the ports, it also signals the extent of the change. In the deregulated shipping and port markets of the 1990s trade union militancy is muted by the ability of globally attuned shipping capitalism to switch routes and ports with ease.

This was the case during the 1995–6 strikes on the Liverpool waterfront, when the international container consortia, ACL, re-routed their North Atlantic services to Thamesport (*Lloyd's List*, 17 April 1996, p. 3). In both examples provided of declining labour supply power it is evident that the trends towards a global market, accompanied by deregulation of both ownership and industrial relations, has proved to be the catalyst for a dramatic change in the relative balance between labour and capital.

■ The bargaining power of buyers

The respective power of buyers is a function of their share of the total market. In maritime trade the power of the commodity-owning multinationals has had a significant influence on change in the shipbuilding and ship owning industries. This is particularly so given the changing pattern of multinational corporate buying behaviour as they severed the strong historic linkages with their original host nations. In the oil trades, radical changes in shipping organisation resulted from intensified attention to cost controls, very much enforced by the economic stringency which followed the oil price shocks of 1973–4 and 1979. The allegiances that such UK-based majors as BP, Shell(UK) and Esso(UK) had, firstly with UK shipyards and, secondly, with the UK registry and crew supply, were severed by a more mercenary approach to investment and operational costings. Increasingly, the oil majors ordered and chartered their new tonnage outside the UK (Parker 1996). The fleet rationalisation and flagging out strategies occurring after 1975 had a significant impact on the total UK fleet. Between 1975 and 1990, the UK flag tanker fleet declined from 16.9m grt to 2.3m grt (*Lloyd's Register Statistical Tables*, 1976 and 1991). Also, in both the UK bulk and ferry fleets, the change in economic strategy which accompanied the privatisation of British Steel and British Rail's Sealink ferries, was to lead to a high loss of UK flag tonnage.

While the relative bargaining power of buyers has not altered significantly between the 1970s and 1990s, the transformation in corporate business behaviour proved the catalyst of change. As the oil majors and the privatised shipping companies began to employ a more global outlook in their search for both lower costs and reduced tax burdens, the retreat from UK flags and crews became inevitable.

■ Rivalry among existing competitors

The level of rivalry amongst competitors is a determinant of prices charged. Under these conditions, unless prices can be protected by product differentiation, the firm will be forced to reduce prices. Economists are aware that intense competition leads to firms making a loss. Not only is sustainable competitive advantage lost but also continued losses will cause the firm's withdrawal from the market. In the North Europe–North America cargo liner market, stability existed until the mid-1970s. Competitive rivalry was limited to service differentiation which accorded more to the traditional prestige of such lines as Cunard, Canadian Pacific, United States Lines, Hamburg-America Lines, Holland-America Lines, Manchester Liners and Bristol City Lines, than to price competition. This was reinforced by their membership of the North Atlantic Liner Conference. This, however, was disrupted by the arrival of new entrants, including Cast Line and Evergreen Line. Operating outside the North Atlantic Conference, these new entrants not only added extra capacity to the route, leading to price competition at the margins, but also sharpened the rivalry between the already existing lines.

Both the Canadian-based Cast Line and the Taiwan-based Evergreen Line were developed as a response by entrepreneurs identifying the attractions of blending flags of convenience and low-cost Far East labour with the availability of easy shipbuilding credit terms that existed in the late 1970s and the 1980s (Drury and Stokes 1983). The outcome for British shipping was that such established regionally based lines as Bristol City and Manchester Liners and (Glasgow's) Donaldson Lines were forced into larger consortia, eventually losing their identity and severing their traditional linkages with regional ports. The entrance of global shipping enterprise to once stable market routes had a disruptive impact on the traditional UK owners by intensifying rivalry. Again this contributed to the decline of UK shipping.

In summarising the utilisation of the five forces it has become apparent that they provide a focus on the structural and strategic factors at work in competitive markets. Overall, the trends towards a globally driven competitive market can be seen at work, bringing changes and dramatically fragmenting and reshaping the organisational, operational and employment factors in the three maritime industries.

■ 10.7 The shock waves of the era of economic liberalism

The retreat from Keynesian macroeconomic policies of full employment and the reappearance of economic liberalism in the 1970s had considerable repercussions on the three maritime industries. No longer was their special role considered a vital link in the nation's economic infrastructure. Instead, their success or failure would be determined by the workings of global competition and the market clearing view of the economy (Mackintosh *et al.* 1996). The following section considers the 'shock' impact of deindustrialisation, diversification, divestment and decentralisation within this context.

■ Deindustrialisation

From the early 1970s it was apparent that many of the UK's staple manufacturing industries were in absolute decline. These included steel, mining, metal manufacturing, heavy engineering and textiles. The process was particularly noticeable in the shipbuilding industry but also had implications for shipowners (see also Chapter 3.1).

Bazen and Thirwall's definition of deindustrialisation is employed here. It identifies:

- a declining share of total employment in manufacturing
- an absolute decline in employment in manufacturing. (Bazen and Thirlwall 1989)

Between 1960 and 1986 the UK suffered a 37.5 per cent decline in manufacturing's share of total employment; in the same period Japan experienced a 14.9 per cent increase (ibid.). In the UK this amounted to a loss of 3.8 million manufacturing jobs.

In explaining this process the mature economy thesis is directly relevant. This predicts that as industrial societies become more advanced, with per capita income rising, a shift occurs from traditional labour-intensive industries to a mixture of capital-intensive and service-based industries.

While this trend can be clearly identified across a range of European economies it is the extent of UK deindustrialisation that stands out. A number of explanations of this exist. The first industry thesis emphasises the long-term inevitability of the early industrial leaders being overtaken by newly industrialised countries (NICs). Clearly this explains the UK–Japan comparison above. The UK's Victorian supremacy in shipbuilding skills became a hindrance in the market post-1960. Partly the problem was technical and partly cultural. Japanese yards were relatively new in contrast to UK yards. They were constructed on the post-Second World War greenfield sites, not those of three-quarters of a century earlier. Whereas Japanese yards were suited to both the increased size in vessels and mass-production processes, UK yards suffered from their geographic history. In the Clyde, Tees, Tyne, and Wear the geographic history of the yards was inseparable from that of the towns. While this urban–industrial conglomeration was suited to the logistics of Victorian shipbuilding it had a restrictive effect on the scale and efficiency of modern production (Todd 1985).

Culturally, shipyard deindustrialisation also has an historic pedigree. Traditionally, the yards were family enterprises. Until the 1960s this ensured continuity in investment and linkages with the regional ship owning communities. The twin pressures of technological change and globalisation severed this continuity. Change in ship sizes and designs meant increased attention was paid to economies of scale and investment in new mass-production techniques. For small yards this proved an insurmountable problem. In a global market which features state-supported shipbuilding – particularly in Japan, Germany and later South Korea – UK yards fell behind in terms of efficiency. In the 1960s the average time for building a tanker was 808 days in the UK, 307 in Germany and only 204 in Sweden (Cantile-Stewart 1993).

Following the end of the Second World War, UK yards had been reluctant to invest, fearing a repeat recession such as that of the 1930s (ibid). As family firms became merged joint stock companies, increased emphasis was placed on tight financial management, leading to short-term cash flow taking precedence over sustainable long-term investment. Cantile-Stewart identified lack of investment as the cause of decline:

'Without doubt, lack of liquidity was at the heart of the problem. Not only did it restrict investment in new plant and machinery, purchase of raw materials and expansion of facilities, but it led also to a number of changes in industrial structure. Whereas at one time accountants were the advisers to the directors, now they were on the board rather than the engineers.'

If the organisational structure was unsuited to implementing a successful shipyard restructuring and modernisation programme, the industrial relations system was also problematic. The myriad trade unions, sectoral disputes and a rigid demarcation of tasks all militated against efficiency gains compatible with global competition. In addition, the famine or feast nature of the industry often led to a tacit 'go slow' by the workforce in an attempt to postpone the trip to the unemployment office when the contract had been completed (Parker 1992). As a postscript to this analysis of shipyard deindustrialisation, nationalisation was undertaken by the Labour Government of James Callaghan in 1976, creating British Shipbuilders (Parker 1996). This, however, did not prevent the rapid decline of the industry throughout the 1980s as the emphasis on economic liberalism in government proved incompatible with any state-initiated recovery planning.

A less obvious example of deindustrialisation resulted from the decline of the coal and steel industries. Rationalisations in South Wales, Clydeside and the North East can now be seen as having a detrimental impact on the trampship owners of these regions. As the commodity trades became increasingly globalised, British tramp owners found it difficult to survive in a market in which cost competition was led by the global mix of capital and labour facilitated by flag of convenience shipping.

■ Diversification strategy

As markets change and products reach the end of their life-cycle, firms seek new ideas, technologies and images to enable them to engage in future opportunities (compare with Chapter 2 and financial services diversification). In the maritime industries the pressure to diversify stems from two main factors:

1. the diversion of the skill and expertise base into new products;
2. the rechanneling of the firm's financial assets into more lucrative markets.

The diversion of skill and expertise is a typical response by a firm in the mature industrial nation context. As labour becomes a relatively expensive commodity in the global market, emphasis will be placed on labour-saving, capital-intensive methods. This recognises the core skill and expertise composition of the firm. The question becomes, how can this be geared to new market challenges and opportunities?

For the Glasgow trampship owners, Denholms, the response to a global market dominated by below break-even freight rates, endemic over-capacity and low-cost third world ships and crews, was to diversify into ship management and away from owning ships. This permitted the use of traditional core management skills and expertise developed over the 130-year history of the family firm. Staying ahead of the competition has become something of a trademark of the firm. Demonstrating entrepreneurial vision and drive the Denholm family were quick to grasp the opportunities for new vessels in the post-1945 period while competitors wavered:

> 'When the Second World War was over, my brother and I decided we had to get out or go right for it. We'd have done nicely if we had sold out then, but . . . we went ahead while other firms waited or the slump that never came.' (Hope 1990)

By the late 1970s, however, Denholms realised the limitations of owning trampships. They drastically reduced their fleet of ships, switching their entrepreneurial skills towards a range of ship management services controlled from a number of worldwide locations, as well as the traditional Glasgow base. This extended to a cosmopolitan mix of crews, finance and flags. By the late 1980s, Denholms had 120 ships and 3,500 seafarers on their management books. Their ownership of vessels had been reduced to one. The family firm's diversification was heralded in the maritime press as a 'professional high-quality service organisation . . . used by . . . blue chip names in shipping' (*Lloyd's List*, 24 October 1988). The wisdom of this diversification becomes evident when the decline of the UK deepsea shipping entrepreneur is considered. Between 1975 and 1990 this sector suffered a loss of 91 ships (51 per cent of the total), amounting to 2.5m gross registered tonnes (*Lloyd's Register List of Shipowners*).

The second type of diversification stems from the quest for higher returns on investment. This applies to firms that have made the transition from family enterprises to business conglomerates. The most obvious example of this is provided by the evolution of the P & O Shipping Company from strictly ship owning to a multinational business conglomerate with assets in a range of industrial and service markets – engineering, road haulage, shopping malls, catering, building and construction. The emphasis in the shipping section of P & O's investment portfolio has been on high value and/or stable markets – container shipping, cruising, ferry-boats and fixed charters in the coal, iron ore and grain trades. The desire to move outside the traditional spheres of operation marks an organisational and cultural change.

P & O had made a speedy transition from its family roots in the mid nineteenth century, so that by the 1930s it had taken over a large number of smaller UK shipping lines. However, until the late 1960s the group saw itself as exclusively shipping oriented. Partly this was explained by its particular brand of management culture. Despite the well-established public company status, senior management still clung to the family oriented style. This was typified by the longevity of the company chairman's reign. Sir William Currie retained control between 1938 and 1960, much to the chagrin of younger executives who felt that their ideas on moving the company into new market opportunities were stifled (Howarth 1986). In 1971 consultants provided a scathing attack on the senior management, with words such as 'feudal', 'autocratic' and 'Victorian' being banded about (ibid). By the 1980s, the change in organisation and management manifested itself in the more relevant approach to investment cited by one of its Directors:

> 'In P & O because we have so many areas of investment opportunity, clearly capital is competing between those various opportunities within the group. I think that shipping has to be looked at in that way; it's not something we just do because of our historical association with shipping.' (Black 1986)

This statement clearly provides evidence of change as P & O sought the highest possible returns for its shareholders. In the property and service oriented economy of the early to mid 1980's this could only mean diversification away from low-performing shipping sectors, concentrating instead on the more lucrative business opportunities.

■ Divestment strategy

As with diversification, divestment strategy can be seen as a response by firms adapting to a changing commercial environment. It may be described as selling one or more parts of itself in order to further the firm's objectives (Coyne and Wright 1986). For many UK trampship and tanker owners, divestment of ships was seen as the only way to attain financial solvency during the 1980s. In some cases it can be seen that divestment was complementary to diversification; as the firm headed into new market opportunities it needed to rationalise existing core activities. The above example of Denholm's diversification is typical. This option was usually open to a firm with sufficient capital resources and expertise to make the necessary transition. For some smaller firms, less abundant in factor endowments, divestment became a last-ditch attempt to avoid the slide into business failure and insolvency.

In the port industry, divestment was seen as a way of enhancing core areas of activity while also rationalising the workforce. Throughout the 1980s a number of management–worker buy-outs occurred in ports such as Southampton, Cardiff and Hull. As the parent company, ABP, redefined its core business objectives, the direct employment of dock workers was seen as a service to the core activity which could be franchised. Whilst these were seen as ports with a secure economic future, ports with less cause for optimism experienced divestment of their traditional cargo handling activities. This can be seen in the withdrawal of services from the London Docklands, the Upper Clyde and the upper reaches of the Manchester Ship Canal. Here divestment was seen as a way of realising property assets. The Manchester Ship Canal Company took this to extreme proportions in its attempts to close at least twenty miles of the thirty-six-mile waterway to navigation. This was seen as a necessary concomitant of the shift towards property landlord status with a portfolio of tenants ranging from private householders, supermarkets and sports complexes to light industries. The divestment strategy was seen to be working against the maritime interest when a Netherlands consortium's plans for revitalising the waterway with European liner linkages to the inland port of Manchester were seen to be in conflict with a property development strategy (*Fairplay*, 7 September 1989, p.5, and *Town and Country Planning*, May 1986, p. 135).

In the ship owning sector, divestment and diversification were pursued by those firms possessing sufficient capital and expertise to complete the strategy. The Ocean Transport and Trading Company featured the fleets of two Liverpool-based family lines, Blue Funnel and Elder Dempster. The severance of the traditional linkage between ownership and control, that had been a feature of the family firms until the 1960s, led to a divestment and diversification strategy. By 1980, the group's shipping activities were being critically appraised in comparison with its 'land-based' investment (*Fairplay Shipping Yearbook 1980*, pp. 170–1). The process became absolute in 1989 when the group's last ship was sold. Shipping had been unable to achieve corporate targets of 15 per cent rate of return on capital employed and, as such, was seen as an incumbrance to the group. This was justified as a necessity if diversification was to succeed. The extent of the firm's transition from a family and regionally oriented ship owning concern to a modern business conglomerate through the sale of the remaining ships in 1989, was justified on the grounds that 'the sale had yielded funds for investment in the Group's new growth activities and that the move had been well received in the City' (*Ocean Mail*, February 1980).

The opportunity cost of shipping, when directly compared with more profitable investments in the group's portfolio, was the rationale for this example of divestment. This process further needs to be seen within the context of the shift to corporate business discipline at the expense of the historical shipping tradition.

Divestment in the shipyards was a compulsory strategy as early as the 1960s. The Geddes Report (1965) argued that if the UK was to compete globally a more scientific and strategic approach was needed leading to a centralisation of the twenty-seven top yards, as measured by capacity. In practice the outcome of this strategy was hardly as intended since the industry lurched from crisis to crisis, with decline continuing unabated. The perceived synergy of the consolidated yards clearly had not worked. It quickly became evident that the strategy was problematic. The distinct cultures and traditions of the individual yards clearly militated against any co-ordinated modernisation/rationalisation strategy (Cantile-Stewart 1993). Both on the Clyde and on the Tyne and Wear the distinct histories of the yards obstructed any scientific approach towards modernisation, despite the large amounts of state investment by the Shipbuilding Industry Board (Parker 1992).

■ Decentralisation strategy

For maritime firms remaining in business in the 1990s change was implemented through decentralisation in their organisations. This section considers decentralisation in the ports, in BP Shipping and in the remaining shipyards.

Industrial decentralisation can be seen as a move away from the corporatist structures inherent in organised capitalism. Trends in centralisation in industrial relations, in organisational structure and decision-making were evident in the mergers of the twentieth century; as smaller firms became concentrated into managerial structures based on functional lines they lost their autonomy to the centralised head office (Lash and Urry 1987). The 1920s and 1930s saw concentration in most major industries including ports and liner shipping (Pollard 1969). Keynes, noting this trend, was particularly alert to the implications of powerful, centralised, management organisation which created a schism between ownership and control:

'A point arrives in the growth of a big institution . . . at which the owners of the capital, i.e., the shareholders, are almost entirely disassociated from the management, with the result that . . . profit becomes quite secondary.' (Keynes 1926)

From this it can be seen how the large joint-stock firm was a departure from entrepreneurialism. Under these conditions profit was relegated in the long-term interests of prestige and stability. This was suited to the limited global market conditions which existed until the 1970s. Secure and stable markets allowed for the monolithic workings of the centralised organisation; but as markets became more volatile, and as more maritime nations joined the global supply chain, a more functional and streamlined organisational model was required. If costs were to be reduced and if decision-making was to respond to the immediacy of change pressures, decentralisation was needed.

In the port industry, centralised organisations had dominated. As discussed previously, major ports such as Cardiff, Hull and Southampton had been nationalised along with their railway company parents in 1947. As components of the British Transport grouping they remained under state control until 1984. In Liverpool, London and Glasgow municipal enterprise prevailed from the 1930s. In addition to centralised organisation, the supply of dock labour was controlled and administered by the National Dock Labour Scheme (NDLS). The situation, however, was not completely homogeneous, since some ports benefited from a less centralised organisational structure, remaining outside of NDLS. The success of the Suffolk port, Felixstowe, in becoming the nation's leading provider of deepsea container handling, is a result of its relatively less centralised history. Globally oriented liner shipping was attracted to the port because of its increased labour flexibility and relatively low level of union militancy.

Felixstowe's development is at the expense of Liverpool, Tilbury and Southampton, although the evidence of the 1990s suggests that privatisation and deregulation have brought these ports back into competitive contention.

The mixture of public ownership and a corporatist industrial relations system was clearly inimical to Conservative Governments from 1979. Both were to be reformed by a process of privatisation and abolition of the NDLS. The result of these reforms had a significant impact on the ports and radically affected the nature of waterfront employment. Privatisation of the British Transport ports, forming Associated British Ports (ABP), cleared the way for a more decentralised organisation and its labour force. Early moves in this direction were signalled by the franchising-out of dock workers' employment and the return of casual labour on the waterfront.

In merchant shipping some of the bigger, centralised lines saw decentralisation as a survival strategy. This was the case with two of the UK's biggest fleet operators, Shell Tankers and BP Shipping. Both had formed a major component of the UK fleet, amounting to 14 per cent of total UK tonnage and 31 per cent of total UK tanker tonnage in 1975 (*Lloyd's Register List of Shipowners*). BP in particular, with its history of part state ownership, was seen as a fundamental element in the technological advancement of the UK fleet. Research and development was perceived as an important aspect of the company which was to pioneer a range of safety and pollution-reducing measures. In 1975 the company operated 88 vessels, employed 5,820 seafarers and a headquarters staff of 532 (*Transport Committee, vol. 2, 1986–7*). By 1986 the fleet had declined by almost 72 per cent with just 25 tankers remaining. No seafarers were directly employed, these being franchised out to dedicated crewing agencies. The ships were reflagged from the UK flag to those of Hong Kong, Bermuda and the Bahamas. BP had made the transition from a leading UK merchant shipping institution to a decentralised, offshore operator, indirectly employing developing nation crews under FOC terms. The extent of the oil majors' transition was endorsed by the embarrassing Gothenburg detention of the BP tanker, *British Wye*, in 1987. Swedish trade union officials were particularly aggrieved by the low rates of pay of the Filipino ratings (*The Seaman*, 1987).

Decentralisation in the shipbuilding sector very clearly parallels divestment. The wholesale retreat from the remnants of merchant shipbuilding in the 1980s left only a few core yards. In those that remained, a decentralisation of the industrial relations system occurred, resulting in the widespread use of casual labour. Overseas capital staked a claim in such once-prestigious yards as John Brown on Clydeside and Swan Hunter on Tyneside. The attraction was an abundance of core skills which could be supplemented by the surplus of skilled labour available for casual work projects.

One of the few areas of optimism has been in the less capital-intensive ship repair business. The radically downsized Camell Laird yard on Merseyside and the A & P Appledore dry dock in Southampton reported brisk business in 1996. This mini revival was endorsed by the Southampton dry docks' successful tenders, in a highly competitive global market, for the refit of the prestigious liners, *Norway* and *QE2* in 1996. The latter's contract had been lost to German yards over the previous decade (*Southern Daily Echo*, 6 September 1996). On Tyneside the social and economic problems caused by the demise of shipbuilding have been partly offset by the revival of ship and oil-rig repairing (*The Guardian*, 21 May 1996).

It next remains to illustrate a wide range of change factors which have to consorted to bring change in the maritime industries. The decline of the Port of Manchester is offered as a case study of industrial change.

■ 10.8 Case study: the decline of the port of Manchester

This case study concentrates on change in the inland Port of Manchester. Globalisation and the international division of labour can be seen at work in these changes. In particular, the loss of the port's principal deepsea shipping line was an outcome of the takeover of Manchester Liners by the entrepeneurial Hong Kong shipping group, C. Y. Tung. Relating this process to Porter's five forces, the impact of the new entrant coupled to the bargaining power of the buyer are particularly pertinent here. The entrance of the Tung group into the North Atlantic liner trades signalled a departure from the regional affinity that Manchester Liners had with their home port, crew supplies and the local economy. The Tung group were able to exercise buyer bargaining power, switching ports – to Liverpool initially, then Felixstowe – switching the registry of the ships to Hong Kong, and replacing UK crews by third world labour. For the port this amounted to a loss of critical mass in that the departure of the North Atlantic trade proved to be the catalyst of decline, divestment and diversification.

The years 1975–90 saw a complete reversal of the port's fortunes as trade was lost. During the mid-1980s the port and its 36-mile canal system faced closure. Within the context of globalisation, the port's destiny was shaped by a number of competitive factors which contributed to its decline.

The canal and the port continued to enjoy growth throughout the twentieth century, the position in the 1950–70 period being one of intense activity. Chemicals, steel and grain processing had concentrated on the canal side. Also, the Manchester Docks network was situated virtually in the Trafford Park industrial complex, which until the 1970s employed 70,000 people and was regarded as one of the world's leading centres of industrial capital concentration. Despite Manchester's limitations on vessel size (9000 grt) and the time penalties of navigating the Canal system (12–18 hours), the port was consistently in the top five of UK ports as measured by tonnage handled, and 3,000 dock workers were kept fully employed. The modern fleet of Manchester Liners enjoyed leadership in containerisation on the North Atlantic. The importance of Manchester Liners to the regional economy was acknowledged by the Monopolies and Mergers Commission in 1975 when it recommended against the Line's merger.

The mid-1970s saw a range of global forces conspiring to erode Manchester's traffic. Deindustrialisation in the regional economy diminished trade as overseas competition in textiles, coal, steel and engineering impacted on the region. Moreover, global competition on the North Atlantic throughout the 1970s had weakened the finances of Manchester Liners. This precipitated the early 1980s takeover by the Hong Kong shipping entrepreneur, C. Y. Tung, and led to the regional linkage provided by Manchester Liners being severed, the North Atlantic trade diverting to Felixstowe. Without its premier trade, the port and the upper reaches of the canal quickly fell into economic decay or made the transition to property development. Although by the mid-1990s there was some signs of a mini-revival in trade, Manchester's deepsea linkage with world markets was lost.

■ 10.9 Summary and conclusions

The emphasis on the globalisation effect has been stressed in order to provide analysis of change in three selected maritime industries. The question of why change occurred, and that of decline in particular, has been especially salient in considering their fate. The emergence of new forces in trade and shipping have been identified. The impact of Japan in shipbuilding for example and, to a lesser extent, ship owning has become apparent as a catalyst for change in the global market. The increasing supply of third world crews and flag of convenience registries has shifted the balance of shipping operations away from the UK. Likewise third world industrialisation has impacted on British shipbuilding.

The historic problem of the UK maritime industries has been identified, as has how this has proved problematic in responding to the challenge of the global market. The value of theory has become evident in gauging both the impact of international competition and the strategic challenges facing the UK's maritime industries. The new international division of labour in shipping has its roots in classical economic theory. The shift in maritime activity from developed to developing nations can be seen within the context of comparative advantage as lower-cost labour supplies are sought in the global market. Additionally, it has been shown that this process results from an asymmetrical trading relationship between capital-rich developed nations and the low-wage and off-shore registries of the developing nations. For the UK companies responding to this global shift, low operational costs and tax avoidance were the prize of diversification: for those unwilling or unable to pursue the global path, decline was in many instances inevitable.

Porter's five forces have been employed in order to demonstrate the competitive impact on UK maritime industries, given the intensification of globalisation. New entrants to both the global shipbuilding and trampship industries were recognised as the cause of UK decline. The threat of substitutes has been illustrated in the globally aligned container trades, and the example of the detrimental impact of long-distance road haulage on the regional ports of the West Coast has been provided. Changes in the bargaining power of suppliers was recognised in the evolving structure of seafaring and waterfront employment caused by deregulation in the labour market. This led to a reduction in the relative bargaining power of the unions and a fragmented and casualised labour supply. The bargaining power of buyers was exampled in the dominance of the oil majors in the tanker trades and, also, that of British Steel and British Rail's Sealink in the iron ore and ferry trades, respectively. As these companies went through a complete transformation in their economic behaviour, bargaining power (as buyers) was reflected in the ability to exit from the UK flag. Finally, the rivalry amongst existing competitors was discussed within the context of the disruptive impact of global competition on the North Atlantic trades.

As the nation made the transition from the Keynesianism of the 1960–70s to the economic liberalism of the 1980–90s, the shock waves of deindustrialisation, diversification, divestment and decentralisation ran through the maritime industries. Overall, the process of a globally initiated change in the three maritime industries has been discussed. This resulted in industrial fragmentation with significant shifts in the size, organisation and economic behaviour of the maritime industries as they sought to respond to the global market. The fourth arm industries of the 1950–70 period had been replaced by the globally oriented forces of international maritime capital.

■ 10.10 Questions for discussion

1. Describe the globalisation process which has destroyed Manchester's trade
2. Despite the Monopolies and Mergers Commission's earlier reservations, Manchester Liners were allowed to disintegrate a decade later. What changes in economic ideology can be detected here?
3. Examine how 'new entrants' (Porter) help to explain changes in the global shipping and shipbuilding market.
4. Discuss the impact of the reduced 'bargaining power of suppliers' (Porter) with reference to the influence of trade unions in the three maritime industries.
5. Analyse the specific mixture of labour and capital factors that have created a global division of labour in the three maritime industries.

■ Bibliography

Anon, 'P&O Veer off the Road', *Containerisation International*, February 1996, p. 29.
Anon, 'Dutch Shipowner in Manchester Ship Canal Link', *Fairplay*, 7 September 1996, p. 5.
Anon, 'The Tyne It Is A-Changin', *The Guardian*, 21 May 1996, p. 21.
Anon, 'Journal of Commerce Freight-Age 70', *The Journal of Commerce Annual Review*, 1970, p. 135.
Anon, 'NUS', *The Seaman*, Oct.–Nov. 1987, p. 1.
Anon, 'Don't Let the Motorists Mess up Manchester!', *Town and Country Planning*, May 1986, p. 135.
Bazen, S. and Thirlwall, T., *Deindustrialisation* (Oxford: Heinemann, 1989).
Black, A., 'Evidence Given to the House of Commons Transport Committee', Session 1986–1987, *Decline in the UK Registered Merchant Fleet*, p. 298 (London: HMSO, 1986).
Boczek, B. A., *Flags of Convenience* (Cambridge, Mass.: Harvard UP, 1986).
British Maritime Charitable Foundation (BMCF), *Why the Ships Went* (Colchester: Lloyds of London Press, 1986, supplemented 1988).
Bruce, A., 'State to Private Sector Divestment: The Case of Sealink', in Coyne, J. and Wright, M., *Divestment and Strategic Change* (Oxford: Philip Allan, 1986).
Burton, A., *The Rise and Fall of British Shipbuilding* (London: Constable, 1994).
Cantile-Stewart, J., *The Sea Our Heritage: British Maritime Interests Past and Present* (Banffshire: Rowan, 1993).
Carlisle, R. P., *Sovereignty for Sale: The Origins of Panamanian and Liberian Flags of Convenience* (Annapolis, Maryland: Naval Institute Press, 1981).
Coates, D., *The Question of UK Decline: The Economy, State and Society* (Hemel Hempstead: Harvester Wheatsheaf, 1994).
Coyne, J. and Wright, M., *Divestment and Strategic Change* (Oxford: Philip Allen, 1986).
Daily Telegraph, 'MOD Charter Condemned', NUMAST, p. 13, June 1993.
Davies, M., *Belief in the Sea: State Encouragement of British Merchant Shipping and Shipbuilding* (London: Lloyds of London Press, 1992).
Drury, C. and Stokes, P., *Ship Finance: The Credit Crisis. Can the Debt/Equity Balance be Restored?* (Colchester: Lloyds of London Press, 1983).
Evans, N. *et al.*, *The Abolition of the Dock Labour Scheme* (Sheffield: Employment Department, 1993).

Farnie, D. A., *The Manchester Ship Canal and the Rise of the Port of Manchester* (Manchester: Manchester University Press, 1990).

Ferguson, P. R. and Ferguson, G. J., *Industrial Economics: Issues and Perspectives* (Basingstoke: Macmillan, 1994).

General Council of British Shipping (GCBS) *Annual Reports*, London: GCBS.

Gallagher, J. G., *British and Commonwealth* (Cranfield Institute of Technology: European Case Study Clearing House, 1992).

Geddes Report. Report of the Shipbuilding Inquiry Committee, Command 2937 vi. (London: HMSO, 1965).

Hogwood, B. W., *Government and Shipbuilding: The Politics of Industrial Change* (Farnborough: Saxon Press, 1979).

Hope, R., *A New History of British Shipping* (London: Murray Press, 1990).

House of Commons Employment Committee, 3rd Report, *The Future of Maritime Skills and Employment in the UK* (London: HMSO, 1993).

Howarth, D., *The Story of P&O* (London: Weidenfield & Nicholson, 1986).

Keynes, J. M., *The End of Laissez-Faire* (1926) (London: Leonard and Virginia Woolf, Hogarth Press, 1926).

Kindleberger, C. P. and Lindert, P. H., *International Economics* (Homewood, Illinois: Richard Irwin, 1978).

Knowles, J., 'Exploring the Idea of International Business Strategy', in Preston, J., *International Business Text and Cases* (London: Pitman, 1993).

Lash, S. and Urry, J., *The End of Organised Capitalism* (Oxford: Blackwell, 1987).

Lloyd's List, 24 October 1988, 'Blue Chip Independent Seeks to Gain from Global Association', p. 7.

Lloyd's List, 17 April 1996, 'Both Sides Entrenched in Stand-off in Liverpool', p. 3.

Lloyds Register of Shipping (London: Lloyds of London Press, Annual).

Lorenz, E. H., *Economic Decline in Britain: The Shipbuilding Industry, 1890–1970* (Oxford: 1991).

Mackintosh, M. et al., *Economics and Changing Economies* (Milton Keynes: Open University Press, 1996).

Marcus, H. S., *Maritime Transportation Management* (Beckenham: Croom Helm, 1987).

Marsh, A. and Ryan, V., *The Seamen: A History of the National Union of Seamen* (Oxford: Malthouse Press, 1989).

Monopolies and Mergers Commission, *EuroCanadian Shipholdings Limited and Furness Withy Limited and Manchester Liners Limited: A Report on the Proposed Merger* (London: HMSO, 1976). National Union of Marine, Aviation and Shipping Transport Officers (NUMAST), 'MOD Charters Condemned', *The Telegraph*, June 1993, p. 13.

Organisation for Economic Cooperation and Development (OECD), *Maritime Transport* (Paris: OECD, Annually).

Parker, G. H., *At the Sharp End* (Glasgow: Brown, Son & Ferguson, 1992).

Parker, G. H., *Astern Business: 75 Years of UK Shipbuilding* (Kendal: World Ship Society, 1996).

Pearson Report, *Final Report of the Committee of Inquiry into Certain Matters Concerning the Shipping Industry*, Command 3211 (London: HMSO, 1967).

Pollard, S. *The Development of the British Economy, 1914–67*, 2nd Edition, (London: Edward Arnold, 1969).

Porter, M., *The Competitive Advantage of Nations* (Basingstoke: Macmillan, 1990).

Ricardo, D., *On the Principles of Political Economy and Taxation* (1817). Edited by Sraffa, P. (Cambridge: Cambridge University Press, 1951).

Rochdale Inquiry, *Report of the Committee of Inquiry into the Major Ports of Great Britain* (London: HMSO, 1962).

Rochda Report, *HM Committee of Inquiry into Shipping*, Command 4337 (London: HMSO, 1970).

Rowlinson, M., 'The Decline of UK Merchant Shipping 1975–90 Beyond the Market View', Ph.D. thesis, London Guildhall University, 1994.

Rowlinson, M. and Salveson, P., *Green Links to Europe* (Manchester: CLES, 1991).

The Seaman, 'BP Ship of Shame is Held', National Union of Seamen. 1987.

Smith, A., *An Inquiry into the Nature and Causes of the Wealth of Nations* (1776) (London: David Campbell, 1991).

Southern Daily Echo, 'Bullish A&P Buck the Trend with £2.5m Expansion', p. 23, 6 September 1996.

Stopford, M., *Maritime Economics* (London: Harper Collins, 1988).

Todd, D., *The World Shipbuilding Industry* (Beckenham: Croom Helm, 1985).

UNCTAD, *Beneficial Ownership of Open Registry* (Geneva: UNCTAD, 1980).

UNCTAD, *Review of Maritime Transport* (Geneva: UNCTAD 1990).

Wilson, D. F., *Dockers: The Impact of Industrial Change* (London: Fontana, 1972).

Index